THE RHETORIC OF NO

RAY FABRIZIO
EDITH KARAS
RUTH MENMUIR

Monterey Peninsula College

Holt, Rinehart and Winston, Inc.

New York   Chicago   San Francisco
Atlanta   Dallas   Montreal   Toronto

Copyright © 1970 by Holt, Rinehart and Winston, Inc.
Library of Congress Catalog Card Number: 77–104812
SBN: 03–083185–7
Printed in the United States of America
1 2 3 4 5 6 7 8 9

What is a rebel? A man who says no, but whose refusal does not imply a renunciation. He is also a man who says yes, from the moment he makes his first gesture of rebellion.

—ALBERT CAMUS
The Rebel

Preface

Today's college freshman brings the world into the classroom with him, like it or not. He wants to read about his world, to think about ideas germane to it, and to communicate with it. The current demand for "relevance" in education demonstrates young people's concern for understanding contemporary issues and for responding to these issues. *The Rhetoric of NO* is our response to this concern.

Bored by a daily pablum of advertisements, political gamesmanship, and innocuous "position" essays disguised as controversy, the student begins to hunger for real argument, for responsible conviction. This collection speaks to that student by concentrating on a dominant characteristic of our contemporary dialogue—that of dissent. Each essay, with its own distinctive voice, is saying *no* in one way or another to the "unexamined lives" of men and the blind assumptions of a fearful and violent age. Taken together, they deal with many of the unresolved controversies of our time.

In many ways, and for a long time, men have been saying *no*. We have included essays from the past to show that there is a heritage of dissent which sheds light on and lends eloquence to the dissent of today. An exposure to some of the best examples can help the student evaluate the quality of current discontent. Perhaps he will discover that yesterday's outrageous or dangerous challenge often turns out to be today's *status quo,* that the most virulent accusation of an Eldridge Cleaver may one day be accepted as an element of human progress.

Dissent, by definition, is "unpopular," and thus any collection of protest cannot avoid expressing unpopular positions. However, we have tried to refrain from making ideological judgments of our own both in our selections of material and in our questions. Furthermore, recognizing that the nature of the material may offend some readers, we can only hope that stimulation of any kind will lead the reader to question and analyze both what he has read and what he thinks about it. In an effort to treat dissent in a broad sense, we have also included some writers who dissent from a minority view which they feel is threatening to become a majority one (see, for example, Goldwater and Boorstin).

Finally, dissent has its own rhetoric, one that can be studied in its full range of tones—resentful or resigned, angry or agonized, irate or ironic, furious or downright funny. It is the rhetoric of human protest against human injustice, varying in intensity, purpose, and effect. With this rhetorical consideration in mind, we have grouped the essays under four "voices": *The Impassioned NO, The Discursive NO, The Reflective NO,* and *The Ironic NO,* according to each author's tone and purpose. An introduction to each of the sections discusses more completely the rationale for such a grouping, and the questions following each essay explore in more detail the relationship of style and rhetoric to content. In addition, we have included a second table of contents which suggests an alternate of the essays for a thematic approach.

acknowledgments

The editors wish to thank the following persons for their kind help: Mrs. Allye Fabrizio and Dr. Ronald Menmuir for their valuable suggestions and advice, and Dr. Idelle Sullens and Miss Irene Davis for their aid in preparing the manuscript.

R. F.

Monterey, California   E. K.
January 1970   R. M.

Contents

THE DISCURSIVE NO

THE REFLECTIVE *NO* 249

THE IRONIC *NO* 339

Thematic Contents

NO TO HYPOCRISY

NO TO INJUSTICE

NO TO IRRESPONSIBILITY

PUBLIC IRRESPONSIBILITY

PRIVATE IRRESPONSIBILITY

THE IMPASSIONED NO

*You taught me language; and my profit on't
Is, I know how to curse.*

CALIBAN
in *The Tempest*

The voiceless Caliban could only feel; the articulate Caliban could now curse, and in his curse express an impassioned *no* to his condition of slavery. Like Caliban, each writer in this section speaks with strong emotion and reveals the depth of his feeling in the way he approaches his subject—and his reader.

When a writer is emotionally close to his subject all of the things that constitute his style—his choice of words, the rhythm of his sentences, the comparisons he makes—convey his emotion and shape his ideas. With the good writer this is not chance or luck but the result of a conscious act. The good writer is able to move far enough away from his feelings to form his ideas and control his writing. When he does, he communicates not only ideas but also the convictions that make those ideas vital to him.

The same emotions which lend force to these ideas often impel the writer to reach out to the reader in some way. He may plead with him, cajole him, or even attack him. He may flatter him or call him names. But whatever he does, he tries to make the reader understand that he is feeling something and that his feeling is a part of what he is trying to say.

1

Some may say that a person should not attempt to be emotional and logical at the same time. But if we think about this, we see that it is perfectly natural and right for us to "feel" what we "think." Emotion does not necessarily cancel out reason, nor does reason exclude emotion. The only danger comes when a writer, intentionally or unintentionally, disguises emotion as logic. Then the result is *propaganda,* and the unperceptive reader is led to accept pseudologic as truthful communication. (In *The Ironic NO* we will see how writers can intentionally disguise feelings in other ways for different purposes.)

The rhetorical relationship between reason and emotion can be more clearly illustrated through a specific example. Consider the following way of making an argument:

All men are mortal.
Socrates is a man.
Therefore, Socrates is mortal.

This is an example of deductive reasoning, stated without emotion. What happens if we make the argument another way?

I love old man Socrates very much. At certain times, though, the sudden realization hits me that all men must die. And then I know with desperate certainty that I will lose him.

The second statement is no less logical than the first. But it is different in that its logic is not the total content; it also communicates the author's feeling about his subject. Furthermore, the reader reacts differently to the second statement because of the added dimension of feeling which the writer has chosen to reveal. The feeling, then, becomes part of the communication, shaping both it and the reader's response.

All of the essays in this section are strongly emotional. The emotion each expresses is an essential ingredient of its subject and must be "listened to" as such. Some selections are more passionate than others, some more logical; but all say *no* in a voice which speaks with conviction.

Matthew 23

The Gospel of Matthew, written about 75 A.D., was addressed to a Jewish audience, probably in Antioch. The unknown author's purpose was: (1) to declare to the Jews of his day that Jesus was the Messiah, even though he was rejected by the religious establishment—the Scribes, the Pharisees, and the Sadducees; and (2) to justify the turning of the Messiah from the Jews to the Gentiles with His Gospel of "righteousness"—the religion of the free spirit. The rejection of Jesus, as well as the failure by the establishment to respond to the spiritual vision, occasions and justifies the "woes" reproduced here. Chapters 19–25 should be read as a unit to give the full apocalyptic flavor of this Gospel.

Then spake Jesus to the multitudes and to his disciples, saying, The scribes and the Pharisees sit on Moses' seat: all things therefore whatsoever they bid you, *these* do and observe: but do not ye after their works; for they say, and do not. Yea, they bind heavy burdens and grievous to be borne, and lay them on men's shoulders; but they themselves will not move them with their finger. But all their works they do to be seen of men: for they make broad their phylacteries, and enlarge the borders *of their garments,* and love the chief place at feasts, and the chief seats in the synagogues, and the salutations in the market-places, and to be called of men, Rabbi. But be not ye called Rabbi: for one is your teacher, and all ye are brethren. And call no man your father on the earth: for one is your Father, *even* he who is in heaven. Neither be ye called masters: for one is your master, *even* the Christ. But he that is greatest among you shall be your servant. And whosoever shall exalt himself shall be humbled; and whosoever shall humble himself shall be exalted.

But woe unto you, scribes and Pharisees, hypocrites! because ye shut

From *The Holy Bible,* American Standard Revision. © 1946 by Thomas Nelson. Reprinted by permission.

3

the kingdom of heaven against men: for ye enter not in yourselves, neither suffer ye them that are entering in to enter.

Woe unto you, scribes and Pharisees, hypocrites! for ye compass sea and land to make one proselyte; and when he is become so, ye make him twofold more a son of hell than yourselves.

Woe unto you, ye blind guides, that say, Whosoever shall swear by the temple, it is nothing; but whosoever shall swear by the gold of the temple, he is a debtor. Ye fools and blind: for which is greater, the gold, or the temple that hath sanctified the gold? And, Whosoever shall swear by the altar, it is nothing; but whosoever shall swear by the gift that is upon it, he is a debtor. Ye blind: for which is greater, the gift, or the altar that sanctifieth the gift? He therefore that sweareth by the altar, sweareth by it, and by all things thereon. And he that sweareth by the temple, sweareth by it, and by him that dwelleth therein. And he that sweareth by the heaven, sweareth by the throne of God, and by him that sitteth thereon.

Woe unto you, scribes and Pharisees, hypocrites! for ye tithe mint and anise and cummin, and have left undone the weightier matters of the law, justice, and mercy, and faith: but these ye ought to have done, and not to have left the other undone. Ye blind guides, that strain out the gnat, and swallow the camel!

Woe unto you, scribes and Pharisees, hypocrites! for ye cleanse the outside of the cup and of the platter, but within they are full from extortion and excess. Thou blind Pharisee, cleanse first the inside of the cup and of the platter, that the outside thereof may become clean also.

Woe unto you, scribes and Pharisees, hypocrites! for ye are like unto whited sepulchres, which outwardly appear beautiful, but inwardly are full of dead men's bones, and of all uncleanness. Even so ye also outwardly appear righteous unto men, but inwardly ye are full of hypocrisy and iniquity.

Woe unto you, scribes and Pharisees, hypocrites! for ye build the sepulchres of the prophets, and garnish the tombs of the righteous, and say, If we had been in the days of our fathers, we should not have been partakers with them in the blood of the prophets. Wherefore ye witness to yourselves, that ye are sons of them that slew the prophets. Fill ye up then the measure of your fathers. Ye serpents, ye offspring of vipers, how shall ye escape the judgment of hell? Therefore, behold, I send unto you prophets, and wise men, and scribes: some of them shall ye kill and crucify; and some of them shall ye scourge in your synagogues, and persecute from city to city: that upon you may come all the righteous blood shed on the earth, from the blood of Abel the righteous unto the blood of Zachariah son of Barachiah, whom ye slew between the sanctuary and the altar. Verily I say unto you, All these things shall come upon this generation.

O Jerusalem, Jerusalem, that killeth the prophets, and stoneth them that are sent unto her! how often would I have gathered thy children together, even as a hen gathereth her chickens under her wings, and ye would not! Behold, your house is left unto you desolate. For I say unto you, Ye shall not see me henceforth, till ye shall say, Blessed is he that cometh in the name of the Lord.

For Discussion

1. What general criticism does Jesus make of the Scribes and Pharisees? Who would be their modern counterparts?
2. To what extent are the criticisms Jesus makes valid for the church today? For the world?
3. What other descriptions in this selection have modern equivalents?
4. Locate several metaphors and discuss their effectiveness.
5. Discuss the emotional content of the language. Point out those words with the strongest feeling.
6. Epithet and invective are universal weapons of persuasion. In this respect, compare the style of Matthew 23 to that of Miller, Bruce, and Farber.

FREDERICK W. NIETZSCHE

On the New Idol

Nietzsche (1844–1900), a German philosopher, is one of the fore-runners of existential philosophy. His central theme is that *will*—the blind thrust of power in all things—makes life what it is. Yet everything he knew had subverted the life of man. Reason had supplanted the will, the slave ethic of Christianity had corrupted the true nobleman, the democratic state had produced the mass mediocracy of the "herd"—and all were jointly responsible for the degenerate state of man. Man's salvation, according to Nietzsche, lies in the principle of the individual aristocratic will to power. This selection is taken from *Thus Spake Zarathustra*, the work which best expressed his views.

Somewhere there are still peoples and herds, but not where we live, my brothers: here there are states. State? What is that? Well then, open your ears to me, for now I shall speak to you about the death of peoples.

State is the name of the coldest of all cold monsters. Coldly it tells lies too; and this lie crawls out of its mouth: "I, the state, am the people." That is a lie! It was creators who created peoples and hung a faith and a love over them: thus they served life.

It is annihilators who set traps for the many and call them "state": they hang a sword and a hundred appetites over them.

Where there is still a people, it does not understand the state and hates it as the evil eye and the sin against customs and rights.

This sign I give you: every people speaks its tongue of good and evil, which the neighbor does not understand. It has invented its own language of customs and rights. But the state tells lies in all the tongues of good and evil; and whatever it says it lies—and whatever it has it has stolen. Everything about it is false; it bites with stolen teeth, and bites easily. Even its entrails are false. Confusion of tongues of good and evil: this sign I give you as the

From *The Portable Nietzsche* translated by Walter Kaufmann. Copyright 1954 by The Viking Press, Inc. Reprinted by permission of The Viking Press, Inc.

sign of the state. Verily, this sign signifies the will to death. Verily, it beckons to the preachers of death.

All-too-many are born: for the superfluous the state was invented.

Behold, how it lures them, the all-too-many—and how it devours them, chews them, and ruminates!

"On earth there is nothing greater than I: the ordering finger of God am I"—thus roars the monster. And it is not only the long-eared and short-sighted who sink to their knees. Alas, to you too, you great souls, it whispers its dark lies. Alas, it detects the rich hearts which like to squander themselves. Indeed, it detects you too, you vanquishers of the old god. You have grown weary with fighting, and now your weariness still serves the new idol. With heroes and honorable men it would surround itself, the new idol! It likes to bask in the sunshine of good consciences—the cold monster!

It will give you everything if you will adore it, this new idol: thus it buys the splendor of your virtues and the look of your proud eyes. It would use you as bait for the all-too-many.

Indeed, a hellish artifice was invented there, a horse of death, clattering in the finery of divine honors. Indeed, a dying for many was invented there, which praises itself as life: verily, a great service to all preachers of death!

State I call it where all drink poison, the good and the wicked; state, where all lose themselves, the good and the wicked; state, where the slow suicide of all is called "life."

Behold the superfluous! They steal the works of the inventors and the treasures of the sages for themselves; "education" they call their theft—and everything turns to sickness and misfortune for them.

Behold the superfluous! They are always sick; they vomit their gall and call it a newspaper. They devour each other and cannot even digest themselves.

Behold the superfluous! They gather riches and become poorer with them. They want power and first the lever of power, much money—the impotent paupers!

Watch them clamber, these swift monkeys! They clamber over one another and thus drag one another into the mud and the depth. They all want to get to the throne: that is their madness—as if happiness sat on the throne. Often mud sits on the throne—and often also the throne on mud. Mad they all appear to me, clambering monkeys and overardent. Foul smells their idol, the cold monster: foul they smell to me altogether, these idolators.

My brothers, do you want to suffocate in the fumes of their snouts and appetites? Rather break the windows and leap to freedom.

Escape from the bad smell! Escape from the idolatry of the superfluous!

Escape from the bad smell! Escape from the steam of these human sacrifices!

The earth is free even now for great souls. There are still many empty seats for the lonesome and the twosome, fanned by the fragrance of silent seas.

A free life is still free for great souls. Verily, whoever possesses little is possessed that much less: praised be a little poverty!

Only where the state ends, there begins the human being who is not superfluous: there begins the song of necessity, the unique and inimitable tune.

Where the state *ends*—look there, my brothers! Do you not see it, the rainbow and the bridges of the overman?

Thus spoke Zarathustra.

For Discussion

1. Nietzsche calls the state a "cold monster." See how he extends this metaphor and identify any literal situations that the figurative language represents.
2. Who are the "superfluous"?
3. How does the author relate wealth and power to the state? (Find possible comparisons in Malcolm X, Carmichael, Shoup, and Kunen.)
4. What is Nietzsche's message? What other philosophers share similar beliefs?
5. The Nazis leaned heavily on Nietzsche to reinforce their concept of Aryan superiority. However, what aspects of Nietzsche's philosophy revealed in this essay contradict Nazism?
6. What poetic devices or techniques does this essay utilize?
7. What is the predominant emotion of this piece? Consider the changes in mood from the beginning to the end.

MARK TWAIN

Reflections on Religion

Samuel L. Clemens, perhaps America's most famous author and humorist, took the pen name of "Mark Twain" while a reporter in Virginia City in 1862. His many novels, short stories, essays, and lectures drew upon his varied experiences as a tramp printer, riverboat pilot, prospector, lecturer, traveler, and unsuccessful financial investor. Although they are philosophically consistent with his early humorous works, his later writings are more profoundly cynical and more bitterly satiric. The following "reflections" were dictated by Twain in June, 1906, approximately four years before his death; but at the request of his daughter, they were not released for publication until 1960, the 125th anniversary of Clemens' birth, when Mrs. Samossoud lifted the ban on all of his previously unpublished works.

One

Tuesday, June 19, 1906

Our Bible reveals to us the character of our God with minute and remorseless exactness. The portrait is substantially that of a man—if one can imagine a man charged and overcharged with evil impulses far beyond the human limit; a personage whom no one, perhaps, would desire to associate with now that Nero and Caligula are dead. In the Old Testament His acts expose His vindictive, unjust, ungenerous, pitiless and vengeful nature constantly. He is always punishing—punishing trifling misdeeds with thousand-fold severity; punishing innocent children for the misdeeds of their parents; punishing unoffending populations for the misdeeds of their rulers; even descending to wreak bloody vengeance upon harmless calves and lambs and sheep and bullocks as punishment for inconsequential trespasses committed by their proprietors. It is perhaps the most damnatory biography that exists in print anywhere. It makes Nero an angel of light and leading by contrast.

It begins with an inexcusable treachery, and that is the keynote of the entire biography. That beginning must have been invented in a pirate's nursery, it is so malign and so childish. To Adam is forbidden the fruit of a certain tree—and he is gravely informed that if he disobeys he shall die. How could that be expected to impress Adam? Adam was merely a man in stature; in knowledge and experience he was in no way the superior of a baby of two years of age; he could have no idea of what the word death meant. He had never seen a dead thing; he had never heard of a dead thing before. The word meant nothing to him. If the Adam child had been warned that if he ate of the apples he would be transformed into a meridian of longitude, that threat would have been the equivalent of the other, since neither of them could mean anything to him.

The watery intellect that invented the memorable threat could be depended on to supplement it with other banalities and low grade notions of justice and fairness, and that is what happened. It was decreed that all of Adam's descendants, to the latest day, should be punished for the baby's trespass against a law of his nursery fulminated against him before he was out of his diapers. For thousands and thousands of years his posterity, individual by individual, has been unceasingly hunted and harried with afflictions in punishment of the juvenile misdemeanor which is grandiloquently called Adam's Sin. And during all that vast lapse of time there has been no lack of rabbins and popes and bishops and priests and parsons and lay slaves eager to applaud this infamy, maintain the unassailable justice and righteousness of it, and praise its Author in terms of flattery so gross and extravagant that none but a God could listen to it and not hide His face in disgust and embarrassment. Hardened to flattery as our Oriental potentates are through long experience, not even they would be able to endure the rank quality of it which our God endures with complacency and satisfaction from our pulpits every Sunday.

We brazenly call our God the source of mercy, while we are aware all the time that there is not an authentic instance in history of His ever having exercised that virtue. We call Him the source of morals, while we know by His history and by His daily conduct as perceived with our own senses that He is totally destitute of anything resembling morals. We call Him Father, and not in derision, although we would detest and denounce any earthly father who should inflict upon his child a thousandth part of the pains and miseries and cruelties which our God deals out to His children every day, and has dealt out to them daily during all the centuries since the crime of creating Adam was committed.

We deal in a curious and laughable confusion of notions concerning God. We divide Him in two, bring half of Him down to an obscure and infinitesimal corner of the world to confer salvation upon a little colony of Jews—and only Jews, no one else—and leave the other half of Him throned in Heaven and looking down and eagerly and anxiously watching for results. We reverently study the history of the earthly half and deduce from it the conviction that the earthly half has reformed, is equipped with morals and virtues, and in no way resembles the abandoned, malignant half that abides upon the throne. We conceive that the earthly half is just, merciful, charitable, benevolent, forgiving and full of sympathy for the sufferings of mankind and anxious to remove them. Apparently we deduce this character not by examining facts but by diligently declining to search them, measure them and weigh them. The earthly half requires us to be merciful and sets us an example by inventing a lake of fire and brimstone in which all of us who fail to recognize and worship Him as God are to be burned through all eternity. And not only *we*, who are offered these terms, are to be thus burned if we neglect them, but also the earlier billions of human beings are to suffer this awful fate, although they all lived and died without ever having heard of Him or the terms at all. This exhibition of mercifulness may be called gorgeous. We have nothing approaching it among human savages, nor among the wild beasts of the jungle. We are required to forgive our brother seventy times seven times and be satisfied and content if on our deathbed, after a pious life, our soul escape from our body before the hurrying priest can get to us and furnish it a pass with his mumblings and candles and incantations. This example of the forgiving spirt may also be pronounced gorgeous.

We are told that the two halves of our God are only seemingly disconnected by their separation; that in very fact the two halves remain one, and equally powerful, notwithstanding the separation. This being the case, the earthly half—who mourns over the sufferings of mankind and would like to remove them, and is quite competent to remove them at any moment He may choose—satisfies Himself with restoring sight to a blind person here and there instead of restoring it to all the blind; cures a cripple here and there instead of curing all the cripples; furnishes to five thousand famishing persons a meal and lets the rest of the millions that are hungry remain hungry— and all the time He admonishes inefficient man to cure these ills which God Himself inflicted upon him, and which He could extinguish with a word if He chose to do it, and thus do a plain duty which He had neglected from the beginning and always will neglect while time shall last. He raised several dead persons to life. He manifestly regarded this as a kindness. If it was a kindness it was not just to confine it to half-a-dozen persons. He should have raised the rest of the dead. I would not do it myself, for I think the dead are the only human beings who are really well off—but I merely mention it in passing as one of those curious incongruities with which our Bible history is heavily overcharged.

Whereas the God of the Old Testament is a fearful and repulsive character He is at least consistent. He is frank and outspoken. He makes no pretense to the possession of a moral or a virtue of any kind—except with His mouth. No such thing is anywhere discoverable in His conduct. I think He comes infinitely nearer to being respectworthy than does His reformed self as guilelessly exposed in the New Testament. Nothing in all history—nor even His massed history combined—remotely approaches in atrocity the invention of Hell.

His heavenly self, His Old Testament self, is sweetness and gentleness and respectability, compared with His reformed earthly self. In Heaven he claims not a single merit and hasn't one—outside of those claimed by His mouth—whereas in the earth He claims every merit in the entire catalogue of merits, yet practised them only now and then, penuriously, and finished by conferring Hell upon us, which abolished all His fictitious merits in a body.

Two

Wednesday, June 20, 1906

There are one or two curious defects about Bibles. An almost pathetic poverty of invention characterizes them all. That is one striking defect. Another is that each pretends to originality without possessing any. Each borrows from the others and gives no credit, which is a distinctly immoral act. Each in turn confiscates decayed old stage-properties from the others and with naïve confidence puts them forth as fresh new inspirations from on high. We borrow the Golden Rule from Confucius after it has seen service for centuries and copyright it without a blush. When we want a Deluge we go away back to hoary Babylon and borrow it, and are as proud of it and as satisfied with it as if it had been worth the trouble. We still revere it and admire it to-day and claim that it came to us direct from the mouth of the Deity; whereas we know that Noah's flood never happened, and couldn't have happened. The flood is a favorite with Bible makers. If there is a Bible— or even a tribe of savages—that lacks a General Deluge it is only because the religious scheme that lacks it hadn't any handy source to borrow it from.

Another prime favorite with the authors of sacred literature and founders of religions is the Immaculate Conception. It had been worn threadbare before we adopted it as a fresh new idea—and we admire it as much now as did the original conceiver of it when his mind was delivered of it a million years ago. The Hindus prized it ages ago when they acquired Krishna by the Immaculate process. The Buddhists were happy when they acquired Gautama by the same process twenty-five hundred years ago. The Greeks of the same period had great joy in it when their Supreme Being and his cabinet used to come down and people Greece with mongrels half human and half divine. The Romans borrowed the idea from Greece and found great happiness in Jupiter's Immaculate Conception products. We got it direct from Heaven, by way of Rome. We are still charmed with it. And only a fortnight go, when an Episcopal clergyman in Rochester was summoned before the governing body of his church to answer the charge of intimating that he did not believe that the Savior was miraculously conceived, the Rev. Dr. Briggs, who is perhaps the most daringly broad-minded religious person now occupying an American pulpit, took up the cudgels in favor of the Immaculate Conception in an article in the *North American Review,* and from the tone of that article it seemed apparent that he believed he had settled that vexed question once and for all.[1] His idea was that there could be no doubt about it, for the reason that the Virgin Mary knew it was authentic because the Angel of the Annunciation told her so. Also, it must have been so, for the additional reason that Jude—a later son of Mary, the Virgin, and born in wedlock—was still living and associating with the adherents of the early church many years after the event, and that he said quite decidedly that it was a case of Immaculate Conception; therefore it must be true, for Jude was right there in the family and in a position to know.

If there is anything more amusing than the Immaculate Conception doctrine it is the quaint reasonings whereby ostensibly intelligent human beings persuade themselves that the impossible fact is proven.

If Dr. Briggs were asked to believe in the Immaculate Conception process as exercised in the cases of Krishna, Osiris, Buddha and the rest of the tribe he would decline with thanks and probably be offended. If pushed, he would probably say that it would be childish to believe in those cases, for the reason that they were supported by none but human testimony and that it would be impossible to prove such a thing by human testimony, because if the entire human race were present at a case of Immaculate Conception they wouldn't be able to tell when it happened, nor whether it happened at all—and yet this bright man with the temporarily muddy mind is quite able to believe an impossibility whose authenticity rests entirely upon human testimony—the testimony of but one human being, the Virgin herself, a witness not disinterested, but powerfully interested; a witness incapable of knowing the fact as a fact, but getting all that she supposed she knew about it at second hand—at second hand from an entire stranger, an alleged angel, who could have been an angel, perhaps, but also could have been a tax collector. It is not likely that she had ever seen an angel before or knew their trade-marks. He was a stranger. He brought no credentials. His evidence was worth nothing at all to anybody else in the community. It is worth noth-

[1] Dr. Briggs' article discusses the Virgin Birth and not the Immaculate Conception. The latter refers to the conception of Mary, while the former refers to the birth of Jesus. However, Twain's misuse of the term *Immaculate Conception,* common even among Catholics, does not affect the substance of his argument. [Ed.]

ing to-day to any but minds which are like Dr. Briggs's—which have lost their clarity through mulling over absurdities in the pious wish to dig something sane and rational out of them. The Immaculate Conception rests wholly upon the testimony of a single witness—a witness whose testimony is without value—a witness whose very existence has nothing to rest upon but the assertion of the young peasant wife whose husband needed to be pacified. Mary's testimony satisfied him but that is because he lived in Nazareth instead of New York. There isn't any carpenter in New York that would take the testimony at par. If the Immaculate Conception could be repeated in New York to-day there isn't a man, woman or child of those four millions who would believe in it—except perhaps some addled Christian Scientists. A person who can believe in Mother Eddy wouldn't strain at an Immaculate Conception, or six of them in a bunch. The Immaculate Conception could not be repeated successfully in New York in our day. It would produce laughter, not reverence and adoration.

To a person who doesn't believe in it, it seems a most puerile invention. It could occur to nobody but a god that it was a large and ingenious arrangement and had dignity in it. It could occur to nobody but a god that a divine Son procured through promiscuous relations with a peasant family in a village could improve the purity of the product, yet that is the very idea. The product acquires purity—purity absolute—purity from all stain or blemish—through a gross violation of both human and divine law, as set forth in the constitution and by-laws of the Bible. Thus the Christian religion, which requires everybody to be moral and to obey the laws, has its very beginning in immorality and in disobedience to law. You couldn't purify a tomcat by the Immaculate Conception process.

Apparently as a pious stage-property it is still useful, still workable, although it is so bent with age and so nearly exhausted by overwork. It is another case of begats. What's-his-name begat Krishna, Krishna begat Buddha, Buddha begat Osiris, Osiris begat the Babylonian deities, they begat God, He begat Jesus, Jesus begat Mrs. Eddy. If she is going to continue the line and do her proper share of the begatting, she must get at it, for she is already an antiquity.

There is one notable thing about our Christianity: bad, bloody, merciless, money-grabbing and predatory as it is—in our country particularly, and in all other Christian countries in a somewhat modified degree—it is still a hundred times better than the Christianity of the Bible, with its prodigious crime—the invention of Hell. Measured by our Christianity of to-day, bad as it is, hypocritical as it is, empty and hollow as it is, neither the Deity nor His Son is a Christian, nor qualified for that moderately high place. Ours is a terrible religion. The fleets of the world could swim in spacious comfort in the innocent blood it has spilt.

Three

Friday, June 22, 1906

. . .

The Gospel of Peace is always making a good deal of noise with its mouth; always rejoicing in the progress it is making toward final perfection, and always diligently neglecting to furnish the statistics. George the Third reigned sixty years, the longest reign in English history up to his time. When his revered successor, Victoria, turned the sixty-year corner—thus scoring a new long-reign record—the event was celebrated with great pomp and circumstance and public rejoicing in England and her colonies. Among the statistics fetched out for general admiration were these: that for each year of the sixty of her reign Victoria's Christian soldiers had fought in a separate and distinct war. Meantime the possessions of England had swollen to such a degree by depredations committed upon helpless and godless pagans that there were not figures enough in Great Britain to set down the stolen acreage and they had to import a lot from other countries.

There are no peaceful nations now except those unhappy ones whose borders have not been invaded by the Gospel of Peace. All Christendom is a soldier-camp. During all the past generation the Christian poor have been taxed almost to starvation-point to support the giant armaments which the Christian Governments have built up, each to protect itself from the rest of the brotherhood and, incidentally, to snatch any patch of real estate left exposed by its savage owner. King Leopold II of Belgium—probably the most intensely Christian monarch, except Alexander the Sixth,[2] that has escaped Hell thus far—has stolen an entire kingdom in Africa, and in the fourteen years of Christian endeavor there has reduced the population of thirty millions to fifteen by murder, mutilation, overwork, robbery, rapine —confiscating the helpless native's very labor and giving him nothing in return but salvation and a home in Heaven, furnished at the last moment by the Christian priest.

Within this last generation each Christian power has turned the bulk of its attention to finding out newer and still newer and more and more effective ways of killing Christians—and, incidentally, a pagan now and then—and the surest way to get rich quickly in Christ's earthly kingdom is to invent a gun that can kill more Christians at one shot than any other existing gun.

Also, during the same generation each Christian Government has

[2] The reigning Russian monarch was Nicholas II, the son of Alexander III. It is not clear whether Twain has someone in particular in mind or whether he is being ironic. [Ed.]

played with its neighbors a continuous poker game in the naval line. In this game France puts up a battleship; England sees that battleship and goes it one battleship better; Russia comes in and raises it a battleship or two—*did*, before the untaught stranger entered the game and reduced her stately pile of chips to a damaged ferryboat and a cruiser that can't cruise. We are in it ourselves now. This game goes on and on and on. There is never a new shuffle; never a new deal. No player ever calls another's hand. It is merely an unending game of put up and put up and put up; and by the law of probabilities a day is coming when no Christians will be left on the land, except the women. The men will all be at sea, manning the fleets.

This singular game, which is so costly and so ruinous and so silly, is called statesmanship—which is different from assmanship on account of the spelling. Anybody but a statesman could invent some way to reduce these vast armaments to rational and sensible and safe police proportions, with the result that thenceforth all Christians could sleep in their beds unafraid, and even the Savior could come down and walk on the seas, foreigner as He is, without dread of being chased by Christian battleships.

Has the Bible done something still worse than drench the planet with innocent blood? To my mind it has—but this is only an opinion, and it may be a mistaken one. There has never been a Protestant boy or a Protestant girl whose mind the Bible has not soiled. No Protestant child ever comes clean from association with the Bible. This association cannot be prevented. Sometimes the parents try to prevent it by not allowing the children to have access to the Bible's awful obscenities, but this only whets the child's desire to taste that forbidden fruit, and it does taste it—seeks it out secretly and devours it with a strong and grateful appetite. The Bible does its baleful work in the propagation of vice among children, and vicious and unclean ideas, daily and constantly, in every Protestant family in Christendom. It does more of this deadly work than all the other unclean books in Christendom put together; and not only more, but a thousandfold more. It is easy to protect the young from those other books, and they are protected from them. But they have no protection against the deadly Bible.

Is it doubted that the young people hunt out the forbidden passages privately and study them with pleasure? If my reader were here present—let him be of either sex or any age, between ten and ninety—I would make him answer this question himself—and he could answer in only one way. He would be obliged to say that by his own knowledge and experience of the days of his early youth he knows positively that the Bible defiles all Protestant children, without a single exception.

Do I think the Christian religion is here to stay? Why should I think so? There had been a thousand religions before it was born. They are all dead. There had been millions of gods before ours was invented. Swarms of them are dead and forgotten long ago. Ours is by long odds the worst

God that the ingenuity of man has begotten from his insane imagination—
and shall He and His Christianity be immortal against the great array of
probabilities furnished by the theological history of the past? No. I think
that Christianity and its God must follow the rule. They must pass on in
their turn and make room for another God and a stupider religion. Or perhaps a better than this? No. That is not likely. History shows that in the
matter of religions we progress backward and not the other way. No matter,
there will be a new God and a new religion. They will be introduced to
popularity and accepted with the only arguments that have ever persuaded
any people in this earth to adopt Christianity, or any other religion that
they were not born to: the Bible, the sword, the torch and the axe—the
only missionaries that have ever scored a single victory since gods and religions began in the world. After the new God and the new religion have
become established in the usual proportions—one-fifth of the world's population ostensible adherents, the four-fifths pagan missionary field, with the
missionary scratching its continental back complacently and inefficiently—
will the new converts believe in them? Certainly they will. They have always
believed in the million gods and religions that have been stuffed down their
midriffs. There isn't anything so grotesque or so incredible that the average
human being can't believe it. . . .

Four

Saturday, June 23, 1906

. . .

We know that the real God, the Supreme God, the actual Maker of
the universe, made everything that is in it. We know that He made all the
creatures, from the microbe and the brontosaur down to man and the monkey,
and that He knew what would happen to each and every one of them from
the beginning of time to the end of it. In the case of each creature, big or
little, He made it an unchanging law that that creature should suffer wanton
and unnecessary pains and miseries every day of its life—that by that law
these pains and miseries could not be avoided by any diplomacy exercisable
by the creature; that its way, from birth to death, should be beset by traps,
pitfalls and gins, ingeniously planned and ingeniously concealed; and that
by another law every transgression of a law of Nature, either ignorantly or
wittingly committed, should in every instance be visited by a punishment
ten-thousandfold out of proportion to the transgression. We stand astonished
at the all-comprehensive malice which could patiently descend to the
contriving of elaborate tortures for the meanest and pitifulest of the countless
kinds of creatures that were to inhabit the earth. The spider was so contrived
that she would not eat grass but must catch flies and such things and inflict a
slow and horrible death upon them, unaware that her turn would come next.

The wasp was so contrived that he also would decline grass and stab the spider, not conferring upon her a swift and merciful death, but merely half-paralyzing her, then ramming her down into the wasp den, there to live and suffer for days while the wasp babies should chew her legs off at their leisure. In turn, there was a murderer provided for the wasp, and another murderer for the wasp's murderer, and so on throughout the whole scheme of living creatures in the earth. There isn't one of them that was not designed and appointed to inflict misery and murder on some fellow creature and suffer the same in turn from some other murderous fellow creature. In flying into the web the fly is merely guilty of an indiscretion—not a breach of any law—yet the fly's punishment is ten-thousandfold out of proportion to that little indiscretion.

The ten-thousandfold law of punishment is rigorously enforced against every creature, man included. The debt, whether made innocently or guiltily, is promptly collected by Nature—and in this world, without waiting for the ten-billionfold additional penalty appointed—in the case of man—for collection in the next.

This system of atrocious punishments for somethings and nothings begins upon the helpless baby on its first day in the world and never ceases until its last one. Is there a father who would persecute his baby with un-earned colics and the unearned miseries of teething, and follow these with mumps, measles, scarlet-fever and the hundred other persecutions appointed for the unoffending creature? And then follow these, from youth to the grave, with a multitude of ten-thousandfold punishments for laws broken either by intention or indiscretion? With a fine sarcasm we ennoble God with the title of Father—yet we know quite well that we should hang His style of father wherever we might catch him. . . .

In His destitution of one and all of the qualities which could grace a God and invite respect for Him and reverence and worship, the real God, the genuine God, the Maker of the mighty universe is just like all the other gods in the list. He proves every day that He takes no interest in man, nor in the other animals, further than to torture them, slay them and get out of this pastime such entertainment as it may afford—and do what He can not to get weary of the eternal and changeless monotony of it.

Five

Monday, June 25, 1906

. . .

As to the human race. There are many pretty and winning things about the human race. It is perhaps the poorest of all the inventions of all the gods but it has never suspected it once. There is nothing prettier than its naïve and complacent appreciation of itself. It comes out frankly and pro-claims without bashfulness or any sign of a blush that it is the noblest work of God. It has had a billion opportunities to know better, but all signs fail with this ass. I could say harsh things about it but I cannot bring myself to do it—it is like hitting a child.

Man is not to blame for what he is. He didn't make himself. He has no control over himself. All the control is vested in his temperament—which he did not create—and in the circumstances which hedge him round from the cradle to the grave and which he did not devise and cannot change by any act of his will, for the reason that he has no will. He is as purely a piece of automatic mechanism as is a watch, and can no more dictate or influence his actions than can the watch. He is a subject for pity, not blame—and not con-tempt. He is flung head over heels into this world without ever a chance to decline, and straightway he conceives and accepts the notion that he is in some mysterious way under obligations to the unknown Power that inflicted this outrage upon him—and thenceforth he considers himself responsible to that Power for every act of his life, and punishable for such of his acts as do not meet with the approval of that Power—yet that same man would argue quite differently if a human tyrant should capture him and put chains upon him of any kind and require obedience; that the tyrant had no right to do that; that the tyrant had no right to put commands upon him of any kind and require obedience; that the tyrant had no right to compel him to commit murder and then put the responsibility for the murder upon him. Man con-stantly makes a most strange distinction between man and his Maker in the matter of morals. He requires of his fellow man obedience to a very creditable code of morals but he observes without shame or disapproval his God's utter destitution of morals.

God ingeniously contrived man in such a way that he could not escape obedience to the laws of his passions, his appetites and his various unpleasant and undesirable qualities. God has so contrived him that all his goings out and comings in are beset by traps which he cannot possibly avoid and which compel him to commit what are called sins—and then God punishes him for doing these very things which from the beginning of time He had always intended that he should do. Man is a machine and God made it—without invitation from any one. Whoever makes a machine here below is responsi-ble for that machine's performance. No one would think of such a thing as trying to put the responsibility upon the machine itself. We all know per-fectly well—though we all conceal it, just as I am doing, until I shall be dead and out of reach of public opinion—we all know, I say, that God, and God alone, is responsible for every act and word of a human being's life between cradle and grave. We know it perfectly well. In our secret hearts we haven't the slightest doubt of it. In our secret hearts we have no hesitation in pro-claiming as an unthinking fool anybody who thinks he believes that he is by

any possibility capable of committing a sin against God—or who thinks he
thinks he is under obligations to God and owes Him thanks, reverence and
worship.

For Discussion

1. Paraphrase Twain's argument that the first part of Genesis is an "inexcusable treachery." What do you think of this argument? Comment on
   Twain's use of it as a recurring theme throughout the whole piece.
2. What differences does Twain see between the Old and the New Testa-
   ments?
3. Name the striking defects in the Bible, according to Twain.
4. How does Twain discredit the doctrine of the Immaculate Conception?
   Agree or disagree.
5. What does Twain see as the basic dangers of belief in the Biblical God?
   How does he support his argument?
6. What is Twain objecting to in the discussion of the Gospel of Peace?
   What is your opinion?
7. Describe the "real God" as Twain sees him.
8. Twain says that man's difficulties arise from his "moral sense." What does
   he mean?
9. What is Twain's religious philosophy? Would you call him an atheist?
   What is his personal philosophy regarding man's relationship to nature?
10. What universal human follies are being satirized on this piece?
11. Twain uses phrases such as "watery intellect" and "celestial bandits" to
    describe both the authors of the Bible and the Biblical God. Locate at
    least one similar use of invective on each page and discuss its effect.
    (Also see Mencken and Miller for use of invective.)
12. What is the central irony that Twain wants us to see in Christianity?

ADOLF HITLER

Nation and Race

The spectacular ascent to power of Adolf Hitler was the result of numerous causes, not the least of which was his appeal to a national sense of racial superiority. Book I of *Mein Kampf* (1925), from which the following selection is taken, was written while Hitler, a member of the National Socialist party, was in jail after an aborted attempt to overthrow the state government of Bavaria in 1923. Together with Book II (1926), it eventually became the creed for millions of Germans. Within eight years of its publication, Hitler had been elected Führer for life, and the decade that followed saw him conquer most of Europe. The combined strength of the Allies finally defeated the Axis powers, and Hitler is believed to have committed suicide in Berlin on April 20, 1945.

There are some truths which are so obvious that for this very reason they are not seen or at least not recognized by ordinary people. They sometimes pass by such truisms as though blind and are most astonished when someone suddenly discovers what everyone really ought to know. Columbus's eggs lie around by the hundreds of thousands, but Columbuses are met with less frequently.

Thus men without exception wander about in the garden of Nature; they imagine that they know practically everything and yet with few exceptions pass blindly by one of the most patent principles of Nature's rule: the inner segregation of the species of all living beings on this earth.

Even the most superficial observation shows that Nature's restricted form of propagation and increase is an almost rigid basic law of all the innumerable forms of expression of her vital urge. Every animal mates only with a member of the same species. The titmouse seeks the titmouse, the

From "Nation and Race" by Adolf Hitler from Vol. I, Chapter 11 of *Mein Kampf* trans. Ralph Manheim. Copyright 1943 by Houghton Mifflin Company. Reprinted by permission of the publisher.

finch the finch, the stork the stork, the field mouse the field mouse, the dormouse the dormouse, the wolf the she-wolf, etc.

Only unusual circumstances can change this, primarily the compulsion of captivity or any other cause that makes it impossible to mate within the same species. But then Nature begins to resist this with all possible means, and her most visible protest consists either in refusing further capacity for propagation to bastards or in limiting the fertility of later offspring; in most cases, however, she takes away the power of resistance to disease or hostile attacks.

This is only too natural.

Any crossing of two beings not at exactly the same level produces a medium between the level of the two parents. This means: the offspring will probably stand higher than the racially lower parent, but not as high as the higher one. Consequently, it will later succumb in the struggle against the higher level. Such mating is contrary to the will of Nature for a higher breeding of all life. The precondition for this does not lie in associating superior and inferior, but in the total victory of the former. The stronger must dominate and not blend with the weaker, thus sacrificing his own greatness. Only the born weakling can view this as cruel, but he after all is only a weak and limited man; for if this law did not prevail, any conceivable higher development of organic living beings would be unthinkable.

The consequence of this racial purity, universally valid in Nature, is not only the sharp outward delimitation of the various races, but their uniform character in themselves. The fox is always a fox, the goose a goose, the tiger a tiger, etc., and the difference can lie at most in the varying measure of force, strength, intelligence, dexterity, endurance, etc., of the individual specimens. But you will never find a fox who in his inner attitude might, for example, show humanitarian tendencies toward geese, as similarly there is no cat with a friendly inclination toward mice.

Therefore, here, too, the struggle among themselves arises less from inner aversion than from hunger and love. In both cases, Nature looks on calmly, with satisfaction, in fact. In the struggle for daily bread all those who are weak and sickly or less determined succumb, while the struggle of the males for the female grants the right or opportunity to propagate only to the healthiest. And struggle is always a means for improving a species' health and power of resistance and, therefore, a cause of its higher development.

If the process were different, all further and higher development would cease and the opposite would occur. For, since the inferior always predominates numerically over the best, if both had the same possibility of preserving life and propagating, the inferior would multiply so much more rapidly that in the end the best would inevitably be driven into the background, unless a correction of this state of affairs were undertaken. Nature does just this by subjecting the weaker part to such severe living conditions that by them alone the number is limited, and by not permitting the remainder to increase promiscuously, but making a new and ruthless choice according to strength and health.

No more than Nature desires the mating of weaker with stronger individuals, even less does she desire the blending of a higher with a lower race, since, if she did, her whole work of higher breeding, over perhaps hundreds of thousands of years, might be ruined with one blow.

Historical experience offers countless proofs of this. It shows with terrifying clarity that in every mingling of Aryan blood with that of lower peoples the result was the end of the cultured people. North America, whose population consists in by far the largest part of Germanic elements who mixed but little with the lower colored peoples, shows a different humanity and culture from Central and South America, where the predominantly Latin immigrants often mixed with the aborigines on a large scale. By this one example, we can clearly and distinctly recognize the effect of racial mixture. The Germanic inhabitant of the American continent, who has remained racially pure and unmixed, rose to be master of the continent; he will remain the master as long as he does not fall a victim to defilement of the blood.

The result of all racial crossing is therefore in brief always the following:

(a) Lowering of the level of the higher race;
(b) Physical and intellectual regression and hence the beginning of a slowly but surely progressing sickness.

To bring about such a development is, then, nothing else but to sin against the will of the eternal creator.

And as a sin this act is rewarded.

When man attempts to rebel against the iron logic of Nature, he comes into struggle with the principles to which he himself owes his existence as a man. And this attack must lead to his own doom.

Here, of course, we encounter the objection of the modern pacifist, as truly Jewish in its effrontery as it is stupid! "Man's rôle is to overcome Nature!"

Millions thoughtlessly parrot this Jewish nonsense and end up by really imagining that they themselves represent a kind of conqueror of Nature; though in this they dispose of no other weapon than an idea, and at that such a miserable one, that if it were true no world at all would be conceivable.

But quite aside from the fact that man has never yet conquered Nature in anything, but at most has caught hold of and tried to lift one or another corner of her immense gigantic veil of eternal riddles and secrets, that in reality he invents nothing but only discovers everything, that he does not dominate Nature, but has only risen on the basis of his knowledge of various laws and secrets of Nature to be lord over those other living creatures who lack this knowledge—quite aside from all this, an idea cannot overcome the preconditions for the development and being of humanity, since the idea itself depends only on man. Without human beings there is no human idea in this world, therefore, the idea as such is always conditioned by the presence of human beings and hence of all the laws which created the precondition for their existence.

And not only that! Certain ideas are even tied up with certain men. This applies most of all to those ideas whose content originates, not in an exact scientific truth, but in the world of emotion, or, as it is so beautifully and clearly expressed today, reflects an "inner experience." All these ideas, which have nothing to do with cold logic as such, but represent only pure expressions of feeling, ethical conceptions, etc., are chained to the existence of men, to whose intellectual imagination and creative power they owe their existence. Precisely in this case the preservation of these definite races and men is the precondition for the existence of these ideas. Anyone, for example, who really desired the victory of the pacifistic idea in this world with all his heart would have to fight with all the means at his disposal for the conquest of the world by the Germans; for, if the opposite should occur, the last pacifist would die out with the last German, since the rest of the world has never fallen so deeply as our own people, unfortunately, has for this nonsense so contrary to Nature and reason. Then, if we were serious, whether we liked it or not, we would have to wage wars in order to arrive at pacifism. This and nothing else was what Wilson, the American world savior, intended, or so at least our German visionaries believed—and thereby his purpose was fulfilled.

In actual fact the pacifist-humane idea is perfectly all right perhaps when the highest type of man has previously conquered and subjected the world to an extent that makes him the sole ruler of this earth. Then this idea lacks the power of producing evil effects in exact proportion as its practical application becomes rare and finally impossible. Therefore, first struggle and then we shall see what can be done. Otherwise mankind has passed the high point of its development and the end is not the domination of any ethical idea but barbarism and consequently chaos. At this point someone or other may laugh, but this planet once moved through the ether for millions of years without human beings and it can do so again some day if men forget that they owe their higher existence, not to the ideas of a few crazy ideologists, but to the knowledge and ruthless application of Nature's stern and rigid laws.

Everything we admire on this earth today—science and art, technology and inventions—is only the creative product of a few peoples and originally perhaps of *one* race. On them depends the existence of this whole culture. If they perish, the beauty of this earth will sink into the grave with them.

However much the soil, for example, can influence men, the result of the influence will always be different depending on the races in question. The low fertility of a living space may spur the one race to the highest achievements; in others it will only be the cause of bitterest poverty and final undernourishment with all its consequences. The inner nature of peoples is always determining for the manner in which outward influences will be effective. What leads the one to starvation trains the other to hard work.

All great cultures of the past perished only because the originally creative race died out from blood poisoning.

The ultimate cause of such a decline was their forgetting that all culture depends on men and not conversely; hence that to preserve a certain culture the man who creates it must be preserved. This preservation is bound up with the rigid law of necessity and the right to victory of the best and stronger in this world.

Those who want to live, let them fight, and those who do not want to fight in this world of eternal struggle do not deserve to live.

Even if this were hard—that is how it is! Assuredly, however, by far the harder fate is that which strikes the man who thinks he can overcome Nature, but in the last analysis only mocks her. Distress, misfortune, and diseases are her answer.

The man who misjudges and disregards the racial laws actually forfeits the happiness that seems destined to be his. He thwarts the triumphal march of the best race and hence also the precondition for all human progress, and remains, in consequence, burdened with all the sensibility of man, in the animal realm of helpless misery.

. . .

It is idle to argue which race or races were the original representative of human culture and hence the real founders of all that we sum up under the word "humanity." It is simpler to raise this question with regard to the present, and here an easy, clear answer results. All the human culture, all the results of art, science, and technology that we see before us today, are almost exclusively the creative product of the Aryan. This very fact admits of the not unfounded inference that he alone was the founder of all higher humanity, therefore representing the prototype of all that we understand by the word "man." He is the Prometheus of mankind from whose bright forehead the divine spark of genius has sprung at all times, forever kindling anew that fire of knowledge which illumined the night of silent mysteries and thus caused man to climb the path to mastery over the other beings of this earth. Exclude him—and perhaps after a few thousand years darkness will again descend on the earth, human culture will pass, and the world turn to a desert.

For Discussion

1. Discuss the logic of the analogy Hitler uses to introduce his argument for racial purity.
2. How scientifically accurate are Hitler's assertions regarding Nature and its laws?
3. In deductive argument, if the premises are false, the conclusions are false. What unsupported assumptions does Hitler use as premises?
4. Hitler's mastery of propaganda is well known. Discuss the connotations of the following "glittering generalities":
    a) racial progress
    b) highest type of man
    c) will of nature
    d) will of the eternal order
    e) racial laws
5. Hitler frequently pairs words like "higher-lower," "superior-inferior," and "stronger-weaker." What kind of thinking is reflected in these value judgments?
6. Discuss the reasoning that links warfare with the will of nature, with pacifism, and with culture.
7. Hitler was one of the world's most powerful speakers, shouting passionately at his audience and whipping them into a frenzy of patriotism. Find passages which lend themselves to this kind of oratory.

MALCOLM X

After the Bombing

Malcolm Little, the Christian name of the remarkable man whose speech follows, was born in Omaha, Nebraska, in 1925. A school drop-out at fifteen, he was convicted of burglary and sent to prison where he was converted to the Nation of Islam (Black Muslims) and adopted the name he bore until his assassination in New York in February of 1965. After strongly disagreeing with Elijah Muhammed, the leader of the Muslims, Malcolm X left the movement while retaining his faith. Toward the end of his life, as his speeches record and as his autobiography explains, he became more interested in internationalizing the racial struggle, at the same time advocating universal brotherhood. His assertion of the right of self-defense and his aversion to pacifism made him a symbol of racial threat. To a whole generation of militants—black and white—Malcolm X has become the most important of the black martyrs. His assassination remains unsolved. At 2:30 A.M. on the day of the following speech, Molotov cocktails were thrown into his home, but he and his family escaped injury.

Attorney Milton Henry, distinguished guests, brothers and sisters, ladies and gentlemen, friends and enemies: I want to point out first that I am very happy to be here this evening and I am thankful to the Afro-American Broadcasting Company for the invitation to come here this evening. As Attorney Milton Henry has stated—I should say Brother Milton Henry because that's what he is, our brother—I was in a house last night that was bombed, my own. It didn't destroy all my clothes but you know what fire and smoke do to things. The only thing I could get my hands on before leaving was what I have on now.

It isn't something that made me lose confidence in what I am doing, because my wife understands and I have children from this size on down, and even in their young age they understand. I think they would rather have a father or brother or whatever the situation may be who will take a stand in the face of reaction from any narrow-minded people rather than to compromise and later on have to grow up in shame and disgrace.

So I ask you to excuse my appearance. I don't normally come out in front of people without a shirt and tie. I guess that's somewhat a holdover from the Black Muslim movement which I was in. That's one of the good aspects of that movement. It teaches you to be very careful and conscious of how you look, which is a positive contribution on their part. But that positive contribution on their part is greatly offset by too many liabilities.

Also, last night, when the temperature was about 20 above and when this explosion took place, I was caught in what I had on—some pajamas. In trying to get my family out of the house, none of us stopped for any clothes at that point, so we were out in the 20 degree cold. I got them into the house of the neighbor next door. I thought perhaps being in that condition for so long I would get pneumonia or a cold or something like that, so a doctor came today, a nice doctor, and shot something in my arm that naturally put me to sleep. I've been back there asleep ever since the program started in order to get back in shape. So if I have a tendency to stutter or slow down, it's still the effect of that drug. I don't know what kind it was, but it was good; it makes you sleep, and there's nothing like sleeping though a whole lot of excitement.

Tonight one of the things that has to be stressed, which has not only the United States very much worried but also has France, Great Britain and most of the powers who formerly were known as colonial powers worried, and that is the African revolution. They are more concerned with the revolution that is taking place on the African continent than they are with the revolution in Asia and in Latin America. And this is because there are so many people of African ancestry within the domestic confines or jurisdictions of these various governments . . . . There is an increasing number of dark-skinned people in England and also in France.

When I was in Africa in May, I noticed a tendency on the part of the Afro-Americans to—what I call lollygag. Everybody else who was over there had something on the ball, something they were doing, something constructive. Let's take Ghana as an example. There would be many refugees in Ghana from South Africa. . . . Some were being trained in how to be soldiers but others were involved as a pressure group or lobby group to let the people of Ghana never forget what happened to the brother in South Africa. Also you had brothers there from Angola and Mozambique. All of the Africans who were exiles from their particular country and would be in a place like Ghana or Tanganyika, now Tanzania—they would be training. Their every move would be designed to offset what was happening to their people back home where they had left. . . . When they escaped from their respective countries that were still colonized, they didn't try and run away from the family; as soon as they got where they were going, they began to organize into pressure groups to get support at the international level against the injustices they were experiencing back home.

But the American Negroes or the Afro-Americans, who were in these various countries, some working for this government, some working for that government, some in business—they were just socializing, they had turned their back on the cause over here, they were partying, you know. When I went through one country in particular, I heard a lot of their complaints and I didn't make any move. But when I got to another country, I found the Afro-Americans there were making the same complaints. So we sat down and talked and we organized a branch in this particular country of the Organization of Afro-American Unity. That one was the only one in existence at that time. Then during the summer when I went back to Africa, I was able in each country that I visited to get the Afro-American community together and organize them and make them aware of their responsibility to those of us who are still here in the lion's den.

They began to do this quite well, and when I got to Paris and London —there are many Afro-Americans in Paris, and many in London—in November, we organized a group in Paris and within a very short time they had grown into a well-organized unit. In conjunction with the African community, they invited me to Paris Tuesday to address a large gathering of Parisians and Afro-Americans and people from the Caribbean and also from Africa who were interested in our struggle in this country and the rate of progress that we have been making. But the French government and the British government and this government here, the United States, know that I have been almost fanatically stressing the importance of the Afro-Americans uniting with the Africans and working as a coalition, especially in areas which are of mutual benefit to all of us. And the governments in these different places were frightened . . . .

I might point out here that colonialism or imperialism, as the slave system of the West is called, is not something that is just confined to England or France or the United States. The interests in this country are in cahoots with the interests in France and the interests in Britain. It's one huge complex or combine, and it creates what's known not as the American power structure or the French power structure, but an international power structure. This international power structure is used to suppress the masses of dark-skinned people all over the world and exploit them of their natural resources, so that the era in which you and I have been living during the past ten years most specifically has witnessed the upsurge on the part of the black man in Africa against the power structure.

He wants his freedom and now. Mind you, the power structure is international, and its domestic base is in London, in Paris, in Washington,

D.C., and so forth. The outside or external phase of the revolution which is manifest in the attitude and action of the Africans today is troublesome enough. The revolution on the outside of the house, or the outside of the structure, is troublesome enough. But now the powers that be are beginning to see that this struggle on the outside by the black man is affecting, infecting the black man who is on the inside of that structure—I hope you understand what I am trying to say. The newly awakened people all over the world pose a problem for what is known as Western interests, which is imperialism, colonialism, racism and all these other negative isms or vulturistic isms. Just as the external forces pose a grave threat, they can now see that the internal forces pose an even greater threat. But the internal forces pose an even greater threat only when they have properly analyzed the situation and know what the stakes really are.

Just advocating a coalition of African, Afro-Americans, Arabs, and Asians who live within the structure automatically has upset France, which is supposed to be one of the most liberal countries on earth, and it made them expose their hand. England is the same way. And I don't have to tell you about this country that we are living in now. When you count the number of dark-skinned people in the Western hemisphere you can see that there are probably over 100 million. When you consider Brazil has two-thirds what we call colored, or non-white, and Venezuela, Honduras and other Central American countries, Cuba and Jamaica, and the United States and even Canada—when you total all these people up, you have probably over 100 million. And this 100 million on the inside of the power structure today is what is causing a great deal of concern for the power structure itself . . . .

We thought that the first thing to do was to unite our people, not only internally, but with our brothers and sisters abroad. It was for that purpose that I spent five months in the Middle East and Africa during the summer. The trip was very enlightening, inspiring, and fruitful. I didn't go into any African country, or any country in the Middle East for that matter, and run into any closed door, closed mind, or closed heart. I found a warm reception and an amazingly deep interest and sympathy for the black man in this country in regards to our struggle for human rights . . . .

I hope you will forgive me for speaking so informally tonight, but I frankly think it is always better to be informal. As far as I am concerned, I can speak to people better in an informal way than I can with all of this stiff formality that ends up meaning nothing. Plus, when people are informal, they are relaxed. When they are relaxed, their mind is more open, and they can weigh things more objectively. Whenever you and I are discussing our problems we need to be very objective, very cool, calm and collected. That doesn't mean we should always be. There is a time to be cool and a time to be hot. See—you got messed up into thinking that there is only one time for everything. There is a time to love and a time to hate. Even Solomon said that, and he was in that book too. You're just taking something out of the book that fits your cowardly nature when you don't want to fight, and you say, "Well, Jesus said don't fight." But I don't even believe Jesus said that . . . .

Before I get involved in anything nowadays, I have to straighten out my own position, which is clear. I am not a racist in any form whatsoever. I don't believe in any form of racism. I don't believe in any form of discrimination or segregation. I believe in Islam. I am a Muslim and there is nothing wrong with being a Muslim, nothing wrong with the religion of Islam. It just teaches us to believe in Allah as the God. Those of you who are Christians probably believe in the same God, because I think you believe in the God who created the universe. That's the one we believe in, the one who created the universe—the only difference being you call him God and we call him Allah. The Jews call him Jehovah. If you could understand Hebrew, you would probably call him Jehovah too. If you could understand Arabic, you would probably call him Allah. But since the white man, your friend, took your language away from you during slavery, the only language you know is his language. You know your friend's language, so when he's putting the rope around your neck, you call for God and he calls for God. And you wonder why the one you call on never answers . . . .

Elijah Muhammed had taught us that the white man could not enter into Mecca in Arabia and all of us who followed him, we believed it . . . . When I got over there and went to Mecca and saw these people who were blond and blue-eyed and pale-skinned and all those things, I said, "Well," but I watched them closely. And I noticed that though they were white, and they would call themselves white, there was a difference between them and the white ones over here. And that basic difference was this: In Asia or the Arab world or in Africa, where the Muslims are, if you find one who says he's white, all he's doing is using an adjective to describe something that's incidental about him, one of his incidental characteristics; there is nothing else to it, he's just white.

But when you get the white man over here in America and he says he's white, he means something else. You can listen to the sound of his voice—when he says he's white, he means he's boss That's right. That's what white means in this language. You know the expression, "free, white and twenty-one." He made that up. He's letting you know that white means free, boss. He's up there, so that when he says he's white he has a little different sound in his voice. I know you know what I'm talking about . . . .

Despite the fact that I saw that Islam was a religion of brotherhood, I also had to face reality. And when I got back into this American society, I'm not in a society that practices brotherhood. I'm in a society that might preach it on Sunday, but they don't practice it on any day. America is a society where there is no brotherhood. This society is controlled primarily by the racists and segregationists who are in Washington, D.C., in positions of power. And from Washington, D.C., they exercise the same forms of brutal oppression against dark-skinned people in South and North Vietnam, or in the Congo, or in Cuba or any other place on this earth where they are trying to exploit and oppress. That is a society whose government doesn't hesitate to inflict the most brutal form of punishment and oppression upon dark-skinned people all over the world.

Look right now what's going on in and around Saigon and Hanoi and in the Congo and elsewhere. They are violent when their interests are at stake. But for all that violence they display at the international level, when you and I want just a little bit of freedom, we're supposed to be nonviolent. They're violent in Korea, they're violent in Germany, they're violent in the South Pacific, they're violent in Cuba, they're violent wherever they go. But when it comes time for you and me to protect ourselves against lynchings, they tell us to be nonviolent.

That's a shame. Because we get tricked into being nonviolent, and when somebody stands up and talks like I just did, they say, "Why, he's advocating violence." Isn't that what they say? Everytime you pick up your newspaper, you see where one of these things has written into it that I am advocating violence. I have never advocated any violence. I have only said that black people who are the victims of organized violence perpetrated upon us by the Klan, the Citizens Councils, and many other forms, should defend ourselves. And when I say we should defend ourselves against the violence of others, they use their press skilfully to make the world think that I am calling for violence, period. I wouldn't call on anybody to be violent without a cause. But I think the black man in this country, above and beyond people all over the world, will be more justified when he stands up and starts to protect himself, no matter how many necks he has to break and heads he has to crack . . . .

The Klan is a cowardly outfit. They have perfected the art of making Negroes be afraid. As long as the Negro is afraid, the Klan is safe. But the Klan itself is cowardly. One of them never come after one of you. They all come together. They're scared of you. And you sit there when they're putting the rope around your neck saying, "Forgive them, Lord, they know not what they do." As long as they've been doing it, they're experts at it, they know what they're doing. No, since the federal government has shown that it isn't going to do anything about it but *talk*, then it is a duty, it's your and my duty as men, as human beings, it is our duty to our people, to organize ourselves and let the government know that if they don't stop that Klan, we'll stop it ourselves. *Then* you'll see the government start doing something about it. But don't ever think that they're going to do it just on some kind of morality basis. No. So I don't believe in violence—that's why I want to stop it. And you can't stop it with love, not love of those things down there. No!

So, we only mean vigorous action in self-defense, and that vigorous action we feel we're justified in initiating by any means necessary.

Now, for saying something like that, the press calls us racist and people who are "violent in reverse." This is how they psycho you. They make you think that if you try to stop the Klan from lynching you, you're practicing violence in reverse. Pick up on this, I hear a lot of you parrot what the man says. You say, "I don't want to be a Ku Klux Klan in reverse." Well, if a criminal comes around your house with his gun, brother, just because he's got a gun and he's robbing your house, and he's a robber, it doesn't make you a robber because you grab your gun and run him out. No, the man is using some tricky logic on you. I say it is time for black people to put together the type of action, the unity, that is necessary to pull the sheet off of them so they won't be frightening black people any longer. That's all. And when we say this, the press calls us "racist in reverse." "Don't struggle except within the ground rules that the people you're struggling against have laid down." Why, this is insane, but it shows how they can do it. With skilful manipulating of the press they're able to make the victim look like the criminal and the criminal look like the victim.

Right now in New York we have a couple of cases where the police grabbed a brother and beat him unmercifully—and charged him was assaulting them. They used the press to make it look like he is the criminal and they are the victims. This is how they do it, and if you study how they do it here then you'll know how they do it over there. It's the same game going all the time, and if you and I don't awaken and see what this man is doing to us, then it will be too late. They may have the gas ovens built before you realize that they're already hot.

One of the shrewd ways that they project us in the image of a criminal is that they take statistics and with the press feed these statistics to the public, primarily the white public. Because there are some well-meaning persons in the white public as well as bad-meaning persons in the white public. And whatever the government is going to do, it always wants the public on its side—whether it is the local government, state government or federal government. At the local level, they will create an image by feeding statistics to the public through the press showing the high crime rate in the Negro community. As soon as this high crime rate is emphasized through the press, then people begin to look upon the Negro community as a community of criminals.

And then any Negro in the community can be stopped in the street. "Put your hands up," and they pat you down. Might be a doctor, a lawyer, a preacher or some other kind of Uncle Tom, but despite your professional standing, you'll find that you're the same victim as the man who's in the alley. Just because you're black and you live in a black community which has been projected as a community of criminals. And once the public accepts this image, it also paves the way for police-state type of activity in the Negro community—they can use any kind of brutal methods to suppress blacks because they're criminals anyway. And what has given us this image? The press again, by letting the power structure or the racist element in the power structure use them in that way.

A very good example was the riots that took place during the summer. I was in Africa, I read about them over there. If you noticed, they referred to the rioters as vandals, hoodlums, thieves, and they skilfully took the burden off the society for its failure to correct these negative conditions in the black community. They took the burden completely off the society and put it right on the community by using the press to make it appear that the looting and all of this was proof that the whole act was nothing but vandals and robbers and thieves, who weren't really interested in anything other than that which was negative. And I hear many dumb, brainwashed Negroes who parrot the same old party line that the man handed down in his paper.

It was not the case that they were just knocking out store windows ignorantly. In Harlem, for instance, all of the stores are owned by white people, all of the buildings are owned by white people. The black people are just there—paying rent, buying the groceries; but they don't own the stores, clothing stores, food stores, any kind of stores; don't even own the homes that they live in. These are all owned by outsiders, and for these run-down apartment dwellings, the black man in Harlem pays more money than the man down in the rich Park Avenue section. It costs us more money to live in the slums than it costs them to live down on Park Avenue. Black people in Harlem know this, and that the white merchants charge us more money for food in Harlem—and it's the cheap food, the worst food; we have to pay more money for it than the man has to pay for it downtown. So black people know that they're being exploited and that their blood is being sucked and they see no way out.

When the thing is finally sparked, the white man is not there—he's gone. The merchant is not there, the landlord is not there, the one they consider to be the enemy isn't there. So, they knock at his property. This is what makes them knock down the store windows and set fire to things, and things of that sort. It's not that they're thieves. But they [the newspapers] are trying to project the image to the public that this is being done by thieves, and thieves alone. And they ignore the fact that it is not thievery alone. It's a corrupt, vicious, hypocritical system that has castrated the black man, and the only way the black man can get back at it is to strike it in the only way he knows how.

[When I say] they use the press, that doesn't mean that all reporters are bad. Some of them are good, I suppose. But you can take their collective approach to any problem and see that they can always agree when it gets to you and me. They knew that the Afro-American Broadcasting Company was giving this affair—which is designed to honor outstanding black Americans, is it not? But you find nothing in the newspapers that gives the slightest hint that this affair was going to take place—not one hint, though there are supposed to be many sources of news. If you don't think that they're in cahoots, watch. They're all interested, or none of them are interested. It's not a staggering thing. They're not going to say anything in advance about an affair that's being given by any black people who believe in functioning beyond the scope of the ground rules that are laid down by the liberal elements of the power structure.

When you start thinking for yourselves, you frighten them, and they try and block your getting to the public, for the fear that if the public listens to you then the public won't listen to them anymore. And they've got certain Negroes whom they have to keep blowing up in the papers to make them look like leaders. So that the people will keep on following them, no matter how many knocks they get on their heads following them. This is how the man does it, and if you don't wake up and find out how he does it, I tell you, they'll be building gas chambers and gas ovens pretty soon—I don't mean those kind you've got at home in your kitchen—[and] . . . you'll be in one of them, just like the Jews ended up in gas ovens over there in Germany. You're in a society that's just as capable of building gas ovens for black people as Hitler's society was . . . .

Now what effect does [the struggle over Africa] have on us? Why should the black man in America concern himself since he's been away from the African continent for three or four hundred years? Why should we concern ourselves? What impact does what happens to them have upon us? Number one, you have to realize that up until 1959 Africa was dominated by the colonial powers. Having complete control over Africa, the colonial powers of Europe projected the image of Africa negatively. They always project Africa in a negative light: jungle savages, cannibals, nothing civilized. Why then naturally it was so negative that it was negative to you and me, and you and I began to hate it. We didn't want anybody telling us anything about Africa, much less calling us Africans. In hating Africa and in hating the Africans, we ended up hating ourselves, without even realizing it. Because you can't hate the roots of a tree, and not hate the tree. You can't hate your origin and not end up hating yourself. You can't hate Africa and not hate yourself.

You show me one of these people over here who has been thoroughly brainwashed and has a negative attitude toward Africa, and I'll show you one who has a negative attitude toward himself. You can't have a positive attitude toward yourself and a negative attitude toward Africa at the same time. To the same degree that your understanding of and attitude toward Africa become positive, you'll find that your understanding of and your attitude toward yourself will also become positive. And this is what the white man knows. So they very skilfully make you and me hate our African identity, our African characteristics.

You know yourself that we have been a people who hated our African characteristics. We hated our heads, we hated the shape of our nose, we wanted one of those long dog-like noses, you know; we hated the color of our skin, hated the blood of Africa that was in our veins. And in hating our features and our skin and our blood, why, we had to end up hating ourselves. And we hated ourselves. Our color became to us a chain—we felt that it was holding us back; our color became to us like a prison which we felt was keeping us confined, not letting us go this way or that way. We felt that all of these restrictions were based solely upon our color, and the psychological reaction to that would have to be that as long as we felt imprisoned or chained or trapped by black skin, black features and black blood, that skin and those features and that blood holding us back automatically had to become hateful to us. And it became hateful to us.

It made us feel inferior; it made us feel inadequate; made us feel helpless. And when we fell victims to this feeling of inadequacy or inferiority or helplessness, we turned to somebody else to show us the way. We didn't have confidence in another black man to show us the way, or black people to show us the way. In those days we didn't. We didn't think a black man could do anything except play some horns—you know, make some sound and make you happy with some songs and in that way. But in serious things, where our food, clothing, shelter and education were concerned, we turned to the man. We never thought in terms of bringing these things into existence for ourselves, we never thought in terms of doing things for ourselves. Because we felt helpless. What made us feel helpless was our hatred for ourselves. And our hatred for ourselves stemmed from our hatred for things African . . . .

After 1959 the spirit of African nationalism was fanned to a high flame and we then began to witness the complete collapse of colonialism. France began to get out of French West Africa, Belgium began to make moves to get out of the Congo, Britain began to make moves to get out of Kenya, Tanganyika, Uganda, Nigeria and some of these other places. And although it looked like they were getting out, they pulled a trick that was colossal.

When you're playing ball and they've got you trapped, you don't throw the ball away—you throw it to one of your teammates who's in the clear. And this is what the European powers did. They were trapped on the African continent, they couldn't stay there—they were looked upon as colonial and imperialist. They had to pass the ball to someone whose image was different, and they passed the ball to Uncle Sam. And he picked it up and has been running it for a touchdown ever since. He was in the clear, he was not looked upon as one who had colonized the African continent. At that time, the Africans couldn't see that though the United States hadn't colonized the African continent, it had colonized 22 million blacks here on this continent. Because we're just as thoroughly colonized as anybody else.

When the ball was passed to the United States, it was passed at the time when John Kennedy came to power. He picked it up and helped to run it. He was one of the shrewdest backfield runners that history has ever recorded. He surrounded himself with intellectuals—highly educated, learned and well-informed people. And their analysis told him that the government of America was confronted with a new problem. And this new problem stemmed from the fact that Africans were now awakened, they were enlightened, they were fearless, they would fight. This meant that the Western powers couldn't stay there by force. Since their own economy, the European economy and the American economy, was based upon their continued influence over the African continent, they had to find some means of staying there. So they used the friendly approach.

They switched from the old openly colonial imperialistic approach to the benevolent approach. They came up with some benevolent colonialism, philanthropic colonialism, humanitarianism, or dollarism. Immediately everything was Peace Corps, Operation Crossroads, "We've got to help our African brothers." Pick up on that: Can't help us in Mississippi. Can't help us in Alabama, or Detroit, or out here in Dearborn where some real Ku Klux Klan lives. They're going to send all the way to Africa to help. I know Dearborn; you know, I'm from Detroit, I used to live out here in Inkster. And you had to go through Dearborn to get to Inkster. Just like driving through Mississippi when you got to Dearborn. Is it still that way? Well, you should straighten it out.

So, realizing that it was necessary to come up with these new approaches, Kennedy did it. He created an image of himself that was skilfully designed to make the people on the African continent think that he was Jesus, the great white father, come to make things right. I'm telling you, some of these Negroes cried harder when he died than they cried for Jesus when he was crucified. From 1954 to 1964 was the era in which we witnessed the emerging of Africa. The impact that this had on the civil-rights struggle in America has never been fully told.

For one thing, one of the primary ingredients in the complete civil-rights struggle was the Black Muslim movement. The Black Muslim movement took no part in things political, civic—it didn't take too much part in anything other than stopping people from doing this drinking, smoking, and so on. Moral reform it had, but beyond that it did nothing. But it talked such a strong talk that it put the other Negro organizations on the spot. Before the Black Muslim movement came along, the NAACP was looked upon as radical; they were getting ready to investigate it. And then along came the Muslim movement and frightened the white man so hard that he began to say, "Thank God for old Uncle Roy, and Uncle Whitney and Uncle A. Philip and Uncle"—you've got a whole lot of uncles in there; I can't remember their names, they're all older than I so I call them "uncle." Plus, if you use the word "Uncle Tom" nowadays, I hear they can sue you for libel, you know. So I don't call any of them Uncle Tom anymore. I call them Uncle Roy.

One of the things that made the Black Muslim movement grow was its emphasis upon things African. This was the secret to the growth of the Black Muslim movement. African blood, African origin, African culture, African ties. And you'd be surprised—we discovered that deep within the subconscious of the black man is this country, he is still more African than he is American. He *thinks* that he's more American than African, because the man is jiving him, the man is brainwashing him every day. He's telling him, "You're an American, you're an American." Man, how could you think you're an American when you haven't ever had any kind of an American treat over here? You have never, never. Ten men can be sitting at a table eating, you know, dining, and I can come and sit down where they're dining. They're dining; I've got a plate in front of me, but nothing is on it. Because all of us are sitting at the same table, are all of us diners? I'm not a diner until you let me dine. Just being at the table with others who are dining doesn't make me a diner, and this is what you've got to get in your head here in this country.

Just because you're in this country doesn't make you an American. No, you've got to go farther than that before you can become an American. You've got to enjoy the fruits of Americanism. You haven't enjoyed those fruits. You've enjoyed the thorns. You've enjoyed the thistles. But you have not enjoyed the fruits, no sir. You have fought harder for the fruits than the white man has, you have worked harder for the fruits than the white man has, but you've enjoyed less. When the man put the uniform on you and sent you abroad, you fought harder than they did. Yes, I know you—when you're fighting for them, you can fight.

The Black Muslim movement did make that contribution. They made the whole civil-rights movement become more militant, and more acceptable to the white power structure. He would rather have them than us. In fact, I think we forced many of the civil-rights leaders to be even more militant than they intended. I know some of them who get out there and "boom, boom, boom" and don't mean it. Because they're right on back in their corner as soon as the action comes.

John F. Kennedy also saw that it was necessary for a new approach among the American Negroes. And during his entire term in office, he specialized in how to psycho the American Negro. Now, a lot of you all don't like my saying that—but I wouldn't ever take a stand on that if I didn't know what I was talking about. By living in this kind of society, pretty much around them, and you know what I mean when I say "them," I learned to study them. You can think that they mean you some good ofttimes, but if you look at it a little closer you'll see that they don't mean you any good. That doesn't mean there aren't some of them who mean good. But it does mean that most of them don't mean good.

Kennedy's new approach was pretending to go along with us in our struggle for civil rights. He was another proponent of rights. But I remember the expose that *Look* magazine did on the Meredith situation in Mississippi. *Look* magazine did an expose showing that Robert Kennedy and Governor Barnett had made a deal, wherein the Attorney General was going to come down and try to force Meredith into school, and Barnett was going to stand at the door, you know, and say, "No, you can't come in." He was going to get in anyway, but it was all arranged in advance and then Barnett was supposed to keep the support of the white racists, because that's who he was upholding, and Kennedy would keep the support of the Negroes, because that's who he'd be upholding. It was a cut-and-dried deal. And it's not a secret; it was written, they write about it. But if that's a deal, how many other deals do you think go down? What you think is on the level is crookeder, brothers and sisters, than a pretzel, which is most crooked.

So in my conclusion I would like to point out that the approach that was used by the administration right up until today was designed skilfully to make it appear they were trying to solve the problem when they actually weren't. They would deal with the conditions, but never the cause. They only gave us tokenism. Tokenism benefits only a few. It never benefits the masses, and the masses are the ones who have the problem, not the few. That one who benefits from tokenism, he doesn't want to be around us anyway—that's why he picks up on the token . . . .

The masses of our people still have bad housing, bad schooling and inferior jobs, jobs that don't compensate with sufficient salaries for them to carry on their life in this world. So that the problem for the masses has gone absolutely unsolved. The only ones for whom it has been solved are people like Whitney Young, who is supposed to be placed in the cabinet, so the rumor says. He'll be the first black cabinet man. And that answers where he's at. And others have been given jobs, like Carl Rowan, who was put over the USIA, and is very skilfully trying to make Africans think that the problem of black men in this country is all solved.

The worst thing the white man can do to himself is to take one of these kinds of Negroes and ask him, "How do your people feel, boy?" He's going to tell that man that we are satisfied. That's what they do, brothers and sisters. They get behind the door and tell the white man we're satisfied. "Just keep on keeping me up here in front of them, boss, and I'll keep them behind you." That's what they talk when they're behind closed doors. Because, you see, the white man doesn't go along with anybody who's not for him. He doesn't care are you for right or wrong, he wants to know are you for him.

And if you're for him, he doesn't care what else you're for. As long as you're for him, then he puts you up over the Negro community. You become a spokesman.

In your struggle it's like standing on a revolving wheel; you're running, but you're not going anywhere. You run faster and faster and the wheel just goes faster and faster. You don't ever leave the spot that you're standing in. So, it is very important for you and me to see that our problem has to have a solution that will benefit the masses, not the upper class—so-called upper class. Actually, there's no such thing as an upper-class Negro, because he catches the same hell as the other class Negro. All of them catch the same hell, which is one of things that's good about this racist system—it make us all one . . . .

If you'd tell them right now what is in store for 1965, they'd think you crazy for sure. But 1965 will be the longest and hottest and bloodiest year of them all. It has to be, not because you want it to be, or I want it to be, or we want it to be, but because the conditions that created these explosions in 1963 are still here; the conditions that created explosions in 1964 are still here. You can't say that you're not going to have an explosion when you leave the conditions, the ingredients, still here. As long as those explosive ingredients remain, then you're going to have the potential for explosion on your hands.

And, brothers and sisters, let me tell you, I spend my time out there in the streets with people, all kinds of people, listening to what they have to say. And they're dissatisfied, they're disillusioned, they're fed up, they're getting to the point of frustration where they begin to feel, "What do we have to lose?" When you get to that point, you're the type of person who can create a very dangerously explosive atmosphere. This is what's happening in our neighborhoods, to our people.

I read in a poll taken by *Newsweek* magazine this week, saying that Negroes are satisfied. Oh, yes, *Newsweek,* you know, supposed to be a top magazine with a top pollster, talking about how satisfied Negroes are. Maybe I haven't met the Negroes he met. Because I know he hasn't met the ones that I've met. And this is dangerous. This is where the white man does himself the most harm. He invents statistics to create an image, thinking that that image is going to hold things in check. You know why they always say Negroes are lazy? Because they want Negroes to be lazy. They always say Negroes can't unite because they don't want Negroes to unite. And once they put this thinking in the Negro's mind, they feel that he tries to fulfill their image. If they say you can't unite black people, and then you come to them to unite them, they won't unite because it's been said that they're not supposed to unite. It's a psycho that they work, and it's the same way with these statistics.

When they think that an explosive era is coming up, then they grab their press again and begin to shower the Negro public, to make it appear that all Negroes are satisfied. Because if you know you're dissatisfied all by yourself and ten others aren't, you play it cool; but if you know that all ten of you are dissatisfied, you get with it. This is what the man knows. The man knows that if these Negroes find out how dissatisfied they really are— even Uncle Tom is dissatisfied, he's just playing his part for now—this is what makes the man frightened. It frightens them in France and frightens them in England, and it frightens them in the United States.

And it is for this reason that it is so important for you and me to start organizing among ourselves, intelligently, and try to find out: "What are we going to do if this happens, that happens or the next thing happens?" Don't think that you're going to run to the man and say, "Look, boss, this is me." Why, when the deal goes down, you'll look just like me in his eyesight; I'll make it tough for you. Yes, when the deal goes down, he doesn't look at you in any better light than he looks at me. . . .

I point these things out, brothers and sisters, so that you and I will know the importance in 1965 of being in complete unity with each other, in harmony with each other, and not letting the man maneuver us into fighting one another. The situation I have been maneuvered into right now, between me and the Black Muslim movement, is something that I really deeply regret, because I don't think anything is more destructive than two groups of black people fighting each other. But it's something that can't be avoided because it goes deep down beneath the surface, and these things will come up in the very near future.

I might say this before I sit down. If you recall, when I left the Black Muslim movement, I stated clearly that it wasn't my intention to even continue to be aware that they existed; I was going to spend my time working in the non-Muslim community. But they were fearful if they didn't do something that perhaps many of those who were in the [Black Muslim] mosque would leave it and follow a different direction. So they had to start doing a takeoff on me, plus, they had to try and silence me because of what they know that I know. I think that they should know me well enough to know that they certainly can't frighten me. But when it does come to light—excuse me for keeping coughing like that, but I got some of that smoke last night—there are some things involving the Black Muslim movement which, when they come to light, will shock you.

The thing that you have to understand about those of us in the Black Muslim movement was that all of us believed 100 per cent in the divinity of Elijah Muhammad. We believed in him. We actually believed that God, in Detroit by the way, that God had taught him and all of that. I always believed that he believed it himself. And I was shocked when I found out that he himself didn't believe it. And when that shock reached me, then I began to look everywhere else and try and get a better understanding of the things that confront all of us so that we can get together in some kind of way to offset them.

I want to thank you for coming out this evening. I think it's wonderful that as many of you came out, considering the blackout on the meeting that took place. Milton Henry and the brothers who are here in Detroit are very progressive young men, and I would advise all of you to get with them in any way that you can to try and create some kind of united effort toward common goals, common objectives. Don't let the power structure maneuver you into a time-wasting battle with others when you could be involved in something that is constructive and getting a real job done . . . .

I say again that I'm not a racist, I don't believe in any form of segregation or anything like that. I'm for brotherhood for everybody, but I don't believe in forcing brotherhood upon people who don't want it. Let us practice brotherhood among ourselves, and then if others want to practice brotherhood with us, we're for practicing it with them also. But I don't think that we should run around trying to love somebody who doesn't love us. Thank you.

For Discussion

1. What purpose does the reference to the bombing serve?
2. What did the author's trip to Mecca teach him about the differences between blacks and whites there? Here?
3. Explain Malcolm X's position on brotherhood. On nonviolence. On being an American.
4. Discuss and evaluate Malcolm X's charges of white exploitation of the ghetto Negro.
5. Malcolm X is considered to be the most influential advocate of "Black Is Beautiful." How does he relate black pride to the concept of hate? (Also see Browne.)
6. What are Malcolm X's objections to Kennedy's liberal administration and to the Civil Rights movement generally?
7. What point does the football analogy illustrate?
8. Why did Malcolm X leave the Black Muslim movement?
9. How does Malcolm X relate the African revolution to the United States? How does he expand on the concept of a power structure? (Also see Kunen, Browne, and Carmichael.)
10. How does the tone of the last sentence affect your understanding of his concept of brotherhood?
11. Examine the quality of Malcolm X's feeling toward his subject and his audience. How might this feeling refute accusations that he was a "hate monger" and a "black racist"?

GEORGE C. WALLACE

The Civil Rights Bill:
Fraud, Sham, and Hoax

The following speech, articulating the position of the Southern segregationist, was delivered by George C. Wallace, then Governor of Alabama, on July 4, 1964, in Atlanta, Georgia. Unable to succeed himself as governor, Wallace campaigned for his wife, Lurleen, who took office in 1966 but died the following year. Wallace became the candidate of the American Independent Party in the Presidential election of 1968, receiving almost ten million votes, primarily but not entirely from the Southern electorate.

We come here today in deference to the memory of those Stalwart patriots who on July 4, 1776, pledged their lives, their fortunes, and their sacred honor to establish and defend the proposition that governments are created by the people, empowered by the people, derive their just powers from the consent of the people, and must forever remain subservient to the will of the people.

Today, 188 years later, we celebrate that occasion and find inspiration and determination and courage to preserve and protect the great principles of freedom enunciated in the Declaration of Independence.

It is therefore a cruel irony that the President of the United States has only yesterday signed into law the most monstrous piece of legislation ever enacted by the United States Congress.

It is a fraud, a sham, and a hoax.

This bill will live in infamy. To sign it into law at any time is tragic. To do so upon the eve of the celebration of our independence insults the intelligence of the American people.

It dishonors the memory of countless thousands of our dead who offered up their very lives in defense of principles which this bill destroys.

Reprinted by permission of the author.

Never before in the history of this nation have so many human and property rights been destroyed by a single enactment of the Congress. It is an act of tyranny. It is the assassin's knife stuck in the back of liberty.

With this assassin's knife and a blackjack in the hand of the federal force-cult, the left-wing liberals will try to force us back into bondage. Bondage to a tyranny more brutal than that imposed by the British Monarchy which claimed power to rule over the lives of our forefathers under sanction of the divine right of kings.

Today, this tyranny is imposed by the central government which claims the right to rule over our lives under sanction of the omnipotent black-robed despots who sit on the bench of the United States Supreme Court.

This bill is fraudulent in intent, in design, and in execution.

It is misnamed. Each and every provision is mistitled. It was rammed through the Congress on the wave of ballyhoo, promotions, and publicity stunts reminiscent of P. T. Barnum.

It was enacted in an atmosphere of pressure, intimidation, and even cowardice, as demonstrated by the refusal of the United States Senate to adopt an amendment to submit the bill to a vote of the people.

To illustrate the fraud—it is not a civil rights bill. It is a federal penal code. It creates federal crimes which would take volumes to list and years to tabulate because it affects the lives of 192 million American citizens. Every person in every walk and station of life and every aspect of our daily lives becomes subject to the criminal provisions of this bill.

It threatens our freedom of speech, of assembly, or association, and makes the exercise of these freedoms a federal crime under certain conditions.

It affects our political rights, our right to trial by jury, our right to the full use and enjoyment of our private property, the freedom from search and seizure of our private property and possessions, the freedom from harassment by federal police and, in short, all the rights of individuals inherent in a society of free men.

Ministers, lawyers, teachers, newspapers, and every private citizen must guard his speech and watch his actions to avoid the deliberately imposed booby traps put into this bill. It is designed to make federal crimes of our customs, beliefs, and traditions. Therefore, under the fantastic powers of the federal judiciary to punish for contempt of court and under their fantastic powers to regulate our most intimate aspects of our lives by injunction, every American citizen is in jeopardy and must stand guard against these despots.

. . .

I am having nothing to do with enforcing a law that will destroy our free enterprise system.

I am having nothing to do with enforcing a law that will destroy neighborhood schools.

I am having nothing to do with enforcing a law that will destroy the rights of private property.

I am having nothing to do with enforcing a law that destroys your right—and my right—to choose my neighbors—or to sell my house to whomever I choose.

I am having nothing to do with enforcing a law that destroys the labor seniority system.

I am having nothing to do with this so-called Civil Rights Bill.

The liberal left-wingers have passed it. Now let them employ some pinknik social engineers in Washington, D.C., to figure out what to do with it.

The situation reminds me of the little boy looking at the blacksmith as he hammered a red-hot horseshoe into the proper shape.

After minutes of hammering, the blacksmith took the horseshoe, splashed it into a tub of water and threw it steaming onto a sawdust pile.

The little fellow picked up the horseshoe, dropped it quickly.

"What's the matter, son," the blacksmith said, "is that shoe too hot to handle?"

"No, sir," the little boy said, "it just don't take me long to look at a horseshoe."

It's not going to take the people of this country long to look at the Civil Rights Bill, either.

And they are going to discard it just as quickly as the little boy tossed away the still hot horseshoe.

But I am not here to talk about the separate provisions of the federal penal code. I am here to talk about principles which have been overthrown by the enactment of this bill. The principles that you and I hold dear. The principles for which our forefathers fought and died to establish and to defend. The principles for which we came here to rededicate ourselves.

But before I get into that, let me point out one important fact. It would have been impossible for the American people to have been deceived by the sponsors of this bill had there been a responsible American press to tell the people exactly what the bill contained. If they had had the integrity and the guts to tell the truth, this bill would never have been enacted.

Whoever heard of truth put to the worst in free and open encounter? We couldn't get the truth to the American people.

You and I know that that's extremely difficult to do where our news papers are owned by out-of-state interests. Newspapers which are run and operated by left-wing liberals, Communist sympathizers, and members of the Americans for Democratic Action and other Communist front organizations with high sounding names.

However, we will not be intimidated by the vultures of the liberal left-wing press. We will not be deceived by their lies and distortions of truth. We will not be swayed by their brutal attacks upon the character and reputation of any honest citizen who dares stand up and fight for liberty.

. . .

As I have said before, that federal penal code could never have been enacted into law if we had had a responsible press who was willing to tell the American people the truth about what it actually provides. Nor would we have had a bill had it not been for the United States Supreme Court.

Now on the subject of the court let me make it clear that I am not attacking any member of the United States Supreme Court as an individual. However, I do attack their decisions, I question their intelligence, their common sense and their judgment, I consider the federal judiciary system to be the greatest single threat to individual freedom and liberty in the United States today, and I'm going to take off the gloves in talking about these people.

There is only one word to describe the federal judiciary today. That word is "lousy."

They assert more power than claimed by King George III, more power than Hitler, Mussolini, or Khrushchev ever had. They assert the power to declare unconstitutional our very thoughts. To create for us a system of moral and ethical values. To outlaw and declare unconstitutional, illegal, and immoral the customs, traditions, and beliefs of the people, and furthermore they assert the authority to enforce their decrees in all these subjects upon the American people without their consent.

. . .

The court today, just as in 1776, is deaf to the voices of the people and their repeated entreaties: They have become arrogant, contemptuous, highhanded, and literal despots.

It has been said that power corrupts and absolute power corrupts absolutely. There was never greater evidence as to the proof of this statement than in the example of the present federal judiciary.

I want to touch upon just a few of the acts of tyranny which have been sanctioned by the United States Supreme Court and compare these acts with the acts of tyranny enumerated in the Declaration of Independence.

The colonists objected most strenuously to the imposition of taxes upon the people without their consent.

Today, the federal judiciary asserts the same tyrannical power to levy taxes in Prince Edward County, Virginia, and without the consent of the people. Not only that, but they insist upon the power to tell the people for what purposes their money must be spent.

The colonists stated, "He has refused to pass other laws for the accommodation of large districts of people, unless those people would relinquish the right of representation in the legislature, a right inestimable to them and formidable to tyrants only."

Today, the federal judiciary, in one of its most recent decisions, has deprived the American people of the right to use the unit system of representation in their own state governments for the accommodation of large districts of people, and has itself prescribed the manner in which the people shall structure the legislative branch of their own government, and have prescribed how the people shall allocate the legislative powers of state government.

More than that they have even told the American people that we may not, with a majority of the people voting for the measure, or with two-thirds of those voting, or even if by unanimous consent, adopt a provision in our state constitutions to allocate the legislative power of state government in any manner other than as prescribed by the court.

One Justice of the United States Supreme Court said in this connection, and I quote, "To put the matter plainly, there is nothing in all the history of this Court's decisions which supports this constitutional rule. The Court's draconian pronouncement which makes unconstitutional the legislatures of most of the fifty states finds no support in the words of the Constitution in any prior decision of this Court or in the 175-year political history of our federal union . . . these decisions mark a long step backward into the unhappy era where a majority of the members of this Court were thought by many to have convinced themselves and each other that the demands of the Constitution were to be measured not by what it says but by their own notions of wise political theory."

Two other Justices of the Court said, "Such a massive repudiation of the experience of our whole past in asserting destructively novel judicial power demands analysis of the role of this Court and our constitutional scheme. . . . It may well impair the Court's position as the ultimate organ of the supreme law of the land. . . ."

The only reason it is the supreme law of the land today is because we have a President who cares so little for freedom that he would send the armed forces into the states to enforce the dictatorial decree.

Our colonist forefathers had something to say about that too.

The Declaration of Independence cited as an act of tyranny the fact that, ". . . kept among us in times of peace standing armies without the consent of the legislature."

Today, 188 years later, we have actually witnessed the invasion of the State of Arkansas, Mississippi, and Alabama by the armed forces of the United States and maintained in the state against the will of the people and without consent of State legislatures.

It is a form of tyranny worse than that of King George III who had sent mercenaries against the colonies because today the federal judicial tyrants have sanctioned the use of brother against brother and father against son by federalizing the National Guard.

In 1776 the colonies also complained that the Monarch ". . . has incited domestic insurrections among us. . . ."

Today, we have absolute proof that the federal Department of Justice has planned, supervised, financed and protected acts of insurrection in the Southern states, resulting in vandalism, property damage, personal injury, and staggering expense to the states.

In 1776 it was charged that the Monarchy had asserted power to ". . . dissolve representative houses and to punish . . . for opposing with manly firmness his invasions of the rights of the people. . . ."

Today, the federal judiciary asserts the power not only to dissolve state legislatures but to create them and to dissolve all state laws and state judicial decrees, and to punish a state governor by trial without jury ". . . for opposing with manly firmness his invasions of the rights of the people. . . ."

The colonists also listed as acts of tyranny: ". . . the erection of a multitude of new offices and sent hither swarms of officers to harass our people and to eat out their substance . . .;"

". . . suspending our own legislatures and declaring themselves invested with the power to legislate for us in all cases whatsoever;"

". . . abolishing the free system of the English laws . . .;"

—it had "abdicated government here;"

—refusing to assent to the laws enacted by the people, ". . . laws considered most wholesome and necessary for the public good;"

—and ". . . for depriving us in many cases, of the benefits of trial by jury . . .; for taking away our charters, abolishing our most valuable laws, and altering fundamentally forms of our government; for suspending our own legislatures and declaring themselves invested with power to legislate for us in all cases whatsoever."

The United States Supreme Court is guilty of each and every one of these acts of tyranny.

Therefore, I echo the sentiments of our forefathers who declared: "A prince, whose character is thus marked by every act which may define a tyrant, is unfit to be the ruler of a free people."

Ladies and gentlemen, I have listed only a few of the many acts of tyranny which have been committed or specifically sanctioned by the United States Supreme Court.

I feel it important that you should know and understand what it is that these people are trying to do. The written opinions of the Court are filled with double talk, semantics, jargon, and meaningless phrases. The words they use are not important. The ideas that they represent are the things which count.

It is perfectly obvious from the left-wing liberal press and from the left-wing law journals that what the Court is saying behind all the jargon is that they don't like our form of government.

They think they can establish a better one. In order to do so it is necessary that they overthrow our existing form, destroy the democratic institutions created by the people, change the outlook, religion, and philosophy, and bring the whole area of human thought, aspiration, action and organization, under the absolute control of the Court. Their decisions reveal this to be the goal of the liberal element on the Court which is in a majority at present.

It has reached the point where one may no longer look to judicial decisions to determine what the Court may do. However, it is possible to predict with accuracy the nature of the opinions to be rendered. One may find the answer in the Communist Manifesto.

The Communists are dedicated to the overthrow of our form of government. They are dedicated to the destruction of the concept of private property. They are dedicated to the object of destroying religion as the basis of moral and ethical values.

The Communists are determined that all natural resources shall be controlled by the central government, that all productive capacity of the Nation shall be under the control of the central government, that the political sovereignty of the people shall be destroyed as an incident to control of local schools. It is their objective to capture the minds of our youth in order to indoctrinate them in what to think and not how to think.

I do not call the members of the United States Supreme Court Communists. But I do say, and I submit for your judgment the fact that every single decision of the Court in the past ten years which related in any way to each of these objectives has been decided against freedom and in favor of tyranny.

A politician must stand on his record. Let the Court stand on its record.

The record reveals, for the past number of years, that the chief, if not the only beneficiaries of the present Court's rulings, have been duly and lawfully convicted criminals, Communists, atheists, and clients of vociferous left-wing minority groups.

You can't convict a Communist in our federal court system.

Neither can you convict one of being a Communist in Russia, China, or Cuba. The point is that the United States Supreme Court refuses to recognize the Communist conspiracy and their intent to "bury us."

Let us look at the record further with respect to the Court's contribution to the destruction of the concept of God and the abolition of religion.

The federal court rules that your children shall not be permitted to read the Bible in our public school systems.

Let me tell you this, though. We still read the Bible in Alabama schools and as long as I am Governor we will continue to read the Bible no matter what the Supreme Court says.

Federal courts will not convict a "demonstrator" invading and destroying private property. But the federal courts rule you cannot say a simple "God is great, God is good, we thank Thee for our food," in kindergartens supported by public funds.

Now, let us examine the manner in which the court has continously chipped away at the concept of private property.

It is contended by the left-wing liberals that private property is merely a legal fiction. That one has no inherent right to own and possess property. The courts have restricted and limited the right of acquisition of property in life and have decreed its disposition in death and have ruthlessly set aside the wills of the dead in order to attain social ends decreed by the court. The court has substituted its judgment for that of the testator based on social theory.

The courts assert authority even to decree the use of private cemeteries.

They assert the right to convert a private place of business into a public place of business without the consent of the owner and without compensation to him.

One Justice asserts that the mere licensing of a business by the state is sufficient to convert it into control by the federal judiciary as to its use and disposition.

Another asserts that the guarantees of equal protection and due process of law cannot be extended to a corporation.

In one instance, following the edicts of the United States Supreme Court, a state supreme court has ordered and directed a private citizen to sell his home to an individual contrary to the wishes of the owner.

In California we witnessed a state supreme court taking under advisement the question as to whether or not it will compel a bank to make a loan to an applicant on the basis of his race.

. . .

All of us know what the court has done to capture the minds of our children.

The federal judiciary has asserted the authority to prescribe regulations with respect to the management, operation, and control of our local schools. The second Brown decision in the infamous school segregation case authorized federal district courts to supervise such matters as teacher hiring, firing, promotion, the expenditure of local funds, both administratively and for capital improvements, additions, and renovations, the location of new schools, the drawing of school boundaries, busing and transportation of school children, and, believe it or not, it has asserted the right in the federal judiciary to pass judgment upon the curricula adopted in local public schools.

A comparatively recent federal court decision in a Florida case actually entered an order embracing each and every one of these assertions of federal supervision.

In ruling after ruling, the Supreme Court has overstepped its constitutional authority. While appearing to protect the people's interest, it has in reality become a judicial tyrant.

It's the old pattern. The people always have some champion whom they set over them . . . and nurse into greatness. This, and no other, is the foot from which a tyrant springs, after first appearing as a protector.

This is another way of saying that the people never give up their liberties . . . and their freedom . . . but under some delusion.

But yet there is hope.

There is yet a spirit of resistance in this country which will not be oppressed. And it is awakening. And I am sure there is an abundance of good sense in this country which cannot be deceived.

. . .

I shall never forget last spring as I stood in the midst of a great throng of South Milwaukee supporters at one of the greatest political rallies I have ever witnessed.

A fine-looking man grabbed my hand and said:

"Governor, I've never been South of South Milwaukee, but I am a Southerner!"

Of course, he was saying he believed in the principles and philosophy of the Southern people . . . of you here today and the people of my state of Alabama.

He was right.

Being a Southerner is no longer geographic. It's a philosophy and an attitude.

One destined to be a national philosophy—embraced by millions of Americans—which shall assume the mantle of leadership and steady a governmental structure in these days of crisis.

. . .

Conservatives of this nation constitute the balance of power in Presidential elections.

I am a conservative.

I intend to give the American people a clear choice. I welcome a fight between our philosophy and the liberal left-wing dogma which now threatens to engulf every man, woman, and child in the United States.

I am in this race because I believe the American people have been pushed around long enough and that they, like you and I, are fed up with the continuing trend toward a socialist state which now subjects the individual to the dictates of an all-powerful central government.

I am running for President because I was born free. I want to remain free. I want your children and mine and our prosperity to be unencumbered by the manipulation of a soulless state.

I intend to fight for a positive, affirmative program to restore constitutional goverment and to stop the senseless bloodletting now being performed on the body of liberty by those who lead us willingly and dangerously close to a totalitarian central government.

. . .

A left-wing monster has risen up in this nation. It has invaded the government. It has invaded the news media. It has invaded the leadership of many of our churches. It has invaded every phase and aspect of the life of freedom-loving people.

It consists of many and various and powerful interests, but it has combined into one massive drive and is held together by the cohesive power of the emotion, setting forth civil rights as supreme to all.

But, in reality, it is a drive to destroy the rights of private property, to destroy the freedom and liberty of you and me.

And, my friends, where there are no property rights, there are no human rights. Red China and Soviet Russia are prime examples.

Politically evil men have combined and arranged themselves against us. The good people of this nation must now associate themselves together, else we will fall one by one, an unpitied sacrifice in a struggle which threatens to engulf the entire nation.

We can win. We can control the election of the President in November.

Our object must be our country, our whole country and nothing but our country.

If we will stand together—the people of this state—the people of my state—the people throughout this great region—yes, throughout the United States—then we can be the balance of power. We can determine who will be the next President.

Georgia is a great state. Atlanta is a great city. I know you will demonstrate that greatness in November by joining Alabama and other states throughout the South in electing the next President of the United States.

We are not going to change anything by sitting on our hands hoping that things will change for the better. Those who cherish individual freedom have a job to do.

First, let us let it be known that we intend to take the offensive and carry our fight for freedom across this nation. We will wield the power that is ours—the power of the people.

Let it be known that we will no longer tolerate the boot of tyranny. We will no longer hide our heads in the sand. We will reschool our thoughts in the lessons our forefathers knew so well.

We must destroy the power to dictate, to forbid, to require, to demand, to distribute, to edict, and to judge what is best and enforce that will of judgment upon free citizens.

We must revitalize a government founded in this nation on faith in God.

I ask that you join with me and that together, we give an active and courageous leadership to the millions of people throughout this nation who look with hope and faith to our fight to preserve our constitutional system of government with its guarantees of liberty and justice for all within the framework of our priceless freedoms.

For Discussion

1. Briefly discuss the provisions of the Civil Rights Bill.
2. Wallace attacks three groups—the liberals (including the liberal press), the Supreme Court, and communists. What are his specific charges against each?
3. Evaluate Wallace's accusations of fraud, tyranny, and invasion.
4. Discuss Wallace's references to past history.
5. Wallace declares himself a conservative. What picture of the conservative does he give you, and how does it compare with your own understanding of the term?
6. Examine Wallace's use of language in terms of the following categories:
    a) specific—general
    b) concrete—abstract
    c) denotative—connotative
    d) literal—figurative
    e) formal—colloquial
   Find examples of invective.
7. What emotional appeal is made to the audience at the beginning? How is this appeal sustained throughout the speech?
8. Describe Wallace's attitude toward his audience. To what extent does it affect the content and organization of his argument?

ROBERT McAFEE BROWN

In Conscience
I Must Break the Law

Robert McAfee Brown, born in 1920, is both an educator and a clergyman. He was ordained to the ministry of the Presbyterian Church, received his Ph.D. from Columbia University, and has studied in the United States, England, and Scotland. Active in achieving better relations between Protestants and Catholics, Brown was invited to attend Vatican Council II during 1963 and 1964 as a Protestant observer and to contribute a regular column to the Catholic weekly, *Commonweal*. He demonstrated his belief in social equality by taking part in a Freedom Ride in July, 1961, which resulted in his spending twenty-four hours in a Tallahassee, Florida, jail. Since 1963, he has been a professor of religion at Stanford University.

"Vietnam? I've got other things to worry about." There was a time when it was easy for me to say that. I was worried about the California battle over Proposition 14, in which the real estate interests were trying to palm off on the California voters legislation designed to discriminate against minority groups, a measure later declared unconstitutional by the United States Supreme Court. I was worried about the plight of the migrant workers in the San Joaquin Valley, who were striking for the right to bargain collectively. I was also, if truth be told, worried about other things as well: getting tomorrow's lecture finished, scrounging up the extra dollars I was going to need when state income-tax time rolled around, finding time to get acquainted with my kids, recouping some of the losses on the writing project on which I was currently so far behind.

In this, I was like many millions of Americans. In addition, also like

By permission of the editors. From the October 31, 1967, issue of Look Magazine. Copyright 1967 by Cowles Communications, Inc.

many millions of Americans, I was probably afraid to face the issue of Vietnam, afraid that if I learned enough about it, I would have to join those radical, far-out types who two or three years ago were saying in such lonely fashion what many middle-class people are saying now: that our policy in Vietnam is wrong, that it is callous and brutalizing to those who must implement it, that it cannot be supported by thinking or humane people and that if one comes to feel this way, he has to engage in the uncomfortable and annoying and possibly threatening posture of putting his body where his words are.

In the interval since I discovered that I couldn't duck Vietnam any longer, I have tried to do my homework, read some history, examine the Administration's position, listen to its critics and come to a stand of my own. I've come to a stand, all right. And I only regret, not just for the sake of my own conscience, but for the sake of the thousands of Americans and the hundreds of thousands of Asians who have died in Vietnam, that I did not come to it with much greater speed. For I have now gone the full route—from unconcern

to curiosity
to study
to mild concern
to deep concern
to signing statements
to genteel protest
to marching
to moral outrage
to increasingly vigorous protest
to . . . civil disobedience.

The last step, of course, is the crucial one, the one where I part company with most of my friends in the liberal groups where I politic, with most of my friends in the academic community where I work and with most of my friends in the church where I worship. And since I am a reasonable man, not given to emotive decisions, one who by no stretch of the imagination could be called far-out, one who is not active in the New Left, one who still shaves and wears a necktie—a typical Establishment-type middle-class American wasp—I feel it important to record why it is that such a person as myself finds it impossible to stop merely at the level of vigorous protest of our policy in Vietnam and feels compelled to step over the line into civil disobedience.

My basic reason is also my most judgmental: I have utterly lost confidence in the Johnson Administration. Those who do not share that premise may shrink from the consequences I draw from it. All I can say by way of reply is that I tried for many months to work from the presuppposition that the Administration was genuinely seeking peace and that it was trying to conduct foreign policy in honorable terms. But the record now makes patently clear to me that our Government is not willing to negotiate seriously save on terms overwhelmingly favorable to it and that it has refused to respond to many feelers that have come from the other side. I can no longer trust the spokesmen for the administration when they engage in their customary platitudes about a desire to negotiate. What they do belies what they say, and at the moment they express willingness to talk with Hanoi, they engage in further frantic acts of escalation that bring us closer to the brink of World War III and a nuclear holocaust. I do not believe that they are any longer reachable in terms of modifying their senseless policy of systematically destroying a small nation of dark-skinned people so that American prestige can emerge unscathed. All of us who have written, spoken, marched, petitioned, reasoned and organized must surely see that in the moments when Mr. Johnson is not calling us unpatriotic, he is simply ignoring a mounting chorus of moral horror with benign disdain and proceeding day by day, week by week, month by month, to escalate the war far past the point of no return.

This means that if one believes that what we are doing in Southeast Asia is immoral, he has no effective way of seeking to change such a policy, for the policy, in the face of two or three years of increasing criticism, is only becoming more hard-nosed, more irrational, more insane. The procedures through which change can normally be brought about in a democracy are increasingly futile. Mr. Johnson emasculated Congress in August 1964 with the Gulf of Tonkin agreement, which he now uses to justify air war over China. Public protests are written off as examples of lack of patriotism or lack of fidelity to the Americans now in Vietnam or even, by members of the House Armed Services Committee, as treasonable. With each act of military escalation, the moral horror of the war is escalated. We have been killing women and children all along; now, we kill more of them. We have been destroying the villages of civilians all along; now, we destroy more of them. We have been breaking almost every one of the rules that civilized men have agreed constitute the minimal standards of decency men must maintain even in the indecency of war; now, we break them more often.

This escalation of military power demands the escalation of moral protest. Those of us who condemn this war, who are repulsed by it and who realize that history is going to judge our nation very harshly for its part in it, must see more and more clearly that it is not enough any longer to sign another advertisement or send another telegram or give another speech— or write another article. The ways of genteel, legal protest have shown themselves to be ineffective. During the time of their impact, escalation has not lessened, it has increased. (I leave as a purely academic matter the question of whether escalation would have been worse without the genteel protests. Undoubtedly, it would have been. But it is too easy a rationalization to argue that we might have killed 500,000 Vietnamese, whereas, thanks to the protests, we may have only killed 100,000. Howard Zinn has remarked that World War II furnished us with a very convenient moral calculus: it is not permitted to kill 6,000,000 Jews, but anything short of that number can be justified in comparison.)

Military escalation has become our Government's stock response to every problem, and in its exercise, our leaders have demonstrated themselves incapable of change. Their only response, now no more than a conditioned reflex, is to hit a little harder. They have become prisoners of their own propaganda. Their rationalizations of their policy become more frantic, their attacks on their critics more strident, their defense of their actions more removed from the realm of reality. In justifying the decision to bomb within ten miles of the China border, Mr. Johnson, in a not-untypical burst of omniscience, assured us that he knew the mind of the Peking government and that the Peking government would not interpret our action as a widening of the war. But who, even in Peking, can predict how that government will respond? Such acts and gestures and declarations on our part indicate the awful temptation of using power irresponsibly and the way in which our blithe self-confidence may sow the seeds of our own—and everybody else's—destruction. I do not know which is more terrifying to contemplate: the possibility that Administration leaders really believe the reasons they give to defend their policy or the possibility that behind their public reasons, there lies another set of motivations and justifications that they dare not share with the rest of us. On either count, their right to lead the most powerful nation on earth is faulted.

I have already suggested that history will judge them harshly. But such a statement is a little too smug, however true it may be. History will judge *us* harshly, that is to say, those of us who continue to support our present policy makers, either overtly by echoing their tattered clichés or covertly by our silence. He who is not against them is for them.

In the face of such conclusions, one is counseled, "Work for '68. Wait for '68." I will, of course, work for '68, just as, inevitably, being a child of time, I must wait for it. But I am no longer content to throw all my energies in that direction, and for the following reasons: (1) It seems clear that no Democrat will have either the courage or the power to challenge Mr. Johnson. In the face of his virtually certain nomination, it is important that millions of persons like myself get on record as indicating that under no circumstances whatsoever would we vote for him. (2) There is little indication that the Republican party will offer a real choice. Nixon and Reagan are more hawkish than Johnson, and Romney has displayed an indecisiveness about Vietnam seldom matched in the history of American politics. (3) The vacuum within the two major parties leaves voters opposed to our Vietnam policy with rather bleak alternatives. The decision to cast no vote at all cannot be justified by those who believe in the democratic process. All that is left, then, is to vote for a protest candidate who will not win. Several million voters so acting might serve notice on whoever wins that there is a body of opposition that cannot be discounted. But serving notice is a far cry from influencing policy. (4) All of this remains desperately abstract, however, because 1968 is a full year off. What is not in the least abstract is that in the meantime, men and women and children are dying. They are dying horrible deaths, inflicted not only by the Vietcong but also by our own soldiers. As our casualty rate increases in the next 12 months, the casualty rate of the enemy will increase perhaps ten times as fast. Meanwhile, our escalation will be bringing us closer and closer to war with China and possibly with Russia.

In the face of such facts, an informed conscience does not have the luxury of waiting 12 months to see what the political machinery may or may not produce. Therefore, I find myself forced, by the exclusion of alternatives as well as by an increasing sense of moral imperative, to escalate my own protest to the level of civil disobedience. The war is so wrong, and ways of registering concern about it have become so limited, that civil disobedience seems to me the only honorable route left.

I make this judgment, foreseeing two possible consequences.

First, there is always the remote possibility (on which it is not wise to count too heavily) that civil disobedience might make a significant enough impact on the nation as a whole that the policy makers could not any longer ignore the voice and act of protest. If engaged in by significant enough numbers of people (and significant enough people) it could conceivably shock the nation and the world into a recognition that our actions in Vietnam are so intolerable that a drastic shift in our policy could no longer be avoided. There is the further remote possibility that others, not yet ready to escalate their protest to civil disobedience, might at least escalate somewhere in the spectrum and thus produce a total yield noticeably higher than in the past.

I would like to believe that such things might happen. I see little likelihood that they will. Why, then, protest by breaking the law, if such protest is not going to do any discernible good? Because there comes a time when the issues are so clear and so crucial that a man does not have the choice of waiting until all the possible consequences can be charted. There comes a time when a man must simply say, "Here I stand, I can do no other, God help me." There comes a time when it is important for the future of a nation that it be recorded that in an era of great folly, there were at least some within that nation who recognized the folly for what it was and were willing, at personal cost, to stand against it. There comes a time when, in the words of Father Pius-Raymond Régamey, one has to oppose evil even if one cannot prevent it, when one has to choose to be a victim rather than an accomplice. There comes a time when thinking people must give some indication for their children and their children's childen that the national conscience was not totally numbed by Washington rhetoric into supporting a policy that is evil, vicious and morally intolerable.

If such language sounds harsh and judgmental, it is meant precisely to be such. The time is past for gentility, pretty speeches and coy evasions of blunt truths. Evil deeds must be called evil. Deliberate killing of civilians— by the tens of thousands—must be called murder. Forcible removal of people from their homes must be called inhumane and brutal. A country that permits such things to be done in its name deserves to be condemned, not only by the decent people of other countries but particularly by the decent people who are its citizens, who will call things what they are and who recognize finally and irrevocably that the most evil deed of all is not to do bestial things but to do bestial things and call them humane.

In light of this, I no longer have any choice but to defy those laws of our land that produce such rotten fruits. I believe with Martin Luther King that such civil disobedience as I engage in must be done nonviolently, and that it must be done with a willingness to pay the penalties that society may impose upon me. I recognize the majesty of Law and its impregnable quality as a bulwark of a free society, and it is in the name of Law that I must defy given laws that are an offense against morality, making this witness wherever need be—in the churches, on the streets, in the assembly halls, in the courts, in jails.

Each person who takes this route must find the level at which his own conscience comes into conflict with laws relating to American presence in Vietnam, and the cardinal rule for those engaging in civil disobedience must be a respect for the consciences of those who choose a different point along the spectrum at which to make their witness; words like "chicken" or "rash" must have no place in their lexicon. Some will refuse to pay that portion of their Federal income tax directly supporting the war. Others will engage in "unlawful assembly" in front of induction centers. For myself, it is clear what civil disobedience will involve. I teach. I spend my professional life with American youth of draft age. And while I will not use the classroom for such purposes, I will make clear that from now on my concerns about Vietnam will be explicitly focused on counseling, aiding and abetting all students who declare that out of moral conviction they will not fight in Vietnam. I will "counsel, aid and abet" such students to find whatever level of moral protest is consonant with their consciences, and when for them this means refusing service in the armed forces, I will support them in that stand. In doing so, I am committing a Federal offense, for the Military Selective Service Act of 1967 specifically states that anyone who "knowingly counsels, aids or abets another to refuse or evade registration or service in the armed forces" opens himself to the same penalties as are visited upon the one he so counsels, aids and abets, namely up to five years in jail or up to $10,000 in fines, or both.

I will continue to do this until I am arrested. As long as I am not arrested, I will do it with increasing intensity, for I am no longer willing that 18- or 19-year-old boys should pay with their lives for the initially bumbling but now deliberate folly of our national leaders. Nor am I willing to support them in action that may lead them to jail, from a safe preserve of legal inviolability for myself. I must run the same risks as they, and therefore I break the law on their behalf, so that if they are arrested, I too must be arrested. If this means jail, I am willing to go with them, and perhaps we can continue there to think and learn and teach and reflect and emerge with a new set of priorities for American life. If, as is far more likely, this means merely public abuse or ridicule, then perhaps a minority of us can be disciplined, chastened and strengthened by that kind of adversity.

But whatever it means, the time has come when some of us can no longer afford the luxury of gentility or the luxury of holding "moderate" positions. The issue must be joined. Our country is committing crimes so monstrous that the only thing more monstrous would be continuing silence or inaction in the face of them.

For Discussion

1. How does the author characterize himself in relation to other Americans?
2. What in principle is Brown's objection to the Vietnam conflict?
3. Why does Brown finally advocate civil disobedience? What reasons does he offer to support his view?
4. What is Brown's rationale for increased protest?
5. Discuss the author's concept of responsibility of the individual as a member of society. (Also see Thoreau and Wald.)
6. Discuss the form of Brown's civil disobedience. What other avenues of protest exist?
7. Buffon said, "Style is the man himself." If this is true, what kind of man is Brown? How does he qualify as impassioned?

STOKELY CARMICHAEL

Black Power

Stokely Carmichael was born in Trinidad in 1941 and came to the United States in 1952. A graduate of New York City's Bronx High School of Science and of Howard University, Carmichael took part in the civil rights movement in Lowndes County, Alabama, and was one of the first "freedom riders" to be arrested. Voicing the position of the intellectual black militant, Carmichael was elected chairman of the Student Nonviolent Coordinating Committee (SNCC) in 1966. After serving for one year, he traveled to Cuba. He has since spent time in England, appearing in Peter Brook's controversial motion picture *Tell Me Lies*, as well as writing and lecturing. Presently, he resides in Conakry, Guinea, with his wife, the well-known singer Miriam Makeba. The following speech was delivered at the Congress on the Dialectics of Liberation in London in July of 1967.

We had intended to prepare a written speech for this Congress, and had started to prepare it three weeks before the trip, but the US government thought that as I was starving it would be better if they saw to it that I got some meals every day, so they confined me to their prison system, and I lost all the notes. So I tried to get another one together.

Now since I've been at the Congress from Saturday I've been very confused, because I'm not a psychologist or a psychiatrist, I'm a political activist and I don't deal with the individual. I think it's a cop out when people talk about the individual. What we're talking about around the US today, and I believe around the Third World, is the system of international white supremacy coupled with international capitalism. And we're out to smash that system. And people who see themselves as part of that system are going to be smashed with it—or we're going to be smashed.

From *To Free a Generation: The Dialectics of Liberation,* ed. David Cooper (New York: Collier Books, 1968), pp. 150–174. Reprinted by permission of the Institute of Phenomenological Studies.

So that I'm not going to centre on the individual—I'm not even going to talk about him at all. I want to talk about the system. I want to use some quotes to back up my feeling about talking of the system, and the first one comes from one of my patron saints: Frantz Fanon. His quote is that

> Freud insisted that the individual factor be taken into account through psychoanalysis. It will be seen that the black man's alienation is not an individual question. It is a question of socio-diagnostics. The Negro problem does not resolve itself into the problem of Negroes living among white men, but rather of Negroes exploited, enslaved, despised by the colonialist, capitalist society that is only accidentally white.

But since it is accidentally white, that's what we talk about—white western society.

Now the other reason that I don't talk about the individual is that I feel that whenever you raise questions about racial problems to white western society, each white man says 'Well don't blame me, I'm only one person and I really don't feel that way. Actually I have nothing against you, I see you as an equal. You're just as good as I am—almost.' And to try and clear that up I want to point out the difference between individual racism as opposed to institutionalized racism.

It is important to this discussion of racism to make a distinction between the two types: individual racism and institutional racism. The first type consists of overt acts by individuals, with usually the immediate result of the death of victims, or the traumatic and violent destruction of property. This type can be recorded on TV cameras and can frequently be observed in the process of commission.

The second type is less overt, far more subtle, less identifiable in terms of specific individuals committing the acts, but is no less destructive of human life. The second type is more the overall operation of established and respected forces in the society, and thus does not receive the condemnation that the first type receives.

Let me give you an example of the first type: When unidentified white terrorists bomb a black church and kill five black children, that is an act of individual racism, widely deplored by most segments of the world. But when in that same city, Birmingham, Alabama, not five but 500 black babies die each year because of lack of proper food, shelter and medical facilities; and thousands more are destroyed and maimed physically, emotionally and intellectually because of conditions of poverty and discrimination in the black community, that is a function of institutionalized racism. When a black family moves into a home in a white neighbourhood, and it is stoned, burned or routed out, the latter is an overt act of individual racism, and many people condemn that, in words at least. But it is institutionalized racism that keeps the black people locked in dilapidated slums, tenements, where they must live out their daily lives subject to the prey of exploiting slum landlords, merchants, loan-sharks and the restrictive practices of real-estate agents. We're talking now about the US, but I think you can apply a little of it to London. But the society either pretends it does not know of institutionalized racism, or is incapable of doing anything meaningful about the conditions of institutionalized racism. And the resistance to doing anything meaningful about institutionalized racism stems from the fact that western society enjoys its luxury from institutionalized racism, and therefore, were it to end institutionalized racism, it would in fact destroy itself.

O.K. then, now I want to talk about de-mystifying human beings, and I'm talking about the Third World, I'm not talking about the white West. I think that the Third World are the people whom, at least in the US, black people are concerned with. The white West has been able to do very well for itself. I want to talk, then, very specifically about a number of things under that.

The first is the importance of definitions. The second: we want to talk about cultural integrity versus cultural imposition. And then we want to talk about the US, specifically the cities and the rebellions (as opposed to 'riots' as they are called by the white press) that are occurring in the US, which are going to lead to guerrilla warfare. And we want to talk about violence because the West is always upset by violence when a black man uses it. Yeah.

I want to start off with definitions by using a quote from one of my favourite books, which is *Alice in Wonderland,* by Lewis Carroll. In the book there's a debate between Humpty Dumpty and Alice around the question of definitions. It goes like this:

> 'When I use a word,' Humpty Dumpty said, in a rather scornful tone, 'It means just what I choose it to mean. Neither more nor less.'
> 'The question is,' said Alice, 'whether you can make words mean so many different things.'
> 'The question is,' said Humpty Dumpty, 'who is to be master. That is all.'

Now I think that Lewis Carroll is correct. Those who can define are the masters. And white western society has been able to define, and that's why she has been the master. And we want to follow up with a lot of those examples, because I think that the white youth of my generation in the West today does not understand his own subconscious racism, because he accepts the writings of the West, which has destroyed, distorted and lied about history, so that he starts off with a basic assumption of superiority which is not even recognizable.

Frederick Douglass, the great black leader of the 1800s, said that when a slave stops obeying a master, then and only then does he seek his liberation. Camus said the same thing 100 years later on the first page of *The Rebel*, when he said that when a slave stops accepting definitions imposed upon him by his master, then and only then does he begin to move and create a life for himself. That's very important, because what the people of the Third World are going to have to do today is to stop accepting the definitions imposed on them by the West. Let's give some examples.

The first one is that the history books tell you that nothing happens until a white man comes along. If you ask any white person who discovered America, they'll tell you 'Christopher Columbus'. And if you ask them who discovered China, they'll tell you 'Marco Polo'. And if you ask them, as I used to be told in the West Indies, I was not discovered until Sir Walter Raleigh needed pitch lake for his ship, and he came along and found me and said 'Whup—I have discovered you.' And my history began.

But let us examine the racism in that statement. Let us examine it very closely. Columbus did not discover America. Columbus may be the first recorded white man to have set foot in America. That is all. There were people there before Columbus. Unfortunately, those people were not white— unfortunately for the white West, fortunately for us, they weren't white. But what happens is that white western society never recognizes the existence of non-white people, either consciously or subconsciously. So that all around the world, the peoples of the Third World never did anything until some white man came along—and that's why China's non-existent, because Mao won't let no white folk in there. Yeah. And pretty soon Hong Kong is going to be non-existent because they're going to kick them out.

So that the situation you have is that history has been written—but indeed it has been so distorted. One of the biggest lies, I think, that western society could have told was to name itself Western Civilization. And now all through history we were studying Western Civilization, and that meant that all else was uncivilized. And white kids who read that today never recognize that they're being told that they are superior to everybody else because they have produced civilization. At best, that's a misnomer, at worst, and more correctly, it's a damn lie. Yes. Western Civilization has been anything but civilized. It has been most barbaric, as a matter of fact. We are told that Western Civilization begins with the Greeks, and the epitome of that is Alexander the Great. The only thing that I can remember about Alexander the Great was that at age twenty-six he wept because there were no other people to kill, murder and plunder. And that is the epitome of Western Civilization. And if you're not satisfied with that, you could always take the Roman Empire. Their favourite pastime was watching men kill each other or lions eating up men. They were a civilized people. The fact is that their civilization, as they called it, stemmed from the fact that they oppressed other peoples. And that the oppression of other people allowed them a certain luxury, at the expense of those other people. That has been interpreted as 'civilization' for the West, and that is precisely what it has done. The only difference is that after the Roman Empire, when the British Empire—on which the sun never used to set, but today it sets, sometimes it don't even rise—began to exploit non-white people, what they did was they let colour be the sole choice of the people they would exploit.

Now that's very important because as we go along you can see one of the best examples you can see today. You see, because you've been able to lie about terms, you've been able to call people like Cecil Rhodes a philanthropist, when in fact he was a murderer, a rapist, a plunderer and a thief. But you call Cecil Rhodes a philanthropist because what he did was that after he stole our diamonds and our gold, he gave us some crumbs so that we can go to school and become just like you. And that was called philanthropy. But we are renaming it: the place is no longer called Rhodesia, it is called Zimbabwe, that's its proper name. And Cecil Rhodes is no longer a philanthropist, he's known to be a thief—you can keep your Rhodes Scholars, we don't want the money that came from the sweat of our people.

Now let us move on to present times. I'm always appalled when some white person tells me that 'progress is being made'. I always ask him 'progress for whom? And from whom?' Progress for white people might be made, because I would say that since World War II they have learned a little about how to get along with people of colour. But I don't think there's been progress for the black people, there's not been progress for the people of colour around the Third World. And progress will not be measured for us by white people. We will have to tell you when progress is being made. You cannot tell us when progress is being made, because progress for us means getting you off our backs, and that's the only progress that we can see.

Now then, we want to talk about cultural integrity versus cultural imposition, because that stems from definitions. Because the white West felt somehow that it was better than everybody else—I remember when I was a young man in the West Indies, I had to read Rudyard Kipling's *The White Man's Burden*. I thought the best thing the white man could do for me was to leave me alone, but Rudyard Kipling told them to come and save me because I was half savage, half child. It was very white of him. What has happened is that the West has used force to impose its culture on the Third World wherever it has been. If a few settlers left England to go to Zimbabwe, there was no reason for them to rename that country after themselves, Rhodesia, and then force everybody to speak their language, English. If they had respect for the cultures of other people, they would have spoken the language of those people and adopted their religions. But what in fact happened was because the West was so powerful—that's the word nobody wants to talk about, power. It was only power that made people bow their heads to the West, you know. They didn't bow it because they liked Jesus Christ, or because they liked white folks. No, Machiavelli said a long time ago that 'people obey masters for one of two reasons. Either they love them, or they fear them.' I often ask myself whether or not the West believes the Third World really loves them and that's why they've obeyed them. But it's clear that they feared them. The West with its guns and its power and its might came into Africa, Asia, Latin America and the USA and raped it. And while they raped it they used beautiful terms. They told the Indians 'We're civilizing you, and we're taming the West. And if you won't be civilized, we'll kill you.' So they committed genocide and stole the land, and put the Indians on reservations, and they said that they had civilized the country.

They weren't satisfied with that. They came to Africa and stole Africans and brought them to the USA, and we were being brought there to be 'civilized', because we were cannibals and we ate each other, and they were going to give us a better life, which was, of course, slavery.

Now I want to make just one clear distinction, before I move on, in terms of cultural integrity. Inside the countries of the West there was democracy for the whites, at least some form of it. But that democracy was at the expense of non-white people. While Britain surely enjoyed her papers, and her Parliamentary nonsense about constitutionality, she was suppressing all of Africa. The same thing holds true for France, and De Gaulle still suppresses Somaliland, I would like to inform him; and the same thing, of course, is true today for the US.

White people are very funny, you know. De Gaulle got out of Vietnam a few years ago, and now he's gotten very broad-minded. But he's still in Somaliland.

So what the West was able to do is impose its culture and it told everyone 'we are better, we are civilized'. And because of its force, all of the non-white countries began to try to imitate Europe and to imitate its ways, and to try and copy it because nobody wanted to be uncivilized. . . . Our ancestors had recognized that they knew what civilization was long before Europeans even got out of their caves, and that they should have stuck to their way of life. Had they done that, perhaps we shouldn't be in the shape we are in today.

So that all other non-western people have been stripped of their own culture. They have been forced to accept a culture that does not belong to them. And so messed up are the minds of people of colour around the world, that in certain sections of Vietnam today, and in Japan certainly, women who have slanted eyes are cutting their eyes so that they can get round eyes to look like the West. Needless to say what black people have been doing to their hair, especially females: they have been putting hot combs in their hair, straightening it, attempting to look like white people, because the West has defined beauty as that which was theirs—the white woman, who was supposed to be taboo.

And so the non-white world began to copy and to imitate, began to do all the things of the West. I think what is happening in the world today is that there's a fight for cultural integrity. Each group of people wants to retain its own integrity, and say 'To Hell with the West and its culture. Let it keep it. We want ours.' I don't propose to speak for the Red Guards, but I would assume that that's part of the fight that they're waging. It's a healthy fight and it needs to be waged. I know in the US that one of the fights that we're waging is the fight for our own cultural integrity. We want to be able to recognize the contributions that the non-white peoples of the world have made. It's amazing that, when you do some reading, you find out that they did most of what the white people claim that they did. They just distorted history. Pythagoras didn't give you geometry, the Egyptians gave it to you.

I have something against England, I really do. Because when I was young I had to read all that rot about how good England was to Trinidad, while she was raping us left and right. And all I used to read about London when I was small was the beauty of London, and how peacefully everybody lived, and how nice life was—at my expense. And I used to say 'I sure would like to get to London and burn it down to the ground.' But that's violence!

Now the trouble with the West is that it feels it has the right to *give* everybody their independence. That's totally absurd. You can never *give* anyone their independence. All men are born free. They are enslaved by other men. So that the only act that the men who enslaved them can do is, not give them their independence, but stop oppressing them. There's a very important difference, and I don't think people make that distinction all the time. I'm amazed when I pick up the paper and read that 'England today decided to give independence to the West Indies.' Who the hell is England to give me my independence? All they can do is stop oppressing me, get off my back. But it sounds so much nicer when they say, 'We're giving you your independence. You're ready for it now.' Rather than for them to admit to themselves 'We're going to stop oppressing you because we're becoming a little bit more civilized; or because you're making it uncomfortable for us and we can no longer afford to oppress you at the price that you're asking us to pay.' Which is correct. But you wouldn't expect self-condemnation.

So that you cannot grant anybody independence, they just take it. And that is what White America is going to learn. They cannot *give* us anything. No white liberal can give me anything. The only thing a white liberal can do for me is to help civilize other whites, because they need to be civilized.

Now in order to move on to the US—because I know what's on everybody's mind is the rebellions and the guerrilla warfare that is taking place inside the US—I'd just like to read some of the notes that I jotted down, so that you can maybe get a clearer picture, because you don't live in the States. However, I don't think you really need that much of a clearer picture, because England isn't far behind.

It is estimated that in another five to ten years two thirds of the 20 million black people that inhabit the US will be living in the ghettoes, in the heart of the cities. Joining us are going to be hundreds of thousands of Puerto Ricans, Mexican Americans, and people of the American Indian population. The American city, in essence, is going to be populated by the peoples of the Third World while the white middle classes will flee to the suburbs. Now the black people do not control, nor do we own, the resources —we do not control the land, the houses or the stores. These are all owned by whites who live outside the community. These are very real colonies, in the sense that there is cheap labour exploited by those who live outside the cities. It is white power that makes the laws, and enforces those laws with guns and sticks in the hands of white racist policemen and their black mercenaries. It does not seem that at any point the men who control the power and resources of the US ever sat down and designed those black enclaves, and formally articulated the terms of their colonial and dependent status, as was done, for example, by the Apartheid government of South Africa which both Britain and the US and France backs. Yet one cannot distinguish between one ghetto and another as one moves around the US. It appears as if each ghetto is the same. Note that the US has, within its continental borders, forty-eight states, and each of these states has a ghetto in all of its major cities. As one moves from city to city it is as though some malignant, racist, planning unit has done precisely this: designed each one from the same master blue-print. And indeed, if the ghetto had been formally and deliberately planned, instead of growing spontaneously and inevitably from the racist functionings of the various institutions that combine to make the society, it would somehow be less frightening. The situation would be less frightening, because if these ghettoes were the result of design and conspiracy, one could understand their similarity as being artificially and consciously imposed, rather than the result of identical patterns of white racism which repeat themselves in cities as far apart as Boston is from Watts—that is, 3,000 miles.

We understand that a capitalist system automatically contains within itself racism, whether by design or not. Capitalism and racism seem to go hand in hand. The struggle for Black Power in the US, and certainly the world, is the struggle to free these colonies from external domination. But we do not seek merely to create communities where, in place of white rulers, black rulers control the lives of black masses, and where black money goes into a few black pockets. We want to see it go into the communal pocket. The society we seek to build among black people is not an oppressive capitalist society. Capitalism, by its very nature, cannot create structures free from exploitation.

The question may be asked, how does the struggle to free these internal colonies relate to the struggle against imperialism all around the world? We realistically survey our numbers and know that it is not possible for black people to take over the whole country militarily. In a highly industrialized nation the struggle is different. The heart of production and the heart of trade is in the cities. *We* are in the cities. We can become, and are becoming, a disruptive force in the flow of services, goods and capital. While we disrupt internally and aim for the eye of the octopus, we are hoping that our brothers are disrupting externally to sever the tentacles of the US.

That's very important, because Newark, New Jersey, is where Engelhart has his capital—and for the last five days he couldn't do any work. Good move for the Africans. You know who Engelhart is, don't you—you don't—you should read about South Africa, he controls most of it, along with Rockefeller, the liberal from the US.

It is sometimes said that the African-American movement in the US does not understand the true nature of the struggle in the world today; that the movement is involved in fighting only racial discrimination, and only with the weapon of non-violence. It used to be. As you know, the Black Power movement which SNCC initiated moved away from the movement for integration. This was not only because the movement's goals were middle class—such as job opportunities for college graduates, equal public facilities—and not only because white Americans' concept of integration was based on the assumption that there was nothing of value in the black community and that little of value would ever come from the black community—and that's very important, because the West doesn't understand its own racism when they talk about integration. When they talk about integration, they talk about accepting black people—isn't that ridiculous? I have to talk about whether or not I want to accept *them,* and they're never willing to talk about that, because they know they'll come up losing. So that integration is absolutely absurd unless you can talk about it on a two-way streak, where black people sit down and decide about integration. That means if you're really going to talk about integration, you don't talk about black people moving into white neighbourhoods, you talk about white people moving into black neighbourhoods.

Because of the middle-class orientation of the integration movement, and because of its subconscious racism, and because of its non-violent approach, it has never been able to involve the black proletariat. It could never attract and hold the young bloods who clearly understood the savagery of white America, and who were ready to meet it with armed resistance. It is the young bloods who contain especially the hatred Che Guevera speaks of when he says, and I quote:

'Hatred as an element of the struggle, relentless hatred of the enemy that impels us over and beyond the natural limitations of man, and transforms us into effective, violent, selected and cold killing machines.'

The Black Power movement has been the catalyst for the bringing together of these young bloods—the real revolutionary proletariat, ready to fight by any means necessary for the liberation of our people.

The Black Power movement in the US is exposing the extent of the racism and exploitation which permeates all the institutions in the country. It has unique appeal to young black students on campuses across the US. These students have been deluded by the fiction in white America that if the black man would educate himself and behave himself, he would be acceptable enough to leave the ranks of the oppressed and have tea with the Queen. However, this year, when provoked by savage white policemen, students on many campuses fought back, whereas before they had accepted these incidents without rebellion. As students are a part of these rebellions, they begin to acquire a resistance-consciousness. They begin to realize that white America might let a very few of them escape, one by one, into the mainstream of a society, but as soon as blacks move in concert around their blackness she will reply with the fury which reveals her true racist nature.

It is necessary, then, to understand that our analysis of the US and international capitalism is one that begins in race. Colour and culture were, and are, key factors in our oppression. Therefore our analysis of history and our economic analysis are rooted in these concepts. Our historical analysis for example views the US as being conceived in racism. Although the first settlers themselves were escaping from oppression, and although their armed uprising against their mother country was around the aggravation of colonialism, and their slogan was 'no taxation without representation', the white European settlers could not extend their lofty theories of democracy to the red men, whom they systematically exterminated as they expanded into the territory of the country which belonged to the red men. Indeed, in the same town in which the settlers set up their model of government based on the theory of representative democracy, the first slaves were brought from Africa. In the writings of the glorious Constitution, guaranteeing 'life, liberty, the pursuit of happiness' and all that other garbage, these were rights for white men only, for the black man was counted only as three fifths of a person. If you read the US Constitution, you will see that this clause is still in there to this very day—that the black man was three fifths of a man.

It was because white America needed cheap or free labour that she raped our African homeland of millions of black people. Because we were black and considered inferior by white Americans and Europeans, our enslavement was justified and rationalized by the so-called white Christians, who attempted to explain their crimes by spouting lies about civilizing the heathens, pagans, savages from Africa, whom they portrayed as being 'better off' in the Americas than they were in their homeland. These circumstances laid the systematic base and framework for the racism which has become institutionalized in white American society.

In our economic analysis, our interpretation of Marx comes not only

from his writing, but, as we see it, from the relationship of capitalistic countries to people of colour around the world. Now I'm going to use the Labour
Movement as an example to show what happens when people in a white
country in the West organize themselves when they're being oppressed. I
want to use the Labour Movement in the US because it's always quoted
around the world as the real movement, or friend, of the black man, who is
going to be able to help him. This is true for all other little white countries
when the white workers organize—here's how they get out of the bind.

The Labour Movement of the US—while in the beginning certainly
some of their great leaders in the struggle were against the absolute control
of the economy by the industrial lords—essentially fought only for money.
And that has been the fight of white workers in the West. The fight for one
thing—more money. Those few who had visions of extending the fight for
workers' control of production never succeeded in transmitting their entire
vision to the rank and file. The Labour Movement found itself asking the
industrial lords, not to give up their control, but merely to pass out a few
more of the fruits of this control. Thereby did the US anticipate the prophecy
of Marx, and avoided the inevitable class struggle within the country by
expanding into the Third World and exploiting the resources and slave
labour of people of colour. Britain, France, did the same thing. US capi-
talists never cut down on their domestic profits to share with the workers.
Instead, they expanded internationally, and threw the bones of their profits
to the American working class, who lapped them up. The American working
class enjoys the fruits of the labours of the Third World workers. The pro-
letariat.has become the Third World, and the bourgeoisie is white western
society.

And to show how that works—and not only how it works just in
terms of the bourgeoisie—I've watched the relationships of whites to whites
who are communist, and whites to non-whites whom they call communist.
Now every time the US wants to take somebody's country, they get up and
say 'Communists are invading them and terrorist guerrilla warfare is on the
way, and we must protect democracy, so send thousands of troops to
Vietnam to kill the Communists.' Italy is a white country. Over one third
of its population is communist. Why doesn't the US invade Italy? Tito is an
acknowledged communist. The US gives him aid. Why don't they invade
Tito's country, if they really care about stopping communism? The US is
not kidding anybody. When they want to take over somebody's land who is
non-white, they talk about communist aggression—that's what they did in
Cuba, in Santo Domingo, and it's what they're doing in Vietnam. They're
always telling people how they're going to stop them from going communist.
And don't talk about dictatorship. Franco is perhaps the worst dictator in the
world today, but the US gives him aid.

So that it is clear it is not a question of communist invasion; it's really a question of being able to take the countries they want most from the people, and the countries they want most are obviously the non-white countries because that is where the resources of the world are today. That's where they have been for the last few centuries. And that's why white western society has to be there.

Now we want to make two distinctions, because when rebellions break out in the large cities of America, the first thing that people say is that they're riots. And white western society is very good, the first thing they want is order; law and order. 'We must have law and order.' They never talk about justice, because they're incapable of talking about it. Hitler had the most efficient system of law and order I've ever seen. He happened to have been a fascist. He did not have justice coupled with his law and order. The US knows about law and order, it doesn't know about justice. It is for white western society to talk about law and order. It is for the Third World to talk about justice.

Now we want to talk just a little about violence. For God's sake, I don't understand how the white West can ever talk against violence. They are the most violent people on the face of the earth. They have used violence to get everything they have. And yet they're the first to talk against violence. The armed rebellions and the guerrilla warfare going on in the US today is not the most violent thing going on in the world. Vietnam, South Africa, Zimbabwe, Hong Kong, Aden, Somaliland—that's where your violence really is. For violence takes many forms. It can take the form of physical warfare, or it can take the form of a slow death.

The Jews in the Warsaw ghettoes were suffering from violence. It didn't take an actual physical form until they were put in the gas chambers, but they were suffering from mental violence. Wherever you go in Africa today, the Africans are suffering from violence, violence inflicted on them by the white West, be it that they are stripped of their culture, of their human diginity, or of the resources of their very land.

And it is crystal clear to the peoples of the Third World today that it's time out for talk. There can be no talk about how to stop violence. That's clear because even Camus talks about that, even though he cops out. Camus talks about executioner/victim. He says, well, there's executioner/victim relationships in society, and the executioner uses force to keep his victim down. But the victim gets tired of that. And what happens is that when the victim moves either to a position of equality or to try to conquer the executioner, he uses the force and the means and the methods that his oppressor used to keep him down. That happens to be violence. I never get caught up with violence. As a matter of fact, one of my favourite quotes on that, to stop all the talk about it, is a quote from Sartre, which my patron saint used. Sartre says:

What then did you expect when you unbound the gag that had muted those black mouths? That they would chant your praises? Did you think that when those heads that our fathers had forcefully bowed down to the ground were raised again, you would find adoration in their eyes?

That's Jean-Paul Sartre, not me.

We are working to increase the revolutionary consciousness of black people in America to join with the Third World. Whether or not violence is used is not decided by us, it is decided by the white West. We are fighting a political warfare. Politics is war without violence. War is politics with violence. The white West will make the decision on how they want the political war to be fought. We are not any longer going to bow our heads to any white man. If he touches one black man in the US, he is going to go to war with every black man in the US.

We are going to extend our fight internationally and we are going to hook up with the Third World. It is the only salvation—we are fighting to save our humanity. We are indeed fighting to save the humanity of the world, which the West has failed miserably in being able to preserve. And the fight must be waged from the Third World. There will be new speakers. They will be Che, they will be Mao, they will be Fanon. You can have Rousseau, you can have Marx, you can even have the great libertarian John Stuart Mill.

I want to tell you why violence is important in terms of building a re-sistance-consciousness in the US. Now I want to use a quote which we learned from Germany:

> The triumph of the Storm Troopers required that the tortured victim allow himself to be led to the gallows without protesting, that he repudiate and abandon himself to the point where he ceases to affirm his identity.

There is nothing more terrible than these processions of human beings going to their deaths like human beings. I'm afraid black Americans cannot afford to march to the gallows the way Jews did. If the US, white America, decides to play Nazis, we're going to let them know the black Americans are not Jews, we're going to fight back to the death. And in case you think that sounds very violent, let me remind you of a poem that your great, great Prime Minister, Sir Winston Churchill, read when you were getting ready to attack Germany, even though you were told that you were a minority. He read a poem, incidentally, I don't know if he told you, which was written by a black man named Claude McKay from Jamaica, and he wrote it for black people. It is called 'If we must die'. It is our poem today in the US. Its message goes something like this:

'We will nobly die, fighting back, and for each of the thousand blows we will deal one death blow. But we're going to die like men. We are not going to take the oppression of white society any longer. That is clear in our minds. How it is in white society's mind is another question, but they are not defining for us any longer our struggle. We will define our struggle and we will carry it out as we see fit.'

We have to extend our fight internationally, not only because such a consciousness would destroy within black communities the minority complex so carefully calculated by the American press, but also because we know that if the black man realizes that the counter-insurgency efforts of the US are directed against his brothers, he will not fight in any of their wars. He will not go. Then it will become crystal clear to the world that the imperialist wars of the US are nothing less than racist wars. During the past year we have initiated a black resistance movement to the Draft, which is being led by our hero, the World Champion, Mr. Mohammed Ali. Not only because we're against black men fighting their brothers in Vietnam, but also because we're certain that the next Vietnam will either be in the Congo, in South Africa, in Zimbabwe, Bolivia, in Guatemala, in Brazil, in Peru, or indeed in the West Indies. And we are not going to fight our brothers.

And to answer your question about violence, the African-American has tried for the past 400 years to peacefully coexist inside the US. It has been to no avail. We have never lynched a white man, we have never burned their churches, we have never bombed their houses, we have never beaten them in the streets. I wish we could say the same for white people around the world. Our history demonstrates that the reward for trying to peacefully coexist has been the physical and psychological murder of our peoples. We have been lynched, our houses have been bombed, and our churches burned. We are now being shot down like dogs in the streets by white racist policemen. We can on longer accept this oppression without retribution. We understand that as we expand our resistance, and internationalize the consciousness of our people, as our martyred brother Malcolm X did, we will get retaliation from the government, as he did. As the resistance struggle escalates we are well aware of the reality of Che's words, when he says:

'The struggle will not be a mere street fight, but it will be a long and harsh struggle.'

And to the end, we are going to work with our common brothers and sisters in the Third World to fight this oppression.

I would like to conclude, then, by telling you just precisely what black people in America are going to do, and when we're going to do it, and how we're going to do it, and why we're going to do it. This is your only chance to hear it clear, because you'll be hearing it from the BBC next time.

Black people in the US have no time to play nice polite parlour games, especially when the lives of our children are at stake. Some white Americans can afford to speak softly, tread lightly, employ the soft sell and put-off—or it is put-down?—because they own the society. For black people to adopt their methods of relieving our oppression is certainly ludicrous. We blacks must respond in our own way, on our own terms, in a manner which fits our temperaments. The definition of ourselves, the road we pursue, the goals we seek are our responsibility. It is crystal clear that society is capable of, and willing to, reward those individuals who do not forcefully condemn it —to reward them with prestige, status and material benefits. But these crumbs of corruption will be rejected. The plain fact is that as a people we have absolutely nothing to lose by refusing to play such games. Anything less than clarity, honesty and forcefulness perpetuates the centuries of sliding over, dressing up and soothing down the true feelings, hopes and demands of an oppressed black people. Mild demands and hypocritical smiles mislead white America into thinking that all is fine and peaceful; they lead white America into thinking that the path and pace chosen to deal with racial problems are acceptable to the masses of black Americans. It is far better to speak forcefully and truthfully. Only when one's true self, black or white, is exposed can society proceed to deal with the problems from a position of clarity, and not from one of misunderstanding.

Thus we have no intention of engaging in the rather meaningless language so common to discussions of race in the world today. They say:

'Things were and are bad, but we are making progress. Granted, your demands are legitimate, but we cannot move hastily. Stable societies are best built slowly. Be careful that you do not anger or alienate your white allies. Remember, after all, you are only ten per cent of the population.'

We reject the language and these views, whether expressed by blacks or by whites. We leave them to others to mouth, because we don't feel that this rhetoric is either relevant or useful. Rather we suggest a more meaningful language—that of Frederick Douglass, a great black man who understood the nature of protest in society. He said:

> Those who profess to favour freedom, yet deprecate agitation, are men who want crops without ploughing up the ground. They want rain without thunder and lightning. They want the ocean without the awful wrath of its many waters. Power concedes nothing without demands—it never did and it never will. Find out just what any people will quietly submit to, and you have found out the exact measure of injustice and wrong which will be imposed upon them. And these will continue until they are resisted with either words or blows, or with both. The limits of tyrants are prescribed by the endurance of those whom they oppress.

He was a slave.

Black Power, to us, means that black people see themselves as a part of a new force, sometimes called the Third World; that we see our struggle as closely related to liberation struggles around the world. We must hook up with these struggles. We must, for example, ask ourselves: when black people in Africa begin to storm Johannesburg, what will be the reaction of the US? What will be the role of the West, and what will be the role of black people living inside the US? It seems inevitable that the US will move to protects its financial interests in South Africa, which means protecting the white rule in South Africa, as England has already done. Black people in the US have the responsibility to oppose, and if not to oppose, certainly to neutralize the effort by white America. This is but one example of many such situations which have already arisen around the world; there are more to come.

There is only one place for Black Americans in these struggles and that is on the side of the Third World.

Now I want to draw two conclusions. I want to give a quote from Fanon. Frantz Fanon in *The Wretched of the Earth* puts forth clearly the reasons for this, and the relationships of the concept called Black Power to the concept of a new force in the world. This is Mr. Fanon's quote:

> Let us decide not to imitate Europe. Let us try to create the whole man, whom Europe has been incapable of bringing to triumphant birth. Two centuries ago a former European colony decided to catch up with Europe. It succeeded so well that the USA became a monster in which the taints, the sickness and the inhumanity of Europe has grown to appalling dimensions. The Third World today faces Europe like a colossal mass, whose aim should be to try to resolve the problems to which Europe has not been able to find the answers. It is a question of the Third World starting a new history of man, a history which will have regard to the sometimes prodigious thesis which Europe has put forward, but which will also not forget Europe's crimes, of which the most horrible was committed in the heart of man and consisted of the pathological tearing apart of his functions and the crumbling away of his unity.
>
> No, there is no question of a return to nature. It is simply a very concrete question of not dragging men towards mutilation, of not imposing upon the brain rhythms which very quickly obliterate it and wreck it. The pretext of catching up must not be used for pushing men around, to tear him away from himself or from his privacy, to break and to kill him.
>
> No, we do not want to catch up with anyone. What we want to do is go forward all the time, night and day, in the company of man, in the company of all men.

Since there's been a lot of talk about psychology. I've thought up a psychological problem. White liberals are always saying 'What can we do?' I mean they're always coming to help black people. And I thought of an analogy. If you were walking down the street and a man had a gun on another man—let's say both of them were white—and you had to help somebody, whom would you help? It's obvious to me that if I were walking down the street, and a man had a gun on another man, and I was going to help, I'd help the man who didn't have the gun, if the man who had the gun was just pulling the gun on the other man for no apparent reason— if he was just going to rob him or shoot him because he didn't like him. The only way I could help is either to get a gun and shoot the man with the gun, or join the fellow who doesn't have a gun and both of us gang up on the man with the gun. But white liberals never do that. When the man has the gun, they walk around him and they come to the victim, and they say 'Can I help you?' And what they mean is 'help you adjust to the situation with the man who has the gun on you'.

So that if indeed white liberals are going to help, their only job is to get the gun from the man and talk to him, because he is in fact the sick man. The black man is not the sick man, it is the white man who is sick, he's the one who picked up the gun first.

So the psychologists ought to stop investigating and examining people of colour, they ought to investigate and examine their own corrupt society. That's where they belong. And once they are able to do that, then maybe we can move on to build in the Third World.

I want to conclude, then, by reading a poem that was written by a young man who works in SNCC, the organization for which I work. His name is Worth Long. It's called 'Arson and Cold Grace, or How I Yearn to Burn, Baby, Burn'.*

> We have found you out, four faced Americans, we have found you out.
> We have found you out, false faced farmers, we have found you out.
> The sparks of suspicion are melting your waters
> And waters can't drown them, the fires are burning
> And firemen can't calm them with falsely appeasing
> And preachers can't pray with hopes for deceiving
> Nor leaders deliver a lecture on losing
> Nor teachers inform them the chosen are choosing
> For now is the fire and fires won't answer
> To logical reason and hopefully seeming
> Hot flames must devour the kneeling and feeling
> And torture the masters whose idiot pleading
> Gets lost in the echoes of dancing and bleeding.
> We have found you out, four faced farmers, we have found you out.
> We have found you out, four faced America, we have found you out.

* Reprinted by permission of the Student National Coordinating Committee.

For Discussion

1. What is the Third World?
2. What distinction does Carmichael make between individual and institutionalized racism? Why does he make a point of this?
3. How does Carmichael connect Western civilization with racism?
4. Compare Carmichael's ideas on the white liberal with those of other black leaders. (Also see King, Baldwin, and Malcolm X.)
5. Explain Carmichael's idea of independence in relation to imperialism.
6. How does the new colonialism operate in the United States? Can you recognize any trends working against it?
7. Carmichael popularized the phrase Black Power, which was the title of a book by Richard Wright published in 1954. How is the concept of Black Power incompatible with integration? (Also see Browne.)
8. What relationship does Carmichael establish between capitalism and racism?
9. What ironies does Carmichael point out in discussing U.S. opposition to communism?
10. How does violence relate to politics? To war?
11. What are the advantages for the black American in becoming a part of the Third World movement? What might be the disadvantages?
12. Boorstin has criticized the new movements as lacking in intellectual content. How does this essay refute his judgment?
13. Describe Carmichael's attitude toward his specific audience. How does it influence his treatment of his argument?
14. What is Carmichael's outlook toward the future?

ELDRIDGE CLEAVER

A Letter from Jail

Eldridge Cleaver became the Black Panther Minister of Information and the 1968 candidate for the Presidency of the United
States on the Peace and Freedom Party ticket. Convicted of a
marijuana charge at eighteen and sent to Folsom Prison, he was
later released on parole, only to be returned in 1958 as a parole
violator. While in prison he became a Muslim convert and a firm
follower of Malcolm X, whose leadership of the black militants
he has inherited. Released from prison nine years later, he was
again arrested on a parole violation and scheduled to return to
prison when he disappeared in November of 1968. Since then
he has been reported in Cuba and Algeria. Cleaver began to
write the letters and essays which are collected in *Soul on Ice*
when he was in prison. The insight and force of this book have
led to his acclaim as a brilliant social critic, able to articulate the
black American's condition with passion, strength, and beauty.
The following letter was handwritten by Cleaver and later
smuggled out of his cell for publication in *Ramparts*.

I fell in love with the Black Panther Party for Self-Defense immediately upon my first encounter with it; it was literally love at first sight. It
happened one night at a meeting in a dingy little storefront on Scott Street
in the Fillmore district, the heart of San Francisco's black ghetto. It was
February 1967. The meeting was the latest in a series of weekly meetings
held by a loose coalition functioning under the name of the Bay Area
Grassroots Organizations Planning Committee. The purpose of the coalition
was to coordinate three days of activities with the worthy ambition of involving the total black community in mass action commemorating the fourth
anniversary of the assassination of Malcolm X. The highlight and culmina-

From *Eldridge Cleaver: Post-Prison Writings and Speeches*, edited by Robert Scheer.
© Copyright 1967, 1968, 1969 by Ramparts Magazine, Inc. Reprinted by permission of
Random House, Inc.

tion of the memorial was to be the appearance of Sister Betty Shabazz, Malcolm X's widow, who was to deliver the keynote speech at a mass meeting at the Bayview Community Center in Hunters Point.

Among the topics on the agenda for this fortuitous meeting was the question of providing security for Sister Betty during the 24 hours she was to be our guest in the Bay Area. There was a paranoia around—which I did not share—that assassins by the dozens were lurking everywhere for the chance to shoot Sister Betty down. This fear, real or imagined, was a fact and it kept everybody up-tight.

I had arrived at the meeting late, changing at the last minute a previous decision not to attend at all. I was pissed off at everyone in the room. Taking a seat with my back to the door I sat there with, I'm sure, a scornful frown of disdain upon my face. Roy Ballard (if the normal brain had three cylinders his would have one) sat opposite me, across the circle formed by the placement of the chairs. He, above all, understood the expression on my face, for he had done the most to put it there; this accounted, I thought, for the idiot grin on his own.

On Roy's left sat Ken Freeman, chairman of the now defunct Black Panther Party of Northern California, who always looked to me like Dagwood, with his huge round bifocals and the bald spot in the front of his natural. On Roy's right sat a frightened-looking little mulatto who seemed to live by the adage, "It's better to remain silent and be thought a fool than to open one's mouth and remove all doubt." He probably adopted that rule from observing his big fat yellow wife, who was seated on his right and who had said when I walked in, just loud enough for me to hear, "Shit! I thought we agreed after last week's meeting that *he* wouldn't be allowed to attend any more meetings!"

Next to her sat Jack Trueblood, a handsome, earnest youth in a black Russian cap who represented San Francisco State College's Black Students Union and who always accepted whatever tasks were piled upon him, insuring that he would leave each weekly meeting with a heavy load. On his right sat a girl named Lucky. I could never tell why they called her that—not, I'm sure, because she happened to be Roy Ballard's old lady; maybe because she had such a beautiful smile.

Between Lucky and myself sat Marvin Jackmon who was known as a poet, because after Watts went up in flames he had composed a catchy ditty entitled "Burn, Baby, Burn!" and a play entitled "Flowers for the Trashman." (It is hard for me to write objectively about Marvin. My association with him, dating from the third week of December 1966, ended in mutual bitterness with the closing of the Black House. After getting out of prison that month, he was the first person I hooked up with. Along with Ed Bullins, a young playwright who now has a few things going for himself off-Broadway, and Willie Dale, who had been in San Quentin with me and was trying to make it as a singer, we had founded the Black House in January 1967. Within the next two months the Black House, located in San Francisco, became the center of non-Establishment black culture throughout the Bay Area.)

On my right sat Bill Sherman, an ex-member of the Communist Party and at that time a member of the Central Committee of the Black Panther Party of Northern California. Next to Bill was Victoria Durant, who dressed with what the black bourgeoisie would call "style" or, better yet, "class." She seemed so out of place at those meetings. We were supposed to be representing the common people—grassroots—and here was Victoria ready to write out a $50 check at the drop of a hat. She represented, as everyone knew, the local clique of Black Democrats who wanted inside info on everything even hinting of "organizing" in their stomping grounds—even if the price of such info was a steady flow of $50 checks.

Then there was Marianne Waddy, who kept everybody guessing because no one was ever sure of where or what she really was. One day she'd be dressed in flowing African gowns with her hair wrapped up in a pretty *skashok,* the perfect picture of the young Afro-American lady who had established a certain identity and relationship to traditional African culture. The next day she would be dressed like a man and acting like a man who would cut the first throat that got in his way.

Next to Marianne sat a sneaky-looking fellow called Nasser Shabazz. Sitting between Nasser and Ken Freeman, completing the circle, was Vincent Lynch, as smooth and black as the ebony statues he had brought back from his trip to Nigeria and the only member of the Black Panther Party of Northern California I ever liked or thought was sincere. Somewhere in the room, too, was Ann Lynch, Vincent's wife, with their bright-eyed little son, Patrice Lumumba Lynch. Ann was the head of Black Care, the women's auxiliary to this Panther Party. These sisters spent all of their time talking about the impending violent stage of the black revolution, which was inevitable and how they, the women, must be prepared to care for the men who would be wounded in battle.

I had come out of prison with plans to revive the Organization of Afro-American Unity, the vehicle finally settled upon by Malcolm X to spearhead the black revolution. The OAAU had never really gotten off the ground, for it was cut short by the assassins' bullets that felled Malcolm on the stage of the Audubon Ballroom in New York City. I was amazed that no one else had moved to continue Malcolm's work in the name of the organization he had chosen, which seemed perfect to me and also logically necessary in terms of historical continuity. The three-day memorial, which was but part of the overall plan to revive the OAAU, was to be used as a forum for launching the revival. In January, I had put the plan on paper and circulated it throughout the Bay Area, then issued a general call for a meeting to establish a temporary steering committee that would see after things until the start of the memorial. At this time we would have a convention, found the Bay Area branch of the Organization of Afro-American Unity and elect officers whom Sister Betty Shabazz would install, giving the whole effort her blessings in a keynote address on the final day of the memorial.

By February the plan had been torn to shreds. If the plan was a pearl, then I had certainly cast it before swine, and the biggest swine of all, Roy Ballard, had hijacked the plan and turned it into a circus. It soon became clear that if the OAAU was to be reborn, it would not be with the help of this crew, because all they could see was the pageantry of the memorial. Beyond that, their eyes blotted out all vision. Far from wanting to see an organization develop that would put an end to the archipelago of one-man showcase groups that plagued the black community with division, they had each made it their sacred cause to insure the survival of their own splinter group.

From the beginning, when the plan was first put before them, they took up each separate aspect and chewed it until they were sure it was either maimed for life or dead. Often after an idea had gone around the circle, if it still showed signs of life they would pounce upon it and rend it some more. When they finished, all that was left of the original plan was a pilgrimage to the site where a sixteen-year-old black youth, Matthew Johnson, had been murdered by a white cop, putting some pictures of Malcolm X on the walls of the Bayview Community Center, a hysterical speech by Ken Freeman and 24 hours of Sister Betty Shabazz's time.

In all fairness, however, I must confess that the whole plan was impossible to achieve, mostly because it did not take into account certain negative aspects of the black man's psychological heritage from 400 years of oppression here in Babylon. Then, too, I was an outsider. Having gone to prison from Los Angeles, I had been paroled to San Francisco. I was an interloper unfolding a program to organize *their* community. Fatal. It didn't matter to them that we were dealing with the concept of the Black Nation, of colonized Afro-America, and that all the boundaries separating our people were the stupid impositions of the white oppressors and had to be obliterated. Well, no matter; I had failed. Proof of my failure was Roy Ballard, sitting there before me like a gaunt buzzard, presiding over the carcass of a dream.

Suddenly the room fell silent. The crackling undercurrent that for weeks had made it impossible to get one's point across when one had the floor was gone; there was only the sound of the lock clicking as the front door opened, and then the sofe shuffle of feet moving quietly toward the circle.

Shadows danced on the walls. From the tension showing on the faces of the people before me, I thought the cops were invading the meeting, but there was a deep female gleam leaping out of one of the women's eyes that no cop who ever lived could elicit. I recognized that gleam out of the recesses of my soul, even though I had never seen it before in my life; the total admiration of a black woman for a black man. I spun round in my seat and saw the most beautiful sight I had ever seen: four black men wearing black berets, powder blue shirts, black leather jackets, black trousers, shiny black shoes—and each with a gun! In front was Huey P. Newton with a riot pump shotgun in his right hand, barrel pointed down to the floor. Beside him was Bobby Seale, the handle of a .45 caliber automatic showing from its holster on his right hip, just below the hem of his jacket. A few steps behind Seale was Bobby Hutton, the barrel of his shotgun at his feet. Next to him was Sherwin Forte, an M1 carbine with a banana clip cradled in his arms.

Roy Ballard jumped to his feet. Licking his lips, he said, "For those of you who've never met the brothers, these are the Oakland Panthers."

"You're wrong," said Huey P. Newton. "We're not the Oakland Panthers. We happen to live in Oakland. Our name is the Black Panther Party for Self-Defense."

With that the Panthers seated themselves in chairs along the wall, outside the circle. Every eye in the room was riveted upon them. What amazed me was that Roy Ballard did not utter one word in contradiction, nor was there any other yakkity-yak around the room. There was absolute silence. Even little Patrice Lumumba Lynch seemed to sit up and take notice.

Where was my mind at? Blown! Racing through time, racing through the fog of a perspective that had just been shattered into a thousand fragments. Who are these cats? I wondered at them, checking them out carefully. They were so cool and it seemed to me not unconscious of the electrifying effect they were having on everybody in the room. Then I recalled a chance remark that Marvin Jackmon had once made. We were discussing the need for security at the Black House because the crowds were getting larger and larger and we had had to bodily throw out a cat who was high and acting like he owned the place. I said that Marvin, Ed, Dale and I had better each get ourself a gun. As I elaborated on the necessity as I saw it, Marvin said: "You need to forget about the Black House and go across the bay and get with Bobby Seale." And then he laughed.

"Who is Bobby Seale?" I asked him.

At first he gave no answer, he seemed to be carefully considering what to say. Finally he said, "He's arming some brothers across the bay." Though I pressed him, he refused to got into it any further, and at the time it didn't seem important to me, so I forgot about it. Now, sitting there looking at those Panthers, I recalled the incident with Marvin. I looked at him. He seemed to have retreated inside himself, sitting there looking like a skinny black Buddha with something distasteful and menacing on his mind.

"Do you brothers want to make a speech at the memorial?" Roy Ballard asked the Panthers.

"Yes," Bobby Seale said.

"O.K.," said Ballard. "We have the program broken down into subjects: Politics, Economics, Self-Defense and Black Culture. Now which section do you brothers want to speak under?" This was the sort of question which in my experience had always signaled the beginning of a two-hour debate with this group.

"It doesn't matter what section we speak under," Huey said. "Our message is one and the same. We're going to talk about black people arming themselves in a political fashion to exert organized force in the political arena to see to it that their desires and needs are met. Otherwise there will be a political consequence. And the only culture worth talking about is a revolutionary culture. So it doesn't matter what heading you put on it, we're going to talk about political power growing out of the barrel of a gun."

"O.K.," Roy Ballard said. He paused, then added, "Let's put it under Politics." Then he went on to start the specific discussion of security for Sister Betty, who would pick her up at the airport, etc. Bobby Seale was jotting down notes in a little black book. The other Panthers sat quietly, watchfully.

Three days before the start of the memorial, I received a phone call from Los Angeles. The man on the other end identified himself as Mr. Hakim Jamal, Malcolm X's cousin by marriage. He would be arriving with Sister Betty, he said, and both of them wanted to talk with me. They had liked, it turned out, an article on Malcolm that I had written and that was published in Ramparts. We agreed that when they got in from the airport I would meet them at the Ramparts office in San Francisco.

On the day that Sister Betty and Hakim Jamal were to arrive in San Francisco, I was sitting in my office tinkering with some notes for an article. One of the secretaries burst through the door. Her face was white with fear and she was shouting, "We've being invaded! We're being invaded!"

I couldn't tell just who her "we" referred to. Were the Chinese coming? Had the CIA finally decided to do Ramparts in?" Then she said, "There are about 20 men outside with guns!"

I knew that Hakim Jamal and Sister Betty had arrived with their escort of armed Black Panthers.

"Don't worry," I said, "they're friends."

"Friends?" she gasped. I left her there with her eyes bugging out of her head and rushed to the front of the building.

I waded through Ramparts' staff jammed into the narrow hallway, fending off the frightened inquiries by repeating, "It's all right, it's all right." The lobby resembled certain photographs coming out of Cuba the day Castro took Havana. There were guns everywhere, pointed towards the ceiling like metallic blades of grass growing up out of the sea of black faces beneath the black berets of the Panthers. I found Hakim Jamal and Sister Betty surrounded by a knot of Panthers, who looked calm and self-possessed in sharp contrast to the chaotic reactions their appearance had set off. Outside where Broadway ran in four lanes to feed the freeway on-ramp and to receive the heavy traffic from the off-ramp, a massive traffic jam was developing and sirens could be heard screaming in the distance as cops sped our way.

I took Jamal and Sister Betty to an office down the hall. We talked for about 15 minutes about Malcolm. Sister Betty, her eyes concealed behind dark glasses, said nothing after we were introduced. She looked cool enough on the surface, but it was clear that she felt hard-pressed. Huey P. Newton was standing at the window, shotgun in hand, looking down into the upturned faces of a horde of police. I left the room to get Sister Betty a glass of water, squeezing past Bobby Seale and what seemed like a battalion of Panthers in the hall guarding the door. Seale's face was a chiseled mask of determination.

A few yards down the hall, Warren Hinckle III, editor of Ramparts, was talking to a police lieutenant.

"What's the trouble?" the lieutenant asked, pointing at the Black Panthers with their guns.

"No trouble," Hinckle said. "Everything is under control."

The policeman seemed infuriated by this answer. He stared at Bobby Seale for a moment and then stalked outside. While I was in the lobby a TV cameraman, camera on his shoulder, forced his way through the front door and started taking pictures. Two white boys who worked at Ramparts stopped the TV man and informed him that he was trespassing on private property. When he refused to leave they picked him up and threw him out the door, camera and all.

When it was agreed that it was time to leave, Huey Newton took control. Mincing no words, he sent five of his men out first to clear a path through the throng of spectators clustered outside the door, most of whom were cops. He dispatched a phalanx of ten Panthers fast on their heels, with Hakim Jamal and Sister Betty concealed in their midst. Newton himself along with Bobby Seale and three other Panthers, brought up the rear.

I went outside and stood on the steps of Ramparts to observe the departure. When Huey left the building, the TV cameraman who had gotten tossed out was grinding away with his camera. Huey took an envelope from his pocket and held it up in front of the camera, blocking the lens.

"Get out of the way!" the TV man shouted. When Huey continued to hold the envelope in front of the lens, the TV man started cursing, and reached out and knocked Huey's hand away with his fist. Huey coolly turned to one of the score of cops watching and said:

"Officer, I want you to arrest this man for assault."

An incredulous look came into the cop's face, then he blurted out: "If I arrest anybody it'll be you!"

Huey turned on the cameraman, again placing the envelope in front of the lens. Again the cameraman reached out and knocked Huey's hand away. Huey reached out, snatched the cameraman by the collar and slammed him up against the wall, sending him spinning and staggering down the sidewalk, trying to catch his breath and balance the camera on his shoulder at the same time.

Bobby Seale tugged at Huey's shirt sleeve. "C'mon, Huey, let's get out of here."

Huey and Bobby started up the sidewalk toward their car. The cops stood there on the point, poised as though ready to start shooting at a given signal.

"Don't turn your backs on these back-shooting dogs!" Huey called out to Bobby and the other three Panthers. By this time the other Panthers with Sister Betty and Jamal had gotten into cars and melted into the traffic jam. Only these five were still at the scene.

At that moment a big, beefy cop stepped forward. He undid the little strap holding his pistol in his holster and started shouting at Huey, "Don't point that gun at me! Stop pointing that gun at me!" He kept making gestures as though he was going for his gun.

This was the most tense of moments. Huey stopped in his tracks and stared at the cop.

"Let's split, Huey! Let's split!" Bobby Seale was saying.

Ignoring him, Huey walked to within a few feet of the cop and said, "What's the matter, you got an itchy finger?"

The cop made no reply.

"You want to draw your gun?" Huey asked him.

The other cops were calling out for this cop to cool it, to take it easy, but he didn't seem to be able to hear them. He was staring into Huey's eyes, measuring him.

"O.K.," Huey said. "You big fat racist pig, draw your gun!"

The cop made no move.

"Draw it, you cowardly dog!" Huey pumped a round into the chamber of the shotgun. "I'm waiting," he said, and stood there waiting for the cop to draw.

All the other cops moved back out of the line of fire. I moved back, too, onto the top step of Ramparts. I was thinking, staring at Huey surrounded by all those cops and daring one of them to draw, "Goddam, that nigger is c-r-a-z-y!"

Then the cop facing Huey gave it up. He heaved a heavy sigh and lowered his head. Huey literally laughed in his face and then went off up the street at a jaunty pace, disappearing in a blaze of dazzling sunlight.

"Work out soul-brother," I was shouting to myself. "You're the baddest motherfucker I've ever seen!" I went back into Ramparts and we all stood around chattering excitedly, discussing what he had witnessed with disbelief.

"*Who was that?*" asked Vampira, Warren Hinckle's little sister.

"That was Huey P. Newton," I said, "Minister of Defense of the Black Panther Party for Self-Defense."

"Boy, is he gutsy!" she said dreamily.

"Yeah," I agreed. "He's out of sight!"

The quality in Huey P. Newton's character which I had seen that morning in front of Ramparts and which I was to see demonstrated over and over again after I joined the Black Panther Party for Self-Defense was *courage*. I had called it "crazy," as people often do to explain away things they do not understand. I don't mean the courage "to stand up and be counted," or even the courage it takes to face certain death. I speak of that revolutionary courage it takes to pick up a gun with which to oppose the oppressor of one's people. That's a different kind of courage.

Oppressed people, Fanon points out, kill each other all the time. A glance through any black newspaper will prove that black people in America kill each other with regularity. This is the internalized violence of oppressed people. Angered by the misery of their lives but cowed by the overt superior might of the oppressor, the oppressed people shrink from striking out at the true objects of their hostility and strike instead at their more defenseless brothers and sisters near at hand. Somehow this seems safer, less fraught with dire consequences, as though one is less dead when shot down by one's brother than when shot down by the oppressor. It is merely criminal to take up arms against one's brother, but to step outside the vicious circle of the internalized violence of the oppressed and take up arms against the oppressor is to step outside of life itself, to step outside of the structure of this world, to enter, almost alone, the no-man's-land of revolution.

Huey P. Newton took that step. For the motto of the Black Panther Party he chose a quotation from Mao Tse-tung's Little Red Book: "We are advocates of the abolition of war; we do not want war; but war can only be abolished through war; and in order to get rid of the gun it is necessary to pick up the gun."

When I decided to join the Black Panther Party the only hang-up I had was with its name. I was still clinging to my conviction that we owed it to Malcolm to pick up where he left off. To me, this meant building the organization that he had started. Picking up where Malcolm left off, however, had different meanings for different people. For cats like Marvin Jackmon, for instance, it meant returning to the ranks of Elijah Muhammad's Nation of Islam, denouncing Malcolm as a heretic and pledging loyalty to Elijah, all in Malcolm's name. For Huey, it meant implementing the program that Malcolm advocated. When that became clear to me, I knew what Huey P. Newton was all about.

For the revolutionary black youth of today, time starts moving with the coming of Malcolm X. Before Malcolm, time stands still, going down in frozen steps into the depths of the stagnation of slavery. Malcolm talked shit, and talking shit is the iron in a young nigger's blood. Malcolm mastered language and used it as a sword to slash his way through the veil of lies that for 400 years gave the white man the power of the word. Through the breach in the veil, Malcolm saw all the way to national liberation, and he showed us the rainbow and the golden pot at its end. Inside the golden pot, Malcolm told us, was the tool of liberation. Huey P. Newton, one of the millions of black people who listened to Malcolm, lifted the golden lid off the pot and blindly, trusting Malcolm, stuck his hand inside and grasped the tool. When he withdrew his hand and looked to see what he held, he saw the gun, cold in its metal and implacable in its message: Death-Life, Liberty or Death, mastered by a black hand at last! Huey P. Newton is the ideological descendant, heir and successor of Malcolm X. Malcolm prophesied the coming of the gun to the black liberation struggle. Huey P. Newton picked up the gun and pulled the trigger, freeing the genie of black revolutionary violence in Babylon.

The genie of black revolutionary violence is here, and it says that the oppressor has no rights which the oppressed are bound to respect. The genie also has a question for white Americans: which side do you choose? Do you side with the oppressor or with the oppressed? The time for decision is upon you. The cities of America have tested the first flames of revolution. But a hotter fire rages in the hearts of black people today: total liberty for black people or total destruction for America.

The prospects, I confess, do not look promising. Besides being a dumb nation, America is mad with white racism. Whom the gods would destroy, they first make mad. Perhaps America has been mad far too long to make any talk of sanity relevant now. But there is a choice and it will be made, by decision or indecision, by action or inaction, by commission or omission. Black people have made their choice; a revolutionary generation that has the temerity to say to America that Huey P. Newton must be set free, also invested with the courage to kill, pins its hopes on the revolutionary's faith and says, with Che: *Wherever death may surprise us, it will be welcome, provided that this, our battlecry, reach some receptive ear, that another hand reach out to pick up weapons, and that other fighting men come forward to intone our funeral dirge with the staccato of machine guns and new cries of battle and victory.*

For Discussion

1. What is accomplished by the detailed description of the participants in the meeting? What picture of Cleaver emerges from this description?
2. What is the main organizational weakness in the black community that Cleaver wanted to correct?
3. What attitude of black women toward black men does Cleaver project at the entrance of the Black Panthers? How does this differ from the traditional one?
4. How does Newton's behavior with the "beefy cop" illustrate those qualities which Cleaver admires?
5. How does Cleaver's picture of the Black Panthers differ from that presented by the news media?
6. Discuss Cleaver's idea that oppressed peoples strike out at each other rather than at their oppressors.
7. Look at the motto of the Black Panther Party. What would be your feeling about its meaning if it were written by
   a) Huey Newton?
   b) Adolf Hitler?
   c) Dwight Eisenhower?
   d) President Nixon?
8. What does Cleaver mean when he says, "Malcolm talked shit, and talking shit is the iron in a young nigger's blood"? (See "After the Bombing" by Malcolm X.)
9. Discuss the concept of madness, which Cleaver focuses on in the final paragraph, as it applies to both black and white.
10. How do Cleaver's tone and style change after the incident at the *Ramparts* office?

JAMES KUNEN

Why We're Against the Biggees

James Kunen was nineteen years old and a student at Columbia University when the student protest erupted there in 1968. Sparked by Columbia's plans to build a gym in Morningside Park (which separates Columbia from Harlem) without consulting the community, the revolt became a protest against all the ills the university had come to represent. Subsequently the revolt has had counterparts in colleges and universities across the United States and Europe. Although Kunen denies any importance for his writing, the following essay begins to make clear what much of student dissent is all about. In 1969, his chronicle of the events at Columbia was published in a book entitled *The Strawberry Statement.*

I have surveyed the opinions of the well-intentioned American middle class regarding Columbia. That is, I have spoken to my mother about it. She's been reading the *New Republic,* and is currently fond of saying that the Columbia rebellion was set up in advance by people who are not students at Columbia, and who do not have its interests at heart. This is entirely true.

The Columbia rebellion was set in motion by a nebulous group of outsiders who are variously known as the corporate power elite, the military-industrial complex, the Establishment. A friend of mine refers to them as the Biggees.

The Biggees are a small group of men. Little else about them is known. They are probably old. They possess wealth surpassing the bounds of imagination. They have no real needs or desires, but cultivate avarice as a sort of obsessive hobby. They sit in smoke-filled rooms, so it may be presumed that they smoke cigars. In the councils of the Biggees, one might hear decisions that one thought no one could make. Buy Uruguay. Sell Bolivia. Hold India. Pollute New York. The decisions are of incomprehensible variety, but they have in common the fact that they are swiftly implemented and invariably soak the Little Man.

Sometimes the Biggees slug it out with each other, as in the gold market, where they get down to the nitty-gritty of buying and selling *money* (a commerce that no one else can understand, let alone participate in), but more often they are after *our* coin.

The Biggees lie. They shout up and down that Vitalis has V_7, but they don't say what V_7 *is*. They say that Arrid stops wetness, but they don't explain why wetness should be stopped. (I can think of a lot of things that qualify for stoppage way ahead of wetness.) They lie about little things like that, and big things like Vietnam, the ghetto, Democracy. It's all the same— truth in lending, truth in labeling, truth in government; none of them exist.

The Biggees *control*. I read a sixth-grader's history paper about the Spanish-American War. The young boy, having put away his Mattel M-16 automatic rifle for the evening to do his homework, wrote that the 1898 war was fought by America to set the poor Cubans free from tyranny. He added that America traditionally fights on the side of right for justice and freedom and therefore always wins, "like in Vietnam today." The Biggees have that kid right where they want him. They've got his mind; when he's eighteen they'll take his body.

Look around you. The Biggees are everywhere. Look in your driveway. They build cars that dissociate in three years, and they make everybody buy them, and they're in on the gas biz too, so you can forget about mileage. And no one can make them change. You get organized and ask them to please just put all bumpers at a standard level so maybe a little less than that 50,000 of us will die on the roads next year, but no, they can't do it. They can't do it because it will *cost* to do it, and anyway, if all bumpers were at the same height, then there wouldn't be any choice, and that's what democracy's all about. If you didn't know that that's what democracy's all about, there are frequent ads to remind you. It seems, for instance, that in socialist countries there are only three colors of lipstick, whereas capitalism provides forty.

And with these forty shades of lipstick the Biggees turn our women into nauga-babes (vinyl girls) who in pre-fab sexiness sit tracing cheap pictures in the air with cigarettes they never made up their minds to start smoking. And, arguing about what to-do to do next, one of these naugas might be heard to say, "It's a free country."

But it isn't a free country. You can't drop out of school because you'd be drafted, and you have to study certain things to get a degree, and you have to have a degree to make it, and you have to make it to get what you want, and you can't even decide what you want, because it's all programmed into you beforehand. You can *say* whatever you want, but you won't be heard because the media control that, but if you do manage to be heard, the People won't like it, because the people have been told what to like. And if they don't like you, they might even kill you, because the government endorses killing by exemplification.

All of which brings us to Columbia, because at Columbia we're all together and we teach each other and feel strong. The Biggees are killing people in Vietnam and keeping the blacks down at home, because they have to keep some people at the bottom for their system to work, or so they thought. Now they're finding out that the downs can really screw them up bad, so they'd like to raise them just a bit, but that would certainly cost, so for the moment they'll try to keep them down by promising them rewards if they behave.

So here we all are at Columbia not comprehending this great money motivation because we didn't grow up in a depression and have always had coin and therefore don't value it as highly as we might. We're right at Harlem, so we see how it is. And we've got the draft right on us, so we know how that is. And we don't like it. We don't like it at all, because we've got a lot of life ahead of us and we're for it. Killing and dying just don't make it with us.

And lo and behold, right here at Columbia where all we young angries are seething, who should be president but Grayson Kirk, a Biggee if ever there was one. Consolidated Edison, IBM, Socony Mobil, Asia Foundation, I.D.A.—he's got an iron in every fire that's consuming us. And it turns out that Military Intelligence has offices at the university, and Electronic Research Laboratories is raking in about $5 million per annum on radar, and we're in the Institute for Defense Analysis in a big way, and the School of International Affairs is hitting it off really well with the CIA. All the while the university is systematically desiccating the integrated community of Morningside Heights, and has its eyes on land all the way over to Seventh Avenue, so that some fine day there'll be a nice white suburban buffer zone in the middle of Manhattan, which people will know, by the inevitable iron gates around it, to be Columbia.

Seeing all this, we decided to change it. Of course, if you don't like it you can leave, but if you leave you're going to run into something else you don't like, and you can't go on leaving forever because you'll run out of places to go. So we decided to change it. We petitioned, we demonstrated, we wrote letters, and we got nowhere. We weren't refused; we were ignored. So one day we went into the buildings, and one day somewhat later we were pulled out and arrested and many people were beaten. In the intervening days we were widely accused of having ourselves a good time in the buildings. We did have a good time. We had a good time because for six days we regulated our own lives and were free.

But Dr. Kirk and his associates saw that we were free and they knew of course that that sort of thing must not be permitted. They knew also that they could not deal with our demands, because that would mean a breakdown of their law and a violation of their order. So they called in the police. And they expressed regret that the police injured 150 people, and they really did regret it, because the brutal bust showed everybody how far the powerful will go to retain their power, how far they will go rather than answer a single question, rather than admit that questions can be asked.

As I write this and as you read it people are dying. So you see it isn't really a topic for suburban conversation or magazine articles. It's something that must be dealt with. That's what's happening at Columbia, not a revolution but a counterattack. We are fighting to recapture a school from business and war and rededicate it to learning and life. Right now nobody controls Columbia, but if we get it, we will never give it back. And there are 5 million college students in the country watching us. And a lot of them have just about had it with the Biggees.

For Discussion

1. Logically, the term "Biggees" is an oversimplification (like Boorstin's "Barbarians"), which relies upon individual connotation for its specific meaning. Name your own Biggees.
2. Kunen sometimes combines great and small ills. Find an example of this combination and analyze its effect.
3. Discuss the idea that what happened at Columbia was a counterattack rather than a revolution.
4. How might Columbia be considered a symbol of other protest movements? What elements would they share?
5. Argue for or against Kunen's contention that this is not a free country.
6. Do you think that Kunen speaks for the majority of college students today? What do you think the purpose of the university should be? (Also see Ridgeway.)
7. Reread the first and last paragraphs. Explain how and why the tone changes.
8. How does Kunen's style reveal his attitude toward his subject?

DANIEL J. BOORSTIN

The New Barbarians

What future historians will say of the present generation can only be conjectured, but the following assessment, written by Daniel J. Boorstin, denies the current charge of radicalism and suggests that the real threat is a new form of barbarism. Mr. Boorstin holds degrees in law and history and has lectured at major universities throughout the world. Author of numerous books, he is presently a professor of history at the University of Chicago.

For centuries, men here have been discovering new ways in which the happiness and prosperity of each individual revolves around that of the community. Now suddenly we are witnessing the explosive rebellion of small groups, who reject the American past, deny their relation to the community, and, in a spiritual Ptolemaism insist that the U.S.A. must revolve around each of them. This atavism, this New Barbarism, cannot last, if the nation is to survive.

Because the New Barbarians seek the kudos of old labels—"Non-violence," "Pacifism," "Leftism," "Radicalism," etc.—we too readily assume that they really are just another expression of "good old American individualism," of "healthy dissent," of the red-blooded rambunctious spirit which has kept his country alive and kicking.

Nothing could be further from the truth. We are now seeing something new under the American sun. And we will be in still deeper trouble if we do not recognize what has really happened. The New Barbarism is not simply another expression of American vitality. It is not simply another expression of the utopianism of youth. On the contrary. What it expresses, in tornado-potence, is a new view of America and of the world. It expresses a new notion of how the world should be grasped.

The Depression Decade beginning in 1929 saw in the United States

First published in Esquire Magazine, October, 1968. Copyright 1968 by Daniel J. Boorstin, author of *The Americans*. Reprinted by permission of the author.

a host of radicalisms, perhaps more numerous and more influential than at any earlier period of our history. Many of these were left-wing movements, which included large numbers of our academics, intellectuals, and men of public conscience, who became members or fellow travelers of groups dominated by Marxist ideas. They favored a reconstruction of American life on a base of socialism or communism. They had a great deal to do with promoting a new and wider American labor movement, with helping F.D.R. popularize the need for a welfare state, and with persuading Americans to join the war to stop Hitler. Although they fenced in American social scientists by new orthodoxies, they did have a generally tonic effect on American society. However misguided were many of the policies they advocated, these radicals did awaken and sensitize the American conscience. They confronted Americans with some facts of life which had been swept under the rug.

That was radicalism. And those of us who were part of it can attest to some of its features. It was radicalism in the familiar and traditional sense of the word. The word "radical" does, of course, come from the Latin "radix," meaning "root," and a radical, then, is a person trying to go to the root of matters.

Of course those radicals never were quite respectable. Their message was that things were not what they seemed, and that inevitably makes respectable people uncomfortable. But we would be mistaken if we assumed, as many do nowadays, that a radical is anybody who makes a lot of other people uncomfortable.

What makes a radical radical is not *that* he discomfits others but *how* he does it. A drunk is not a radical, neither is a psychotic, though both can make us quite uncomfortable. Nor does mere rudeness or violence make a person a radical, though a rude or violent man can make everybody around him quite miserable. Nor is a man who is unjustly treated and resents it necessarily a radical. Caryl Chessman may not have been guilty as charged— yet that did not make him a radical.

The most vocal and most violent disrupters of American society today are not radicals at all, but a new species of barbarian. In the ancient world, "barbarian" was a synonym for foreigner, and meant an alien who came from some far-off savage land. He himself was "barbarous," wild, and uncivilized. He was a menace not because he wanted to reform or reshape the society he invaded but because he did not understand or value that society, and he aimed to destroy it.

The New Barbarians in America today come not from without, but from within. While they are not numerous anywhere—comprising perhaps less than two percent of our two hundred million Americans—they pose a special threat precisely because they are diffuse, wild, and disorganized. They have no one or two headquarters to be surveyed, no one or two philosophies to be combated. But they are no less rude, wild, and uncivilized than if they had come from the land of the Visigoths or the Vandals. The fact that they come from within—and are somehow a product of—our society makes them peculiarly terrifying, but it does not make them any the less barbarians.

We must not be deceived by our own hypersensitive liberal consciences, nor by the familiar, respected labels under which the New Barbarians like to travel. If American civilization is to survive, if we are to resist and defeat the New Barbarism, we must see it for what it is. Most important, we must see that in America the New Barbarism is something really new.

A first step in this direction is to cease to confuse the New Barbarians with the members of other, intellectually respectable groups which can and must claim tolerance in a free society. The New Barbarians are not radicals. This will be obvious if we recall the characteristics of the radicalisms that in one form or another have discomfited and awakened generations of Americans.

Radicalism in the United States has had several distinctive and inter-related characteristics:

1. *Radicalism Is a Search for Meaning.* The search for meaning is the search for significance, for what else something connotes. The socialist, for example, denies that the capitalist system of production and distribution makes sense; he wants to reorganize it to produce a new meaning in the institutions of property and in the economy of the whole society. The religious pacifist, if he is a Christian, seeks the meaning of society in the Christian vision of peace and the brotherhood of man. When the true radical criticizes society he demands that the society justify itself according to some new measure of meaning.

2. *Radicalism Has a Specific Content.* The radical is distinguished from the man who simply has a bad digestion by the fact that the radical's belief has some solid subject matter, while the other man is merely dyspeptic. A stomachache or sheer anger or irritability cannot be the substance of radicalism. Thus, while a man can be ill-natured or irritable in general, he cannot be a radical in general. Every radicalism is a way of asserting *what* are the roots. Radicalism, therefore, involves affirmation. It is distinguished from conservatism precisely in that the conservative can be loose and vague about his affirmation. The conservative is in fact always tempted to let his affirmation become mere complacency. But the true radical cannot refuse to affirm, and to be specific, although of course he may be utopian. The radical must affirm that *this* is more fundamental than *that*. One great service of the radical, then, is that by his experimental definitions he puts the conservative on the defensive and makes him discover, decide, and define what is really worth preserving. The radical does this by the specificity (sometimes also by the rashness) of his affirmation—of the dictatorship of the proletariat, of the Kingdom of God on earth, or of whatever else.

3. *Radicalism Is an Affirmation of Community.* It affirms that we all share the same root problems, that we are all in the same boat, though the

radical may see the boat very differently than do others. For example, if he is a pacifist radical he insists that the whole society bears the blame for even a single man killed in war; if he is an anarchist radical he insists that the whole society bears the blame for the injustice of property and the violence of government. Radicalism, then, involves a commitment to the interdependence of men, and to the sharing of their concerns, which the radical feels with an especially urgent, personal intensity.

These are only general characteristics. Of course, there are borderline cases. We might be uncertain whether Henry George's Single Taxers or Tom Watson's Populists were real radicals. But a full-fledged radicalism, of the kind which can serve and has served as a tonic to the whole society, does have at least the three characteristics I have mentioned. There have been many such radicalisms in American History—from the Antinomians of Massachusetts Bay, through the Quakers of Pennsylvania, the Abolitionists and the Mormons down to the Jehovah's Witnesses and the Communists in our own day. But the most prominent, the most vocal, the most threatening, and the most characteristic disruptive movements in the United States within the last few years do not belong in this tradition. Whatever they or their uncritical observers may say to the contrary, they are not radicalisms. They do not exhibit the characteristics I have listed.

It is characteristic of the Student Power and the Black Power "movements" that in them the quest for meaning has been displaced by the quest for power. Among students, the Bull Session tends to be displaced by the Strategy Session. The "discussions" of activist students are not explorations of the great questions that have troubled civilized men as they come to manhood, since the days of the Old Testament and of Ancient Greece. They are not concerned with whether there is a God, with what is the true nature of art, or of civilization, or of morals. The Student Power Barbarians and the Black Power Barbarians pose not questions but answers. Or, as one of their recent slogans says: "Happiness Is Student Power." Their answer to everything is uncharmingly simple: Power. And to the more difficult questions their answer is: More Power.

These New Barbarians offer no content, no ideology, hardly even a jargon. While dissident students thirty-five years ago spoke an esoteric Marxist lingo, and debated "dialectical materialism," "the transformation of quantity into quality," etc., etc., the dissident students and Black Powerites today scream four-letter obscenities and expletives. While the radicals explored an intricate ideology in the heavy volumes of Marx, the cumbersome paragraphs of Lenin, and the elaborate reinterpretations of Stalin and Trotsky, today's power-seekers are more than satisfied by the hate slogans of Mao Tse-tung, Che Guevara, or Malcolm X. They find nothing so enchanting as the sound of their own voices, and their bibliography consists mainly of the products of their own mimeographing. They seem to think they can be radicals without portfolio. If they call themselves "anarchists" they have not bothered to read their Thoreau or Proudhon, Bakunin or Tolstoy. If they call themselves "leftists" they have not bothered to read Marx or Engels, Lenin or Trotsky. If they call themselves Black Power Nationalists, they mistake the rattle of ancient chains for the sound of facts and ideas.

Having nothing to say, the New Barbarians cannot interest others by *what* they say. Therefore they must try to shock by *how* they say it. Traditionally, radicals have addressed their society with a question mark, but the new frustrates' favorite punctuation is the exclamation point! Having no new facts or ideas to offer, they strain at novelty with their latrine words. The Black Powerites, whose whole program is their own power, must wrap up their emptiness in vulgarisms and expletives. For racism is the perfect example of a dogma without content.

The appeal to violence and "direct action" as if they were ends rather than means is eloquent testimony of the New Barbarians' lack of subject matter. An act of violence may express hate or anger, but it communicates nothing precise or substantial. Throwing a rock, like hurling an epithet, proclaims that the thrower has given up trying to say anything.

These Student Powerites and Black Powerites are not *egalitarians* seeking a just community; they are *egolitarians,* preening the egoism of the isolationist self. Students seek power for "students," Negroes seek power for "blacks"—and let the community take the hindmost! Unlike the radicalisms which affirm community and are preoccupied or obsessed by its problems, the Student Power and Black Power movements deny any substantial community—even among their own "members." A novel feature of S.N.C.C. and S.D.S., too little noted, is the fact that they are, strictly speaking, "nonmembership" organizations. Members do not carry cards, membership lists are said not to exist. A person does not "join" as a result of long and solemn deliberation, he is not trained and tested (as was the case in the Thirties with candidates for membership in the Communist Party). Instead the New Barbarian simply affiliates, and stays with the group as long as it pleases him. "I'm with you today, baby, but who knows where I'll be tomorrow?" A desperate infantinstantism reveals the uncertainty and vagrancy of these affiliations. The leader better act this afternoon, for maybe they won't be with him tomorrow morning!

All these unradical characteristics of the New Barbarians express a spiritual cataclysm. This is what I mean by the Ptolemaic Revolution: a movement from the community-centered to the self-centered. While radicals see themselves and everything else revolving around the community and its idealized needs, each of these new frustrates tries to make the world revolve around himself. The depth and significance of this shift in focus have remained unnoticed. It has been the harder to grasp because it is in the nature of the New Barbarism that it should lack philosophers. Being closer to a dyspepsia than to an ideology, the New Barbarism has tried to generalize its stomachaches but has been unable to cast them into a philosophy. It is much easier, therefore, to describe the direction in which the chaotic groups comprising the New Barbarism are moving than to fix the precise position where they stand.

The New Barbarism, in a word, is the social expression of a movement from Experience to Sensation. Experience, the dictionary tells us, means *actual observation of or practical acquaintance with facts or events; knowledge resulting from this.* A person's experience is what he has lived through. Generally speaking, experience is (a) cumulative, and (b) communicable. People add up their experiences to become wiser and more knowledgeable. We can learn from our own experience and, most important, we can learn from other people's experiences. Our publicly shared experience is history. Experience is distinguished, then, by the very fact that it can be shared. When we have an experience, we enter into the continuum of a society. But the dramatic shift now is away from Experience and toward Sensation.

Sensation is personal, private, confined, and incommunicable. Our sensations (hearing, seeing, touching, tasting, and smelling) are what we *receive.* Or, as the dictionary says, sensation is *consciousness of perceiving or seeming to perceive some state or affection of one's body or its parts or senses of one's mind or its emotions; the contents of such consciousness.* If an experience were totally incommunicable, if I could not describe it to anyone else, if I could not share it, it would not really be an experience. It would simply be a sensation, a message which came to me and to me alone. Sensations, from their very nature, then, are intimate and ineffable. Experience takes us out of ourselves, sensation affirms and emphasizes the self.

What history is to the person in quest of experience, a "happening" is to the person in quest of sensation. For a "happening" is something totally discrete. It adds to our sensations without increasing our experience.

Experience and Sensation, then, express attitudes to the world as opposite as the poles. The experience-oriented young person suffers Weltschmerz—the discovery of the pain and suffering that are his portion of the world. The sensation-oriented suffers an "identity crisis": he is concerned mostly about defining the boundaries of that bundle of private messages which is himself. The experience-oriented seeks, and finds, continuity, and emphasizes what is shared and what is communicable. The sensation-oriented seeks the instantaneous, the egocentric, the inexpressible. The accumulation of *experience* produces the *expert.* Its cumulative product is *expertise*—competence, the ability to handle situations by knowing what is tried and familiar about them. And the name for accumulated experience is knowledge.

While sensations can be more or less intense, they are not cumulative. A set of simultaneous, intense and melodramatic sensations is not instructive, but it is shocking: we say it is *sensational*. Experience is additive, it can be organized, classified, and rearranged; sensation is miscellaneous, random, and incapable of being generalized.

Everywhere in the United States nowadays—and not only among the New Barbarians—we see a desperate quest for sensation and a growing tendency to value sensation more than experience. We note this in what people seek, in what they find, in what they make, and in what they like to watch. We note a tendency in painting to produce works which do not appeal to a common, shareable fund of experience, but which, instead, set off each viewer on his own private path of sensation. In the theatre and in movies which lack a clear and intelligible story line, the spectators are offered sensations from which each is expected to make his own private inward adventure.

An example of the current quest for the indescribable, the ineffable, the transcendent—aiming to maximize sensation rather than experience—is the current vogue for LSD and for other so-called "consciousness-expanding" drugs. Precisely speaking, they aim to expand not experience but *consciousness*. They aim somehow to increase the intensity and widen the range of the vivid, idiosyncratic self.

The special appeal of an LSD "trip" is that it leads to the ineffable: what one person gets is as different as possible from what is obtained by another. And it is all quite individual and quite unpredictable. "Instead of a communion," one psychologist explains, "it [the LSD state] is a withdrawal into oneself. The *religio* (binding together) is not visible here." This is how Richard Alpert, the archbishop of LSD, explains the sensations under the drug:

> "Nowhere" is Sidney's prediction of where the psychochemical (r)evolution is taking the "young people" who are exploring inner space. I prefer to read that word as NowHere, and fervently hope he is right—that LSD is bringing man back "to his senses". . . . Do not be confused! The issue is not LSD. . . . Your control and access to your own brain is at stake.

LSD sensations, Alpert insists, are "eyewitness reports of what is, essentially, a private experience." "It was," in the words of a girl who had just been on an LSD trip, "like a shower on the inside."

The search for sensation is a search for some way of reminding oneself that one is alive—but without becoming entangled with others or with a community.

> I have never felt so intense, alive, such a sense of well-being. . . . I have chosen to be outside of society after having been very much inside. . . . My plans are unstructured in regards to anything but the immediate future. I believe in freedom, and must take the jump, I must take the chance of action.

This is not the report of an LSD trip, but the explanation by a young white student of his sensations on joining S.N.C.C. The vocabulary of the Student Power movement reveals the same desperate quest for sensation. "Direct Action" is the name for spasmodic acts of self-affirmation. It is a way of making the senses scream. It matters not whether the "Direct Action" has a purpose, much less whether it can attain any purpose, since it gives satisfaction enough by intensifying the Direct Actor's sense of being alive and separate from others. "Direct Action" is to politics what the Frug or the Jerk is to the dance. It identifies and explodes the self without attaching the self to groups or to individuals outside. And now the "New Left" has become the LSD of the intellectuals.

The man who is pathologically experience-oriented will be timid, haunted by respectability. His motto is apt to be that posted over the desk of an English civil servant: "Never do anything for the first time!" On the other hand, the man pathologically obsessed by Sensation makes his motto: "Do everything only for the first time!"

All about us, and especially in the Student Power and Black Power movements of recent years, we see the pathology of the sensation-oriented. Contrary to popular belief, and to the legends which they would like to spread about themselves, they are not troubled by any excessive concern for others. Their feelings cannot accurately be described as a concern, and it is surely not for others. Their ailment might best be called *apathy*. For apathy is a feeling apart from others and, as the dictionary reminds us, *an indolence of mind*. The Direct Actionists, as President W. Allen Wallis of the University of Rochester has explained, "are the students who are truly apathetic." They do not care enough about the problems of their society to burn the midnight oil over them. Impatient to sate their egos with the sensations of "Direct Action," they are too indolent intellectually to do the hard work of exploring the problems to which they pretend a concern. Theirs is the egoism, the personal chauvinism of the isolationist self. Their "Direct Action" slogan means nothing but "Myself, Right or Wrong!"

These people I would call the *Apathetes*. Just as the Aesthetes of some decades ago believed in "Art for Art's Sake," so the Apathetes believe in "Me for My Own Sake." They try to make a virtue of their indolence of mind (by calling it "Direct Action") and they exult in their feeling-apartness (by calling it "Power"). Thus these Apathetes are at the opposite pole from the radicals of the past.

They abandon the quest for meaning, for fear it might entangle their thoughts and feelings with those of others, and they plunge into "Direct Action" for fear that second thoughts might deny them this satisfaction to their ego. Theirs is a mindless, obsessive quest for power. But they give up the very idea of man's need for quest. Instead they seek explosive affirmations of the self.

They deny the existence of subject matter, by denying the need for experience. How natural, then, that Youth should lord it over Age! For in youth, they say, the senses are most sensitive and most attuned. The accumulated experience of books or of teachers becomes absurdly irrelevant. There is no Knowledge, but only Sensation, and Power is its Handmaiden!

They deny the existence of time, since Sensation is instantaneous and not cumulative. They herald the age of Instant Everything! Since time can do nothing but accumulate experience and dull the senses, experience is said to be nothing but the debris which stifles our sensations! There must be no frustration. Every program must be instantaneous, every demand must be an ultimatum.

This movement from Experience to Sensation accelerates every day. Each little victory for Student Power or Black Power—or any other kind of Power—is a victory for the New Barbarism. Appropriately, the New Barbarism makes its first sallies and has its greatest initial successes against the universities, which are the repositories of Experience, and in the cause of Racism, which—whether it is Black or whether it is Aryan—is the emptiness to end all emptinesses.

For Discussion

1. Agree or disagree with Boorstin's assertions that
    a) the search for meaning "has been displaced by a quest for power."
    b) the "Black Powerites" and "Student Powerites" have "nothing to say."
    c) the new barbarism is not an "affirmation of community."
2. How does he differentiate between barbarism and radicalism?
3. Boorstin argues by using definition, extended through classification and generalization. Comment on his use of generalization.
4. Dispute his contention that the new movements lack philosophers.
5. Examine the coherence of the paragraph beginning "These Student Powerites and Black Powerites . . . ." (page 98). Summarize the main point of the paragraph.
6. What distinction does the author make between sensation and experience?
7. According to Boorstin, what are the most serious drawbacks to the sensation-oriented society? What positive advantages might a sensation-oriented society offer?
8. Boorstin establishes a link between the new barbarism and the quest for sensation, but he does not discuss the reasons for either. Suggest possible explanations for this turning toward sensation.

9. The author places in opposition sensation and experience, self-identity and community. Argue that these opposites *can* be reconciled.
10. Boorstin assails the new barbarians because they argue by expletive and invective. Analyze his own method of invective. What examples of the impassioned voice can you find?

GEORGE WALD

A Generation in Search
of a Future

Dr. George Wald, Harvard biologist and 1967 Nobel prize win-
ner in physiology and medicine, delivered the following talk ex-
temporaneously to a meeting of students and faculty at the
Massachusetts Institute of Technology on March 4, 1969, to
protest the misuses of science. Dr. Wald's speech created a strong,
immediate response and has continued to impress young and old
alike. It has received wide circulation through readings on FM
radio and distribution in pamphlet form, and has been hailed as
one of the most important speeches of our time.

All of you know that in the last couple of years there has been student
unrest breaking at times into violence in many parts of the world: in England,
Germany, Italy, Spain, Mexico and needless to say, in many parts of this
country. There has been a great deal of discussion as to what it all means.
Perfectly clearly it means something different in Mexico from what it does in
France, and something different in France from what it does in Tokyo, and
something different in Tokyo from what it does in this country. Yet unless
we are to assume that students have gone crazy all over the world, or that
they have just decided that it's the thing to do, there must be some common
meaning.

I don't need to go so far afield to look for that meaning. I am a teacher,
and at Harvard, I have a class of about 350 students—men and women—
most of them freshmen and sophomores. Over these past few years I have
felt increasingly that something is terribly wrong—and this year ever so much
more than last. Something has gone sour, in teaching and in learning. It's
almost as though there were a widespread fealing that education has become
irrelevant.

A lecture is much more of a dialogue than many of you probably

Reprinted by permission of the author.

appreciate. As you lecture, you keep watching the faces; and information keeps coming back to you all the time. I began to feel, particularly this year, that I was missing much of what was coming back. I tried asking the students, but they didn't or couldn't help me very much.

But I think I know what's the matter, even a little better than they do. I think that this whole generation of students is beset with a profound uneasiness. I don't think that they have yet quite defined its source. I think I understand the reasons for their uneasiness even better than they do. What is more, I share their uneasiness.

What's bothering those students? Some of them tell you it's the Vietnam War. I think the Vietnam War is the most shameful episode in the whole of American history. The concept of War Crimes is an American invention. We've committed many War Crimes in Vietnam; but I'll tell you something interesting about that. We were committing War Crimes in World War II, even before the Nuremburg trials were held and the principle of war crimes started. The saturation bombing of German cities was a War Crime. Dropping atom bombs on Hiroshima and Nagasaki was a War Crime. If we had lost the war, some of our leaders might have had to answer for those actions.

I've gone through all of that history lately, and I find that there's a gimmick in it. It isn't written out, but I think we established it by precedent. That gimmick is that if one can allege that one is repelling or retaliating for an *aggression*—after that everything goes. And you see we are living in a world in which all wars are wars of defense. All War Departments are now Defense Departments. This is all part of the double talk of our time. The aggressor is always on the other side. And I suppose this is why our ex-Secretary of State, Dean Rusk— a man in whom repetition takes the place of reason, and stubbornness takes the place of character—went to such pains to insist, as he still insists, that in Vietnam we are repelling an aggression. And if that's what we are doing—so runs the doctrine—anything goes. If the concept of war crimes is ever to mean anything, they will have to be defined as categories of acts, regardless of alleged provocation. But that isn't so now.

I think we've lost that war, as a lot of other people think, too. The Vietnamese have a secret weapon. It's their willingness to die, beyond our willingness to kill. In effect they've been saying, you can kill us, but you'll have to kill a lot of us, you may have to kill all of us. And thank heavens, we are not yet ready to do that.

Yet we have come a long way—far enough to sicken many Americans, far enough even to sicken our fighting men. Far enough so that our national symbols have gone sour. How many of you can sing about "the rockets' red glare, bombs bursting in air" without thinking, those are *our* bombs and *our* rockets bursting over South Vietnamese villages? When those words were written, we were a people struggling for freedom against oppression. Now we are supporting real or thinly disguised military dictatorships all over the world, helping them to control and repress peoples struggling for their freedom.

But that Vietnam War, shameful and terrible as it is, seems to me only an immediate incident in a much larger and more stubborn situation.

Part of my trouble with students is that almost all the students I teach were born since World War II. Just after World War II, a series of new and abnormal procedures came into American life. We regarded them at the time as temporary aberrations. We thought we would get back to normal American life some day. But those procedures have stayed with us now for more than 20 years, and those students of mine have never known anything else. They think those things are normal. Students think we've always had a Pentagon, that we have always had a big army, and that we always had a draft. But those are all new things in American life; and I think that they are incompatible with what America meant before.

How many of you realize that just before World War II the entire American army including the Air Force numbered 139,000 men? Then World War II started, but we weren't yet in it; and seeing that there was great trouble in the world, we doubled this army to 268,000 men. Then in World War II it got to be 8 million. And then World War II came to an end, and we prepared to go back to a peacetime army somewhat as the American army had always been before. And indeed in 1950—you think about 1950, our international commitments, the Cold War, the Truman Doctrine, and all the rest of it—in 1950 we got down to 600,000 men.

Now we have 3.5 million men under arms: about 600,000 in Vietnam, about 300,000 more in "support areas" elsewhere in the Pacific, about 250,000 in Germany. And there are a lot at home. Some months ago we were told that 300,000 National Guardsmen and 200,000 reservists—so half a million men—had been specially trained for riot duty in the cities.

I say the Vietnam War is just an immediate incident, because so long as we keep that big army, it will always find things to do. If the Vietnam War stopped tomorrow, with that big a military establishment, the chances are that we would be in another such adventure abroad or at home before you knew it.

As for the draft: Don't reform the draft—get rid of it.

A peacetime draft is the most un-American thing I know. All the time I was growing up I was told about oppressive Central European countries and Russia, where young men were forced into the army; and I was told what they did about it. They chopped off a finger, or shot off a couple of toes; or better still, if they could manage it, they came to this country. And we understood that, and sympathized, and were glad to welcome them.

Now by present estimates four to six thousand Americans of draft age have left this country for Canada, another two or three thousand have gone to Europe, and it looks as though many more are preparing to emigrate.

A few months ago I received a letter from the Harvard Alumni Bulletin posing a series of questions that students might ask a professor involving what to do about the draft. I was asked to write what I would tell those students. All I had to say to those students was this: If any of them had decided to evade the draft and asked my help, I would help him in any way I could. I would feel as I suppose members of the underground railway felt in pre-Civil War days, helping runaway slaves to get to Canada. It wasn't altogether a popular position then, but what do you think of it now?

A bill to stop the draft was recently introduced in the Senate (S. 503), sponsored by a group of senators that ran the gamut from McGovern and Hatfield to Barry Goldwater. I hope it goes through; but any time I find that Barry Goldwater and I are in agreement, that makes me take another look.

And indeed there are choices in getting rid of the draft. I think that when we get rid of the draft, we must also cut back the size of the armed forces. It seems to me that in peacetime a total of one million men is surely enough. If there is an argument for American military forces of more than one million men in peacetime, I should like to hear that argument debated.

There is another thing being said closely connected with this: that to keep an adequate volunteer army, one would have to raise the pay considerably. That's said so positively and often that people believe it. I don't think it is true.

The great bulk of our present armed forces are genuine volunteers. Among first-term enlistments, 49 percent are true volunteers. Another 30 percent are so-called "reluctant volunteers," persons who volunteer under pressure of the draft. Only 21 percent are draftees. All re-enlistments, of course are true volunteers.

So the great majority of our present armed forces are true volunteers. Whole services are composed entirely of volunteers: the Air Force for example, the Navy, almost all the Marines. That seems like proof to me that present pay rates are adequate. One must add that an Act of Congress in 1967 raised the base pay throughout the services in three installments, the third installment still to come, on April 1, 1969. So it is hard to understand why we are being told that to maintain adequate armed services on a volunteer basis will require large increases in pay; that they will cost an extra $17 billion per year. It seems plain to me that we can get all the armed forces we need as volunteers, and at present rates of pay.

But there is something ever so much bigger and more important than the draft. That bigger thing, of course, is the militarization of our country. Ex-President Eisenhower warned us of what he called the military-industrial complex. I am sad to say that we must begin to think of it now as the military-industrial-labor union complex. What happened under the plea of the Cold War was not alone that we built up the first big peace time army in our history, but we institutionalized it. We built, I suppose, the biggest government building in our history to run it, and we institutionalized it.

I don't think we can live with the present military establishment and its $80-100 billion a year budget, and keep America anything like we have known it in the past. It is corrupting the life of the whole country. It is buying up everything in sight: industries, banks, investors, universities; and lately it seems also to have bought up the labor unions.

The Defense Department is always broke; but some of the things they do with that $80 billion a year would make Buck Rogers envious. For example: the Rocky Mountain Arsenal on the outskirts of Denver was manufacturing a deadly nerve poison on such a scale that there was a problem of waste disposal. Nothing daunted, they dug a tunnel two miles deep under Denver, into which they have injected so much poisoned water that beginning a couple of years ago Denver began to experience a series of earth tremors of increasing severity. Now there is a grave fear of a major earthquake. An interesting debate is in progress as to whether Denver will be safer if that lake of poisoned water is removed or left in place. (N.Y. Times, July 4, 1968; Science, Sept. 27, 1968).

Perhaps you have read also of those 6000 sheep that suddenly died in Skull Valley, Utah, killed by another nerve poison—a strange and, I believe, still unexplained accident, since the nearest testing seems to have been 30 miles away.

As for Vietnam, the expenditure of fire power has been frightening. Some of you may still remember Khe Sanh, a hamlet just south of the Demilitarized Zone, where a force of U.S. Marines was beleaguered for a time. During that period we dropped on the perimeter of Khe Sanh more explosives than fell on Japan throughout World War II, and more than fell on the whole of Europe during the years 1942 and 1943.

One of the officers there was quoted as having said afterward, "It looks like the world caught smallpox and died." (N.Y. Times, Mar. 28, 1968.)

The only point of government is to safeguard and foster life. Our government has become preoccupied with death, with the business of killing and being killed. So-called Defense now absorbs 60 percent of the national budget, and about 12 percent of the Gross National Product.

A lively debate is beginning again on whether or not we should deploy antiballistic missiles, the ABM. I don't have to talk about them, everyone else here is doing that. But I should like to mention a curious circumstance. In September, 1967, or about 1½ years ago, we had a meeting of M.I.T. and Harvard people, including experts on these matters, to talk about whether anything could be done to block the Sentinel system, the deployment of ABM's. Everyone present thought them undesirable; but a few of the most knowledgeable persons took what seemed to be the practical view, "Why fight about a dead issue? It has been decided, the funds have been appropriated. Let's go on from there."

Well, fortunately, it's not a dead issue.

An ABM is a nuclear weapon. It takes a nuclear weapon to stop a nuclear weapon. And our concern must be with the whole issue of nuclear weapons.

There is an entire semantics ready to deal with the sort of thing I am about to say. It involves such phrases as "those are the facts of life." No—they are the facts of death. I don't accept them, and I advise you not to accept them. We are under repeated pressure to accept things that are presented to us as settled—decisions that have been made. Always there is the thought: let's go on from there! But this time we don't see how to go on. We will have to stick with those issues.

We are told that the United States and Russia between them have by now stockpiled in nuclear weapons approximately the explosive power of 15 tons of TNT for every man, woman and child on earth. And now, it is suggested that we must make more. All very regrettable, of course; but those are "the facts of life." We really would like to disarm; but our new Secretary of Defense has made the ingenious proposal that now is the time to greatly increase our nuclear armaments so that we can disarm from a position of strength.

I think all of you know there is no adequate defense against massive nuclear attack. It is both easier and cheaper to circumvent any known nuclear defense system than to provide it. It's all pretty crazy. At the very moment we talk of deploying ABM's, we are also building the MIRV, the weapon to circumvent ABM's.

So far as I know, the most conservative estimates of Americans killed in a major nuclear attack, with everything working as well as can be hoped and all foreseeable precautions taken, run to about 50 millions. We have become callous to gruesome statistics, and this seems at first to be only another gruesome statistic. You think, Bang!—and next morning, if you're still there, you read in the newspapers that 50 million people were killed.

But that isn't the way it happens. When we killed close to 200,000 people with those first little, old-fashioned uranium bombs that we dropped on Hiroshima and Nagasaki, about the same number of persons was maimed, blinded, burned, poisoned and otherwise doomed. A lot of them took a long time to die.

That's the way it would be. Not a bang, and a certain number of corpses to bury; but a nation filled with millions of helpless, maimed, tortured and doomed persons, and the survivors of a nuclear holocaust will be huddled with their families in shelters, with guns ready to fight off their neighbors, trying to get some uncontaminated food and water.

A few months ago Sen. Richard Russell of Georgia ended a speech in the Senate with the words: "If we have to start over again with another Adam and Eve, I want them to be Americans; and I want them on this continent and not in Europe." That was a United States senator holding a patriotic speech. Well, here is a Nobel Laureate who thinks that those words are criminally insane.

How real is the threat of full scale nuclear war? I have my own very inexpert idea, but realizing how little I know and fearful that I may be a little paranoid on this subject, I take every opportunity to ask reputed experts. I asked that question of a very distinguished professor of government at Harvard about a month ago. I asked him what sort of odds he would lay on the possibility of full-scale nuclear war within the foreseeable future. "Oh," he said comfortably, "I think I can give you a pretty good answer to that question. I estimate the probability of full-scale nuclear war, provided that the situation remains about as it is now, at 2 percent per year." Anybody can do the simple calculation that shows that 2 percent per year means that the chance of having that full-scale nuclear war by 1990 is about one in three, and by 2000, it is about 50-50.

I think I know what is bothering the students. I think that what we are up against is a generation that is by no means sure that it has a future.

I am growing old, and my future so to speak is already behind me. But there are those students of mine who are in my mind always; and there are my children, two of them now 7 and 9, whose future is infinitely more precious to me than my own. So it isn't just their generation; it's mine too. We're all in it together.

Are we to have a chance to live? We don't ask for prosperity, or security; only for a reasonable chance to live, to work out our destiny in peace and decency. Not to go down in history as the apocalyptic generation.

And it isn't only nuclear war. Another overwhelming threat is the population explosion. That has not yet even begun to come under control. There is every indication that the world population will double before the year 2000; and there is a widespread expectation of famine on an unprecedented scale in many parts of the world. The experts tend to differ only in the estimates of when those famines will begin. Some think by 1980, others think they can be staved off until 1990, very few expect that they will not occur by the year 2000.

That is the problem. Unless we can be surer than we now are that this generation has a future, nothing else matters. It's not good enough to give it tender loving care, to supply it with breakfast foods, to buy it expensive educations. Those things don't mean anything unless this generation has a future. And we're not sure that it does.

I don't think that there are problems of youth, or student problems. All the real problems I know are grown-up problems.

Perhaps you will think me altogether absurd, or "academic," or hopelessly innocent—that is, until you think of the alternatives—if I say as I do to you now: we have to get rid of those nuclear weapons. There is nothing worth having that can be obtained by nuclear war: nothing material or ideological, no tradition that it can defend. It is utterly self-defeating. Those atom bombs represent an unusable weapon. The only use for an atom bomb is to keep somebody else from using one. It can give us no protection, but only the doubtful satisfaction of retaliation. Nuclear weapons offer us nothing but a balance of terror; and a balance of terror is still terror.

We have to get rid of those atomic weapons, here and everywhere. We cannot live with them.

I think we've reached a point of great decision, not just for our nation, not only for all humanity, but for life upon the Earth. I tell my students, with a feeling of pride that I hope they will share, that the carbon, nitrogen and oxygen that make up 99 percent of our living substance, were cooked in the deep interiors of earlier generations of dying stars. Gathered up from the ends of the universe, over billions of years, eventually they came to form in part the substance of our sun, its planets and ourselves. Three billion years ago life arose upon the Earth. It seems to be the only life in the solar system. Many a star has since been born and died.

About two million years ago, man appeared. He has become the dominant species on the Earth. All other living things, animal and plant, live by his sufferance. He is the custodian of life on Earth. It's a big responsibility.

The thought that we're in competition with Russians or with Chinese is all a mistake, and trivial. Only mutual destruction lies that way. We are one species, with a world to win. There's life all over this universe, but in all the universe we are the only men.

Our business is with life, not death. Our challenge is to give what account we can of what becomes of life in the solar system, this corner of the universe that is our home and, most of all, what becomes of men—all men of all nations, colors and creeds. It has become one world, a world for all men. It is only such a world that now can offer us life and the chance to go on.

For Discussion

1. What accusations does Wald make against the United States government? Defend the government's actions.
2. According to Wald, what should be the only point of government? To what extent would Thoreau agree?
3. Explore the idea that "all wars are wars of defense."
4. Why does Wald refer to the incidents involving nerve poison?

5. Attack or defend the accusation that Senator Russell's words are "criminally insane."

6. In view of the strength of Wald's argument against nuclear warfare, how do you explain our reluctance to halt nuclear stockpiling?

7. What existing phenomena, other than student unrest, do you think are the result of the fear of an uncertain future?

8. To what extent do you share Wald's fear that *you* are part of a generation without a future?

9. How do you explain the increasing popularity of this essay? How does its force depend upon more than a description of specific grievances?

10. Wald documents his generalizations with statistics and facts—a discursive method—and yet his voice is not discursive. What qualities do you find in his voice that make his argument impassioned? (It will help to read the last paragraph aloud.)

THE
DISCURSIVE *NO*

. . . a decent respect for the opinions of mankind requires that they should declare the causes which impel them to the separation.

Declaration of Independence

Whereas the impassioned writer expresses strong feeling and makes an appeal for the reader's total involvement, the discursive writer minimizes the expression of his feelings and asks the reader to judge his ideas on their own merit. This means that, insofar as he is able, he does not allow his emotions to dominate his argument. This is not to say that the discursive writer does not feel strongly, but rather that he prefers to express his argument as dispassionately as possible. Any emotion that the reader might feel comes from the persuasiveness of the writer's facts and logic.

That reason and logic are the chief concerns of the discursive writer is apparent from a glance at the derivation of the word *discursive*. It is the adjective form of *discourse,* meaning an extended treatment of a subject in an organized and logical manner. It emphasizes orderly progression of evidence and ideas in support of reasonable judgments. The success or failure of discursive writing rests mainly upon the force of its objectivity—its logic, its appeal to our minds—rather than upon the force of its feeling.

The discursive writer, therefore, makes special demands upon his reader. He trusts him to think, to be receptive to reason. He has "a decent respect for the opinions of mankind," to use Jefferson's words—meaning that he assumes the reader has an open mind, is capable of changing his opinion despite any personal leanings he may already have, and is intelligent and interested enough to follow an argument and evaluate it.

This is expecting a great deal from the reader. In fact, the discursive writer expects more from his reader than does the reflective or impassioned writer. He relies upon him to participate fully in the discussion, to continually evaluate and judge. In short, he expects him to be what Mark Twain called the "athletic reader." The discursive writer wants his reader's understanding—not of himself but of his subject. This means that the reader's involvement is primarily intellectual and not emotional.

The essays that follow are predominantly discursive. The degree of their persuasiveness depends upon the degree of their responsibility in presenting ideas for our responsible judgment. Every essay, in its own way, "declares the causes which impel" its author to dissent.

PLATO

Apology

The *Apology* means the "Defense," and the dialogue so-named
was written by Plato and contains an account of Socrates' trial
and defense, made by himself. Because he believed that right
action for men was action based on rational principle, he spent
a good part of his life exposing the ignorance and the unsound-
ness of thought in his political contemporaries. The enmity he
thus produced was finally responsible for his being brought to
trial on charges of atheism and corrupting youth, charges which
carried a possible death penalty. He was found guilty, though it is
commonly believed that he was not, and was executed in 399 B.C.
This selection is the latter part of the *Apology* in which Socrates
enunciates the philosophical-moral principles by which he had
conducted his life.

I have said enough in answer to the charge of Meletus: any elaborate
defence is unnecessary; but I know only too well how many are the enmities
which I have incurred, and this is what will be my destruction if I am
destroyed;—not Meletus, nor yet Anytus, but the envy and detraction of
the world, which has been the death of many good men, and will probably
be the death of many more; there is no danger of my being the last of them.
Some one will say: And are you not ashamed, Socrates, of a course
of life which is likely to bring you to an untimely end? To him I may fairly
answer: There you are mistaken: a man who is good for anything ought
not to calculate the chance of living or dying; he ought only to consider
whether in doing anything he is doing right or wrong—acting the part of
a good man or of a bad. Whereas, upon your view, the heroes who fell
at Troy were not good for much, and the son of Thetis above all, who
altogether despised danger in comparison with disgrace; and when he was
so eager to slay Hector, his goddess mother said to him, that if he avenged
his companion Patroclus, and slew Hector, he would die himself—"Fate,"
she said, in these or the like words, "waits for you next after Hector"; he,

receiving this warning, utterly despised danger and death, and instead of fearing them, feared rather to live in dishonour, and not to avenge his friend. "Let me die forthwith," he replies, "and be avenged of my enemy, rather than abide here by the beaked ships, a laughing stock and a burden of the earth." Had Achilles any thought of death and danger? For where-ever a man's place is, whether the place which he has chosen or that in which he has been placed by a commander, there he ought to remain in the hour of danger; he should not think of death or of anything but of disgrace. And this, O men of Athens, is a true saying.

Strange, indeed, would be my conduct, O men of Athens, if I, who, when I was ordered by the generals whom you chose to command me at Potidaea and Amphipolis and Delium, remained where they placed me, like any other man, facing death—if now, when, as I conceive and imagine, God orders me to fulfill the philosopher's mission of searching into myself and other men, I were to desert my post through fear of death, or any other fear; that would indeed be strange, and I might justly be arraigned in court for denying the existence of the gods, if I disobeyed the oracle because I was afraid of death, fancying that I was wise when I was not wise. For the fear of death is indeed the pretence of wisdom, and not real wisdom, being a pretence of knowing the unknown; and no one knows whether death, which men in their fear apprehend to be the greatest evil, may not be the greatest good. Is not this ignorance of a disgraceful sort, the ignorance which is the conceit that a man knows what he does not know? And in this respect only I believe myself to differ from men in general, and may perhaps claim to be wiser than they are:—that whereas I know but little of the world below, I do not suppose that I know: but I do know that injustice and disobedience to a better, whether God or man, is evil and dishonourable, and I will never fear or avoid a possible good rather than a certain evil. And therefore if you let me go now, and are not convinced by Anytus, who said that since I had been prosecuted I must be put to death; (or if not that I ought never to have been prosecuted at all); and that if I escape now, your sons will all be utterly ruined by listening to my words—if you say to me, Socrates, this time we will not mind Anytus, and you shall be let off, but upon one condition, that you are not to enquire and speculate in this way any more, and that if you are caught doing so again you shall die;—if this was the condition on which you let me go, I should reply: Men of Athens, I honour and love you; but I shall obey God rather than you, and while I have life and strength I shall never cease from the practice and teaching of philosophy, exhorting any one whom I meet and saying to him after my manner: You, my friend,—a citizen of the great and mighty and wise city of Athens,—are you not ashamed of heaping up the greatest amount of money and honour and reputation, and caring so little about wisdom and truth and the greatest improvement of the soul, which you never regard or heed at all? And if the person with whom I am arguing, says: Yes, but I do care; then I do not leave him or let him go at once; but I proceed to interrogate and examine and cross-examine him, and if I think that he has no virtue in him, but only says that he has, I reproach him with undervaluing the greater, and overvaluing the less. And I shall repeat the same words to every one whom I meet, young and old, citizen and alien, but especially to the citizens, inasmuch as they are my brethren. For know that this is the command of God; and I believe that no greater good has ever happened in the State than my service to the God. For I do nothing but go about persuading you all, old and young alike, not to take thought for your persons or your properties, but first and chiefly to care about the greatest improvement of the soul. I tell you that virtue is not given by money, but that from virtue comes money and every other good of man, public as well as private. This is my teaching, and if this is the doctrine which corrupts the youth, I am a mischievous person. But if any one says that this is not my teaching, he is speaking an untruth. Wherefore, O men of Athens, I say to you, do as Anytus bids or not as Anytus bids, and either acquit me or not; but whichever you do, understand that I shall never alter my ways, not even if I have to die many times.

Men of Athens, do not interrupt, but hear me; there was an understanding between us that you should hear me to the end: I have something more to say, at which you may be inclined to cry out; but I believe that to hear me will be good for you, and therefore I beg that you will not cry out. I would have you know, that if you kill such an one as I am, you will injure yourselves more than you will injure me. Nothing will injure me, not Meletus nor yet Anytus—they cannot, for a bad man is not permitted to injure a better than himself. I do not deny that Anytus may, perhaps, kill him, or drive him into exile, or deprive him of civil rights; and he may imagine, and others may imagine, that he is inflicting a great injury upon him: but there I do not agree. For the evil of doing as he is doing—the evil of unjustly taking away the life of another—is greater far.

And now, Athenians, I am not going to argue for my own sake, as you may think, but for yours, that you may not sin against the God by condemning me, who am his gift to you. For if you kill me you will not easily find a successor to me, who, if I may use such a ludicrous figure of speech, am a sort of gadfly,[1] given to the State by God; and the State is a great and noble steed who is tardy in his motions owing to his very size, and requires to be stirred into life. I am that gadfly which God has attached to the State, and all day long and in all places am always fastening upon you, arousing and persuading and reproaching you. You will not easily find another like

---

[1] A biting insect; a person who repeatedly and persistently annoys others with schemes, ideas, demands, and requests.

me, and therefore I would advise you to spare me. I dare say that you may feel out of temper (like a person who is suddenly awakened from sleep), and you think that you might easily strike me dead as Anytus advises, and then you would sleep on for the remainder of your lives, unless God in his care of you sent you another gadfly. When I say that I am given to you by God, the proof of my mission is this:—if I had been like other men, I should not have neglected all my own concerns or patiently seen the neglect of them during all these years, and have been doing yours, coming to you individually like a father or elder brother, exhorting you to regard virtue; such conduct, I say, would be unlike human nature. If I had gained anything, or if my exhortations had been paid, there would have been some sense in my doing so; but now, as you will perceive, not even the impudence of my accusers dares to say that I have ever exacted or sought pay of any one; of that they have no witness. And I have a sufficient witness to the truth of what I say—my poverty.

Some one may wonder why I go about in private giving advice and busying myself with the concerns of others, but do not venture to come forward in public and advise the State. I will tell you why. You have heard me speak at sundry times and in divers places of an oracle or sign which comes to me, and is the divinity which Meletus ridicules in the indictment. This sign, whch is a kind of voice, first began to come to me when I was a child; it always forbids but never commands me to do anything which I am going to do. This is what deters me from being a politician. And rightly, as I think. For I am certain, O men of Athens, that if I had engaged in politics, I should have perished long ago, and done no good either to you or to myself. And do not be offended at my telling you the truth: for the truth is, that no man who goes to war with you or any other multitude, honestly striving against the many lawless and unrighteous deeds which are done in a State, will save his life; he who will fight for the right, if he would live even for a brief space, must have a private station and not a public one.

I can give you convincing evidence of what I say, not words only, but what you value far more—actions. Let me relate to you a passage of my own life which will prove to you that I should never have yielded to injustice from any fear of death and that "as I should have refused to yield" I must have died at once. I will tell you a tale of the courts, not very interesting perhaps, but nevertheless true. The only office of State which I ever held, O men of Athens, was that of senator: the tribe Antiochis, which is my tribe, had the presidency at the trial of the generals who had not taken up the bodies of the slain after the battle of Arginusae; and you proposed to try them in a body, contrary to law, as you all thought afterwards; but at the time I was the only one of the Prytanes who was opposed to the illegality, and I gave my vote against you; and when the orators threatened to impeach and arrest me, and you called and shouted, I made up my mind that I would run the risk, having law and justice with me, rather than take part in your injustice because I feared imprisonment and death. This happened in the days of the democracy. But when the oligarchy of the Thirty was in power, they sent for me and four others into the rotunda, and bade us bring Leon the Salaminian from Salamis, as they wanted to put him to death. This was a specimen of the sort of commands which they were always giving with the view of implicating as many as possible in their crimes; and then I showed, not in word only but in deed, that, if I may be allowed to use such an expression, I cared not a straw for death, and that my great and only care was lest I should do an unrighteous or unholy thing. For the strong arm of that oppressive power did not frighten me into doing wrong; and when we came out of the rotunda the other four went to Salamis and fetched Leon, but I went quietly home. For which I might have lost my life, had not the power of the Thirty shortly afterwards come to an end. And many will witness to my words.

Now, do you really imagine that I could have survived all these years, if I had led a public life, supposing that like a good man I had always maintained the right and had made justice, as I ought, the first thing? No, indeed, men of Athens, neither I nor any other man. But I have been always the same in all my actions, public as well as private, and never have I yielded any base compliance to those who are slanderously termed my disciples, or to any other. Not that I have any regular disciples. But if any one likes to come and hear me while I am pursuing my mission, whether he be young or old, he is not excluded. Nor do I converse only with those who pay; but any one, whether he be rich or poor, may ask and answer me and listen to my words; and whether he turns out to be a bad man or a good one, neither result can be justly imputed to me; for I never taught or professed to teach him anything. And if any one says that he has ever learned or heard anything from me in private which all the world has not heard, let me tell you that he is lying.

But I shall be asked, Why do people delight in continually conversing with you? I have told you already, Athenians, the whole truth about this matter: they like to hear the cross-examination of the pretenders to wisdom; there is amusement in it. Now, this duty of cross-examining other men has been imposed upon me by God; and has been signified to me by oracles, visions, and in every way in which the will of divine power was ever intimated to any one. This is true, O Athenians; or, if not true, would be soon refuted. If I am or have been corrupting the youth, those of them who are now grown up and have become sensible that I gave them bad advice in the days of their youth should come forwards as accusers, and take their revenge; or if they do not like to come themselves, some of their relatives, fathers, brothers, or other kinsmen, should say what evil their families have suffered at my hands. Now is their time. Many of them I see in the court.

There is Crito, who is of the same age and of the same deme[2] with myself, and there is Critobulus, his son, whom I also see. Then again there is Lysanias of Sphettus, who is the father of Aeschines—he is present; and also there is Antiphon of Cephisus, who is the father of Epigenes; and there are the brothers of several who have associated with me. There is Nicostratus the son of Theosdotides, and the brother of Theodotus (now Theodotus himself is dead, and therefore he, at any rate, will not seek to stop him); and there is Paralus the son of Demodocus, who had a brother Theages; and Adeimantus the son of Ariston, whose brother Plato is present; and Aeantodorus, who is the brother of Apollodorus, whom I also see. I might mention a great many others, some of whom Meletus should have produced as witnesses in the course of his speech; and let him still produce them, if he has forgotten—I will make way for him. And let him say, if he has any testimony of the sort which he can produce. Nay, Athenians, the very opposite is the truth. For all these are ready to witness on behalf of the corrupter, of the injurer of their kindred, as Meletus and Anytus call me; not the corrupted youth only—there might have been a motive for that—but their uncorrupted elder relatives. Why should they too support me with their testimony? Why, indeed, except for the sake of truth and justice, and because they know that I am speaking the truth, and that Meletus is a liar.

Well, Athenians, this and the like of this is all the defence which I have to offer. Yet a word more. Perhaps there may be some one who is offended at me, when he calls to mind how he himself on a similar, or even a less serious occasion, prayed and entreated the judges with many tears, and how he produced his children in court, which was a moving spectacle, together with a host of relations and friends; whereas I, who am probably in danger of my life, will do none of these things. The contrast may occur to his mind, and he may be set against me, and vote in anger because he is displeased at me on this account. Now, if there be such a person among you,—mind, I do not say that there is,—to him I may fairly reply: My friend, I am a man, and like other men, a creature of flesh and blood, and not "of wood or stone," as Homer says; and I have a family, yes, and sons, O Athenians, three in number, one almost a man, and two others who are still young; and yet I will not bring any of them hither in order to petition you for an acquittal. And why not? Not from any self-assertion or want of respect for you. Whether I am or am not afraid of death is another question, of which I will not now speak. But, having regard to public opinion, I feel that such conduct would be discreditable to myself, and to you, and to the whole State. One who has reached my years, and who has a name for wisdom, ought not to demean himself. Whether this opinion of me be deserved or not, at any rate the world has decided that Socrates is in some way superior

---

[2] A district.

to other men. And if those among you who are said to be superior in wisdom and courage, and any other virtue, demean themselves in this way, how shameful is their conduct! I have seen men of reputation, when they have been condemned, behaving in the strangest manner: they seemed to fancy that they were going to suffer something dreadful if they died and that they could be immortal if you only allowed them to live; and I think that such are a dishonour to the State and that any stranger coming in would have said of them that the most eminent men of Athens, to whom the Athenians themselves give honour and command, are no better than women. And I say that these things ought not to be done by those of us who have a reputation; and if they are done, you ought not to permit them; you ought rather to show that you are far more disposed to condemn the man who gets up a doleful scene and makes the city ridiculous, than him who holds his peace.

But, setting aside the question of public opinion, there seems to be something wrong in asking a favour of a judge, and thus procuring an acquittal, instead of informing and convincing him. For his duty is, not to make a present of justice, but to give judgment; and he has sworn that he will judge according to the laws, and not according to his own good pleasure; and we ought not to encourage you, nor should you allow yourselves to be encouraged, in this habit of perjury—there can be no piety in that. Do not then require me to do what I consider dishonourable and impious and wrong, especially now, when I am being tried for impiety on the indictment of Meletus. For if, O men of Athens, by force of persuasion and entreaty I could overpower your oaths, then I should be teaching you to believe that there are no gods, and in defending should simply convict myself of the charge of not believing in them. But that is not so—far otherwise. For I do believe that there are gods, and in a sense higher than that in which any of my accusers believe in them. And to you and to God I commit my cause, to be determined by you as is best for you and me.

There are many reasons why I am not grieved, O men of Athens, at the vote of condemnation. I expected it, and am only surprised that the votes are so nearly equal; for I had thought that the majority against me would have been far larger; but now, had thirty votes gone over to the other side, I should have been acquitted. And I may say, I think, that I have escaped Meletus. I may say more; for without the assistance of Anytus and Lycon, any one may see that he would not have had a fifth part of the votes, as the law requires, in which case he would have incurred a fine of a thousand drachmae.

And so he proposes death as the penalty. And what shall I propose on my part, O men of Athens? Clearly that which is my due. And what is my due? What returns shall be made to the man who has never had the wit to be idle during his whole life; but has been careless of what the many care for—wealth, and family interests, and military offices, and speaking in the assembly, and magistracies, and plots, and parties. Reflecting that I was really too honest a man to be a politician and live, I did not go where I could do no good to you or to myself; but where I could do the greatest good privately to every one of you, thither I went, and sought to persuade every man among you that he must look to himself, and seek virtue and wisdom before he looks to his private interests, and look to the State before he looks to the interests of the State; and that this should be the order which he observes in all his actions. What shall be done to such an one? Doubtless some good thing, O men of Athens, if he has his reward; and the good should be of a kind suitable to him. What would be a reward suitable to a poor man who is your benefactor, and who desires leisure that he may instruct you? There can be no reward so fitting as maintenance in the Prytaneum,[3] O men of Athens, a reward which he deserves far more than the citizen who has won the prize at Olympia in the horse or chariot race, whether the chariots were drawn by two horses or by many. For I am in want, and he has enough; and he only gives you the appearance of happiness, and I give you the reality. And if I am to estimate the penalty fairly, I should say that maintenance in the Prytaneum is the just return.

Perhaps you think that I am braving you in what I am saying now, as in what I said before about the tears and prayers. But this is not so. I speak rather because I am convinced that I never intentionally wronged any one, although I cannot convince you—the time has been too short: if there were a law at Athens, as there is in other cities, that a capital cause should not be decided in one day, then I believe that I should have convinced you. But I cannot in a moment refute great slanders; and, as I am convinced that I never wronged another, I will assuredly not wrong myself. I will not say of myself that I deserve any evil, or propose any penalty. Why should I? Because I am afraid of the penalty of death which Meletus proposes? When I do not know whether death is a good or an evil, why should I propose a penalty which would certainly be an evil? Shall I say imprisonment? And why should I live in prison, and be the slave of the magistrate of the year—of the Eleven? Or shall the penalty be a fine, and imprisonment until the fine is paid? There is the same objection. I should have to lie in prison, for money I have none, and cannot pay. And if I say exile (and this may possibly be the penalty which you will affix), I must indeed be blinded by the love of life, if I am so irrational as to expect that when you, who are my own citizens, cannot endure my discourses and words, and have found them so grievous and odious that you will have no more of them, others are likely to endure me. No, indeed, men of Athens, that is not very likely.

[3] A public building used as a meeting place for the administrative body of the community.

And what a life should I lead, at my age, wandering from city to city, ever changing my place of exile, and always being driven out! For I am quite sure that wherever I go, there, as here, the young men will flock to me; and if I drive them away, their elders will drive me out at their request; and if I let them come, their fathers and friends will drive me out for their sakes.

Some one will say: Yes, Socrates, but cannot you hold your tongue, and then you may go into a foreign city, and no one will interfere with you? Now, I have great difficulty in making you understand my answer to this. For if I tell you that to do as you say would be a disobedience to the God, and therefore that I cannot hold my tongue, you will not believe that I am serious; and if I say again that daily to discourse about virtue, and of those other things about which you hear me examining myself and others, is the greatest good of man, and that the unexamined life is not worth living, you are still less likely to believe me. Yet I say what is true, although a thing of which it is hard for me to persuade you. Also, I have never been accustomed to think that I deserve to suffer any harm. Had I money I might have estimated the offence at what I was able to pay, and not have been much the worse. But I have none, and therefore I must ask you to proportion the fine to my means. Well, perhaps I could afford a mina, and therefore I propose that penalty: Plato, Crito, Critobulus, and Apollodorus, my friends here, bid me say thirty minae, and they will be the sureties. Let thirty minae be the penalty; for which sum they will be ample security to you.

Not much time will be gained, O Athenians, in return for the evil name which you will get from the detractors of the city, who will say that you killed Socrates, a wise man; for they will call me wise, even although I am not wise, when they want to reproach you. If you had waited a little while, your desire would have been fulfilled in the course of nature. For I am far advanced in years, as you may perceive, and not far from death. I am speaking now not to all of you, but only to those who have condemned me to death. And I have another thing to say to them: You think that I was convicted because I had no words of the sort which would have procured my acquittal—I mean, if I had thought fit to leave nothing undone or unsaid. Not so; the deficiency which led to my conviction was not of words—certainly not. But I had not the boldness or impudence or inclination to address you as you would have liked me to do, weeping and wailing and lamenting, and saying and doing many things which you have been accustomed to hear from others, and which, as I maintain, are unworthy of me. I thought at the time that I ought not to do anything common or mean when in danger: nor do I now repent of the style of my defence; I would rather die having spoken after my manner, than speak in your manner and live. For neither in war nor yet at law ought I or any man to use every way of escaping death. Often in battle there can be no doubt that if a man will throw away his arms, and fall on his knees before his pursuers, he may escape death; and in other dangers there are other ways of escaping death, if a man is willing to say and do anything. The difficulty, my friends, is not to avoid death, but to avoid unrighteousness; for that runs faster than death. I am old and move slowly, and the slower runner has overtaken me, and my accusers are keen and quick, and the faster runner, who is unrighteousness, has overtaken them. And now I depart hence condemned by you to suffer the penalty of death,—they too go their ways condemned by the truth to suffer the penalty of villainy and wrong; and I must abide by my award—let them abide by theirs. I suppose that these things may be regarded as fated,—and I think that they are well.

And now, O men who have condemned me, I would fain prophesy to you; for I am about to die, and in the hour of death men are gifted with prophetic power. And I prophesy to you who are my murderers, that immediately after my departure punishment far heavier than you have inflicted on me will surely await you. Me you have killed because you wanted to escape the accuser, and not to give an account of your lives. But that will not be as you suppose: far otherwise. For I say that there will be more accusers of you than there are now; accusers whom hitherto I have restrained: and as they are younger they will be more inconsiderate with you, and you will be more offended at them. If you think that by killing men you can prevent some one from censuring your evil lives, you are mistaken; that is not a way of escape which is either possible or honourable; the easiest and the noblest way is not to be disabling others, but to be improving yourselves. This is the prophecy which I utter before my departure to the judges who have condemned me.

Friends, who would have acquitted me, I would like also to talk with you about the thing which has come to pass, while the magistrates are busy, and before I go to the place at which I must die. Stay then a little, for we may as well talk with one another while there is time. You are my friends, and I should like to show you the meaning of this event which has happened to me. O my judges—for you I may truly call judges—I should like to tell you of a wonderful circumstance. Hitherto the divine faculty of which the internal oracle is the source has constantly been in the habit of opposing me even about trifles, if I was going to make a slip or error in any matter; and now as you see there has come upon me that which may be thought, and is generally believed to be, the last and worst evil. But the oracle made no sign of opposition, either when I was leaving my house in the morning, or when I was on my way to the court, or while I was speaking, at anything which I was going to say; and yet I have often been stopped in the middle of a speech, but now in nothing I either said or did touching the matter in hand has the oracle opposed me. What do I take to be the explanation of this silence? I will tell you. It is an intimation that what has happened to me is a good, and that those of us who think that death is an evil are in error. For the customary sign would surely have opposed me had I been going to evil and not to good.

Let us reflect in another way, and we shall see that there is great reason to hope that death is a good; for one of two things—either death is a state of nothingness and utter unconsciousness, or, as men say, there is a change and migration of the soul from this world to another. Now, if you suppose that there is no consciousness, but a sleep like the sleep of him who is undisturbed even by dreams, death will be an unspeakable gain. For if a person were to select the night in which his sleep was undisturbed even by dreams, and were to compare with this the other days and nights of his life, and then were to tell us how many days and nights he had passed in the course of his life better and more pleasantly than this one, I think that any man, I will not say a private man, but even the great king will not find many such days or nights, when compared with the others. Now, if death be of such a nature, I say that to die is gain; for eternity is then only a single night. But if death is the journey to another place, and there, as men say, all the dead abide,[4] what good, O my friends and judges, can be greater than this? If, indeed, when the pilgrim arrives in the world below, he is delivered from the professors of justice in this world, and finds the true judges who are said to give judgment there, Minos and Rhadamanthus and Aeacus and Triptolemus, and other sons of God who were righteous in their own life, that pilgrimage will be worth making. What would not a man give if he might converse with Orpheus and Musaeus and Hesiod and Homer? Nay, if this be true, let me die again and again. I myself, too, shall have a wonderful interest in there meeting and conversing with Palamedes, and Ajax the son of Telamon, and any other ancient hero who has suffered death through an unjust judgment; and there will be no small pleasure, as I think, in comparing my own sufferings with theirs. Above all, I shall then be able to continue my search into true and false knowledge; as in this world, so also in the next; and I shall find out who is wise, and who pretends to be wise, and is not. What would not a man give, O judges, to be able to examine the leader of the great Trojan expedition; or Odysseus or Sisyphus, or numberless others, men and women too! What infinite delight would there be in conversing with them and asking them questions! In another world they do not put a man to death for asking questions: assuredly not. For besides being happier than we are, they will be immortal, if what is said is true.

Wherefore, O judges, be of good cheer about death, and know of a certainty, that no evil can happen to a good man, either in life or after

---

[4] A reference to Hades, for the Greeks not a place of punishment but the dwelling place for all souls after death.

death. He and his are not neglected by the gods; nor has my own approaching end happened by mere chance. But I see clearly that the time had arrived when it was better for me to die and be released from trouble; wherefore the oracle gave no sign. For which reason, also, I am not angry with my condemners, or with my accusers; they have done me no harm, although they did not mean to do me any good; and for this I may gently blame them.

Still, I have a favour to ask of them. When my sons are grown up, I would ask you, O my friends, to punish them; and I would have you trouble them, as I have troubled you, if they seem to care about riches, or anything, more than about virtue; or if they pretend to be something when they are really nothing,—then reprove them, as I have reproved you, for not caring about that for which they ought to care, and thinking that they are something when they are really nothing. And if you do this, both I and my sons will have received justice at your hands.

The hour of departure has arrived, and we go our ways—I to die, and you to live. Which is better God only knows.

For Discussion

1. What are the charges Socrates answers in the *Apology?*
2. How should a man live, according to Socrates? (How does his ethical philosophy compare with Thoreau's?)
3. How valid is Socrates' contention that the taker of life injures himself more than he injures his victim? Discuss his rationale in terms of capital punishment today.
4. What is Socratic wisdom?
5. What explanation does Socrates give for his failure to engage in politics? Apply this to today.
6. Why wouldn't Socrates plead for his life or accept exile?
7. Examine the nature of Socrates' self-criticism. How is it consistent with his philosophy?
8. In what ways can you defend the Athenians' attack against Socrates?
9. Discuss the metaphor of the gadfly.
10. Discursive argumentation is usually supported by facts. On what does Socrates base his defense?
11. What argument can you make for including the *Apology* in *The Reflective NO?*
12. Consider Socrates' special audience. Find examples of language—impassioned, ironic, or otherwise—which reveal his attitude toward this audience.

THOMAS JEFFERSON

Declaration of Independence

Thomas Jefferson, the third President of the United States, was born into an aristocratic Virginia family in 1743. One of the most educated men of his time and class, Jefferson was only thirty-three years old when he was chosen chairman of the committee to frame the Declaration of Independence. Jefferson was genuinely devoted to the idea of the elimination of tyranny of all types, including "the tyranny of the majority." He was a friend of Thomas Paine, whose liberal influence can be seen in Jefferson's writing, notably on slavery and religion. Jefferson died in 1826.

The unanimous declaration of the thirteen United States of America, in Congress, July 4, 1776

When, in the course of human events, it becomes necessary for one people to dissolve the political bands which have connected them with another, and to assume among the powers of the earth the separate and equal station to which the laws of nature and of nature's God entitle them, a decent respect to the opinions of mankind requires that they should declare the causes which impel them to the separation.

We hold these truths to be self-evident: That all men are created equal; that they are endowed by their Creator with certain inalienable rights; that among these are life, liberty, and the pursuit of happiness. That, to secure these rights, governments are instituted among men, deriving their just powers from the consent of the governed; that, whenever any form of government becomes destructive of these ends, it is the right of the people to alter or to abolish it, and to institute a new government, laying its foundation on such principles, and organizing its powers in such form, as to them shall seem most likely to effect their safety and happiness. Prudence, indeed, will dictate that governments long established should not be changed for light and transient causes; and accordingly all experience hath shown that mankind are more disposed to suffer, while evils are sufferable, than to right themselves by abolishing the forms to which they are accustomed. But when a long train of abuses and usurpations, pursuing invariably the same object, evinces a design to reduce them under absolute despotism, it is their right, it is their duty, to throw off such government and to provide new guards for their future security. Such has been the patient suffering of these colonies, and such is now the necessity which constrains them to alter their former systems of government. The history of the present king of Great Britain is a history of repeated injuries and usurpations, all having in direct object the establishment of an absolute tyranny over these states. To prove this, let facts be submitted to a candid world.

He has refused his assent to laws the most wholesome and necessary for the public good.

He has forbidden his governors to pass laws of immediate and pressing importance, unless suspended in their operation till his assent should be obtained, and, when so suspended, he has utterly neglected to attend to them.

He has refused to pass other laws for the accommodation of large districts of people, unless those people would relinquish the right of representation in the legislature—a right inestimable to them and formidable to tyrants only.

He has called together legislative bodies, at places unusual, uncomfortable, and distant from the repository of their public records, for the sole purpose of fatiguing them into compliance with his measures.

He has dissolved representative houses repeatedly for opposing with manly firmness his invasions on the rights of the people.

He has refused for a long time after such dissolutions to cause others to be elected; whereby the legislative powers, incapable of annihilation, have returned to the people at large for their exercise: the state remaining, in the meantime, exposed to all the dangers of invasion from without and convulsions within.

He has endeavored to prevent the population of these states; for that purpose obstructing the laws for naturalization of foreigners; refusing to pass others to encourage their migration hither, and raising the conditions of new appropriations of lands.

He has obstructed the administration of justice by refusing his assent to laws for establishing his judiciary powers.

He has made judges dependent on his will alone for the tenure of their offices and the amount and payment of their salaries.

He has erected a multitude of new offices and sent hither swarms of officers to harass our people and eat out their substance.

He has kept among us, in times of peace, standing armies without the consent of our legislatures.

He has affected to render the military independent of and superior to the civil power.

He has combined with others to subject us to a jurisdiction foreign to our constitutions and unacknowledged by our laws, giving his assent to their acts of pretended legislation:

For quartering large bodies of armed troops among us;

For protecting them by a mock trial from punishment for any murders which they should commit on the inhabitants of these states;

For cutting off our trade with all parts of the world;

For imposing taxes on us without our consent;

For depriving us in many cases of the benefits of trial by jury;

For transporting us beyond seas to be tried for pretended offenses;

For abolishing the free system of English laws in a neighboring province, establishing therein an arbitrary government, and enlarging its boundaries so as to render it at once an example and fit instrument for introducing the same absolute rule into these colonies;

For taking away our charters, abolishing our most valuable laws, and altering fundamentally the forms of our government;

For suspending our own legislatures and declaring themselves invested with power to legislate for us in all cases whatsoever.

He has abdicated government here by declaring us out of his protection and waging war against us.

He has plundered our seas, ravaged our coasts, burnt our towns and destroyed the lives of our people.

He is at this time transporting large armies of foreign mercenaries to complete the work of death, desolation, and tyranny already begun, with circumstances of cruelty and perfidy scarcely parallelled in the most barbarous ages and totally unworthy the head of a civilized nation.

He has constrained our fellow citizens taken captive upon the high seas to bear arms against their country, to become the executioners of their friends and brethren, or to fall themselves by their hands.

He has excited domestic insurrection amongst us, and has endeavored to bring on the inhabitants of our frontiers the merciless Indian savages, whose known rule of warfare is an undistinguished destruction of all ages, sexes, and conditions.

In every stage of these oppressions we have petitioned for redress, in the most humble terms; our repeated petitions have been answered only by repeated injury. A prince whose character is thus marked by every act which may define a tyrant is unfit to be the ruler of a free people.

Nor have we been wanting in attention to our British brethren. We have warned them, from time to time, of attempts by their legislature to extend an unwarrantable jurisdiction over us. We have reminded them of the circumstances of our emigration and settlement here. We have appealed to their native justice and magnanimity; and we have conjured them by the ties of our common kindred, to disavow these usurpations, which would inevitably interrupt our connections and correspondence. They, too, have been deaf to the voice of justice and consanguinity. We must, therefore, acquiesce in the necessity which denounces our separation, and hold them, as we hold the rest of mankind, enemies in war; in peace, friends.

We, therefore, the representatives of the United States of America, in general congress assembled, appealing to the Supreme Judge of the World for the rectitude of our intentions, do, in the name and by the authority of the good people of these colonies, solemnly publish and declare that these united colonies are, and of right ought to be, free and independent states; that they are absolved from all allegiance to the British crown, and that all political connection between them and the state of Great Britain is, and ought to be, totally dissolved; and that as free and independent states they have full power to levy war, conclude peace, contract alliances, establish commerce, and to do all other acts and things which independent states may of right do. And for the support of this declaration, with a firm reliance on the protection of Divine Providence, we mutually pledge to each other our lives, our fortunes, and our sacred honor.

For Discussion

1. The Declaration of Independence is a good example of deductive argument, moving from general assumptions to specific conclusions and using supporting examples along the way. Discuss the assumptions which are "self-evident."
2. When is revolution justified? Do you agree?
3. Discuss the rationale for the sequence in which the grievances are listed.
4. In what way does the Declaration go beyond its historical boundaries and apply to events today? Look at both the underlying principles and the specific grievances.
5. In earlier drafts of the Declaration, the language was much more impassioned. How does the formal language of the present version affect its meaning?

CLARENCE DARROW

Address to the Prisoners in Cook County Jail

Although his eloquence in the courtroom earned him the title of The Great Defender, Clarence Darrow was a controversial figure because of his atheism, his socialism, his opposition to capital punishment, and his frequent support of other unpopular causes. After Darrow delivered the following lecture to the prisoners at Cook County Jail in Chicago in 1902, he was criticized by friends who thought the talk inappropriate for its audience. Darrow then had it printed in rather expensive pamphlet form and sold it for five cents, expressly because he objected to the idea that "the truth should not be spoken to all people."

If I looked at jails and crimes and prisoners in the way the ordinary person does, I should not speak on this subject to you. The reason I talk to you on the question of crime, its cause and cure, is that I really do not in the least believe in crime. There is no such thing as a crime as the word is generally understood. I do not believe there is any sort of distinction between the real moral conditions of the people in and out of jail. One is just as good as the other. The people here can no more help being here than the people outside can avoid being outside. I do not believe that people are in jail because they deserve to be. They are in jail simply because they cannot avoid it on account of circumstances which are entirely beyond their control and for which they are in no way responsible.

I suppose a great many people on the outside would say I was doing you harm if they should hear what I say to you this afternoon, but you cannot be hurt a great deal anyway, so it will not matter. Good people outside would say that I was really teaching you things that were calculated to injure society, but it's worth while now and then to hear something different from what you ordinarily get from preachers and the like. These will tell you that you should be good and then you will get rich and be happy.

131

Of course we know that people do not get rich by being good, and that is the reason why so many of you people try to get rich some other way, only you do not understand how to do it quite as well as the fellow outside.

There are people who think that everything in this world is an accident. But really there is no such thing as an accident. A great many folks admit that many of the people in jail ought to be there, and many who are outside ought to be in. I think none of them ought to be here. There ought to be no jails; and if it were not for the fact that the people on the outside are so grasping and heartless in their dealings with the people on the inside, there would be no such institution as jails.

I do not want you to believe that I think all you people here are angels. I do not think that. You are people of all kinds, all of you doing the best you can—and that is evidently not very well. You are people of all kinds and conditions and under all circumstances. In one sense everybody is equally good and equally bad. We all do the best we can under the circumstances. But as to the exact things for which you are sent here, some of you are guilty and did the particular act because you needed the money. Some of you did it because you are in the habit of doing it, and some of you because you are born to it, and it comes to be as natural as it does, for instance, for me to be good.

Most of you probably have nothing against me, and most of you would treat me the same way as any other person would, probably better than some of the people on the outside would treat me, because you think I believe in you and they know I do not believe in them. While you would not have the least thing against me in the world, you might pick my pockets. I do not think all of you would, but I think some of you would. You would not have anything against me, but that's your profession, a few of you. Some of the rest of you, if my doors were unlocked, might come in if you saw anything you wanted—not out of any malice to me, but because that is your trade. There is no doubt there are quite a number of people in this jail who would pick my pockets. And still I know this—that when I get outside pretty nearly everybody picks my pocket. There may be some of you who would hold up a man on the street, if you did not happen to have something else to do, and needed the money; but when I want to light my house or my office the gas company holds me up. They charge me one dollar for something that is worth twenty-five cents. Still all these people are good people; they are pillars of society and support the churches, and they are respectable.

When I ride on the streetcars I am held up—I pay five cents for a ride that is worth two and a half cents, simply because a body of men have bribed the city council and the legislature, so that all the rest of us have to pay tribute to them.

If I do not want to fall into the clutches of the gas trust and choose to burn oil instead of gas, then good Mr. Rockefeller holds me up, and he uses a certain portion of his money to build universities and support churches which are engaged in telling us how to be good.

Some of you are here for obtaining property under false pretenses— yet I pick up a great Sunday paper and read the advertisements of a merchant prince—"Shirtwaists for 39 cents, marked down from $3.00."

When I read the advertisements in the paper I see they are all lies. When I want to get out and find a place to stand anywhere on the face of the earth, I find that it has all been taken up long ago before I came here, and before you came here, and somebody says, "Get off, swim into the lake, fly into the air; go anywhere, but get off." That is because these people have the police and they have the jails and the judges and the lawyers and the soldiers and all the rest of them to take care of the earth and drive everybody off that comes in their way.

A great many people will tell you that all this is true, but that it does not excuse you. These facts do not excuse some fellow who reaches into my pocket and takes out a five-dollar bill. The fact that the gas company bribes the members of the legislature from year to year, and fixes the law, so that all you people are compelled to be "fleeced" whenever you deal with them; the fact that the streetcar companies and the gas companies have control of the streets; and the fact that the landlords own all the earth—this, they say, has nothing to do with you.

Let us see whether there is any connection between the crimes of the respectable classes and your presence in the jail. Many of you people are in jail because you have really committed burglary; many of you, because you have stolen something. In the meaning of the law, you have taken some other person's property. Some of you have entered a store and carried off a pair of shoes because you did not have the price. Possibly some of you have committed murder. I cannot tell what all of you did. There are a great many people here who have done some of these things who really do not know themselves why they did them. I think I know why you did them—every one of you; you did these things because you were bound to do them. It looked to you at the time as if you had a chance to do them or not, as you saw fit; but still, after all, you had no choice. There may be people here who had some money in their pockets and who still went out and got some more money in a way society forbids. Now, you may not yourselves see exactly why it was you did this thing, but if you look at the question deeply enough and carefully enough you will see that there were circumstances that drove you to do exactly the thing which you did. You could not help it any more than we outside can help taking the positions that we take. The reformers who tell you to be good and you will be happy, and the people on the outside who have property to protect—they think that the only way to do it is by building jails and locking you up in cells on weekdays and praying for you Sundays.

I think that all of this has nothing whatever to do with right conduct. I think it is very easily seen what has to do with right conduct. Some so-called criminals—and I will use this word because it is handy, it means nothing to me—I speak of the criminals who get caught as distinguished from the criminals who catch them—some of these so-called criminals are in jail for their first offenses, but nine tenths of you are in jail because you did not have a good lawyer and, of course, you did not have a good lawyer because you did not have enough money to pay a good lawyer. There is no very great danger of a rich man going to jail.

. . .

First and last, people are sent to jail because they are poor. Sometimes, as I say, you may not need money at the particular time, but you wish to have thrifty forehanded habits, and do not always wait until you are in absolute want. Some of you people are perhaps plying the trade, the profession, which is called burglary. No man in his right senses will go into a strange house in the dead of night and prowl around with a dark lantern through unfamiliar rooms and take chances of his life, if he has plenty of the good things of the world in his own home. You would not take any such chances as that. If a man had clothes on his clothes-press and beefsteak in his pantry and money in the bank, he would not navigate around nights in houses where he knows nothing about the premises whatever. It always requires experience and education for this profession, and people who fit themselves for it are no more to blame than I am for being a lawyer. A man would not hold up another man on the street if he had plenty of money in his own pocket. He might do it if he had one dollar or two dollars, but he wouldn't if he had as much money as Mr. Rockefeller has. Mr. Rockefeller has a great deal better hold-up game than that.

The more that is taken from the poor by the rich, who have the chance to take it, the more poor people there are who are compelled to resort to these means for a livelihood. they may not understand it, they may not think so at once, but after all they are driven into that line of employment.

. . .

There is one way to cure all these offenses, and that is to give the people a chance to live. There is no other way, and there never was any other way since the world began; and the world is so blind and stupid that it will not see. If every man and woman and child in the world had a chance to make a decent, fair, honest living, there would be no jails and no lawyers and no courts. There might be some persons here or there with some peculiar formation of their brain, like Rockefeller, who would do these things simply to be doing them; but they would be very, very few, and those should be sent to a hospital and treated, and not sent to jail; and they would entirely disappear in the second generation, or at least in the third generation.

I am not talking pure theory. I will just give you two or three illustrations.

The English people once punished criminals by sending them away. They would load them on a ship and export them to Australia. England was owned by lords and nobles and rich people. They owned the whole earth over there, and the other people had to stay in the streets. They could not get a decent living. They used to take their criminals and send them to Australia—I mean the class of criminals who got caught. When these criminals got over there, and nobody else had come, they had the whole continent to run over, and so they could raise sheep and furnish their own meat, which is easier than stealing it. These criminals then became decent, respectable people because they had a chance to live. They did not commit any crimes. They were just like the English people who sent them there, only better. And in the second generation the descendants of those criminals were as good and respectable a class of people as there were on the face of the earth, and then they began building churches and jails themselves.

A portion of this country was settled in the same way, landing prisoners down on the southern coast; but when they got here and had a whole continent to run over and plenty of chances to make a living, they became respectable citizens, making their own living just like any other citizen in the world. But finally the descendants of the English aristocracy who sent the people over to Australia found out they were getting rich, and so they went over to ·get possession of the earth as they always do, and they organized land syndicates and got control of the land and ores, and then they had just as many criminals in Australia as they did in England. It was not because the world had grown bad; it was because the earth had been taken away from the people.

. . .

Everybody makes his living along the lines of least resistance. A wise man who comes into a country early sees a great undeveloped land. For instance, our rich men twenty-five years ago saw that Chicago was small and knew a lot of people would come here and settle, and they readily saw that if they had all the land around here it would be worth a good deal, so they grabbed the land. You cannot be a landlord because somebody has got it all. You must find some other calling. In England and Ireland and Scotland less than five per cent own all the land there is, and the people are bound to stay there on any kind of terms the landlords give. They must live the best they can, so they develop all these various professions—burglary, picking pockets, and the like.

Again, people find all sorts of ways of getting rich. These are diseases like everything else. You look at people getting rich, organizing trusts and making a million dollars, and somebody gets the disease and he starts out. He catches it just as a man catches the mumps or the measles; he is not to blame, it is in the air. You will find men speculating beyond their means, because the mania of money-getting is taking possession of them. It is simply a disease—nothing more, nothing less. You cannot avoid catching it; but the fellows who have control of the earth have the advantage of you. See what the law is: when these men get control of things, they make the laws. They do not make the laws to protect anybody; courts are not instruments of justice. When your case gets into court it will make little difference whether you are guilty or innocent, but it's better if you have a smart lawyer. And you cannot have a smart lawyer unless you have money. First and last it's a question of money. Those men who own the earth make the laws to protect what they have. They fix up a sort of fence or pen around what they have, and they fix the law so the fellow on the outside cannot get in. The laws are really organized for the protection of the men who rule the world. They were never organized or enforced to do justice. We have no system for doing justice, not the slightest in the world.

Let me illustrate: Take the poorest person in this room. If the community had provided a system of doing justice, the poorest person in this room would have as good a lawyer as the richest, would he not? When you went into court you would have just as long a trial and just as fair a trial as the richest person in Chicago. Your case would not be tried in fifteen or twenty minutes, whereas it would take fifteen days to get through with a rich man's case.

Then if you were rich and were beaten, your case would be taken to the Appellate Court. A poor man cannot take his case to the Appellate Court; he has not the price. And then to the Supreme Court. And if he were beaten there he might perhaps go to the United States Supreme Court. And he might die of old age before he got into jail. If you are poor, it's a quick job. You are almost known to be guilty, else you would not be there. Why should anyone be in the criminal court if he were not guilty? He would not be there if he could be anywhere else. The officials have no time to look after all these cases. The people who are on the outside, who are running banks and building churches and making jails, they have no time to examine 600 or 700 prisoners each year to see whether they are guilty or innocent. If the courts were organized to promote justice the people would elect somebody to defend all these criminals, somebody as smart as the prosecutor—and give him as many detectives and as many assistants to help, and pay as much money to defend you as to prosecute you. We have a very able man for state's attorney, and he has many assistants, detectives, and policemen without end, and judges to hear the cases—everything handy.

Most all of our criminal code consists in offenses against property. People are sent to jail because they have committed a crime against property. It is of very little consequence whether one hundred people more or less go to jail who ought not to go—you must protect property, because in this world property is of more importance than anything else.

How is it done? These people who have property fix it so they can protect what they have. When somebody commits a crime it does not follow that he has done something that is morally wrong. The man on the outside who has committed no crime may have done something. For instance: to take all the coal in the United States and raise the price two dollars or three dollars when there is no need of it, and thus kill thousands of babies and send thousands of people to the poorhouse and tens of thousands to jail, as is done every year in the United States—this is a greater crime than all the people in our jails ever committed; but the law does not punish it. Why? Because the fellows who control the earth make the laws. If you and I had the making of the laws, the first thing we would do would be to punish the fellow who gets control of the earth. Nature put this coal in the ground for me as well as for them and nature made the prairies up here to raise wheat for me as well as for them, and then the great railroad companies came along and fenced it up.

. . .

I will guarantee to take from this jail, or any jail in the world, five hundred men who have been the worst criminals and lawbreakers who ever got into jail, and I will go down to our lowest streets and take five hundred of the most abandoned prostitutes, and go out somewhere where there is plenty of land, and will give them a chance to make a living, and they will be as good people as the average in the community.

There is a remedy for the sort of condition we see here. The world never finds it out, or when it does find it out it does not enforce it. You may pass a law punishing every person with death for burglary, and it will make no difference. Men will commit it just the same. In England there was a time when one hundred different offenses were punishable with death, and it made no difference. The English people strangely found out that so fast as they repealed the severe penalties and so fast as they did away with punishing men by death, crime decreased instead of increased; that the smaller the penalty the fewer the crimes.

Hanging men in our county jails does not prevent murder. It makes murderers.

And this has been the history of the world. It's easy to see how to do away with what we call crime. It is not so easy to do it. I will tell you how to do it. It can be done by giving the people a chance to live—by destroying special privileges. So long as big criminals can get the coal fields, so long as the big criminals have control of the city council and get the public streets for streetcars and gas rights—this is bound to send thousands of poor people to jail. So long as men are allowed to monopolize all the earth, and compel others to live on such terms as these men see fit to make, then you are bound to get into jail.

The only way in the world to abolish crime and criminals is to abolish the big ones and the little ones together. Make fair conditions of life. Abolish the right of private ownership of land, abolish monopoly, make the world partners in production, partners in the good things of life. Nobody would steal if he could get something of his own some easier way. Nobody will commit burglary when he has a house full. No girl will go out on the streets when she has a comfortable place at home. The man who owns a sweatshop or a department store may not be to blame himself for the condition of his girls, but when he pays them five dollars, three dollars, and two dollars a week, I wonder where he thinks they will get the rest of their money to live. The only way to cure these conditions is by equality. There should be no jails. They do not accomplish what they pretend to accomplish. If you would wipe them out there would be no more criminals than now. They terrorize nobody. They are a blot upon any civilization, and a jail is an evidence of the lack of charity of the people on the outside who make the jails and fill them with the victims of their greed.

For Discussion

1. How is Darrow's view of mankind reflected in his opening remarks?
2. How does Darrow equate the crimes of the respectable classes and those of the prisoners? What differentiates the crimes? What additional examples of respectable crimes can you provide?
3. What evidence does Darrow offer to support his belief that an equitable share of the world's goods will eliminate crime? How would this belief apply to what he calls respectable crime?
4. Discuss Darrow's theory on the inviolability of private property. How does it relate to present conflicts in America?
5. How does Darrow feel about capital punishment? (Also see Gregory.)
6. Discuss the practicability of Darrow's proposal to abolish large and small crimes together.
7. Examine each use of concrete illustration. To what extent would these examples support the same argument today?
8. How would you describe Darrow's manner of speaking? What does it tell you about his attitude toward his audience?

BARRY GOLDWATER

The Delusion of Collectivism

The Conscience of a Conservative, from which the following selection is taken, was published in 1960 when Barry Goldwater was United States Senator from Arizona. In 1964, the right wing of the Republican Party gained control and nominated Goldwater for the Presidency; however, he was defeated in the national election, carrying only five Southern states and Arizona. A millionaire businessman and a major general in the U.S. Air Force Reserve, Goldwater returned to private life until 1968, when he was re-elected to the Senate.

the welfare state

Washington—The President estimated that the expenditures of the Department of Health, Education and Welfare in the fiscal year 1961 (including Social Security payments) would exceed $15,000,000,000. Thus the current results of New Deal legislation are Federal disbursements for human welfare in this country second only to national defense.

The New York Times, January 18, 1960, p. 1.

For many years it appeared that the principal domestic threat to our freedom was contained in the doctrines of Karl Marx. The collectivists—non-Communists as well as Communists—had adopted the Marxist objective of "socializing the means of production." And so it seemed that if collectivization were imposed, it would take the form of a State owned and operated economy. I doubt whether this is the main threat any longer.

The collectivists have found, both in this country and in other industrialized nations of the West, that free enterprise has removed the economic and social conditions that might have made a class struggle possible. Mammoth productivity, wide distribution of wealth, high standards of living, the

From *The Conscience of a Conservative,* by Barry Goldwater (Shepherdsville, Kentucky: Victor Publishing Company, 1960), pp. 68–115; reprinted by permission of the publisher.

trade union movement—these and other factors have eliminated whatever incentive there might have been for the "proletariat" to rise up, peaceably or otherwise, and assume direct ownership of productive property. Significantly, the bankruptcy of doctrinaire Marxism has been expressly acknowledged by the Socialist Party of West Germany, and by the dominant faction of the Socialist Party of Great Britain. In this country the abandonment of the Marxist approach (outside the Communist Party, of course) is attested to by the negligible strength of the Socialist Party, and more tellingly perhaps, by the content of left wing literature and by the programs of left wing political organizations such as the Americans for Democratic Action.

The currently favored instrument of collectivization is the Welfare State. The collectivists have not abandoned their ultimate goal—to subordinate the individual to the State—but their strategy has changed. They have learned that Socialism can be achieved through Welfarism quite as well as through Nationalization. They understand that private property can be confiscated as effectively by taxation as by expropriating it. They understand that the individual can be put at the mercy of the State—not only by making the State his employer—but by divesting him of the means to provide for his personal needs and by giving the State the responsibility of caring for those needs from cradle to grave. Moreover, they have discovered—and here is the critical point—that *Welfarism is much more compatible with the political processes of a democratic society.* Nationalization ran into popular opposition, but the collectivists feel sure the Welfare State can be erected by the simple expedient of buying votes with promises of "free" hospitalization, "free" retirement pay and so on. . . . The correctness of this estimate can be seen from the portion of the federal budget that is now allocated to welfare, an amount second only to the cost of national defense.[1]

I do not welcome this shift of strategy. Socialism-through-Welfarism poses a far greater danger to freedom than Socialism-through-Nationalization precisely because it *is* more difficult to combat. The evils of Nationalization are self-evident and immediate. Those of Welfarism are veiled and tend to be postponed. People can understand the consequences of turning over ownership of the steel industry, say, to the State; and they can be counted on to oppose such a proposal. But let the government increase its contribution to the "Public Assistance" program and we will, at most, grumble about excessive government spending. The effect of Welfarism on freedom will be felt later on—after its beneficiaries have become its victims, after dependence on government has turned into bondage and it is too late to unlock the jail.

But a far more important factor is Welfarism's strong emotional appeal

---

[1] The total figure is substantially higher than the $15,000,000,000 noted above if we take into account welfare expenditures outside the Department of Health, Education and Welfare—for federal housing projects, for example.

to many voters, and the consequent temptations it presents the average politician. It is hard, as we have seen, to make out a case for State ownership. It is very different with the rhetoric of humanitarianism. How easy it is to reach the voters with earnest importunities for helping the needy. And how difficult for Conservatives to resist these demands without appearing to be callous and contemptuous of the plight of less fortunate citizens. Here, perhaps, is the best illustration of the failure of the Conservative demonstration.

I know, for I have heard the questions often. Have you no sense of social obligation? the Liberals ask. Have you no concern for people who are out of work? for sick people who lack medical care? for children in overcrowded schools? Are you unmoved by the problems of the aged and disabled? Are you *against* human welfare?

The answer to all of these questions is, of course, no. But a simple "no" is not enough. I feel certain that Conservatism is through unless Conservatives can demonstrate and communicate the difference between being concerned with these problems and believing that the federal government is the proper agent for their solution.

The long range political consequences of Welfarism are plain enough: as we have seen, the State that is able to deal with its citizens as wards and dependents has gathered unto itself unlimited political and economic power and is thus able to rule as absolutely as any oriental despot.

Let us, however, weigh the consequences of Welfarism on the individual citizen.

Consider, first, the effect of Welfarism on the donors of government welfare—not only those who pay for it but also the voters and their elected representatives who decide that the benefits shall be conferred. Does some credit redound on them for trying to care for the needs of their fellow citizens? Are they to be commended and rewarded, at some moment in eternity, for their "charity"? I think not. Suppose I should vote for a measure providing for free medical care: I am unaware of any moral virtue that is attached to my decision to confiscate the earnings of X and give them to Y.

Suppose, however, that X approves of the program—that he has voted for welfarist politicians with the idea of helping his fellow man. Surely the wholesomeness of his act is diluted by the fact that he is voting not only to have his own money taken but also that of his fellow citizens who may have different ideas about their social obligations. Why does not such a man, instead, contribute what he regards as his just share of human welfare to a private charity?

Consider the consequences to the recipient of welfarism. For one thing, he mortgages himself to the federal government. In return for benefits—which, in the majority of cases, he pays for—he concedes to the government the ultimate in political power—the power to grant or withhold from him the necessities of life as the government sees fit. Even more important, however, is the effect on him—the elimination of any feeling of responsibility for his own welfare and that of his family and neighbors. A man may not immediately, or ever, comprehend the harm thus done to his character. Indeed, this is one of the great evils of Welfarism—that it transforms the individual from a dignified, industrious, self-reliant *spiritual* being into a dependent animal creature without his knowing it. There is no avoiding this damage to character under the Welfare State. Welfare programs cannot help but promote the idea that the government *owes* the benefits it confers on the individual, and that the individual is entitled, by right, to receive them. Such programs are sold to the country precisely on the argument that government has an *obligation* to care for the needs of its citizens. It is possible that the message will reach those who vote for the benefits, but not those who receive them? How different it is with private charity where both the giver and the receiver understand that charity is the product of the humanitarian impulses of the giver, not the due of the receiver.

Let us, then, not blunt the noble impulses of mankind by reducing charity to a mechanical operation of the federal government. Let us, by all means, encourage those who are fortunate and able to care for the needs of those who are unfortunate and disabled. But let us do this in a way that is conducive to the spiritual as well as the material well-being of our citizens— and in a way that will preserve their freedom. Let welfare be a private concern. Let it be promoted by individuals and families, by churches, private hospitals, religious service organizations, community charities and other institutions that have been established for this purpose. If the objection is raised that private institutions lack sufficient funds, let us remember that every penny the federal government does *not* appropriate for welfare is potentially available for private use—and without the overhead charge for processing the money through the federal bureaucracy. Indeed, high taxes, for which government Welfarism is so largely responsible, is the biggest obstacle to fund raising by private charities.

Finally, if we deem public intervention necessary, let the job be done by local and state authorities that are incapable of accumulating the vast political power that is so inimical to our liberties.

The Welfare State is *not* inevitable, as its proponents are so fond of telling us. There is nothing inherent in an industrialized economy, or in democratic processes of government that *must* produce de Tocqueville's "guardian society." Our future, like our past, will be what we make it. And we can shatter the collectivists' designs on individual freedom if we will impress upon the men who conduct our affairs this one truth: that the material and spiritual sides of man are intertwined; that it is impossible for the State to assume responsibility for one without intruding on the essential nature of the other; that if we take from a man the personal responsibility for caring for his material needs, we take from him also the will and the opportunity to be free.

the soviet menace

And still the awful truth remains: We can establish the domestic conditions for maximizing freedom, along the lines I have indicated, and yet become slaves. We can do this by losing the Cold War to the Soviet Union.

American freedom has always depended, to an extent, on what is happening beyond our shores. Even in Ben Franklin's day, Americans had to reckon with foreign threats. Our forebearers knew that "keeping a Republic" meant, above all, keeping it safe from foreign transgressors; they knew that a people cannot live and work freely, and develop national institutions conducive to freedom, except in peace and with independence. In those early days the threat to peace and independence was very real. We were a fledgling-nation and the slightest misstep—or faint hearts—would have laid us open to the ravages of predatory European powers. It was only because wise and courageous men understood that defense of freedom required risks and sacrifice, as well as their belief in it, that we survived the crisis of national infancy. As we grew stronger, and as the oceans continued to interpose a physical barrier between ourselves and European militarism, the foreign danger gradually receded. Though we always had to keep a weather eye on would-be conquerors, our independence was acknowledged and peace, unless we chose otherwise, was established. Indeed, after the Second World War, we were not only master of our own destiny; we were master of the world. With a monopoly of atomic weapons, and with a conventional military establishment superior to any in the world, America was—in relative and absolute terms—the most powerful nation the world had ever known. American freedom was as secure as at any time in our history.

Now, a decade and a half later, we have come full circle and our national existence is once again threatened as it was in the early days of the Republic. Though we are still strong physically, we are in clear and imminent danger of being overwhelmed by alien forces. We are confronted by a revolutionary world movement that possesses not only the will to dominate absolutely every square mile of the globe, but increasingly the capacity to do so: a military power that rivals our own, political warfare and propaganda skills that are superior to ours, an international fifth column that operates conspiratorially in the heart of our defenses, an ideology that imbues its adherents with a sense of historical mission; and all of these resources controlled by a ruthless despotism that brooks no deviation from the revolutionary course. This threat, moreover, is growing day by day. And it has now reached the point where American leaders, both political and intellectual, are searching desperately for means of "appeasing" or "accommodating" the Soviet Union as the price of national survival. The American people are being told that, however valuable their freedom may be, it is even more important to live. A craven fear of death is entering the American consciousness; so much so that many recently felt that honoring the chief despot himself was the price we had to pay to avoid nuclear destruction.

The temptation is strong to blame the deterioration of America's fortunes on the Soviet Union's acquisition of nuclear weapons. But this is self-delusion. The rot had set in, the crumbling of our position was already observable, long before the Communists detonated their first Atom Bomb. Even in the early 1950s, when America still held unquestioned nuclear superiority, it was clear that we were losing the Cold War. Time and again in my campaign speeches of 1952 I warned my fellow Arizonians that "American Foreign Policy has brought us from a position of undisputed power, in seven short years, to the brink of possible disaster." And in the succeeding seven years, that trend, because its cause remains, has continued.

The real cause of the deterioration can be simply stated. Our enemies have understood the nature of the conflict, and we have not. They are determined to win the conflict, and we are not.

I hesitate to restate the obvious—to say again what has been said so many times before by so many others: that the Communists' aim is to conquer the world. I repeat it because it is the beginning and the end of our knowledge about the conflict between East and West. I repeat it because I fear that however often we have given lip-service to this central political fact of our time, very few of us have *believed* it. If we had, our entire approach to foreign policy over the past fourteen years would have been radically different, and the course of world events radically changed.

If an enemy power is bent on conquering you, and proposes to turn all of his resources to that end, he is at war with you: and you—unless you contemplate surrender—are at war with him. Moreover—unless you contemplate treason—your objective, like his, will be victory. Not "peace," but victory. Now, while traitors (and perhaps cowards) have at times occupied key positions in our government, it is clear that our national leadership over the past fourteen years has favored neither surrender nor treason. It is equally clear, however, that our leaders have not made *victory* the goal of American policy. And the reason that they have not done so, I am saying, is that they have never believed deeply that the Communists are in earnest.

Our avowed national objective is "peace." We have, with great sincerity, "waged" peace, while the Communists wage war. We have sought "settlements," while the Communists seek victories. We have tried to pacify the world. The Communists mean to own it. Here is why the contest has been an unequal one, and why, essentially, we are losing it.

Peace, to be sure, *is* a proper goal for American policy—as long as it is understood that peace is not all we seek. For we do not want the peace of surrender. We want a peace in which freedom and justice will prevail, and that—given the nature of Communism—is a peace in which Soviet power will no longer be in a position to threaten us and the rest of the world. A tolerable peace, in other words, must *follow* victory over Communism. We have been fourteen years trying to bury that unpleasant fact. It cannot be buried and any foreign policy that ignores it will lead to our extinction as a nation.

We do not, of course, want to achieve victory by force of arms. If possible, overt hostilities should always be avoided; especially is this so when a shooting war may cause the death of many millions of people, including our own. But we cannot, for that reason, make the avoidance of a shooting war our chief objective. If we do that—if we tell ourselves that it is more important to avoid shooting than to keep our freedom—we are committed to a course that has only one terminal point: surrender. We cannot, by proclamation, make war "unthinkable." For it is not unthinkable to the Communists: naturally, they would prefer to avoid war, but they are pre- pared to risk it, in the last analysis, to achieve their objectives. We must, in our hearts, be equally dedicated to our objectives. If war is unthinkable to us but not to them, the famous "balance of terror" is not a balance at all, but an instrument of blackmail. U.S.-Soviet power may be in balance; but if we, and not they, rule out the possibility of using that power, the Kremlin can create crisis after crisis, and force the U.S., because of our greater fear of war, to back down every time. And it cannot be long before a universal Communist Empire sits astride the globe.

The rallying cry of an appeasement organization, portrayed in a recent novel on American politics, was "I would rather crawl on my knees to Mos- cow than die under an Atom Bomb." This sentiment, of course, repudiates everything that is courageous and honorable and dignified in the human being. We must—as the first step toward saving American freedom—affirm the contrary view and make it the cornerstone of our foreign policy: that we would rather die than lose our freedom. There are ways which I will suggest later on—not easy ways, to be sure—in which we may save both our freedom *and* our lives; but all such suggestions are meaningless and vain unless we first understand what the objective is. We want to stay alive, of course; but more than that we want to be free. We want to have peace; but before that we want to establish the conditions that will make peace tolerable. "Like it or not," Eugene Lyons has written, "the great and inescapable task of our epoch is not to end the Cold War but to win it."

I suggest that we look at America's present foreign policy, and ask whether it is conducive to victory. There are several aspects of this policy. Let us measure each of them by the test: Does it help defeat the enemy? . . .

United Nations

Support of the United Nations, our leaders earnestly proclaim, is one of the cornerstones of American foreign policy. I confess to being more interested in whether American foreign policy has the support of the United Nations.

Here, again, it seems to me that our approach to foreign affairs suffers from a confusion in objectives. Is the perpetuation of an international debating forum, for its own sake, the primary objective of American policy? If so, there is much to be said for our past record of subordinating our national interest to that of the United Nations. If, on the other hand, our primary objective is victory over Communism, we will, as a matter of course, view such organizations at the UN as a possible *means* to that end. Once the question is asked—Does America's participation in the United Nations help or hinder her struggle against world Communism?—it becomes clear that our present commitment to the UN deserves re-examination.

The United Nations, we must remember, is in part a Communist organization. The Communists always have at least one seat in its major policy-making body, the Security Council; and the Soviet Union's permanent veto power in that body allows the Kremlin to block any action, on a substantial issue, that is contrary to its interests. The Communists also have a sizeable membership in the UN's other policy-making body, the General Assembly. Moreover, the UN's working staff, the Secretariat, is manned by hundreds of Communist agents who are frequently in a position to sabotage those few UN policies that *are* contrary to Communist interests. Finally, a great number of non-Communist United Nations are sympathetic to Soviet aims—or, at best, are unsympathetic to ours.

We therefore should not be surprised that many of the policies that emerge from the deliberations of the United Nations are not policies that are in the best interest of the United States. United Nations policy is, necessarily, the product of many different views—some of them friendly, some of them indifferent to our interests, some of them mortally hostile. And the result is that our national interests usually suffer when we subordinate our own policy to the UN's. In nearly every case in which we have called upon the United Nations to do our thinking for us, and to make our policy for us—whether during the Korean War, or in the Suez crisis, or following the revolution in Iraq—we have been a less effective foe of Communism that we otherwise might have been.

Unlike America, the Communists do not respect the UN and do not permit their policies to be affected by it. If the "opinion of mankind," as reflected by a UN resolution, goes against them, they—in effect—tell mankind to go fly a kite. Not so with us; we would rather be approved than succeed, and so are likely to adjust our own views to conform with a United Nations majority. This is not the way to win the Cold War. I repeat: Communism will not be beaten by a policy that is the common denominator of the foreign policies of 80-odd nations, some of which are our enemies, nearly all of which are less determined than we to save the world from Communist domination. Let us, then, have done with submitting major policy decisions to a forum where the opinions of the Sultan of Yemen count equally with ours; where the vote of the United States can be cancelled out by the likes of "Byelorussia."

I am troubled by several other aspects of our UN commitment. First—and here again our Cold War interests are damaged—the United Nations provides a unique forum for Communist propaganda. We too, of course, can voice our views at the UN; but the Communists' special advantage is that their lies and misrepresentations are elevated to the level of serious international debate. By recognizing the right of Communist regimes to participate in the UN as equals, and by officially acknowledging them as "peace-loving," we grant Communist propaganda a presumption of reasonableness and plausibility it otherwise would not have.

Second, the UN places an unwarranted financial burden on the American taxpayer. The Marxist formula, "from each according to his ability . . ." —under which contributions to the UN and its specialized agencies are determined—does not tally with the American concept of justice. The United States is currently defraying roughly a third of all United Nations expenses. That assessment should be drastically reduced. The UN should not operate as a charity. Assessments should take into account the benefits received by the contributor-nation.

Finally, I fear that our involvement in the United Nations may be leading to an unconstitutional surrender of American sovereignty. Many UN activities have already made strong inroads against the sovereign powers of Member Nations. This is neither the time nor place to discuss the merits of yielding sovereign American rights—other than to record my unequivocal opposition to the idea. It is both the time and place, however, to insist that any such discussion take place within the framework of a proposed constitutional amendment—and not, clandestinely, in the headquarters of some UN agency.

Withdrawal from the United Nations is probably not the answer to these problems. For a number of reasons that course is unfeasible. We should make sure, however, that the nature of our commitment is such as to advance American interests; and that will involve changes in some of our present attitudes and policies toward the UN. Let the UN firsters—of whom there are many in this country—put their enthusiasm for "international cooperation" in proper perspective. Let them understand that victory over Communism must come *before* the achievement of lasting peace. Let them, in a word, keep their eyes on the target. . . .

For Discussion

1. Determine Goldwater's use of the terms Nationalization and Welfarism. What attributes does he show them as sharing? How does the threat of each differ?
2. Examine Goldwater's discussion of the effects of charity upon the donor and upon the recipient. What do you believe is his primary concern?
3. How does Goldwater's belief in the Soviet menace relate to his understanding and explanation of its cause? How convincing is his argument?
4. Discuss Goldwater's analysis of national objectives.
5. The author confesses to being "more interested in whether American foreign policy has the support of the United Nations" than whether America supports the United Nations. What does this statement tell you about his political philosophy?
6. According to Goldwater, our aim of victory over communism cannot be realized within the equality of the U.N. What, then, do you think is his implied solution?
7. Both Goldwater and Wallace (see "Civil Rights Bill: Sham, Fraud and Hoax") call themselves conservatives. How accurately does the term describe both points of view?
8. Comment on the organization of this essay. How would you characterize it?

PETER MICHELSON

An Apology for Pornography

The subject of pornography has increasingly occupied the attention of the courts, the lawmakers, and citizens' groups. The following essay, arguing the present minority position, was written
by Peter Michelson, a member of the Department of English at
Notre Dame University.

Trickster, the archetypal fool of Winnebago Indian mythology, was possessed of a phallus so large that he had to carry it over his shoulder. He did
not, according to the legend, know either what it was or how it was to be
used. But its very bulk reassured him against those who ridiculed his subjec-
tion to the huge burden and claimed he could not rid himself of it. For
to carry it required, after all, a substantial and unique strength. This mockery, however, eventually took its toll, and Trickster wearied of the weight
and mystery; he determined therefore to remove them. Whereupon he discovered, of course, that the joke was on him. Great as it was, his strength
could not equably bear the burden, nor his wit devise a release from it.

This is a sobering myth. Rather than celebrating power and potency,
like most phallic legends, it documents man's sexual anxiety and ignorance.
But it is honest, more honest than men customarily are about their sexuality.
There are, for instance, primitive Austrialian tribes whose traditional teaching
does not recognize that copulation causes pregnancy. And the traditions are
honored; pregnancy is explained by the woman having slept under a certain
tree or having been graced by the light of the moon. In their hearts—and presumably their loins—they may know what's what, but they must speak with a
forked tongue.

Nor is this paralyzing duality peculiar to primitive cultures. The stable
civilized culture is even more afraid of its own beastly libido (this neurosis
is the subject of Weyland Young's *Eros Denied*). Whether rational (as in
Plato's *Republic*) or hysterical (as in the Salem witch trials) such a fear

attacks the culture's particular libido image. The literature of sexuality has been every bit as victimized by hysteria as were Sacco and Vanzetti. Pornography, it is supposed, constitutes both a social and psychic threat. Society will be terrorized by the rampant lewdness induced by pornographic books— our wives and daughters raped, law and order dissolved. And our sons (somebody has to do the raping) will either be driven to mad carnality or will become idiots driveling in the wake of luxurious onanism. We—i.e. the patriarchal we—of course remain impervious.

The legal starting point is the social threat. And here the machinations of the courts at all levels to find evidence of social value in "pornographic" books have resulted in monumental irrelevance. While there are responsible decisions, such as Judge Woolsey's judgment in favor of Ulysses, their irony is that, however good they are in particular, they are based on the wrongheaded obscenity laws. Judge Woolsey was critically right to find that Ulysses is a complex work, the end of which is not obscenity. But he felt compelled to explain away the pornography and obscenity that are in the novel in order to grant its freedom. The real issue is articulated by Judge Frank's dissenting opinion about the Roth case in 1956. He defined the issue as whether or not pornography, quite distinctly from its social or artistic merit, constitutes a "clear and present danger" to society. He argues that there is no evidence that it does and that such research as has been done is either inconclusive or negates the idea that crimes or neuroses are caused by pornography. Until such time as there is evidence of this, Judge Frank's seems to me the only reasonable standard. There is nevertheless the kind of decision reached through the Supreme Court's recent caprice in the Ginzberg case. In that decision, incisively criticized by Justice Douglas, the character of the book is determined by the kind of advertising with which it is merchandised! An observation of censorship in Rights and Writers suggests the sort of patriarchal hysteria which seems to prompt such decisions: "We know of no case where any juror or judge has admitted that he found material erotically stimulating or a stimulus to irregular conduct; on the contrary, the expression of concern is always that someone else or some other class of people will be corrupted."

We don't prosecute books or television for misrepresenting marriage, or politics, or religion, or war. But we do prosecute where we think sex has been misrepresented. Plato, for all the dangers of his moral metaphysics, would have at least prosecuted all supposed stupidities equally. It would be neither more nor less criminal in his republic to represent man as pure sexuality than it would be to represent marriage as pure idyll or God as pure saccharine.

As usual in the event of emergency, it's women and children first. But such data as we have (e.g. the Kinsey reports, and the Glueck studies for the Harvard Law School) indicate that pornography has little or no effect on women or children. There probably is a psychic threat, but a threat no greater than that posed by any popular fantasy literature. Emma Bovary shows that a mind deluded by romance will make a bad job of reality. That is the danger of romance or fantasy whenever and in whatever way it dominates the mind. And pornography is a kind of romance but no more socially or psychically pernicious than the romance of passion that dominates the lives of Emma Bovary or Heathcliff or the mundane romance of *Please Don't Eat the Daisies.* The representation of life as all passion or all idyll or all sexuality is a delusion but not one that will determine the behavior of any but an already pathological personality. A *preoccupation* with pornography or any other kind of romance may be an index of mental imbalance or even potential criminality, but it is certainly not a cause.

limitless potency, limitless libido

To understand the contemporary working of pornography we must conceive the term in its widest context. Originally it signified writings about prostitutes. But as amateur promiscuity has increasingly supplied erotic fantasy material, pornography has created a new and larger being, *homo sexualis.* This has two images, the erect phallus and the carnal woman. The phallic symbol has become not only a psychological and literary commonplace, but also a cultural joke, and we are long since accustomed to finding one in everything from a new Buick to the Empire State Building. But the female image of *homo sexualis*—the essential pornographic image—is never funny, even in parody. Al Capp's cartoon women, for example, parody this image, enormously breasted and buttocked. But even the parody rides the edge of lust, and these images are much more desirable than ridiculous. For the pornographic world is peopled with men of limitless potency and women of limitless libido. O, the protagonist in *Story of O,* is a good contemporary example. No concerns in the narrative are allowed to obscure the translation of her total existence into terms of sexuality.

In what is perhaps the best critical study of pornography, *Pornography and the Law,* Eberhard and Phyllis Kronhausen observe that, "Both erotic realism and pornography, each in their own way, fulfill certain functions and answer basic needs in the human psyche which have been recognized by many societies and periods; for instance, in ancient Greece and Rome, in the Near East, as well as in China, Japan and India, where erotic art and literature have always been integral parts of the total culture." In whatever art form, pornography documents both man's neurotic and his archetypal concern with sexuality. The neurotic (not to be confused with the pathological) engagement with pornography is the private confrontation of the individual psyche with its sexual needs. The larger cultural engagement with pornography is the public confrontation with archetypal—and usually sub-liminal—sexual impulses. Pornography then, for better or worse, is the imaginative record of man's sexual will. Let's look briefly at some of the implications of this.

Steven Marcus (*The Other Victorians*) suggests that there is an inverse correspondence between a rising concentration on the dominating and sadistic image of masculine sexuality in pornography and the diminishing actuality of these qualities in real life. He finds evidence for this in the extravagant sense of phallic power so characteristic of pornography, where, as he puts it, "the penis becomes the man: it does the thrusting and not the man; it is its own agent." And in the world of pornography, where sexuality is the prime mover, the penis takes on a kind of omnipotence. Marcus tends to regard this extravagant phallic metaphor as another sign of pornography's juvenility. But its psychological dimensions signify something well beyond the rhetorical crudeness of its masculine vanity.

In her book *Psychic Energy* M. Esther Harding, a colleague and student of Jung, analyzes what might be called the sexual ages of man. The earliest stages are phallic, in which man is synecdochically conceived as penis. There are intermediate stages, where sexuality is stylized and idealized. The graphic representations of the early stages are of course the graffiti of the ages—phallic imagery and symbology. The intermediate stages are represented in the expansion of man's image from penis alone to the whole body—*e.g.* in stylized nude statuary. The advanced stages, dealing in emotional as well as physical sexuality, are more difficult of representation. The dynamics of psychic sexuality are beyond the static restrictions of painting and sculpture, but perhaps the film can overcome this. Yukio Mishima's recent film *Rites of Love and Death* or the Swedish film *Dear John* may be examples. But the point is that we do experience these archetypal sexual ages, perhaps all of them simultaneously, and in both a personal and cultural context. And it is a natural impulse to express them. Pornography, in the sense that I am defining it, is the primal manner of this expression. As our knowledge of sexuality increases and is assimilated into the culture, as psychological studies (we are still explicating Freud, Jung, *et al.*), sociological studies (such as the Kinsey reports), and physiological studies (such as Masters' and Johnson's recent *Human Sexual Response*) give us greater understanding of human sexuality, so will pornography, the literature of that sexuality, exhibit a greater artistic sophistication.

A comparison of the contemporary *Story of O* with the eighteenth century *Memoirs of a Woman of Pleasure* (*Fanny Hill*) will authenticate this evolutionary progress. *Fanny Hill* describes a prostitute's life, with the end of exploiting the obvious orgasmic stimuli in the subject. Fantasy is central to this end, and to induce it a kind of realism is affected through description of an occupation where rampant sexuality is made believable so that the reader can identify with it. Thus the action adopts the epistolary narrative device, the trappings of a specific sociological setting (eighteenth century London) and is resolved with a gratuitous moral apostrophe on virtue and honor. In these respects it parodies the techniques of the eighteenth century novel. Fanny's first letter puts it thus:

> Truth! stark, naked truth, is the word; and I will not so much as take the pains to bestow the strip of a gauze wrapper on it, but paint situations such as they actually rose to me in nature, careless of violating those laws of decency that were never made for such unreserved intimacies as ours; and you have too much sense, too much knowledge of the ORIGINALS themselves, to sniff prudishly and out of character at the PICTURES of them. The greatest men, those of the first and most leading taste, will not scruple adorning their private closets with nudities, though, in compliance with vulgar prejudices, they may not think them decent decorations of the staircase, or salon.

This is a good and true argument. But it is rather a rhetorical gambit persuading the reader to believe in the descriptions and not feel guilt, which would of course ruin their effect. From this point the novel turns a standard eighteenth century plot into a paradise of erotic fantasy. Fanny, a poor, provincial innocent, goes to London where she is deflowered and debauched by urban decadence and aristocratic profligacy. In a nice touch, the story is resolved when Fanny is reunited with her first despoiler and true love; they marry and live ever after in virtue, honor and penitence. The key here is that the story is essentially description of sexual acts to the end of inducing some kind of orgasmic fantasy. Although the standard situations of the early English novel are employed—Fanny's world is shot through with the vicissitudes of poverty and innocence in the clutches of City and Aristocracy— the story is altogether focused on fantastic sexuality. There is a suggestion of moral causality, but it is so slight and so overshadowed by sex that it signifies nothing. There is no attempt to *explore* any of the implicit moral or psychic problems.

The Story of O

The essence of *Fanny Hill* is simplicity, simplicity of theme and simplicity of description. *Story of O,* on the other hand, adopts the complexity of abstraction and metaphor so characteristic of the modern novel. It is a metaphor of love as libido. If that figure contains all the paraphernalia of pornography —whips, chains, tortures, sadism, masochism, masculine power, feminine submission, sexual anonymity (At one point O is blindfolded and brought into a room where "*A* hand seized one of her breasts, *a* mouth fastened on the tip of the other." Sex without superego.), and so on—it also contains the complex apparatus of the psyche. O submits herself to a brotherhood of sexuality which exploits and punishes her body, exorcises her will, dominates her total being, and finally is the cause of her self-destruction. She gives herself again to her surrogate lover, proving and taking refuge in her capacity of love; he abandons her also and she kills herself, but only after securing her master's permission.

The story provides, thus, two erotic points of view. From the masculine perspective it describes a complete liberation of the sexual libido. Men possess and enjoy O anonymously, without consequence or emotional responsibility. Her need for love brings her to them, which is a nice male power fantasy. And once they are through with her she is simply discarded; they have in fact the power of life and death, another nice male power fantasy. But from the female viewpoint the story arouses intense anxiety, a sure antidote to pornographic fantasy. O's captivity may be ended whenever she wishes, but to wish it is to forfeit the love she so desperately needs. Thus she is confronted constantly by the fear of loss. And of course she does lose that love, twice. And the consequence is suicide. Here is another classic female anxiety, that love for a man will subsume self identity, and the loss of the love will leave her without reason to be.

What is important here is that O becomes the ur-woman in quest of love. She is thus exposed to its complete domination and consequent agony. Is she, then, an allegorical figure, perhaps the first *Everywoman?* Certainly everything about her is feminine stereotype—her love, her submissiveness, her sexuality, her annihilation of self, her anxieties, everything. At one point in *Peyton Place* (also written, remember, by a woman) a young girl says to her paramour, "Come on Honey. Love me a little. . . . Come on Honey. . . . Hard. . . . Do it hard, Honey. Bite me a little. Hurt me a little." This is O's position; except she says, "Hurt me a *lot.*" On the one hand, she is the answer to every man's secret dream. On the other hand, she is an object awful in her implications. It is the former quality that makes her story pornographic. And it is the latter quality that takes her story beyond simplistic exploitation of sexual fantasy and lets it metaphorically explore a fundamental human condition.

Admittedly, these examples have higher artistic claims than most pornography. But I am interested here in its nature and artistic potential, and must consider therefore its highest stages of development. The hard core or commercial pornography is static and its ends are served by the simplest of descriptive techniques and rhetorical gambits (see Eberhard and Phyllis Kronhausen's *Pornography and the Law* and Steven Marcus' *The Other Victorians* for analyses of pornographic structure). But there is another and higher form of pornography which might be called *literary;* it is an exploration of human sexuality. This is real pornography (not what the Kronhausens call erotic realism). It does more than exploit its subject. We are, as Freud observed, *all* of us more or less neurotic. One aspect of human neurosis is the rhythm of expectations and frustrations which marks our sexual lives. Pornography on its lowest level exploits this rhythm by providing easy fantasy gratifications. On its highest level it *explores* this rhythm, its moral and psychic implications, and to the degree that it does this it is poetic. This is pornography being absorbed into what we call Literature, and it is represented by such works as *O*. The fact of pornography's evolution out of its own genre and into the larger literature means that pornography must also be considered as a rhetorical device for that literature. Faulkner, for example, although no mere pornographer, is certainly one of the most pornographic of modern writers. He often uses pornographic scenes and situations (the cockpit copulation in *Pylon*, the romance of Mink Snopes in *The Hamlet*, etc.) to articulate his total scheme. It is perhaps in this latter rhetorical role that pornography will assume its final form and have its greatest significance.

denying human sexuality

What I have been arguing is that pornography, like any literature, is a way of knowing. The irony of its subject, sex, is the irony of another social pariah, the whore. We either deny its literary existence or privately acknowledge our private intimacies with it; and we are correspondingly either astonished or embarrassed to meet it on the street. Critically, if we don't ignore pornography altogether, we condescend to it like reformed sugar-daddies. Legally we invoke "contemporary community standards" against it, as if they were not a fantasy morality derived from vestigial Puritanism rather than human experience. And thus we insure our ignorance of what it can tell us about the interaction of moral imagination and sexual being. Meanwhile science, having escaped community standards and academic condescension in the guise of a white coat, goes on documenting a reality we deny our imagination.

For Plato the true was necessarily the beautiful. For us the true is much more likely to be the ugly or grotesque. A whole tradition argues this. Stanley Kowalski calls on his "colored lights," but it is finally the bright white light of revelation that brings the play's moment of truth and beauty— Blanche, Stanley and Mitch all exposed, ugly and helpless. And Martha and George in *Who's Afraid of Virginia Woolf* expend their full energies to show their young guests the true, the blushful Hippocrene—their monumental ugliness. Our literature adopts an aesthetic that aims to reveal the ugly as the true, and it often uses the sexual libido, which our culture has turned into a species of the ugly, as part of its rhetoric.

For the eighteenth and nineteenth centuries ugliness was artistically tolerable only when used as a dialectical agent (*e.g.*, satire) to enforce the idea of a beautiful and harmonious nature. It was an aesthetic that dismissed all aberrations as irrelevant. Contemporary aesthetic practice uses this process but reverses the values. Like Satan, it says, "Evil, be thou my good," and plays the role of devil's advocate, using the ugly to penetrate a cosmos no longer thought to be either benevolent or harmonious. It is at best indifferent, at worst malign. The ugly, then, becomes an ironic figure of revelation, exposing an implacable universe unrelieved by moral or spiritual design. Sartre's concepts of *slime* and *nausea* are eloquent statements of an aesthetic of the ugly. And the Theater of the Absurd is its most prominent practitioner. Pornography, the kind represented by *Story of O,* is a manifestation of the ugly. It does not romanticize sexuality; sex, unlike John's other wife, is not beautiful. It is simply there, at the center of man's life, dominating love, aspiration, happiness, all human experience.

Perhaps, as Freud suggests, our sexual impulses cannot be gratified without being cultural outlaws. Perhaps sexuality requires being worked out through cultural taboos. If so, this argues a fearful human necessity. We take LSD trips in an effort to find (or escape from) the true and maybe the beautiful. The danger is that our vision (perhaps of ourselves) will be destructive and make us flip altogether. But our ignorance is desperate enough so that we take the risk. Although the dangers are much smaller, pornography is part of this contemporaneous urgency to pursue the true. It too explores the unknown and therefore fearful in us. Our glimpses into that world refute our private and public lies. We can keep going—into the psyche as into space—and risk the dislocations that new knowledge brings, or we can collapse at the naked sight of ourselves. Not to explore the impulse to pornography is a form of denying human sexuality. We are, willy-nilly, brought to the overriding question of the modern imagination: how much deceit can we afford?

For Discussion

1. What purpose does the myth serve in opening the essay?
2. In what ways is pornography seen as a social threat? As a psychic threat? How does Michelson assess these threats?
3. Basically, Judge Woolsey's decision in the *Ulysses* case was that an otherwise pornographic book should not be banned if it has redeeming social values. In your opinion how valid is this decision as a criterion for judging what can be read?
4. Explain the purpose of each of the various references to studies of pornography.
5. What does Michelson say is the chief difference between *Fanny Hill* and *The Story of O*?

6. Discuss the levels of pornography as Michelson defines them.
7. What does Michelson say about the relationship of sex and romance? (Also see Lawrence, "Sex Versus Loveliness.")
8. In justifying pornography, how is Michelson justifying literature and art generally?
9. How would you define pornography? What is your position regarding it?
10. What discursive qualities are evident in this essay? How do they affect the strength of the argument?

ROBERT S. BROWNE

The Case for Black Separatism

The following article by Robert S. Browne has received wide
circulation since its appearance in *Ramparts* in 1967, following
the Black Power Conference at which the resolution advocating
separatism was adopted. A member of the Advisory Committee
for the Conference, Browne is an assistant professor at Fairleigh
Dickinson University in New Jersey and a frequent contributor
to *The New Republic*.

If the mass media are to be believed, the most sensational information
leaked to the general public from the closed sessions of the Conference on
Black Power, recently held in Newark, New Jersey, concerned the adoption
of a resolution which favored the partitioning of the U.S. into two separate
nations. Understandably, any effort to split the U.S., or any other major
power, is certainly prime news—witness the storm which President de Gaulle
aroused by his support for French separatism in Canada. Consequently, the
attention which the press has focused on this resolution is not unexpected.
Unfortunately, however, there has been some confusion as to exactly what
the resolution says, and considerably more misunderstanding of the traumatic
agony which lies behind it. As the individual who had the responsibility for
reading this resolution to the Conference for adoption, I should like to clarify
some of this confusion for black and white readers alike. (I wish to make it
clear at the outset that I do not speak in any official capacity for the
Conference.)

With respect to the content of the resolution, it reads as follows (as
amended from the floor):

Whereas the black people in America have been systematically op-
pressed by their white fellow countrymen

Whereas there is little prospect that this oppression can be terminated,
peacefully or otherwise, within the foreseeable future

Reprinted by permission of the author.

Whereas the black people do not wish to be absorbed into the larger white community

Whereas the black people in America find that their interests are in contradiction with those of white America

Whereas the black people in America are psychologically handicapped by virtue of their having no national homeland

Whereas the physical, moral, ethical, and aesthetic standards of white American society are not those of black society and indeed do violence to the self-image of the black man

Whereas black people were among the earliest immigrants to America, having been ruthlessly separated from their fatherland, and have made a major contribution to America's development, most of this contribution having been uncompensated, and

Recognizing that efforts are already well advanced for the convening of a Constitutional Convention for the purpose of revising the Constitution of the U.S. for the first time since America's inception, then

Be it resolved that the Black Power Conference initiate a national dialogue on the desirability of partitioning the U.S. into two separate and independent nations, one to be a homeland for white and the other to be a homeland for black Americans.

Clearly, this is not a radical resolution. Like the Declaration of Independence, it enumerates some of the felt grievances of the people. But it is more moderate in tone than Jefferson's Declaration and its action clause stops considerably short of that of the 1776 document. Significantly, it asks not for separation but merely for dialogue. In this sense, it is possibly the mildest resolution which the Conference adopted.

. . .

I frankly do not know how many blacks would favor a separatist solution of the type proposed. Many of us suffer from a serious inferiority complex about our race and may doubt our ability to operate a successful nation, despite the inspiring example of several of the African countries which came into independence with handicaps of illiteracy and lack of capital far more serious than those we would face. My experience suggests that the number of blacks who would support the idea of partitioning is nevertheless sufficient to warrant serious national consideration of its feasibility. I have listened to the voices of my people and I know that they are desperate. Talk of violence and of revolution hangs heavy in the atmosphere of both black and white America. Not surprisingly, black leadership is in the vanguard of those who recognize and articulate the need for drastic changes in American society. However, the black community's role in effecting these changes remains unresolved. Partition has the significant advantage of offering a path which, with proper goodwill, can be trod nonviolently. It has the disadvantage of speaking primarily to the basic problem facing black America and not to the problems of the total society. Clearly, *some* new path will have to be taken to relieve the desperation of black Americans. Partition is being offered as one way out. Does white America have an equally reasonable counter-proposal?

The sources of this desperation of the Negro should have been fairly well known by now. In case they were not, the resolution's drafters took the Jeffersonian view that "a decent respect of the opinions of mankind requires that they should declare the causes which impel them to the separation." Yet, in their formalized brevity, the "whereas" clauses of the resolution hardly convey the full panoply of frustrations which have driven some blacks to an endorsement of separatism.

Unquestionably, the gloomy statistics on black unemployment, income, housing and disease create the general framework for this despair—statistics which the Negro must read against the background of a decade of both unprecedented national civil rights activity and unprecedented national prosperity. The black community clearly sees itself getting a progressively smaller share of the pie as the pie itself grows ever larger. Coupled with these economic statistics are the sociological ones: schools are more segregated than ever before; cities are more ghettoized in 1967 than in 1937.

For the upper middle class Negro, as for most whites, these figures on the deterioration of the Negro's position since World War II are sometimes difficult to grasp, for on the surface much progress is in evidence. Well scrubbed, nattily dressed Negroes are to be seen working in myriad sorts of establishments from which they were formerly barred; they are increasingly seen at private social functions of upper class whites; they are even to be glimpsed occasionally in advertisements for well known products, and in non-stereotype roles in TV and film entertainment. A Negro sits on the Supreme Court, another sits on the Federal Reserve Board, and one has been elected to the Senate from a primarily white constituency.

Indeed, it is these very strides which have been, at least in part, responsible for the current crisis in Negro leadership. The traditional leaders point with pride to their accomplishments and conclude that they are pushing matters at as fast a pace as the white society will permit. Meanwhile, the great bulk of the black community sinks ever lower, increasingly resentful of its worsening position vis-a-vis the black elite as well as vis-a-vis the whites. As a result, the black masses are becoming politicized, are developing a class consciousness, and are rejecting the existing Negro leadership. An unexpected, although possibly temporary, interruption in this process of polarization of the black community occurred last winter as fallout from the Adam Powell incident. The manner in which virtually all segments of the white community openly supported the attack on Congressman Powell, the supreme symbol of black achievement of power in America, served as an eye-opener to all blacks, whatever their level of sophistication and economic achievement. If Powell, the epitome of power, was not safe, then clearly no black man was safe and it was obviously naive to think otherwise. The Powell incident, by the very grossness of its racism, built a precarious bridge between the increasingly bitter, increasingly segregated black masses, and the increasingly affluent, increasingly integrated black middle class. Their interests were once again shown to be identical, even if involuntarily so.

Clearly, it is as a measure of self-defense that the black community has begun to draw together and even to discuss separatism. Let every liberal white American ponder this.

The bridge between the two segments of the black community is by no means a stable one, largely because of the schizophrenia of the black middle class. Whereas the black masses, both those in the rural South and those who have flooded into Northern cities in the past quarter century, aspire primarily for a higher standard of living and for freedom from the indignities and oppressions which their blackness has attracted to them, the middle-class Negroes have developed more subtle tastes. To varying degrees, these Negroes have become "assimilated" into white society and lead lives which are spiritually dependent upon the white community in a way that the mass of Negroes could never comprehend. For them, an integrated America is fast becoming a reality and the thrust of their effort is to extend the integration concept to every corner of the country. Their schizophrenia arises from the inescapable reminders of their vulnerability. Even with a Ph.D., a Nobel prize, a Congressional Medal of Honor or a vast fortune, a Negro is still a "nigger" to many (most?) white Americans and the society does not let him forget it for very long. Nor does the sensitive Negro really want to forget it; he wants to change it.

But perhaps the most unsettling of all the factors affecting the mental health of the black man in this white society is the matter of identification. It can be exemplified by the poignant, untold agony of raising black, kinky-haired children in a society where the standard of beauty is a milk-white skin and long, straight hair. To convince a black child that she is beautiful when every channel of value formation in the society is telling her the opposite is a heart-rending and well-nigh impossible task. It is a challenge which confronts all Negroes, irrespective of their social and economic class, but the difficulty of dealing with it is likely to vary directly with the degree to which the Negro family leads an integrated existence. A black child in a predominantly black school may realize that she doesn't look like the pictures in the books, magazines and TV advertisements, but at least she looks like her schoolmates and neighbors. The black child in a predominantly white school and neighborhood lacks even this basis for identification.

This identity problem is, of course, not peculiar to the Negro. Minorities of all sorts encounter it in one form or another—the immigrant who speaks with an accent; the Jewish child who doesn't celebrate Christmas; the Oriental whose eyes are slanted. But for the Negro the problem has a special dimension, for in the American ethos a black man is not only "different," he is classed as ugly and inferior. This is not an easy situation to deal with, and the manner in which a Negro chooses to handle it will both be determined by and [become] a determinant of his larger political outlook. He can deal with it as an integrationist, accepting his child as being ugly by prevailing standards and urging him to excel in other ways to prove his worth; or he can deal with it as a black nationalist, telling the child that he is not a freak but rather part of a larger international community of black-skinned, kinky-haired people who have a beauty of their own, a glorious history and a great future. In short, he can replace shame with pride, inferiority with dignity, by imbuing the child with what is coming to be known as black nationalism. The growing population of this viewpoint is evidenced by the appearance of "natural" hair styles among Negro youth and the surge of interest in African and Negro culture and history.

Black Power may not be the ideal slogan to describe this new self-image which the black American is developing, for to guilt-ridden whites the slogan conjures up violence, anarchy and revenge. To frustrated blacks, however, it symbolizes unity and a newly found pride in the blackness with which the Creator endowed us and which we realize must always be our mark of identification. Heretofore this blackness has been a stigma, a curse with which we were born. Black Power means that this curse will henceforth be a badge of pride rather than of scorn. It marks the end of an era in which black men devoted themselves to pathetic attempts to be white men and inaugurated an era in which black people will set their own standards of beauty, conduct and accomplishment.

Is this new black consciousness in irreconcilable conflict with the larger American society? In a sense, the heart of the American cultural problem has always been the need to harmonize the inherent contradiction between racial (or national) identity with integration into the melting pot which was America. In the century since the Civil War, the society has made little effort to find a means to afford the black minority a sense of racial pride and independence while at the same time accepting it as a full participant in the larger society. Now that the implications of this failure are becoming apparent, the black community seems to be saying, "Forget it! We'll solve our own problems." Integration, which never had a high priority among the black masses, is now being written off by them as being not only unattainable but actually harmful—driving a wedge between the black masses and the so-called Negro elite. To these developments has been added the momentous realization by many "integrated" Negroes that, in the U.S., full integration can only mean full assimiliation—a loss of racial identity. This sobering prospect has caused many a black integrationist to pause and reflect, even as have his similarly challenged Jewish counterparts. Thus, within the black community there are two separate challenges to the traditional integration policy which has long constituted the major objective of established Negro leadership. There is the general skepticism that the Negro, even after having transformed himself into a white blackman, will enjoy full acceptance into American society; and there is the longer-range doubt that even should complete integration somehow be achieved, it would prove to be really desirable, for its price may be the total absorption and disappearance of the race —a sort of painless genocide.

Understandably, it is the black masses who have most vociferously articulated these dangers of assimiliation, for they have watched with alarm as the more fortunate among their ranks have gradually risen to the top only to be promptly "integrated" off into the white community—absorbed into another culture, often with undisguised contempt for all that had previously constituted their heritage. Also, it was the black masses who first perceived that integration actually increases the white community's control over the black one by destroying black institutions, and by absorbing black leadership and coinciding its interests with those of the white community. The international "brain drain" has its counterpart in the black community, which is constantly being denuded of its best trained people and many of its natural leaders. Black institutions of all sorts—colleges, newspapers, banks, even community organizations—are all experiencing the loss of their better people to the newly available openings in white establishments, thereby lowering the quality of the Negro organizations and in some cases causing their demise or increasing their dependence on whites for survival. Such injurious, if unintended, side effects of integration have been felt in almost every layer of the black community.

If the foregoing analysis of the integration vs. separatism conflict exhausted the case for partition then we might conclude that the problems have all been dealt with before, by other immigrant groups in America. (It would be an erroneous conclusion, for while other groups may have encountered similar problems, their solutions do not work for us, alas.) But there remains yet another factor which is cooling the Negro's enthusiasm for the integrationist path: he is becoming distrustful of his fellow Americans.

The American culture is one of the youngest in the world. Furthermore, as has been pointed out repeatedly in recent years, it is essentially a culture which approves of violence, indeed enjoys it. Military expenditures absorb roughly half of the national budget. Violence predominates on the TV screen and the toys of violence are best selling items during the annual rites for the much praised but little imitated Prince of Peace. In Vietnam, the zeal with which America has pursued its effort to destroy a poor and illiterate peasantry has astonished civilized people around the globe. In such an atmosphere the Negro is understandably restive about the fate his white compatriots might have in store for him. The veiled threat by President Johnson at the time of the 1966 riots—suggesting that riots might beget pogroms and pointing out that Negroes are only ten per cent of the population—was not lost on most blacks. It enraged them, but it was a sobering thought. The manner in which Germany herded the Jews into concentration camps and ultimately into ovens was a solemn warning to minority peoples everywhere. The casualness with which America exterminated the Indians and later interned the Japanese suggests that there is no cause for the Negro to feel complacent about his security in the U.S. He finds little consolation in the assurance that if it does become necessary to place him in concentration camps it will only be as a means of protecting him from uncontrollable whites: "protective incarceration," to use governmental jargonese.

The very fact that such alternatives are becoming serious topics of discussion has exposed the Negro's already raw and sensitive psyche to yet another heretofore unfelt vulnerability—the insecurity which he suffers as a result of having no homeland which he can honestly feel his own. Among the major ethno-cultural groups in the world he is unique in this respect. As the Jewish drama during and following World War II painfully demonstrated, a national homeland is a primordial and urgent need for a people, even though its benefits do not always lend themselves to ready measurement. For some, the homeland constitutes a vital place of refuge from the strains of a life led too long within a foreign environment. For others, the need to reside in the homeland is considerably less intense than the need for merely knowing that such a homeland exists. The benefit to the expatriate is psychological, a sense of security in knowing that he belongs to a culturally and politically identifiable community. No doubt this phenomenon largely accounts for the fact that both the West Indian Negro and the Puerto Rican exhibit considerably more self-assurance than does the American Negro, for both of the former groups have ties to an identifiable homeland which honors and preserves their cultural heritage.

It has been marveled that we American Negroes, almost alone among the cultural groups of the world, exhibit no sense of nationhood. Perhaps it is true that we do lack this sense, but there seems to be little doubt that the absence of a homeland exacts a severe if unconscious price from our psyche. Theoretically, our homeland is the U.S.A. We pledge allegiance to the stars and stripes and sing the national anthem. But from the age when we first begin to sense that we are somehow "different," that we are victimized, these rituals begin to mean less to us than to our white compatriots. For many of us they become form without substance; for others they become a cruel and bitter mockery of our dignity and good sense; for relatively few of us do they retain a significance in any way comparable to their hold on our white brethren.

The recent coming into independence of many African states stimulated some interest among Negroes that independent Africa might become the homeland which they so desperately needed. A few made the journey and experienced a newly-founded sense of community and racial dignity. For many who went, however, the gratifying racial fraternity which they experienced was insufficient to compensate for the cultural estrangement which accompanied it. They had been away from Africa for too long and the differences in language, food and custom barred them from experiencing the "at home" sensation which they were eagerly seeking. Symbolically, independent Africa could serve them as a homeland: practically, it could not. Their search continues—a search for a place where they can experience the security which comes from being a part of the majority culture, free at last from the inhibiting effects of cultural repression and induced cultural timidity and shame.

If we have been separated from Africa for so long that we are no longer quite at ease there, then we are left with only one place to make our home, and that is this land to which we were brought in chains. Justice would indicate such a solution in any case, for it is North America, not Africa, into which our toil and effort have been poured. This land is our rightful home and we are well within our rights in demanding an opportunity to enjoy it on the same terms as the other immigrants who have helped to develop it. Since few whites will deny the justice of this claim, it is paradoxical that we are offered the option of exercising this birthright only on the condition that we abandon our culture, deny our race and integrate ourselves into the white community. The "accepted" Negro, the "integrated" Negro, are mere euphemisms which hide a cruel and relentless cultural destruction which is sometimes agonizing to the middle-class Negro but which is becoming intolerable to the black masses. A Negro who refuses to yield his identity and to ape the white model finds he can survive only by rejecting the entire white society, which must ultimately mean challenging the law and the law enforcement mechanisms. On the other hand, if he abandons his cultural heritage and succumbs to the lure of integration, he risks certain rejection and humiliation along the way, with absolutely no guarantee of ever achieving complete acceptance. That such unsatisfactory options are leading to almost continuous disruption of our society should hardly be cause for surprise.

Partition offers one way out of this tragic situation. Many will condemn it as a defeatist solution, but what they see as defeatism might better be described as a frank facing up to the realities of American society. A society is stable only to the extent that there exists a basic core of value judgments which is unthinkingly accepted by the great bulk of its members. Increasingly, Negroes are demonstrating that they have some reservations about the common core of values which underlie American society—whether because they had little to do with formulating these values or because they feel them to be weighted against their interests. For the Negro in the ghetto especially, the society's values are often as alien and as damaging to him as is its standard of beauty. They are both built on premises which are for him unattainable and often irrelevant.

The alleged disproportionately large number of Negro law violators, of unwed mothers, of non-working adults *may* be indicators that the supposed community of values is much weaker than had been supposed, although I am not unaware of additional racial socio-economic reasons for these statistics. But whatever the reasons for observed behavioral differences, there is clearly no reason *why* the Negro should not have his own ideas about what the societal organization should be. The Anglo-Saxon system of organizing human relationships has certainly not proved itself to be superior to all other systems, and the Negro is likely to be more acutely aware of this fact than most Americans.

Certainly partition would entail enormous initial hardships. But these hardships should be weighed against the prospects of prolonged and intensified racial strife stretching into the indefinite future. Indeed, the social fabric of America is far more likely to be able to withstand the strains of a partitioning of the country than those of an extended race war. Indeed, if it happened that the principle of partition were harmoniously accepted by most Americans as the preferable solution, it is possible that only voluntary transfers of population would be necessary. Conceivably, no one would be forced to move against his will. Those Negroes who wanted to migrate to the new nation ("New Africa"?) could do so, and their counterparts could move to the United States. The France-Algeria arrangements could be used as a model. (To put the question of mass transference of populations into its proper perspective, it is well to remember that the U.S. is currently witnessing one of history's great demographic movements, although most Americans are totally unaware of it. In the past 25 years, some four million Negroes, roughly 20 per cent of the total Negro population, have migrated from the rural South to the cities of the North and West. History records few such massive population transfers.)

There is an excellent chance that, following partition, neither nation would be overtly racist. The basis for the present racial animosity would be largely removed by the very act of separation. Reciprocal tourism might very well become a leading industry for both nations, for the relations between the races would finally be on a healthy, equalitarian basis. A confederation of the two states, perhaps joined by Canada, Mexico and other nations, could conceivably emerge at some future time.

Divorce is an inherent aspect of the American tradition. It terminates the misery of an enforced but unhappy union, relieves the tension and avoids the risk of more serious consequences. It is increasingly apparent to blacks and whites alike that their national marriage has been a disastrous failure. Consequently, in the search for ways to remedy this tragic situation, divorce should obviously not be ruled out as a possible solution. The Black Power Conference resolution asks America to do no more than to give it serious consideration.

Even in the black ghettos it may require considerable time before the idea of partitioning can be evaluated dispassionately, for the Negro has never rejected the indoctrination which he receives in "Americana"; rather, his problem is that he has accepted it too readily, only to discover that it was not meant to apply to him.

But the mood of the ghetto is in a state of unprecedented change and in this new climate a sense of nationhood is groping for expression. It may hold within it the key to mental health for black America, and its ultimate outcome cannot now be foreseen. It may lead to two separate nations or it may lead us toward some as yet untried type of human community vastly superior to the present system of competing nationalisms. The new world community which mankind so desperately needs may rise phoenix-like from the collapsing, unworkable old order. Intelligent, imaginative men must not shrink from exploring fearlessly any avenue which might lead mankind to this new world community. Men may sometimes hate other men. Fortunately, they do not hate mankind. This is the solid foundation upon which we must try to build.

For Discussion

1. What similarities and differences does the resolution favoring partitioning have with the Declaration of Independence? How does Browne go on to develop the comparison?
2. In the face of seeming progress, how has the Negro's position deteriorated since World War II?
3. What has been happening to the class structure of black society in recent years? Why?
4. What are the problems of black identity? For further exploration, see the article by Malcolm X, who is speaking to a black audience.
5. In what way is Black Power a solution to the black American's identity problem? (Also see Carmichael.) In what way is integration a threat to his identity?
6. What do you think of Browne's analogy between the black American and the German Jew? How real are his fears of possible pogroms? Does our racial history support this possibility?
7. Discuss the pro's and con's of Africa as "homeland."

8. What argument can you make against partitioning? What alternatives can you suggest?
9. The author is primarily concerned with letting his subject speak for itself; however, he cannot help revealing his attitude toward his subject and his audience. What is it?

SYLVIA MEAGHER

Accessories After the Fact

Sylvia Meagher resides in New York City, where she writes for such magazines as *Esquire* and *Studies on the Left*. She has worked in the field of international public health and has lectured widely throughout the United States and Canada. Universally considered the most knowledgeable person in the field of published documents relating to the assassination of President Kennedy, she compiled—on her own—the only index to the hastily assembled twenty-six volumes of Hearings and Exhibits of the Warren Commission, which investigated and reported the circumstances surrounding the assassination. *Accessories After the Fact,* from which the following excerpts are taken, is an exhaustive study of the Report in the light of subsequent research by Meagher and others.

Foreword

During the eight o'clock news that morning the face of Dallas Police Chief Jesse E. Curry filled the television screen with assurances that every possible precaution had been taken to ensure the safety of President John Fitzgerald Kennedy. At two o'clock New York time I sat in my office with white-faced colleagues, listening to news bulletins over a transistor radio. President Kennedy had been shot while riding in a motorcade in Dallas.

We all remembered the indignities suffered by UN Ambassador Adlai Stevenson in Dallas less than a month before when a spitting, savage mob of right-wing extremists had subjected him to the hatred and fury they felt for the United Nations, which he represented and symbolized. The screaming insults, the blows, and the spittle were intended for all who believed in the United Nations. They were intended for those who hoped and worked for an end to the cold war and a beginning of genuine peace, for equality and mutual respect among men, for the rule of law and an end to brute violence—aims which had animated President Kennedy's historic speech at American University in June 1963.

At 2:30 p.m. the voice on the radio said with solemn anquish, "The President is dead." Someone in the room screamed with shock and grief. Someone cursed the John Birch Society and its kind. "Don't worry," I said derisively, "you'll see, it was a Communist who did it."

An hour later, back at the television screen on which Curry earlier had reassured the audience, I heard that Lee Harvey Oswald—a man with a Russian wife and a history of pro-Castro activities—had been taken into custody.

This is the personal background for my instantaneous skepticism about the official version of what happened in Dallas on November 22, 1963. In the three years that have followed, intensive study of the evidence against the alleged lone assassin has convinced me, as intuition alone could not, that the truth about Dallas remains unknown and that Lee Harvey Oswald may well have been innocent.

President John Fitzgerald Kennedy arrived at Love Field in Dallas, Texas, on Friday, November 22, 1963 at 11:40 a.m. In his party were his wife Jacqueline Kennedy, Vice President Lyndon B. Johnson and Mrs. Johnson, Governor of Texas John B. Connally, Jr., and Mrs. Connally, and several prominent members of the Senate and the House. One purpose of the Presidential visit to Texas was to seek a reconciliation between warring factions within the state's Democratic Party. Despite apprehension about the President's safety in this city of right-wing activities, the President proceeded in his open car in a motorcade from the airfield toward the Trade Mart Building, where he was to be guest of honor at a luncheon organized by Dallas civic and business leaders.

At 12:30 p.m. the Presidential car proceeded from Houston Street to Elm Street, approaching a triple underpass. Shots rang out. The President and Governor Connally, who was seated directly in front of him, were hit.

The car raced to Parkland Hospital, where the President was taken to an emergency room and futile attempts were made to save his life. He was declared dead at 1 p.m. Governor Connally was seriously wounded, underwent surgery, and in due course recovered from his bullet wounds.

After President Kennedy was pronounced dead, Vice President Johnson left Parkland Hospital under heavy security protection, proceeding to Love Field. He boarded the Presidential airplane and at 2:38 p.m. took the oath of office and became the thirty-sixth President of the United States.

As Johnson was sworn into office, Lee Harvey Oswald was undergoing interrogation at the Dallas police headquarters on suspicion of shooting to death a patrolman, J. D. Tippit, who was murdered shortly after 1 p.m. on a street in Oak Cliff, a section of Dallas some distance from the scene of the assassination. Oswald was employed at the Texas School Book Depository on Elm Street, where witnesses had reported a man shooting at the motorcade from the sixth-floor southeast corner window. Within little more than a minute after the President and the Governor were shot, Oswald had been encountered on the second floor of the Book Depository by a motorcycle officer and the Book Depository superintendent; they found in Oswald's demeanor and appearance no cause for suspicion and proceeded immediately to the roof of the building.

Some time later, apparently 30 or 40 minutes after the encounter, the superintendent reported to the Dallas police captain in charge of homicide that Oswald was missing. The captain placed Oswald under suspicion of the assassination but before sending out an alarm for the missing man learned that Oswald was under arrest for the Tippit killing.

Oswald remained in police custody from Friday afternoon until Sunday morning. The Dallas police and district attorney quickly identified him as a defector who had lived in the Soviet Union, returned to the United States with a Russian wife, and became active in pro-Castro activities. While they acknowledged that Oswald steadfastly claimed that he was innocent of both the assassination and the murder of the policeman, the Dallas authorities repeatedly told the press and the public that his guilt was certain, giving a running account of evidence—real and imaginary—which they regarded as conclusive.

The police announced that Oswald would be transferred to the county jail on Sunday morning. Anonymous telephone calls the night before the transfer threatened that Oswald would be seized and killed, yet the plans for a public transfer proceeded.

Handcuffed to a detective and flanked by officers, Oswald was escorted to the police basement to begin the removal to the county jail. Suddenly, a man in the crowd of reporters and plainclothesmen fired a revolver pointblank, felling the prisoner. Oswald was removed to Parkland Hospital, where he died about two hours later. His killer, Jack Ruby, proprietor of a stripjoint, was to die of cancer in the same hospital some three years later.

The police charges that Oswald, a Marxist, had committed the assassination caused public misgivings, for it was a most strange denouement to the widespread assumption immediately after the President's death that he had been killed by the same right-wing fanatics who had abused Adlai Stevenson. The public's anxieties were compounded by the murder of Oswald in the police basement by Ruby, a known police buff. Dallas officials were denounced on every side for their mishandling of events at every stage; not even the authoritative weight of the Federal Bureau of Investigation sufficed in this instance to make the police version of the assassination credible to the American public or to observers abroad.

No one outside of Dallas was prepared to agree that, as police spokesmen said upon Oswald's death, "the case is closed." One week after the assassination, on November 29, 1963, President Johnson appointed a Commission, chaired by the Chief Justice of the U.S. Supreme Court, to "satisfy itself that the truth is known as far as it can be discovered and to report its findings and conclusions to him [the President], to the American people, and to the world."

The report of the President's Commission—the Warren Report—was published at the end of September 1964. In essence, its conclusions were the same as those of the Dallas authorities: Lee Harvey Oswald, acting alone and unaided, had assassinated the President and murdered a police officer. Two months later, at the end of November 1964, 26 volumes of Hearings and Exhibits were published, assertedly presenting the testimony and evidence upon which the Warren Report was predicated.

This book examines the correlation, or lack of correlation, between the Report on the one hand and the Hearings and Exhibits on the other. The first pronounces Oswald guilty; the second, instead of corroborating the verdict reached by the Warren Commission, creates a reasonable doubt of Oswald's guilt and even a powerful presumption of his complete innocence of all the crimes of which he was accused.

On the day of the assassination the national climate of arrogance and passivity in the face of relentless violence—beatings, burnings, bombings, and shootings—yielded in some quarters to a sudden hour of humility and self-criticism. The painful moment passed quickly, for the official thesis of the lone, random assassin destroyed the impulse for national self-scrutiny and repentance. Thus, the climate of cruelty and barbaric hatred was restored after what was scarcely an interruption, and it was possible for Cuban émigrés—virtually with impunity and without regard for the hundreds of people who might be killed or injured—to fire a bazooka at the United Nations Headquarters building to express displeasure at the presence there of Che Guevara. Thus, it was possible for American Nazi thugs to assault peaceful citizens assembled at a public meeting in Dallas at Christmas 1965. Thus it is possible for Americans to look upon the napalmed children of Vietnam and listen to their terror and agony nightly over the television tubes, and to go about their daily business as usual.

Few people who have followed the events closely—and who are not indentured to the Establishment—conceive of the Kennedy assassination as anything but a political crime. That was the immediate and universal belief on November 22 before the opinion-makers got to work endorsing the official explanation of the complex mystery as Gospel and entreating all good citizens to do the same.

What is noteworthy about the advocates of the Report is that they defend their position largely by rhetoric, asking how anyone can possibly question the probity of Chief Justice Warren or Senator Russell (much as one may disagree with his views on race) or even Allen Dulles. They do not argue on evidence, because frequently they are uninformed, and in preaching their faith in the Warren Commission there is scarcely a platitude they are not willing to use. As a general rule, partisans of the Report have not read it, much less the 26 volumes of Hearings and Exhibits. In discussion and debate, they expose their unfamiliarity with the facts and expound all kinds of irresponsible errors and assumptions. The critics of the Report, on the other hand, have by and large performed arduous labor and taken great pains to master and document the available information with the scrupulousness which was to be expected but is not found in the Warren Report. Only a few of the critics who question or reject the Report have been guilty of careless or incomplete research; and while that is not to be condoned, it is nevertheless the Commission and not the lone critic which had the responsibility of establishing and reporting the truth, with virtually unlimited manpower and funds at its disposal.

It is not the critic's responsibility to explain why the Chief Justice signed such a Report or why Robert Kennedy accepts it or to answer other similar questions posed by the orthodox defenders. As critic Tom Katen has pointed out, instead of evaluating the evidence in terms of Robert Kennedy's acquiescence, his acquiescence should be evaluated in the light of the evidence. Nor is it the critic's responsibility to name the person or persons who committed the assassination if Oswald did not—another characteristic *non sequitur*. It is, on the other hand, clearly the responsibility of the authors and advocates of the Report to explain and justify its explicit documented defects. If they cannot or will not, then let the Government which has given us such a profoundly defective document—at a cost to the people of well over a million dollars—scrap the Report and commission one that will sustain its assertions and conclusions and survive the test of close scrutiny.

One of the most reprehensible actions of the Warren Commission is that it disbanded the moment it handed over its Report, leaving no individual or corporate entity to answer legitimate questions arising from demonstrable misstatements of fact in the Report. On September 27, 1964 the Commission, in effect, attempted to close the case no less firmly than the Dallas police tried to close it on November 25, 1963. Letters to Commission members or counsel posing factual questions on the basis of material cited in the official volumes have gone either completely unanswered, or unanswered in substance. The policy of silence is an affront to concerned citizens and invites the irresistible inference that the authors are unable to defend or justify the points at issue.[1]

The haste with which the Warren Commission closed its case is arresting, because when all is said and done it is the very same case that the Dallas police tried to close before Oswald's corpse grew cold. Chief Jesse E. Curry and Captain J. Will Fritz of the Dallas police and Dallas District Attorney Henry Wade said that Oswald was guilty. The Commission says so. Curry, Fritz, and Wade said that he acted alone and had no accomplices. The Commission says so. Curry, Fritz, and Wade said that he shot Tippit. The Commission says so. The Commission adds the charge that he tried to kill Major General Edwin A. Walker—but that is no tribute to its investigatory skill as opposed to that of the Dallas police. It is merely a story told by Marina Oswald and accepted by the Commission too readily by far, in disregard for the inconsistency between her story and the objective facts recorded contemporaneously or determined later, and in disregard for the doubts which arose about Marina Oswald's credibility when unyielding facts forced the Commission to reject her matching story of an attempt by her husband to assassinate Richard M. Nixon.

The Commission's blatant bias for and against witnesses and its double standard of judging credibility are in themselves beyond belief. Marina Oswald's testimony is treated as impeccable, despite the ludicrous Nixon story and her poor showing under the sole cross-examination (by Senator Russell) to which she was subjected. Helen Markham is another star witness. If Mrs. Markham did not misstate the truth one can only say—as Counsel Joseph Ball said on a public platform—that she is an "utter screwball." It is not necessary to belabor the Commission's desperation in declaring her wild testimony as having "probative value." Having deemed "reliable" the testimony of Marina Oswald and Helen Markham, how does the Commission deal with witnesses who on the face of it have neither fabricated nor become embroiled in blatant self-contradiction nor raved confusedly? The

[1] In mid-1965 I addressed letters to former members of the Warren Commission (Gerald R. Ford, John Sherman Cooper, Earl Warren) and to members of the staff (lawyers J. Lee Rankin, Albert E. Jenner, Jr., Wesley J. Liebeler, and Melvin E. Eisenberg; and historian Alfred Goldberg), requesting clarification on various points of evidence. In four cases (Cooper, Goldberg, Liebeler, and Rankin) no reply was received. In one case, a former assistant counsel agreed to discuss the questions put to him by telephone, on a confidential basis and not for attribution. He was not able to resolve the relevant problems—indeed, he was not even aware of the existence of one piece of evidence (the actual full-page ad of Klein's Sporting Goods in the February 1963 *American Rifleman*, from which it is evident that the rifle ordered by "Hidell" was a different model from the rifle found in the Depository), which I sent to him at his request.

In the remaining cases, I received replies of a purely formal nature, referring me to others for the requested information, only to have the redirected queries go without reply. One such reply promised that the writer would send a substantive response to the questions raised in my letter during the week of July 19, 1965; the promised response has yet to arrive.

Commission decided that Seth Kantor was "mistaken." Buell Wesley Frazier and his sister—mistaken. W. W. Litchfield—mistaken or "lying." Wanda Helmick—mistaken or "lying." It dealt in the same way with Gertrude Hunter, Edith Whitworth, Roger Craig, Arnold Rowland, Victoria Adams, William Whaley, Albert Guy Bogard, Dial Ryder, C. A. Hamblen, Wilma Tice, and still others.

All those "mistaken" or "lying" witnesses have one thing in common: they gave evidence which in whole or in part was inconsistent with or antithetical to the official thesis of the lone psychotic assassin and the lone psychotic killer of the lone psychotic assassin. That was the thesis of the Dallas police and district attorney on November 25, 1963, and, with minor and inconsequential variations, the thesis of the Warren Commission a year later.

It has been said jokingly that the Dallas police are not so bad—look how quickly they caught Jack Ruby. Not so bad? They are brilliant. In some 48 hours they solved three murders of unparalleled complexity and mystery with the same conclusions as those reached a year later by the Chief Justice and his six eminent colleagues, the stable of bright young lawyers, the legions of investigators, and the regiment of criminology experts. The Dallas police achieved in a matter of some three days what the Commission achieved after an investigation said to be unprecedented in scope, depth, duration, and, we daresay, expense. Not many police departments can match the Dallas force.

In addition to the crimes and brutalities often committed by police and other officers of the law—not only in the South but in other regions— it is frequently alleged that police officers are found increasingly among the members of right-wing extremist organizations, several of which are known to collect arsenals and plan acts of violence and destruction.

The Dallas police permitted the most important prisoner in the history of Texas to be gunned down in their basement while handcuffed to a detective and flanked by officers. A few months later the Dallas police lost another prisoner, a woman who said she had worked for Ruby once, by suicide in one of their jail cells. Yet the same police solved the mystery of the assassination and the murder of Tippit with enough speed, authority, and skill to make one's mind reel. (Unfortunately they did not do nearly so well in the shooting of Warren Reynolds, a witness at the Tippit scene, a case which has remained unsolved since January 1964). It seems unfair that editorial writers first assailed the Dallas force with contempt, and then wrote dazzling tributes to the Warren Commission without retracting their unkind words about the hapless Dallas police. If one accepts and endorses the Warren Report, one must also commend the Dallas police for their swift, sure work, and vindicate them in their finding that Oswald was the lone assassin and that the case was closed.

The difficulty is that the editorial writers and partisans of the Report rushed into a chorus of superlatives before they could read the 888-page Report with requisite care, and long before the supporting documents and testimony were made available for study and comparison. When the Hearings and Exhibits were issued two months after the Report, there was another concert of praise, equally extravagant and premature. None of the favorable appraisals was conditional on study of the Hearings and Exhibits to see if they corroborated the assertions in the Report (except perhaps for a critique by Professor Herbert Packer) and few have been followed by a restatement, reiterating or modifying the initial appraisal on the basis of such study.

There is much mention of the 26 volumes of the Hearings and Exhibits but little familiarity with their contents, organization, or character. The first 15 volumes consist of transcripts of the testimony of witnesses. Volumes I through V present the testimony of witnesses heard by the Warren Commission itself—not by the full Commission, as a rule, but with two or three members present—in the chronological sequence of their appearances. Volumes VI through XV present the testimony taken in depositions—that is, testimony under oath taken by a Commission lawyer, usually in Dallas, in the presence of a court reporter—arranged not chronologically but in rough approximation of the area of evidence on which a witness testified.

Volumes XVI through XXVI consist of Exhibits. The first three volumes in this group consist of exhibits identified by number (CE *1*, CE *2*, etc.) which were read into the record during the examination of the witnesses who testified before the Commission and whose testimony is found in Volumes I through V, as mentioned already. The next three volumes (Volumes XIX through XXI) consist of exhibits read into the record during the testimony of witnesses who provided the depositions contained in Volumes VI through XV; these exhibits, unlike the first group, are identified by the name of the witness and then by number (*Armstrong Exhibit No. 1, Paine Exhibit No. 2*, etc.). Finally, the last five volumes (XXII through XXVI) revert to numbered exhibits (CE *2003*, CE *2905*, etc.) selected by an unspecified criterion and not linked with specific testimony or entered on the record during the Hearings. (Thousands of cubic feet of Commission documents, consisting of reports and papers not converted into exhibits or published, are in the custody of the National Archives in Washington, D.C. Still other documents and materials are "classified" and not available for examination even at the Archives.)

Scrutiny of the Hearings and Exhibits, it must be acknowledged, is a monumental undertaking, involving the mastering of 26 thick volumes consisting of some 20,000 pages and more than ten million words. Few people have the time or fortitude for such a task. There are imposing obstacles even to the study of one or two distinct elements of the evidence in their entirety, to determine whether there is fidelity between the raw data and the account given in the Report. Such clearly delimited study would not require exorbitant time or effort if the Commission had included a subject index to make possible the tracing of the relevant testimony and documents to any single item of evidence.[2] The sheer mass of unclassified, unexplored data is enough to discourage an attempt to take inventory. It would be tantamount to a search for information in the *Encyclopedia Britannica* if the contents were untitled, unalphabetized, and in random sequence. It is hard to be unsympathetic to the student who shuddered and declined to read the Hearings and Exhibits word by word; however, it is equally hard to be sympathetic to the apologist for the Report who read the report superficially without skepticism or notice of its internal contradictions, publicly endorsing the findings and influencing opinion in favor of the Report while not bothering to read the Hearings and Exhibits.

It has been said that the American people are the only jury that Lee Harvey Oswald will ever have. It is our responsibility, then, to examine with utmost care and objectivity the evidence for and against him, and to reach an independent verdict. That responsibility cannot be delegated to others, however exalted their reputations and their honors. The first step must be the patient reading of the Hearings and Exhibits, imposing as the task is. If that reading demonstrates that the Report is an inaccurate, incomplete, or partisan synthesis of the raw material on which it supposedly relies, the authors—the Warren Commission—must account for the discrepancies in a manner that satisfies all doubt about their competence and their motives. If they cannot, or will not, provide such satisfaction, the people are entitled to a new investigation and a new report, by a competent and disinterested body submitting to the adversary procedure and permitting Oswald the maximum defense which can be given an accused man posthumously—an act of justice thus far denied him.

A new investigation utilizing the adversary procedure may theoretically also find that Oswald was the lone assassin. If such a finding is supported by unambiguous evidence which cannot be successfully challenged by the defense and if it is based on procedural decorum and equity, it will be acceptable. If there is a different finding, implicating co-assassins or absolving Oswald entirely, that too must meet the strictest tests of evidence and procedure.

A new investigation is imperative, because study of the Hearings and Exhibits has destroyed the grounds for confidence in the Warren Report. Study has shown the Report to contain (1) statements of fact which are inaccurate and untrue, in the light of the official Exhibits and objective

[2] Sylvia Meagher, *Subject Index to the Warren Report and Hearings and Exhibits* (New York: Scarecrow Press, 1966).

verification; (2) statements for which the citations fail to provide authentication; (3) misrepresentation of testimony; (4) omission of references to testimony inimical to findings in the Report; (5) suppression of findings favorable to Oswald; (6) incomplete investigation of suspicious circumstances which remain unexplained; (7) misleading statements resulting from inadequate attention to the contents of Exhibits; (8) failure to obtain testimony from crucial witnesses; and (9) assertions which are diametrically opposite to the logical inferences to be drawn from the relevant testimony or evidence.

In this constellation, as in the case of the "mistaken" witnesses, there is one constant: the effect of each inaccuracy, omission, or misrepresentation is to fortify the fragmentary and dubious evidence for the lone-assassin thesis and to minimize or suppress the contrary evidence. To that constant must be linked the Commission's unashamed refusal to permit Oswald a defense, as formally requested by his mother, in contravention of the most elementary concept of fairness and judicial procedure. The excuse that Marina Oswald, chief witness for the prosecution, did not desire a defender to represent the man whose guilt she proclaimed and reiterated hardly merits discussion. If that position had any moral or legal merit, it was vitiated completely when the Commission appointed the President of the American Bar Association, Walter Craig, "to participate in the investigation and to advise the Commission whether in his opinion the proceedings conformed to the basic principles of American justice."[3] This compromise was worse than meaningless. The Commission should not have required a reminder from the head of the ABA to recall that an accused person has a fundamental right to self-defense and the benefit of reasonable doubt—even posthumously—and in any case no such reminder issued from Mr. Craig or his appointed observers. Craig and his representatives participated in the examination of witnesses from February 27 to March 12, 1964 (after Marina, Marguerite, and Robert Oswald had completed their 468 pages of testimony), the most memorable of their infrequent interventions being a question hostile to Oswald's interests. Thereafter, by agreement with the Commission's chief counsel, the ABA representatives "made suggestions" to counsel instead of participating directly in the proceedings. Therefore, it became impossible to isolate any contribution on their part, much less to infer that there was any safeguard of the interests of the accused or the propriety of the proceedings. Moreover, the ABA observers took no part whatever in the examination of 395 witnesses who did not appear before the Commission but were deposed by counsel. The whole sorry arrangement was a mockery that further compromised the Commission's claim to impartiality.

Although the Commission excluded the use of the adversary procedure,

[3] WR xiv.

it did not hesitate to take advantage of its prerogatives—for example, engaging in the preparation of witnesses. The records show repeated instances of "dry runs" in which counsel questioned the witness in advance of his formal testimony. Such prior rehearsal is essential in a trial where the witness's story will be challenged in cross-examination, but in a fact-finding investigation resort to dry runs in advance of testimony can only feed suspicion that there was no search for truth but only for testimony which would buttress a preconceived and fixed conclusion.

A reading of the full testimony also leads to the irresistible conclusion that the witnesses fall into two general categories—the "friendly" and the "unfriendly"—which again is alien to the impartial fact-finding process. In the case of some "unfriendly" witnesses the Commission went beyond a show of antipathy and set out to discredit character. As Paul L. Freese wrote in the *New York University Law Review*, "The technique of character impeachment used by the Commission has disturbing implications."[4] While Freese ascribes the Commission's publication of defamatory comments on certain witnesses to its "zeal to publish the full truth,"[5] it is susceptible to other interpretations. It is striking that the Commission regarded as unimpeachable a number of witnesses whose testimony is inherently disordered and strongly suggestive of falsification or mental incompetence, or both. When Jack Ruby, a convicted murderer, gave testimony in conflict with the testimony of Seth Kantor, a responsible and respected member of the White House press corps, the Commission chose to believe Ruby and decided that Kantor was mistaken. As already mentioned, it relied on Marina Oswald and Helen Markham, both of whom became flagrantly ensnarled in self-contradiction if not outright falsification. By contrast, the Commission set out to impeach the character of a number of witnesses who were disinterested and whose testimony was corroborated by others, apparently for the sole reason that their testimony came into conflict with a theory which was not subject to change regardless of the evidence.

Moreover, it is arresting that off-the-record discussion took place well over two hundred times during the examination of witnesses, on occasion at crucial points in the testimony and as frequently as seven or eight times per witness. Some of those off-the-record passages undoubtedly were innocuous; in many instances, this discussion was placed on the record immediately afterward. However, one witness who was deposed by counsel subsequently appeared before the Commission at his own request to report that during an off-the-record interruption, counsel had accused him of perjury and had threatened him with the loss of his job. If the witness had not placed those

---

[4] Paul L. Freese, *New York University Law Review*, Vol. XL, No. 3, May 1965, pp. 424–465.
[5] *Ibid.*, p. 449.

facts on the record himself, they would have remained completely concealed from public knowledge. We are therefore entitled to regard the constant resort to off-the-record discussion as an unsatisfactory if not a suspicious practice.

Of the 489 witnesses who gave testimony, less than one-fourth appeared before the Commission itself. Even in those cases, the seven members of the full Commission were never present as a body or throughout an entire session. The Chairman was in attendance at least part of the time for all 94 witnesses who came before the Commission, but his colleagues heard only the following estimated numbers of witnesses:

Representative Ford	70	Mr. McCloy	35
Mr. Dulles	60	Representative Boggs	20
Senator Cooper	50	Senator Russell	6

Some of the difficulties encountered by the members in finding time to spare from other duties for the Commission's needs were almost comical, as may be seen in the following colloquy.

Chairman: Senator Cooper, at this time I am obliged to leave for our all-day conference on Friday at the Supreme Court, and I may be back later in the day, but if I don't, you continue, of course.

Cooper: I will this morning. If I can't be here this afternoon whom do you want to preside?

Chairman: Congressman Ford, would you be here this afternoon at all?

Ford: Unfortunately, Mr. McCloy and I have to go to a conference out of town.

Chairman: You are both going out of town, aren't you?

Cooper: I can go and come back if it is necessary.

Chairman: I will try to be here myself. Will Mr. Dulles be here?

McCloy: He is out of town.

But if attendance was irregular, at least some members of the Commission heard some of the testimony of some of the 94 witnesses who came before the panel. None of the members heard any of the witnesses (well over 350) who testified by deposition; they included such important witnesses as Forrest V. Sorrels, Billy Lovelady, Seymour Weitzman, Earlene Roberts, Sheriff Bill Decker, Abraham Zapruder, Harry Holmes, Domingo Benavides, Nelson Delgado, George De Mohrenschildt, George Bouhe, Jean Lollis Hill, James Tague, Albert Guy Bogard, Dial Ryder, Sylvia Odio, Carlos Bringuier, Gertrude Hunter, Edith Whitworth, George Senator, Harry Olsen, Karen Carlin, and Curtis (Larry) Crafard. A number of witnesses who should have been examined with particular care are represented in the Hearings only by an affidavit. Most appalling of all are the numbers of persons whose names are found nowhere in the list of the Commission's witnesses, from whom no testimony in any form was taken despite indications that they possessed important or crucial information. The failure to examine or, in some instances, to locate such witnesses—including those who gave an account of the Tippit shooting wholly different from the official one—is one of the most serious defects in the Commission's work, and suggests, at the very least, a high degree of negligence.

The Commission's housekeeping is another area in which its performance was inept and undeserving of public confidence. Because of the Commission's inability to maintain control over its internal records, disclosures flowed steadily to the press, including the complete transcript of the examination of Jack Ruby. The Chairman and other spokesmen made a series of ill-advised public statements; the former made an unwarranted attack on the character of a witness and never retracted it, even when the witness exonerated himself from suspicion and requested a retraction. The Chairman also made the shocking statement, still unexplained, that the whole truth might never be known in our lifetime. At least one Commission member capitalized commercially on his experience by publishing an article[6] and later a book[7] purporting to provide a "portrait of the assassin." Apparently the same Commission member is unwilling or unable to explain ambiguities in the Report, including those revealed in his own book, to the taxpayer.

The Commission's failures manifest a contempt for the citizens whom this body pretended to serve—a contempt not for their rights alone but for their intelligence. It must be said, without apology to the authors and advocates of the Warren Report, that it resembles a tale told for fools, full of sophistry and deceit, signifying capitulation to compromise and the degradation of justice by its most eminent guardians.

In June 1966 publication of Edward Jay Epstein's book, Inquest,[8] sparked a long overdue national debate on the Warren Report. Inquest was followed almost immediately by the private editions Whitewash by Harold Weisberg (issued later by Dell as a paperback)[9] and Forgive My Grief by Penn Jones, Jr.;[10] and by Rush to Judgment by Mark Lane,[11] The Oswald Affair by Léo Sauvage,[12] and The Second Oswald by Richard Popkin.[13] The Oswald Affair had appeared in the original French edition (Éditions Minuit,

[6] Representative Gerald R. Ford, "Piecing Together the Evidence," Life, October 2, 1964, pp. 42–50B.
[7] Representative Gerald R. Ford, Portrait of the Assassin (New York: Simon and Schuster and Ballantine Books, 1965).
[8] Inquest (New York: Viking Press, 1966).
[9] Whitewash (Hyattsville, Maryland: Weisberg, 1966); and Whitewash: The Report on the Warren Report (New York: Dell Publishing Co., Inc., 1966).
[10] Forgive My Grief (The Midlothian (Tex.) Mirror, 1966).
[11] Rush to Judgment (New York: Holt, Rinehart, & Winston, 1966).
[12] The Oswald Affair (New York: World Publishing Co., 1966).
[13] The Second Oswald (New York: Avon Books/The New York Review of Books, 1966).

Paris) early in 1965, the first full-length book to assess the official findings on the basis of both the Warren Report and the 26 volumes of Hearings and Exhibits. Unfortunately, it did not become available to American readers until a year and a half after publication in France.

The writers of these books began to be heard on radio and television; news stories and editorials began to appear in respected newspapers, reflecting serious concern about the validity of the Warren Report and suggesting—or demanding, in some cases—that the Commission answer the charges against its Report or that a new investigation be carried out. As this is written, a long list of prominent names are on record as favoring one or another form of new inquiry. Representative Theodore R. Kupferman (R., N.Y.) has presented a joint resolution in the Congress calling for a reappraisal of the Warren Report and, if need be, a new investigation. Former Assistant Counsel Wesley J. Liebeler, embarrassed by his acknowledged contributions to *Inquest*—the book without which no public controversy might now be raging—has launched an attempt to rehabilitate himself. He has organized a new investigation with the stated purpose of reinstating the discredited findings of the Warren Commission, perhaps by re-interpreting the evidence or finding new information. Liebeler is conducting this new investigation with the assistance of 20 law students at the University of California. (*New York Times*, October 23, 1966, p. 66; News broadcast, WINS (N.Y.C.) radio, Oct. 22, 1966.) That a spokesman for the Commission cannot defend the Report as it stands but is seeking a means by which to restore its respectability is in itself a total default to the opposition. Liebeler seems unaware of that.

The critical books and articles that began to appear in June 1966 (and those published earlier that had been ignored before the new wave of skepticism) served as catalytic agents for several major events. One was the sudden announcement early in November 1966 that the notorious autopsy photographs and X rays had been deposited in the National Archives by the Kennedy family, at the request of the Justice Department (admittedly made as a result of the mounting criticism and questions about the Warren Report). But the terms of the transfer of this evidence to the Archives were such that the photographs and X rays will not be made available to any individual or organization except a new governmental investigatory body, if one is appointed to further investigate the assassination.[14]

On the third anniversary of President Kennedy's death, *Life*,[15] *Ramparts*,[16] and other influential publications called editorially for further investigation and openly questioned the evidence and the findings of the Warren Commission. The silent principals suddenly spoke up; Governor

[14] *The Reporter*, December 15, 1966, p. 46.
[15] *Life*, November 25, 1966, pp. 38–48.
[16] *Ramparts*, November 1966, p. 3.

Connally, Senator Russell, Commander Boswell, and J. Edgar Hoover, among others, tripped over each other in their haste to issue public statements, which, deliberately or inadvertently—and in some instances, unintentionally contravening the purpose of the statement—created new doubt and mystery. The gambit of "producing" the missing autopsy photographs and X rays, if it was a gambit, in no way stilled the controversy.

We now have a climate in which the news media and public opinion acknowledge what was formerly unthinkable: that the Warren Commission may have erred, or worse. This healthier climate perhaps signifies recovery of the skepticism, independence of mind, and sense of justice to which Americans as a people lay claim as national attributes. Too often, and especially in the Oswald case, the public has been apathetic, ready to accept government "truth," callously indifferent to injustice.

If closed minds continue to open, to receive and evaluate objectively the facts which are on the record, we may yet proceed to pursue the truth to its ultimate reaches—regardless of attendant dangers and doubts—so that history will know with certainty what happened in Dallas, and why.

To that end, investigation into the assassination and the related murders should be reopened, entrusted to an uncompromisingly independent, competent, and impartial body—a body committed to the use of adversary procedure, the rules of evidence, and total respect for justice, in both the letter and the spirit. In other words, a body different from the Warren Commission.

Whether or not that comes to pass in the immediate future, the country owes profound gratitude to the critics and researchers whose work, published or unpublished, has helped to destroy the myth of the Warren Report. Because of their courage, intelligence, and integrity, "it is the majestic Warren Commission itself that is in the dock today, rather than the lonely Oswald," as Anthony Howard wrote in the *London Observer* on August 7, 1966.[17] The Commission must receive justice—that justice which was denied to Oswald in death as in life—but nothing less than justice.

CHAPTER 20

Truth Was Their Only Client

The 26 volumes of Hearings and Exhibits provide little material that offers an insight into the Warren Commission's process of reasoning or evaluation of testimony and evidence which ultimately produced the official conclusions. We are therefore indebted to Representative Gerald R. Ford,

17 "The Clamour Rises for Kennedy X Rays," *The London Observer,* August 7, 1966, p. 10.

not only for the piquant information that the unofficial motto of the Commission on which he served was "truth is our only client here," but for the whole first chapter of his book *Portrait of the Assassin*,[1] which provides a brief glimpse behind the Commission's closed doors. (The remainder of Ford's work consists mainly of excerpts from the Hearings.) Here we learn for the first time the dramatic story of the Commission's reaction to the rumors that Oswald was an undercover agent for the FBI, and of its efforts to deal with that delicate matter that had been placed into its hands.

According to Ford, the Commission held an emergency meeting on January 22, 1964, after a telephone call from Waggoner Carr, Attorney-General of the State of Texas, alleging that Oswald was an FBI undercover operative. The Commission heard in secret what Carr and Dallas District Attorney Henry Wade had to say about this potentially explosive allegation, and then reconvened on January 27 to consider what steps to take on the report from the Texas officials and the similar allegations that had appeared in the press. It had been claimed at the secret meeting with Carr and Wade that Oswald was on the FBI payroll as undercover agent No. 179 at $200 a month, from September 1962 to the day of the assassination. Rumors to that effect had appeared in stories by Joe Goulden in the *Philadelphia Inquirer* of December 8,1963,[2] Lonnie Hudkins in the *Houston Post* of January 1, 1964,[3] and Harold Feldman in *The Nation* of January 26, 1964.[4]

At the January 27 meeting, General Counsel J. Lee Rankin suggested that the Commission should take the story to J. Edgar Hoover with a request that he produce facts to put an end to the speculations, but making it clear that the Commission would feel free to take any necessary steps in order to satisfy the American people that Oswald had not been an FBI undercover agent. (Rankin seems to have assumed from the first that there would be no substance to the rumors.)

Chairman Warren, on the other hand, considered that the Commission should first find out from "these people" if there was any substance to the allegations or if "just plain rumor" was at work. Warren felt that Hudkins should be questioned; if he claimed privilege and refused to reveal the source for his story, the Commission could go to his publisher and enlist his services to "have this man tell us where he got his information." Warren said, according to the transcript quoted in Ford's book, that he was not in favor of going to any agency and saying, "We would like to do this." He believed that "We ought to know what we are going to do, and do it, and take our chances one way or the other. I don't believe we should apologize

---

[1] *Portrait of the Assassin*, pp. 13–25.
[2] Joe Goulden, *Philadelphia Inquirer*, December 8, 1963, Section A, p. 22.
[3] Lonnie Hudkins, "Oswald Rumored as Informant for U.S.," *Houston Post*, January 1, 1964.
[4] Harold Feldman, "Oswald and the FBI," *The Nation*, January 27, 1964, pp. 86–89.

or make it look that we are in any way reticent about making any investigation that comes to the Commission."

No one will deny that the Commission was confronted with a painful and delicate problem when it appeared that the very investigative agency on which it had to rely for its detective work was itself the subject of allegations of a most compromising nature. The situation was all the more difficult because the head of that agency, J. Edgar Hoover, has long been immune to criticism from any quarter. Warren's position was therefore courageous and faithful to the high responsibility with which the Commission was charged. Apparently he had a decisive influence on the other Commissioners. According to Ford, the discussion resulted in a consensus of all seven men that the only way to proceed was to conduct "extensive and thorough hearings of as many witnesses as was necessary. . . . Where doubts were cast on any United States agency, independent experts would be hired and the investigation conducted in such a way as to avoid reliance on a questioned authority."[5]

With this preface, I searched the Hearings and Exhibits for the "extensive and thorough hearings" of Lonnie Hudkins, Joe Goulden, Harold Feldman and others who had published speculations or made allegations that Oswald was on the FBI payroll. None of the three writers was a witness before the Commission. An undated, unsigned interview with Lonnie Hudkins is included in one exhibit (CE 2003, p. 327), but it deals with the events of Sunday, November 24, 1963 and not with the possibility that Oswald was an FBI undercover man. There is no trace of Goulden or Feldman at all. The Hearings and Exhibits contain no testimony from or interview with Waggoner Carr on this subject, or with Dallas Assistant District Attorney William Alexander, who appears to be the principal advocate of the hypothesis that there was a clandestine relationship between Oswald and the FBI. Alexander's views are reflected in the testimony of District Attorney Henry Wade; although Wade's testimony suggests that Alexander continued to hold that opinion long after the first rumblings which caused the emergency meetings in January, Alexander himself was not asked to testify before the Commission or interviewed on the question.

J. Edgar Hoover did appear before the Warren Commission on May 14, 1964. In the light of the Commission's consensus less than four months earlier to conduct its investigation in such a way "as to avoid reliance on a questioned authority," it is surprising to find the following passage in Hoover's testimony.

I think a Houston reporter was the first one who wrote that Oswald was an informant of the FBI. We went to the newspaper reporter. He refused to

5 *Portrait of the Assassin*, p. 25.

tell us his source. He said he had also heard it from other persons. We asked him the names of these persons and we interviewed them but none of them would provide the source. In other words, I was trying to nail down where this lie started.

(5H 116)

Despite what the Commission had professed earlier, the questioned authority was permitted to investigate the charges against itself and to find itself not guilty. The questioned authority, not the Commission itself or independent experts engaged by it, went to Hudkins "to nail down where this lie started." Who would expect Hudkins to reveal his sources under such circumstances?

An indication of Hudkins' source came to light in Edward Jay Epstein's book, *Inquest*, which referred to a Secret Service report of an interview with Hudkins in which the reporter stated that his information that Oswald was on the FBI payroll came from Allan Sweatt, Chief of the Criminal Division of the Dallas Sheriff's Office.[6] In July 1966, researcher Paul Hoch turned up this Secret Service report, Commission Document 320, at the National Archives. The report is dated January 3, 1964, and contains an account of an interview with Alonso H. Hudkins III of the *Houston Post* which includes the following passage:

> On December 17, Mr. Hudkins advised that he had just returned from a weekend in Dallas, during which time he talked to Allan Sweatt, Chief Criminal Division, Sheriff's Office, Dallas; Chief Sweatt mentioned that it was his opinion that Lee Harvey Oswald was being paid $200 a month by the FBI as an informant in connection with their subversive investigations. He furnished the alleged informant number assigned to Oswald by the FBI as "S172."

This Secret Service report as well as other documents dealing with the allegation that Oswald was on the FBI payroll were withheld from the Report and the Exhibits. Allan Sweatt, like Hudkins and the other reporters, was not called before the Commission to give testimony.

On the basis of this "investigation" the Warren Commission "found" that Oswald was not an agent for the FBI. In support of its conclusion, the Commission cites affidavits from J. Edgar Hoover and his assistant, Alan H. Belmont, and from FBI Agents Fain, Hosty, and Quigley, and an "independent review of the FBI files on the Oswald investigation." (WR 327) But no such independent review took place. Chairman Warren refused to accept the FBI files on the grounds that if the Commission looked at it, claims would be made that everyone should have the same right, even if

---

[6] *Op. cit.*, p. 39.

prohibited security matters were included in the dossier. (5H 13) According to Edward Jay Epstein, Counsel Samuel Stern said that Oswald's files were returned to the FBI without examination and no independent check was ever made of the contents.[7]

Compelling questions must arise. What moved the Commission to reverse its original position? Were pressures exerted? Who had sufficient power to force a Presidential Commission of unparalleled prestige and broad authority to nullify its previous unanimous decision? What considerations exerted greater force than the dictates of the Commission's conscience?

It is not possible to accept a "finding" based on procedures which violate the Commission's own criteria. The possibility of a clandestine link between Oswald and the FBI has not been eliminated. The Commission has disposed of neither the allegations which originated with Hudkins nor the Hosty entries in Oswald's notebook. They are two pieces in a single puzzle.

It comes as comic relief after tracing this travesty of the investigative process to read in Ford's book that "the Commission labored . . . with soul-searching thoroughness" and that its unofficial motto was "Truth is our only client here."[8] One must laugh, lest one weep, at his self-satisfied pronouncement that "the monumental record of the President's Commission will stand like a Gibraltar of factual literature through the ages to come."

History inevitably will pronounce a ruder verdict on the report of an investigation tainted at every crucial point by the hopeless reliance of the authors on a questioned authority.

For Discussion

1. Evaluate Meagher's summary of the events beginning with the day of the assassination and terminating with the death of Ruby. What are the advantages and limitations of this summary?
2. Why does Meagher attempt to characterize the mood of Dallas and of the nation at the time of the assassination? What can you add from your own personal experience and reading?
3. What basic contradiction does Meagher see between the Warren Report and the Hearings and Exhibits?
4. Compare the position of the advocates of the Report with that of its critics. What does each consider important? What do you?
5. What basic concept of justice does Meagher find abused in regard to Oswald? What other irregularities does she find in the conduct of the

[7] Op. cit., p. 38.
[8] Op. cit., pp. 491–492.

Commission? Consider the differences between an investigation and a trial.

6. What does the fact that Meagher independently produced the only index to the Commission's Hearings and Exhibits tell you about her? About the Warren Report?

7. What does Meagher's presentation in Chapter 20 prove? What is your response? Evaluate this method of argumentation.

8. How convincing is J. Edgar Hoover's denial that Oswald was an agent for the F.B.I.?

9. Malcolm X called the Kennedy assassination "a case of 'the chickens coming home to roost.'" Give your interpretation of his meaning.

10. What is the current status of the Warren Report?

11. What examples of ironic humor can you find?

12. To what extent does Meagher allow her feelings to be shown? What is the effect?

NICHOLAS JOHNSON

The Media Barons and the
Public Interest

The role of crusader is not new to Nicholas Johnson, the youngest member of the Federal Communications Commission. When,
at twenty-nine, he headed the Maritime Administration, he
fought for shipping industry reforms against the protests of both
management and labor. Since the following article appeared,
Johnson has come under increasing attack from broadcasting
interests because of his forthright demands that steps be taken
to stop the trend toward concentration of power in the media
industry.

Before I came to the Federal Communications Commission my concerns about the ownership of broadcasting and publishing in America were
about like those of any other generally educated person.

Most television programming from the three networks struck me as
bland at best. I had taken courses dealing with propaganda and "thought
control," bemoaned (while being entertained by) *Time* magazine's "slanted"
reporting, understood that Hearst had something to do with the Spanish-
American War, and was impressed with President Eisenhower's concern
about "the military-industrial complex." The changing ownership of the
old-line book publishers and the disappearance of some of our major newspapers made me vaguely uneasy. I was philosophically wedded to the fundamental importance of the "marketplace of ideas" in a free society, and a
year as law clerk to my idol, Supreme Court Justice Hugo L. Black, had
done nothing to weaken that commitment.

But I didn't take much time to be reflective about the current significance of such matters. It all seemed beyond my ability to influence in
any meaningful way. Then, in July, 1966, I became a member of the FCC.

Here my interest in the marketplace of ideas could no longer remain a casual article of personal faith. The commitment was an implicit part of the oath I took on assuming the office of commissioner, and, I quickly learned, an everyday responsibility.

Threats to the free exchange of information and opinion in this country can come from various sources, many of them outside the power of the FCC to affect. Publishers and reporters are not alike in their ability, education, tolerance of diversity, and sense of responsibility. The hidden or overt pressures of advertisers have long been with us.

But one aspect of the problem is clearly within the purview of the FCC—the impact of *ownership* upon the content of the mass media. It is also a part of the responsibility of the Antitrust Division of the Justice Department. It has been the subject of recent congressional hearings. There are a number of significant trends in the ownership of the media worth examining—local and regional monopolies, growing concentration of control of the most profitable and powerful television stations in the major markets, broadcasting-publishing combines, and so forth. But let's begin with a look at the significance of media ownership by "conglomerate corporations"—holding companies that own, in addition to publishing and broadcasting enterprises, other major industrial corporations.

During my first month at the FCC I studied the cases and attended the meetings, but purposefully did not participate in voting on any items. One of the agenda items at the July 20 commissioners' meeting proposed two draft letters addressed to the presidents of International Telephone and Telegraph and the American Broadcasting Company, ITT and ABC, Messrs. Harold Geneen and Leonard Goldenson. We were asking them to supply "a statement specifying in further detail the manner in which the financial resources of ITT will enable ABC to improve its program services and thereby better to serve the public interest." This friendly inquiry was my first introduction to the proposed ITT-ABC merger, and the Commission majority's attitudes about it. It was to be a case that would occupy much of my attention over the next few months.

There wasn't much discussion of the letters that morning, but I read carefully the separate statements filed with the letter by my two responsible and experienced colleagues, Commissioners Robert T. Bartley and Kenneth A. Cox, men for whom I was already feeling a respect that was to grow over the following months.

Commissioner Bartley, a former broadcaster with the deep and earthy wisdom one would expect in a Texas-born relative of the late Speaker Sam Rayburn, wrote a long and thoughtful statement. He warned of "the probable far-reaching political, social and economic consequences for the public interest of the increasing control of broadcast facilities and broadcast service by large conglomerate corporations such as the applicants." Commissioner Cox, former lawyer, law professor, counsel to the Senate

Commerce Committee, and chief of the FCC's Broadcast Bureau, characterized the proposed merger as "perhaps the most important in the agency's history." He said the issues were "so significant and far-reaching that we should proceed immediately to designate the matter for hearing."

Their concerns were well grounded in broadcasting's history and in the national debate preceding the 1934 Communications Act we were appointed to enforce. Precisely what Congress intended the FCC to do was not specified at the time or since. But no one has ever doubted Congress' great concern lest the ownership of broadcasting properties be permitted to fall into a few hands or to assume monopoly proportions.

The 1934 Act was preceded by the 1927 Radio Act and a series of industry Radio Conferences in the early 1920s. The conferences were called by then Secretary of Commerce Herbert C. Hoover. Hoover expressed concern lest control over broadcasting "come under the arbitrary power of any person or group of persons." During the congressional debates on the 1927 Act a leading congressman, noting that "publicity is the most powerful weapon that can be wielded in a republic," warned of the domination of broadcasting by "a single selfish group." Should that happen, he said, "then woe be to those who dare to differ with them." The requirement that licenses not be transferred without Commission approval was intended, according to a sponsoring senator, "to prevent the concentration of broadcast facilities by a few." Thirty years later, in 1956, Senate Commerce Committee Chairman Warren G. Magnuson was still warning the Commission that it "should be on guard against the intrusion of big business and absentee ownership."

These concerns of Congress and my colleagues were to take on fuller meaning as the ITT-ABC case unfolded, a case which eventually turned into an FCC *cause célèbre*. It also demonstrated the enormity of the responsibility vested in this relatively small and little-known Commission, by virtue of its power to grant or withhold membership in the broadcast industry. On a personal level, the case shook into me the realization, for the first time in my life, of the dreadful significance of the ownership structure of the mass media in America.

the ITT-ABC merger case

ITT is a sprawling international conglomerate of 433 separate boards of directors that derives about 60 percent of its income from its significant holdings in at least forty foreign countries. It is the ninth largest industrial corporation in the world in size of work force. In addition to its sale of electronic equipment to foreign governments, and operation of foreign countries' telephone systems, roughly half of its domestic income comes from U.S. Government defense and space contracts. But it is also in the business of consumer finance, life insurance, investment funds, small loan companies, car rentals (ITT Avis, Inc.), and book publishing.

This description of ITT's anatomy is taken (as is much of this ITT-ABC discussion) from opinions written by myself and Commissioners Bartley and Cox. We objected, vigorously, to the four-man majority's decision to approve the merger. So did some senators and congressmen, the Department of Justice, the Commission's own staff, the American Civil Liberties Union, a number of independent individuals and witnesses, and a belated but eventually insistent chorus of newspaper and magazine editorialists.

What did we find so ominous about the take-over of this radio and television network by a highly successful conglomerate organization?

In 1966, ABC owned 399 theaters in 34 states, 5 VHF television stations, 6 AM and 6 FM stations (all in the top 10 broadcasting markets), and, of course, one of the 3 major television networks and one of the 4 major radio networks in the world. Its 137 primary television network affiliates could reach 93 percent of the then 50 million television homes in the United States and its radio network affiliates could reach 97 percent of the then 55 million homes with radio receivers. ABC had interests in, and affiliations with stations in 25 other nations, known as the "Worldvision Group." These, together with ABC Films, made the parent corporation perhaps the world's largest distributor of filmed shows for theaters and television stations throughout this country and abroad. ABC was heavily involved in the record production and distribution business, and other subsidiaries published three farm papers.

The merger would have placed this accumulation of mass media, and one of the largest purveyors of news and opinion in America, under the control of one of the largest conglomerate corporations in the world. What's wrong with that? Potentially a number of things. For now, consider simply that the integrity of the news judgment of ABC might be affected by the economic interests of ITT—that ITT might simply view ABC's programming as a part of ITT's public relations, advertising, or political activities. This seemed to us a real threat in 1966, notwithstanding the character of the management of both companies, and their protestations that no possibility of abuse existed. By 1967 the potential threat had become reality.

JTT's empire

ITT's continuing concern with political and economic developments in foreign countries as a result of its far-flung economic interests was fully documented in the hearing. It showed, as one might expect, ITT's recurrent concern with internal affairs in most major countries of the world, including rate problems, tax problems, and problems with nationalization and re-imbursement, to say nothing of ordinary commercial dealing. Its involvement with the United States government, in addition to defense contracts, included the Agency for International Development's insurance of 5.8 percent of all ITT assets.

Testimony was offered on the fascinating story of intrigue surrounding "Operation Deep Freeze" (an underwater cable). It turned out that ITT officials, using high-level government contracts in England and Canada, had brought off a bit of profitable international diplomacy unknown to the United States State Department or the FCC, possibly in violation of law. Further inquiry revealed that officers and directors of ITT's subsidiaries included two members of the British House of Lords, one in the French National Assembly, a former premier of Belgium, and several ministers of foreign governments and officials of government-owned companies.

As it seemed to Commissioners Bartley and Cox and to me when we dissented from the Commission's approval of the merger in June, 1967, a company whose daily activities require it to manipulate governments at the highest levels would face unending temptation to manipulate ABC news. Any public official, or officer of a large corporation, is necessarily clearly concerned with the appearance of some news stories, the absence of others, and the tone and character of all affecting his personal interests. That's what public relations firms and press secretaries are all about. We concluded, "We simply cannot find that the public interest of the American citizenry is served by turning over a major network to an international enterprise whose fortunes are tied to its political relations with the foreign officials whose actions it will be called upon to interpret to the world."

Even the highest degree of subjective integrity on the part of chief ITT officials could not ensure integrity in ABC's operations. To do an honest and impartial job of reporting the news is difficult enough for the most independent and conscientious of newsmen. Eric Sevareid has said of putting on a news program at a network relatively free of conglomerate control: "The ultimate sensation is the feeling of being bitten to death by ducks." And ABC newsmen could not help knowing that ITT had sensitive business relations in various foreign countries and at the highest levels of our government, and that reporting on any number of industries and economic developments would touch the interests of ITT. The mere awareness of these interests would make it impossible for those news officials, no matter how conscientious, to report news and develop documentaries objectively, in the way that they would do if ABC remained unaffiliated with ITT. They would advance within the news organization, or be fired, or become officers of ABC—perhaps even of ITT—or not, and no newsman would be able to erase from his mind the idea that his chances of doing so might be affected by his treatment of issues on which ITT is sensitive.

Only last year CBS was reportedly involved, almost Hearst-like, in a nightmarish planned armed invasion of Haiti. It was an exclusive, and would have made a very dramatic start-to-finish documentary but for the inglorious end: U.S. Customs wouldn't let them leave the United States. Imagine ITT, with its extensive interests in the Caribbean, engaged in such undertakings.

The likelihood of at least some compromising of ABC's integrity seemed inherent in the structure of the proposed new organization. What were the *probabilities* that these potentials for abuse would be exercised? We were soon to see the answer in the bizarre proceedings right before our eyes.

During the April, 1967, hearings, while this very issue was being debated, the *Wall Street Journal* broke the story that ITT was going to extraordinary lengths to obtain favorable press coverage of this hearing. Eventually three reporters were summoned before the examiner to relate for the official record the incidents that were described in the *Journal's* exposé.

An AP and a UPI reporter testified to several phone calls to their homes by ITT public relations men, variously asking them to change their stories and make inquiries for ITT with regard to stories by other reporters, and to use their influence as members of the press to obtain for ITT confidential information from the Department of Justice regarding its intentions. Even more serious were several encounters between ITT officials and a New York *Times* reporter.

On one of these occasions ITT's senior vice president in charge of public relations went to the reporter's office. After criticizing her dispatches to the *Times* about the case in a tone which she described as "accusatory and certainly nasty," he asked whether she had been following the price of ABC and ITT stock. When she indicated that she had not, he asked if she didn't feel she had a "responsibility to the shareholders who might lose money as a result of what" she wrote. She replied, "my responsibility is to find out the truth and print it."

He then asked if she was aware that I (as an FCC Commissioner) was working with a prominent senator on legislation that would forbid any newspaper from owning any broadcast property. (The New York *Times* owns station WQXR in New York.) In point of fact, the senator and I had never met, let alone collaborated, as was subsequently made clear in public statements. But the ITT senior vice president, according to the *Times* reporter, felt that this false information was something she "ought to pass on to [her] . . . publisher before [she wrote] . . . anything further" about the case. The obvious implication of this remark, she felt, was that since the *Times* owns a radio station, it would want to consider its economic interests in deciding what to publish about broadcasting in its newspaper.

To me, this conduct, in which at least three ITT officials, including a senior vice president, were involved, was a deeply unsettling experience.

It demonstrated an abrasive self-righteousness in dealing with the press, insensitivity to its independence and integrity, a willingness to spread false stories in furtherance of self-interest, contempt for government officials as well as the press, and an assumption that even as prestigious a news medium as the New York *Times* would, as a matter of course, want to present the news so as to serve best its own economic interests (as well as the economic interests of other large business corporations).

But for the brazen activities of ITT in this very proceeding, it would never have occurred to the three of us who dissented to suggest that the most probable threat to the integrity of ABC news could come from *overt* actions or written policy statements. After the hearing it was obvious that that was clearly possible. But even then, we believed that the most substantial threat came from a far more subtle, almost unconscious, process: that the questionable story idea, or news coverage, would never even be proposed—whether for reasons of fear, insecurity, cynicism, realism, or unconscious avoidance.

concentration of control over the media

Since the ITT-ABC case left the Commission I have not ceased to be troubled by the issues it raised—in many ways more serious (and certainly more prevalent) for wholly domestic corporations. Eventually the merger was aborted by ITT on New Year's Day of this year, while the Justice Department's appeal of the Commission's action was pending before the U.S. Court of Appeals. However, I ponder what the consequences might have been if ITT's apparent cynicism toward journalistic integrity had actually been able to harness the enormous social and propaganda power of a national television network to the service of a politically sensitive corporate conglomerate. More important, I have become concerned about the extent to which such forces *already* play upon important media of mass communication. Perhaps such attitudes are masked by more finesse than that displayed in the ITT-ABC case. Perhaps they are even embedded in the kind of sincere good intentions which caused former Defense Secretary (and former General Motors president) Charles Wilson to equate the interests of his company with those of the country.

I do not believe that most owners and managers of the mass media in the United States lack a sense of responsibility or lack tolerance for a diversity of views. I do not believe there is a small group of men who gather for breakfast every morning and decide what they will make the American people believe that day. Emotion often outruns the evidence of those who argue a conspiracy theory of propagandists' manipulation of the masses. On the other hand, one reason evidence is so hard to come by is that the media tend to give less publicity to their own abuses than, say, to those of politicians. The media operate as a check upon other institutional power centers in our country. There is, however, no check upon the media. Just as it is a mistake to overstate the existence and potential for abuse, so, in my judgment, is it a mistake to ignore the evidence that does exist.

In 1959, for example, it was reported that officials of the Trujillo regime in the Dominican Republic had paid $750,000 to officers of the Mutual Radio Network to gain favorable propaganda disguised as news. (Ownership of the Mutual Radio Network changed hands once again last year without any review whatsoever by the FCC of old or new owners. The FCC does not regulate networks, only stations, and Mutual owns none. RCA was once charged with using an NBC station to serve unfairly its broader corporate interests, including the coverage of RCA activities as "news," when others did not. There was speculation that after RCA acquired Random House, considerable pressure was put on the book publishing house's president, Bennett Cerf, to cease his Sunday evening service as a panelist on CBS's *What's My Line?* The Commission has occasionally found that individual stations have violated the "fairness doctrine" in advocating causes serving the station's economic self-interest, such as pay television.

Virtually every issue of the *Columbia Journalism Review* reports instances of such abuses by the print media. It has described a railroad-owned newspaper that refused to report railroad wrecks, a newspaper in debt to the Teamsters Union which gave exceedingly favorable coverage to Jimmy Hoffa, the repeated influence of the DuPont interests in the editorial functions of the Wilmington papers which it owned, and Anaconda Copper's use of its company-owned newspapers to support political candidates favorable to the company.

Edward P. Morgan left ABC last year to become the commentator on the Ford Foundation-funded Public Broadcasting Laboratory. He has always been straightforward, and he used his final news broadcast to be reflective about broadcasting itself. "Let's face it," he said. "We in this trade use this power more frequently to fix a traffic ticket or get a ticket to a ballgame than to keep the doors of an open society open and swinging. . . . The freest and most profitable press in the world, every major facet of it, not only ducks but pulls its punches to save a supermarket of commercialism or shield an ugly prejudice and is putting the life of the republic in jeopardy thereby."

Economic self-interest *does* influence the content of the media, and as the media tend to fall into the control of corporate conglomerates, the areas of information and opinion affecting those economic interests become dangerously wide-ranging. What *is* happening to the ownership of American media today? What dangers does it pose? Taking a look at the structure of the media in the United States, I am not put at ease by what I see.

Most American communities have far less "dissemination of information from diverse and antagonistic sources" (to quote a famous description by the Supreme Court of the basic aim of the First Amendment) than is available nationally. Of the 1500 cities with daily newspapers, 96 percent are served by single-owner monopolies. Outside the top 50 to 200 markets there is a substantial dropping off in the number of competing radio and television signals. The FCC prohibits a single owner from controlling two AM radio, or two television, stations with overlapping signals. But it has only recently expressed any concern over common ownership of an AM radio station and an FM radio station and a television station in the same market. Indeed, such ownership is the rule rather than the exception and probably exists in your community. Most stations are today acquired by purchase. And the FCC has, in part because of congressional pressure, rarely disapproved a purchase of a station by a newspaper.

There are few statewide or regional "monopolies"—although some situations come close. But in a majority of our states—the least populous—there are few enough newspapers and television stations to begin with, and they are usually under the control of a small group. And most politicians find today, as Congress warned in 1926, "woe be to those who dare to differ with them." Most of our politics is still state and local in scope. And increasingly, in many states and local communities, congressmen and state and local officials are compelled to regard that handful of media owners (many of whom are out-of-state), rather than the electorate itself, as their effective constituency. Moreover, many mass media owners have a significant impact in more than one state. One case that came before the FCC, for example, involved an owner with AM-FM-TV combinations in Las Vegas and Reno, Nevada, along with four newspapers in that state, seven newspapers in Oklahoma, and two stations and two newspapers in Arkansas. Another involved ownership of ten stations in North Carolina and adjoining southern Virginia. You may never have heard of these owners, but I imagine the elected officials of their states return their phone calls promptly.

national power

The principal national sources of news are the wire services, AP and UPI, and the broadcast networks. Each of the wire services serves on the order of 1200 newspapers and 3000 radio and television stations. Most local newspapers and radio stations offer little more than wire service copy as far as national and international news is concerned. To that extent one can take little heart for "diversity" from the oft-proffered statistics on proliferating radio stations (now over 6000) and the remaining daily newspapers (1700). The networks, though themselves heavily reliant upon the wire services to find out what's worth filming, are another potent force.

The weekly newsmagazine field is dominated by *Time, Newsweek,* and *U.S. News.* (The first two also control substantial broadcast, news-paper, and book or publishing outlets. *Time* is also in movies (MGM) and is hungry for three or four newspapers.) Thus, even though there are thousands of general and specialized periodicals and program sources with significant national or regional impact, and certainly no "monopoly" exists, it is still possible for a single individual or corporation to have vast na-tional influence.

What we sometimes fail to realize, moreover, is the political signifi-cance of the fact that we have become a nation of cities. Nearly half of the American people live in the six largest states: California, New York, Illinois, Pennsylvania, Texas, and Ohio. Those states, in turn, are substan-tially influenced (if not politically dominated) by their major population-industrial-financial-media centers, such as Los Angeles, New York City, Chicago, and Philadelphia—the nation's four largest metropolitan areas. Thus, to have a major newspaper or television station influence in *one* of these cities is to have significant national power. And the number of inter-ests with influence in *more* than one of these markets is startling.

Most of the top fifty television markets (which serve approximately 75 percent of the nation's television homes) have three competing commer-cial VHF television stations. There are about 150 such VHF commercial stations in these markets. Less than 10 percent are today owned by entities that do not own other media interests. In 30 of the 50 markets at least one of the stations is owned by a major newspaper published in that market—a total of one third of these 150 stations. (In Dallas-Fort Worth *each* of the network affiliates is owned by a local newspaper, and the fourth, an unaffiliated station, is owned by Oklahoma newspapers.) Moreover, half of the newspaper-owned stations are controlled by seven groups—groups that also publish magazines as popular and diverse as *Time, Newsweek, Look, Parade, Harper's, TV Guide, Family Circle, Vogue, Good Housekeep-ing,* and *Popular Mechanics.* Twelve parties own more than one third of all the major-market stations.

In addition to the vast national impact of their affiliates the three tele-vision networks each *own* VHF stations in all of the top three markets—New York, Los Angeles, and Chicago—and each has two more in other cities in the top ten. RKO and Metromedia each own stations in both New

York City and Los Angeles. Metromedia also owns stations in Washington, D.C., and California's other major city, San Francisco—as well as Philadelphia, Baltimore, Cleveland, Kansas City, and Oakland. RKO also owns stations in Boston, San Francisco, Washington, Memphis, Hartford, and Windsor, Ontario—as well as the regional Yankee Network. Westinghouse owns stations in New York, Chicago, Philadelphia *and* Pittsburgh, Pennsylvania, Boston, San Francisco, Baltimore, and Fort Wayne. These are but a few examples of today's media barons.

There are many implications of their power. Groups of stations are able to bargain with networks, advertisers, and talent in ways that put lesser stations at substantial economic disadvantage. Group ownership means, by definition, that few stations in major markets will be locally owned. (The FCC recently approved the transfer of the last available station in San Francisco to the absentee ownership of Metromedia. The only commercial station locally owned today is controlled by the San Francisco *Chronicle*.) But the basic point is simply that the national political power involved in ownership of a group of major VHF television stations in, say, New York, Los Angeles, Philadelphia, and Washington, D.C., is greater than a democracy should unthinkingly repose in one man or corporation.

conglomerate corporations

For a variety of reasons, an increasing number of communications media are turning up on the organization charts of conglomerate companies. And the incredible profits generated by broadcast stations in the major markets (television broadcasters *average* a 90 to 100 percent return on tangible investment annually) have given FCC licensees, particularly owners of multiple television stations like the networks, Metromedia, Storer Broadcasting, and others, the extra capital with which to buy the New York Yankees (CBS), Random House (RCA), or Northeast Airlines (Storer). Established or up-and-coming conglomerates regard communications acquisitions as prestigious, profitable, and often a useful or even a necessary complement to present operations and projected exploitation of technological change.

The national problem of conglomerate ownership of communications media was well illustrated by the ITT-ABC case. But the conglomerate problem need not involve something as large as ITT-ABC or RCA-NBC. Among the national group owners of television stations are General Tire (RKO), Avco, Westinghouse, Rust Craft, Chris Craft, Kaiser, and Kerr-McGee. The problem of *local* conglomerates was forcefully posed for the FCC in another case earlier this year. Howard Hughes, through Hughes

Tool Company, wanted to acquire one of Las Vegas' three major television stations. He had recently acquired $125 million worth of Las Vegas real estate, including hotels, gambling casinos, and an airport. These investments supplemented 27,000 acres previously acquired. The Commission majority blithely approved the television acquisition without a hearing, overlooking FCC precedents which suggested that a closer examination was in order. In each of these instances the potential threat is similar to that in the ITT-ABC case—that personal economic interests may dominate or bias otherwise independent media.

concentration and technological change

The problem posed by conglomerate acquisitions of communications outlets is given a special but very important twist by the pendency of sweeping technological changes which have already begun to unsettle the structure of the industry.

President Johnson has appointed a distinguished task force to evaluate our national communications policy and chart a course for realization of these technological promises in a manner consistent with the public interest. But private interests have already begun to implement their own plans on how to deal with the revolution in communications technology.

General Sarnoff of RCA has hailed the appearance of "the knowledge industry"—corporate casserole dishes blending radio and television stations, networks, and programming; films, movie houses, and record companies; newspaper, magazine, and book publishing; advertising agencies; sports or other entertainment companies; and teaching machines and other profitable appurtenances of the $50 billion "education biz."

And everybody's in "cable television"—networks, book publishers, newspapers. Cable television is a system for building the best TV antenna in town and then wiring it into everybody's television set—for a fee. It improves signal quality and number of channels, and has proved popular. But the new technology is such that it has broadcasters and newspaper publishers worried. For the same cable that can bring off-the-air television into the home can also bring programming from the cable operator's studio, or an "electronic newspaper" printed in the home by a facsimile process. Books can be delivered (between libraries, or to the home) over "television" by using the station's signal during an invisible pause. So everybody's hedging their bets—including the telephone company. Indeed, about all the vested interests can agree upon is that none of them want us to have direct, satellite-to-home radio and television. But at this point it is not at all clear who will have his hand on the switch that controls what comes to the American people over their "telephone wire" a few years hence.

what is to be done

It would be foolish to expect any extensive restructuring of the media in the United States, even if it were considered desirable. Technological change can bring change in structure, but it is as likely to be change to even greater concentration as to wider diversity. In the short run at least, economics seems to render essentially intractable such problems as local monopolies in daily newspapers, or the small number of outlets for national news through wire service, newsmagazines, and the television networks. Indeed, to a certain extent the very high technical quality of the performance rendered by these news-gathering organizations is aided by their concentration of resources into large units and the financial cushions of oligopoly profits.

Nevertheless, it seems clear to me that the risks of concentration are grave.

Chairman Philip Hart of the Senate Antitrust and Monopoly Subcommittee remarked by way of introduction to his antitrust subcommittee's recent hearings about the newspaper industry, "The products of newspapers, opinion and information, are essential to the kind of society that we undertake to make successful here." If we are serious about the kind of society we have undertaken, it is clear to me that we simply must not tolerate concentration of media ownership—except where concentration creates actual countervailing social benefits. These benefits cannot be merely speculative. They must be identifiable, demonstrable, and genuinely weighty enough to offset the dangers inherent in concentration.

This guideline is a simple prescription. The problem is to design and build machinery to fill it. And to keep the machinery from rusting and rotting. And to replace it when it becomes obsolete.

America does have available governmental machinery which is capable of scotching undue accumulations of power over the mass media, at least in theory and to some extent. The Department of Justice has authority under the antitrust laws to break up combinations which "restrain trade" or which "tend to lessen competition." These laws apply to the media as they do to any other industry.

But the antitrust laws simply do not get to where the problems are. They grant authority to block concentration only when it threatens *economic* competition in a particular economic *market*. Generally, in the case of the media, the relevant market is the market for advertising. Unfortunately, relatively vigorous advertising competition can be maintained in situations where competition in the marketplace of ideas is severely threatened. In such cases, the Justice Department has little inclination to act.

Look at the Chicago *Tribune's* recent purchase of that city's most popular and most successful FM radio station. The *Tribune* already controlled two Chicago newspapers, one (clear channel) AM radio station, and the city's only independent VHF television station. It controls numerous broadcast, CATV, and newspaper interests outside Chicago (in terms of circulation, the nation's largest newspaper chain). But, after an investigation, the Antitrust Division let this combination go through. The new FM may be a needless addition to the *Tribune's* already impressive battery of influential media; it could well produce an unsound level of concentration in the production and supply of what Chicagoans see, read, and hear about affairs in their community, in the nation, and in the world. But it did not threaten the level of competition for advertising money in any identifiable advertising market. So, it was felt, the acquisition was not the business of the Justice Department.

Only the FCC is directly empowered to keep media ownership patterns compatible with a democracy's need for diversified sources of opinion and information.

In earlier times, the Commission took this responsibility very seriously. In 1941, the FCC ordered NBC to divest itself of one of its two radio networks (which then became ABC), barring any single network from affiliating with more than one outlet in a given city. (The Commission has recently waived this prohibition for, ironically, ABC's four new national radio networks.) In 1941 the Commission also established its power to set absolute limits on the total number of broadcast licenses any individual may hold, and to limit the number of stations any individual can operate in a particular service area.

The American people are indebted to the much maligned FCC for establishing these rules. Imagine, for example, what the structure of political power in this country might look like if two or three companies owned substantially all of the broadcast media in our major cities.

But since the New Deal generation left the command posts of the FCC, this agency has lost much of its zeal for combating concentration. Atrophy has reached so advanced a state that the public has of late witnessed the bizarre spectacle of the Justice Department, with its relatively narrow mandate, intervening in FCC proceedings, such as ITT-ABC, to create court cases with names like *The United States vs. The FCC.*

This history is an unhappy one on the whole. It forces one to question whether government can ever realistically be expected to sustain a vigilant posture over an industry which controls the very access of government officials themselves to the electorate.

I fear that we have already reached the point in this country where the media, our greatest check on other accumulations of power, may themselves be beyond the reach of any other institution: the Congress, the President, or the Federal Communications Commission, not to mention governors, mayors, state legislators, and city councilmen. Congressional hearings are begun and then quietly dropped. Whenever the FCC stirs fitfully as if in wakefulness, the broadcasting industry scurries up the Hill for a congressional bludgeon. And the fact that roughly 60 percent of all campaign expenses go to radio and television time gives but a glimmer of the power of broadcasting in the lives of senators and congressmen.

However, the picture at this moment has its more hopeful aspect. There does seem to be an exceptional flurry of official concern. Even the FCC has its proposed rulemaking oustanding. The Department of Justice, having broken into the communications field via its dramatic intervention before the FCC in the ITT-ABC merger case, has also been pressing a campaign to force the dissolution of joint operating agreements between separately owned newspapers in individual cities, and opposed a recent application for broadcasting properties by newspaper interests in Beaumont, Texas. It has been scrutinizing cross-media combinations linking broadcasting, newspaper, and cable television outlets. On Capitol Hill, Senator Phil Hart's Antitrust and Monopoly Subcommittee and Chairman Harley Staggers' House Interstate and Foreign Commerce Committee have both summoned the Federal Communications Commission to appear before them in recent months, to acquaint the Commission with the committees' concern about FCC-approved increases in broadcast holdings by single individuals and companies, and about cross-ownership of newspapers, CATV systems, and broadcast stations. Representatives John Dingell, John Moss, and Richard Ottinger have introduced legislation which would proscribe network ownership of any nonbroadcast interests. And as I previously mentioned, President Johnson has appointed a task force to undertake a comprehensive review of national communications policy.

Twenty years ago Robert M. Hutchins, then chancellor of the University of Chicago, was named chairman of the "Commission on Freedom of the Press." It produced a thoughtful report, full of recommendations largely applicable today—including "the establishment of a new and independent [nongovernmental] agency to appraise and report annually upon the performance of the press," and urged "that the members of the press engage in vigorous mutual criticism." Its proposals are once again being dusted off and reread.

What is needed now, more than anything else, is to keep this flurry of interest alive, and to channel it toward constructive reforms. What this means, in practical fact, is that concern for media concentration must find an institutional home.

The Department of Justice has already illustrated the value of participation by an external institution in FCC decision-making. The developing concept of a special consumers' representative offers a potentially broader base for similar action.

But the proper place to lodge continuing responsibility for promoting diversity in the mass media is neither the FCC nor the Justice Department nor a congressional committee. The initiative must come from private sources. Plucky Nader-like crusaders such as John Banzhaf (who single-handedly induced the FCC to apply the "fairness" doctrine to cigarette commercials) have shown how responsive government can be to the skillful and vigorous efforts of even a lone individual. But there are more adequately staffed and funded private organizations which could play a more effective role in policy formation than a single individual. Even the FCC, where the public interest gets entirely too little representation from private sources, has felt the impact of the United Church of Christ, with its interest in the influence of broadcasting on race relations and in the programming responsibility of licensees, and of the American Civil Liberties Union, which submitted a brief in the ITT-ABC case.

Ideally, however, the resources for a sustained attack on concentration might be centered in a single institution, equipped to look after this cause with the kind of determination and intelligence that the Ford Foundation and the Carnegie Corporation, for example, have brought to bear in behalf of the cause of public broadcasting and domestic satellites. The law schools and their law reviews, as an institution, have performed well in this way for the courts, but have virtually abdicated responsibility for the agencies.

Such an organization could devote itself to research as well as representation. For at present any public body like the FCC, which has to make determinations about acceptable levels of media concentration, has to do so largely on the basis of hunch. In addition, private interest in problems of concentration would encourage the Justice Department to sustain its present vigilance in this area. It could stimulate renewed vigilance on the part of the FCC, through participation in Commission proceedings. And it could consider whether new legislation might be appropriate to reach the problem of newspaper-magazine-book publishing combinations.

If changes are to be made (or now dormant standards are to be enforced) the most pressing political question is whether to apply the standards prospectively only, or to require divestiture. It is highly unlikely, to say the least, that legislation requiring massive divestiture of multiple station ownership, or newspaper ownership of stations, would ever pass through Congress. Given the number of station sales every year, however, even prospective standards could have some impact over ten years or so.

In general, I would urge the minimal standard that no accumulation of media should be permitted without a specific and convincing showing of a continuing countervailing social benefit. For no one has a higher calling in an increasingly complex free society bent on self-government than he who informs and moves the people. Personal prejudice, ignorance, social pressure, and advertiser pressure are in large measure inevitable. But a nation that has, in Learned Hand's phrase, "staked its all" upon the rational dialogue of an informed electorate simply cannot take any unnecessary risk of polluting the stream of information and opinion that sustains it. At the very least, the burden of proving the social utility of doing otherwise should be upon him who seeks the power and profit which will result.

Whatever may be the outcome, the wave of renewed interest in the impact of ownership on the role of the media in our society is healthy. All will gain from intelligent inquiry by Congress, the Executive, the regulatory commissions—and especially the academic community, the American people generally, and the media themselves. For, as the Supreme Court has noted, nothing is more important in a free society than "the widest possible dissemination of information from diverse and antagonistic sources." And if we are unwilling to discuss *this* issue fully today we may find ourselves discussing none that matter very much tomorrow.

For Discussion

1. What function of the FCC does Johnson focus upon in this article?
2. Briefly explain Johnson's objections to the proposed ITT-ABC merger.
3. In addition to the "aborted" ITT-ABC merger, what other examples of dangerous media concentration of ownership does Johnson discuss?
4. What incipient threat does Johnson see in "cable television"?
5. Discuss Johnson's guidelines for "tolerating concentration of media ownership."
6. What provisions of the antitrust laws limit their effectiveness in relationship to media ownership?
7. What assessment does Johnson make of the FCC?
8. Discuss the merits and shortcomings of Johnson's proposal for handling future media barons. Also consider the point at which he would take action.
9. What do the first three paragraphs tell you about Johnson's personality? How is it reflected in the rest of the essay?
10. What qualities make this essay discursive?

JAMES RIDGEWAY

The Machine

James Ridgeway began writing for *The Wall Street Journal,*
then moved to England where he was a contributor to *The Econ-
omist, The Observer,* and *The Guardian.* In 1962, when he returned to the United States, he joined the staff of *The New
Republic.* The selection which follows is the opening chapter of
his recent book, *The Closed Corporation.*

"The function of college is not to prepare you for life," the philosopher
Paul Weiss said. "It is to prepare you to be a man, and when you are a man
you can face life, whatever the conditions."

In all likelihood most Americans believe, like Weiss, that universities
are places where professors teach students. They are wrong. In fact, the
university looks more like a center for industrial activity than a community
of scholars.

The general citizenry may be surprised to learn that they pay such
high prices for medicines partly because the universities ganged together
and lobbied Congress in behalf of the drug companies; that the professor of
medieval history at Princeton university runs from his classes to the Central
Intelligence Agency, where he helps straighten out the spies; and that Yale
University hawks about a mutual fund.

In the *Notes on the Post Industrial State,* Daniel Bell makes it plain
enough:

> The university, which is the place where theoretical knowledge is sought,
> tested and codified in a disinterested way, becomes the primary institution
> of the new society. Perhaps it is not too much to say that if the business
> firm was the key institution of the past one hundred years because of its role
> in organizing production for the mass creation of products, the university
> will become the central institution of the next hundred years because of its
> role as the new source of innovation and knowledge.

This book is an inquiry into the different sorts of relationships universities and professors have with the rest of society, carried forward in large part to find out what their impact is and whether there is anything to the notion that the university is central to industrial activity.

The university industry basically consists of 2200 institutions, with total annual revenues of $10 billion and a growth rate of some 10 percent. The business employs half a million people as instructors, and holds 6.7 million students. The shape of the industry changes, depending as it does on the shifting alliances with government, which supplies much of the money for research, and on business, which makes the products resulting from the research.

It is difficult to gain any clear understanding of the university because it remains as one of the few large secret organizations within the nation. One can find out more about the activities of a public corporation than about a university. The trustees of private universities are invariably self-perpetuating bodies of businessmen who meet in private and do not publish accounts of their activities. In public institutions, where there are more apt to be periodic open meetings of the regents and trustees who are elected or appointed by the state governor, the real business goes on behind the scenes in executive sessions, and the minutes of these back-room deals are either nonexistent or never made public. Institutions of higher learning are tax exempt, yet unlike the foundations which enjoy the same status but are required by the Internal Revenue Service to make public certain financial information, universities are not subject to such provisions. And so far as the private colleges are concerned, the government allows them to operate in total secrecy if they desire. Many of the large private universities do publish financial reports to reassure their alumni, but this is not a standard practice. Columbia University will make available on request a list of its securities investments but refuses to disclose real estate holdings, a delicate matter since some of them are located in slum areas. The University of Chicago will not disclose any of its investments. Even though Long Island University, a private university, is chartered by the state of New York and numbers among its trustees a U.S. congressman, Ogden Reid, it refused to provide a financial report to a state legislative committee investigating its activities. The University of California, a public institution—the largest university in the world—with a budget of nearly $1 billion, steadfastly refused to disclose its holdings, and even the members of the regents committee which invests the money have expressed their ignorance of where it goes. At the University of Maryland the budget is figured with the administration by a planning bureau, which will not even make known the full details to different academic departments, on the general theory that if one department doesn't know what the others are getting, it won't be likely to argue about the course of university expansion.

While it is usual to distinguish between private and public universities, this can be misleading. Two thirds of American students go to public institutions, and the government spends large amounts of money in both types of schools, so much so that Clark Kerr, former president of the University of California, calls the modern university the "Federal Grant University."

In the Northwest Ordinance of 1787, the Federal government set forth its intention of encouraging education, but as a practical matter this meant little until the passage of the Morrill Act of 1862 and subsequent legislation which provided land for public institutions and funds for instruction in agriculture. This led to the establishment of university-operated agricultural extension programs and farm experiment stations. In World War I the government spent a little money at universities for research in improving aircraft and established the ROTC programs for training officers. By the 1930's it was spending money for research in cancer through the creation of the National Cancer Institute. During the depression the universities assisted the government with New Deal public-works measures.

The U.S. government's involvement with the universities had a distinctly utilitarian bent, tied for the most part to industrial or military ends; by contrast, the European universities had become research centers. Consequently, many of the great scientists in the United States during the early part of the century were schooled abroad. Because of the demands of the second world war, the scientists and the military formed a working partnership which resulted first in dramatic scientific breakthroughs leading to the atomic bomb, and subsequently widened into the present pervasive relationship between government and all segments of the Academic Community.

The first controlled chain reaction which led to the development of the atomic bomb was achieved in laboratories at the University of Chicago. Johns Hopkins ran the Applied Physics Laboratory which developed the self-deteriorating proximity fuse. The Radiation Laboratory at MIT was the main center for radar research. During the period of the cold war the ties between university scientists and the government broadened and solidified. Many of the studies which led to the development of the hydrogen bomb were made by university scientists who spent their summers at Los Alamos; the father of the bomb, Edward Teller, of course, is from the University of California. The Lincoln Labs at MIT carried forward work on radar defense warning systems, as well as on missile guidance systems. The Jason Division of the Institute for Defense Analysis, a think tank run for the Defense Department by twelve universities, made studies for the military on missile re-entry problems, counterinsurgency and tactical uses of nuclear warfare in Southeast Asia. Professors at Harvard and MIT worked on building clever communications systems for the military, and others worked secretly during the summers on breaking codes. It was during the 1950's that the CIA began its covert financing through universities. It was interested in building up anti-communist student movements at home and creating anti-communist labor unions abroad.

Today more than two thirds of the university research funds come from the Department of Defense, the Atomic Energy Commission or the National Aeronautics and Space Administration, all closely concerned with defense matters. Much of this money is channeled to a small number of well-known universities. A congressional study in 1964 indicated that of 2100 universities, ten received 38 percent of the federal funds for research and development. (They are the University of California, MIT, Cornell, Columbia, University of Michigan, Harvard, Illinois, Stanford, Chicago and Minnesota.) This money often accounts for large portions of the universities' total budgets. Thus, 80 percent of MIT's funds are estimated to come from the government; Columbia and Princeton get about 50 percent of their money from Washington. In addition, there has been widespread covert funding by the CIA of university projects through front foundations.

The universities' growing liaison with the defense agencies over the past decade has coincided with the expanding importance of the Defense Department, which under Robert McNamara wandered rather far afield from military matters. The Defense Department, which bought the professors' expertise, helped shape the aerospace industry, then laid the groundwork for and supported the new education business. As a hedge against disarmament, the Defense Department encouraged the electronics firms which relied on it for business to get into other fields, one of which was to develop the computer for use in teaching children. The Defense planners also were leaders among those who pointed out that there might be businesses in slum rebuilding, water and air pollution abatement. The Defense Department helped write the poverty program, and when under the stewardship of Sargent Shriver it failed to meet expectations, McNamara sent along efficiency experts to restore order. McNamara's assistants were put in the Department of Health, Education and Welfare, where they remodeled it in imitation of the Pentagon. As they moved from one endeavor to the next, McNamara's staff towed along professors to add their expertise.

In a good many instances the liaisons between the defense agencies and the universities were accomplished through the federal contract research centers. There are forty-seven of them; the centers do $1.2 billion worth of research and development work annually, almost all of it sponsored by the Defense Department or the Atomic Energy Commission. Nearly half the money goes to centers managed by universities. The center idea has provided a convenient way for inveigling bright scientists into defense work. The government can pay the scientists higher wages by hiring them through universities, thereby getting around the civil service pay scales. As for the scientists themselves, they appear more distinguished to their colleagues as members of the faculty of some great university than if they were working on bomb sites in some dingy Pentagon office. And the centers give the universities a bit of prestige and a management fee. (Johns Hopkins gets $1 million annually in fees for administering the $50 million budget of the Applied Physics Laboratory.)

In theory, the government gets the best independent scientific advice in this manner, but in fact, what happens is that the major universities become first captive and then active advocates for the military and paramilitary agencies of government in order to get more money for research. This leads to bizarre situations; last spring Senator Fulbright, the chairman of the Senate Foreign Relations Committee, announced he had been denied certain information concerning the war in Vietnam, prepared for the Defense Department by the Institute for Defense Analysis, although the presidents of the sponsoring universities had access to it.

During the presidency of John Kennedy the Defense Department civilians were important in fashioning and implementing schemes for limited war and counter-insurgency, which resulted in the army's being viewed as an instrument of foreign policy in Southeast Asia and Latin America. Previously it had been widely assumed that the conduct of foreign affairs was the job of the State Department. Whereas during past wars the military relied on relatively straightforward methods of pitting armies against one another, during the Kennedy and early Johnson periods the civilians in the Defense Department got excited about the possibilities of using propaganda devices to manipulate the internal policies of foreign countries, and this in turn led to financing grandiose projects by university social scientists to study the behavior of the enemy, and involving foreign universities in the same work through grants. In 1968, the military will be spending approximately $50 million for projects related to developments in U.S. foreign policy. While there is some pressure within the Congress for stopping these projects, it is more likely that they will instead be expanded, for the social scientists have lately been smitten with what the Defense Department calls "Peacefare," ways of transposing the ideas and machinery employed by the military for civilian uses, such as counter-insurgency tactics in the ghetto, or teaching blacks to behave themselves by putting them all in the army, where, as Patrick Moynihan argues, they may learn a trade before being packed into a coffin in Vietnam.

It was through the Defense Department that the universities and business first worked together in consortia arrangements to develop complicated weapons systems. This troika arrangement is slowly evolving into a new sort of corporate machine, or more precisely, machine parts which engage or disengage depending on the job to be done. Basically, the parts consist of the university, where products or processes are conceived, the government, which finances their development, and private business, which makes and sells the finished item.

The emerging forms of corporate organization are very much in flux, but the professor entrepreneurs, who dart back and forth from university to government to business, help shape corporate structures and policies.

The theory is that the activities of the corporations can be planned and set in motion by scholars who scheme together at their innards. Other scholars within the government make sure the goals of production are worthy, and to control the activity of the corporations, they ring changes through the economic machinery, as, for example, in the late Senator Robert Kennedy's slum rehabilitation plan. Its central feature is to bring outside economic support into the ghetto and yet promote the illusion of black control. In fact, the control remains with the large corporations, which in return for widening their power base are slightly more beneficent, hiring some blacks but passing on the cost of their involvement to the consumers through higher prices.

So the scholars dash back and forth, building the new economic and political machinery. They see themselves as renaissance men, the proprietors of the new factories.

For Discussion

1. What is the traditional image of the university? What role does Ridgeway see for the university in the next 100 years?
2. What evidence does Ridgeway give to show that the university is an industry? A secret organization? An arm of the military?
3. How have the universities become involved with both foreign and domestic policy?
4. What are the implications for the United States of the "troika" which Ridgeway describes? What is being done by those who oppose this troika? What else might be done?
5. Discuss your idea of what a university should be.
6. What is the attitude toward the scholar reflected in the last two sentences? How does it compare to your idea of a scholar?
7. Find examples in which Ridgeway's emotional involvement with his subject is revealed through his choice of language.
8. Although Ridgeway's chief appeal is to reason, what emotions does he arouse in you?

DAVID M. SHOUP

The New American Militarism

General David M. Shoup has been called a "marine's marine."
Born in Battleground, Indiana, on December 30, 1904, he graduated from DePauw University in 1926, where he also began his
military training in the ROTC. His rise to prominence was
marked by his distinguished service as Commander of the Second
Marine Division at Tarawa in World War II, where he won the
Congressional Medal of Honor. In 1960, he was appointed Com-
mandant of the United States Marine Corps and served on the
Joint Chiefs of Staff with the rank of general until his retirement
in 1963. The following essay, written in collaboration with
another retired Marine officer, Colonel James A. Donovan, begins
to explain why Shoup has been called the most outspoken
military critic of the military.

America has become a militaristic and aggressive nation. Our massive
and swift invasion of the Dominican Republic in 1965, concurrent with the
rapid buildup of U.S. military power in Vietnam, constituted an impressive
demonstration of America's readiness to execute military contingency plans
and to seek military solutions to problems of political disorder and potential
Communist threats in the areas of our interest.

This "military task force" type of diplomacy is in the tradition of our
more primitive, pre-World War II "gunboat diplomacy," in which we landed
small forces of Marines to protect American lives and property from the
perils of native bandits and revolutionaries. In those days the U.S. Navy
and its Marine landing forces were our chief means, short of war, for showing the flag, exercising American power, and protecting U.S. interests
abroad. The Navy, enjoying the freedom of the seas, was a visible and
effective representative of the nation's sovereign power. The Marines could
be employed ashore "on such other duties as the President might direct"

without congressional approval or a declaration of war. The U.S. Army was not then used so freely because it was rarely ready for expeditionary service without some degree of mobilization, and its use overseas normally required a declaration of emergency or war. Now, however, we have numerous contingency plans involving large joint Air Force-Army-Navy-Marine task forces to defend U.S. interests and to safeguard our allies wherever and whenever we suspect Communist aggression. We maintain more than 1,517,000 Americans in uniform overseas in 119 countries. We have 8 treaties to help defend 48 nations if they ask us to—or if we choose to intervene in their affairs. We have an immense and expensive military establishment, fueled by a gigantic defense industry, and millions of proud, patriotic, and frequently bellicose and militaristic citizens. How did this militarist culture evolve? How did this militarism steer us into the tragic military and political morass of Vietnam?

Prior to World War II, American attitudes were typically isolationist, pacifist, and generally antimilitary. The regular peacetime military establishment enjoyed small prestige and limited influence upon national affairs. The public knew little about the armed forces, and only a few thousand men were attracted to military service and careers. In 1940 there were but 428,000 officers and enlisted men in the Army and Navy. The scale of the war, and the world's power relationships which resulted, created the American military giant. Today the active armed forces contain over 3.4 million men and women, with an additional 1.6 million ready reserves and National Guardsmen.

America's vastly expanded world role after World War II hinged upon military power. The voice and views of the professional military people became increasingly prominent. During the postwar period, distinguished military leaders from the war years filled many top positions in government. Generals Marshall, Eisenhower, MacArthur, Taylor, Ridgeway, LeMay, and others were not only popular heroes but respected opinion-makers. It was a time of international readjustment; military minds offered the benefits of firm views and problem-solving experience to the management of the nation's affairs. Military procedures—including the general staff system, briefings, estimates of the situation, and the organizational and operational techniques of the highly schooled, confident military professionals—spread throughout American culture.

World War II had been a long war. Millions of young American men had matured, been educated, and gained rank and stature during their years in uniform. In spite of themselves, many returned to civilian life as indoctrinated, combat-experienced military professionals. They were veterans, and for better or worse would never be the same again. America will never be the same either. We are now a nation of veterans. To the 14.9 million veterans of World War II, Korea added another 5.7 million five years later, and ever since, the large peacetime military establishment has been training and releasing draftees, enlistees, and short-term reservists by the hundreds of thousands each year. In 1968 the total living veterans of U.S. military service numbered over 23 million, or about 20 percent of the adult population.

Today most middle-aged men, most business, government, civic, and professional leaders, have served some time in uniform. Whether they liked it or not, their military training and experience have affected them, for the creeds and attitudes of the armed forces are powerful medicine, and can become habit-forming. The military codes include all the virtues and beliefs used to motivate men of high principle: patriotism, duty and service to country, honor among fellowmen, courage in the face of danger, loyalty to organization and leaders, self-sacrifice for comrades, leadership, discipline, and physical fitness. For many veterans the military's efforts to train and indoctrinate them may well be the most impressive and influential experience they have ever had—especially so for the young and less educated.

In addition, each of the armed forces has its own special doctrinal beliefs and well-catalogued customs, traditions, rituals, and folklore upon which it strives to build a fiercely loyal military character and esprit de corps. All ranks are taught that their unit and their branch of the military service are the most elite, important, efficient, or effective in the military establishment. By believing in the superiority and importance of their own service they also provide themselves a degree of personal status, pride, and self-confidence.

As they get older, many veterans seem to romanticize and exaggerate their own military experience and loyalties. The policies, attitudes, and positions of the powerful veterans' organizations such as the American Legion, Veterans of Foreign Wars, and AMVETS, totaling over 4 million men, frequently reflect this pugnacious and chauvinistic tendency. Their memberships generally favor military solutions to world problems in the pattern of their own earlier experience, and often assert that their military service and sacrifice should be repeated by the younger generations.

Closely related to the attitudes and influence of America's millions of veterans is the vast and powerful complex of the defense industries, which have been described in detail many times in the eight years since General Eisenhower first warned of the military-industrial power complex in his farewell address as President. The relationship between the defense industry and the military establishment is closer than many citizens realize. Together they form a powerful public opinion lobby. The several military service associations provide both a forum and a meeting ground for the military and its industries. The associations also provide each of the armed services with a means of fostering their respective roles, objectives, and propaganda. Each of the four services has its own association, and there are also additional military function associations, for ordnance, management, defense industry, and defense transportation, to name some of the more prominent. The Air Force Association and the Association of the U.S. Army are the largest, best organized, and most effective of the service associations. The Navy League, typical of the "silent service" traditions, is not as well coordinated in its public relations efforts, and the small Marine Corps Association is not even in the same arena with the other contenders, the Marine Association's main activity being the publication of a semi-official monthly magazine. Actually, the service associations' respective magazines, with an estimated combined circulation of over 270,000, are the primary medium serving the several associations' purposes.

Air Force and Space Digest, to cite one example, is the magazine of the Air Force Association and the unofficial mouthpiece of the U.S. Air Force doctrine, "party line," and propaganda. It frequently promotes Air Force policy that has been officially frustrated or suppressed within the Department of Defense. It beats the tub for strength through aerospace power, interprets diplomatic, strategic, and tactical problems in terms of air power, stresses the requirements for quantities of every type of aircraft, and frequently perpetuates the extravagant fictions about the effectiveness of bombing. This, of course, is well coordinated with and supported by the multibillion-dollar aerospace industry, which thrives upon the boundless desires of the Air Force. They reciprocate with lavish and expensive ads in every issue of *Air Force.* Over 96,000 members of the Air Force Association receive the magazine. Members include active, reserve, retired personnel, and veterans of the U.S. Air Force. Additional thousands of copies go to people engaged in the defense industry. The thick mixture of advertising, propaganda, and Air Force doctrine continuously repeated in this publication provides its readers and writers with a form of intellectual hypnosis, and they are prone to believe their own propaganda because they read it in *Air Force.*

The American people have also become more and more accustomed to militarism, to uniforms, to the cult of the gun, and to the violence of combat. Whole generations have been brought up on war news and wartime propaganda; the few years of peace since 1939 have seen a steady stream of war novels, war movies, comic strips, and television programs with war or military settings. To many Americans, military training, expeditionary service, and warfare are merely extensions of the entertainment and games of childhood. Even the weaponry and hardware they use at war are similar to the highly realistic toys of their youth. Soldiering loses appeal for some of the relatively few who experience the blood, terror, and filth of battle; for many, however, including far too many senior professional officers, war and combat are an exciting adventure, a competitive game, and an escape from the dull routines of peacetime.

It is this influential nucleus of aggressive, ambitious professional military leaders who are the root of America's evolving militarism. There are over 410,000 commissioned officers on active duty in the four armed services. Of these, well over half are junior ranking reserve officers on temporary active duty. Of the 150,000 or so regular career officers, only a portion are senior ranking colonels, generals, and admirals, but it is they who constitute the elite core of the military establishment. It is these few thousand top-ranking professionals who command and manage the armed forces and plan and formulate military policy and opinion. How is it, then, that in spite of civilian controls and the national desire for peace, this small group of men exert so much martial influence upon the government and life of the American people?

The military will disclaim any excess of power or influence on their part. They will point to their small numbers, low pay, and subordination to civilian masters as proof of their modest status and innocence. Nevertheless, the professional military, as a group, is probably one of the best organized and most influential of the various segments of the American scene. Three wars and six major contingencies since 1940 have forced the American people to become abnormally aware of the armed forces and their leaders. In turn the military services have produced an unending supply of distinguished, capable, articulate, and effective leaders. The sheer skill, energy, and dedication of America's military officers make them dominant in almost every government or civic organization they may inhabit, from the federal Cabinet to the local PTA.

The hard core of high-ranking professionals are, first of all, mostly service academy graduates: they had to be physically and intellectually above average among their peers just to gain entrance to an academy. Thereafter for the rest of their careers they are exposed to constant competition for selection and promotion. Attrition is high, and only the most capable survive to reach the elite senior ranks. Few other professions have such rigorous selection systems; as a result, the top military leaders are top-caliber men.

Not many industries, institutions, or civilian branches of government have the resources, techniques, or experience in training leaders such as are now employed by the armed forces in their excellent and elaborate school systems. Military leaders are taught to command large organizations and to plan big operations. They learn the techniques of influencing others. Their education is not, however, liberal or cultural. It stresses the tactics, doctrines, traditions, and codes of the military trade. It produces technicians and disciples, not philosophers.

The men who rise to the top of the military hierarchy have usually demonstrated their effectiveness as leaders, planners, and organization managers. They have perhaps performed heroically in combat, but most of all they have demonstrated their loyalty as proponents of their own service's doctrine and their dedication to the defense establishment. The paramount sense of duty to follow orders is at the root of the military professional's performance. As a result the military often operate more efficiently and effectively in the arena of defense policy planning than do their civilian counterparts in the State Department. The military planners have their doctrinal beliefs, their loyalties, their discipline—and their typical desire to compete and win. The civilians in government can scarcely play the same policy-planning game. In general the military are better organized, they work harder, they think straighter, and they keep their eyes on the objective, which is to be instantly ready to solve the problem through military action while ensuring that their respective service gets its proper mission, role, and recognition in the operation. In an emergency the military usually have a ready plan; if not, their numerous doctrinal manuals provide firm guidelines for action. Politicians, civilian appointees, and diplomats do not normally have the same confidence about how to react to threats and violence as do the military.

The motivations behind these endeavors are difficult for civilians to understand. For example, military professionals cannot measure the success of their individual efforts in terms of personal financial gain. The armed forces are not profit-making organizations, and the rewards for excellence in the military profession are acquired in less tangible forms. Thus it is that promotion and the responsibilities of higher command, with the related fringe benefits of quarters, servants, privileges, and prestige, motivate most career officers. Promotions and choice job opportunities are attained by constantly performing well, conforming to the expected patterns, and pleasing the senior officers. Promotions and awards also frequently result from heroic and distinguished performance in combat, and it takes a war to become a military hero. Civilians can scarcely understand or even believe that many ambitious military professionals truly yearn for wars and the opportunities for glory and distinction afforded only in combat. A career of peacetime duty is a dull and frustrating prospect for the normal regular officer to contemplate.

The professional military leaders of the U.S. Armed Forces have some additional motivations which influence their readiness to involve their country in military ventures. Unlike some of the civilian policy-makers, the military has not been obsessed with the threat of Communism per se. Most military people know very little about Communism either as a doctrine or as a form of government. But they have been given reason enough to presume that it is bad and represents the force of evil. When they can identify "Communist aggression," however, the matter then becomes of direct concern to the armed forces. Aggressors are the enemy in the war games, the "bad guys," the "Reds." Defeating aggression is a gigantic combat-area competition rather than a crusade to save the world from Communism. In the military view, all "Communist aggression" is certain to be interpreted as a threat to the United States.

The armed forces' role in performing its part of the national security policy—in addition, to defense against actual direct attack on the United States and to maintaining the strategic atomic deterrent forces—is to be prepared to employ its *General Purpose Forces* in support of our collective security policy and the related treaties and alliances. To do this it deploys certain forces to forward zones in the Unified Commands, and maintains an up-to-date file of scores of detailed contingency plans which have been thrashed out and approved by the Joint Chiefs of Staff. Important features of these are the movement or deployment schedules of task forces assigned to each plan. The various details of these plans continue to create intense rivalries between the Navy-Marine sea-lift forces and the Army-Air Force team of air-mobility proponents. At the senior command levels parochial pride in service, personal ambitions, and old Army-Navy game rivalry stemming back to academy loyalties can influence strategic planning far more than most civilians would care to believe. The game is to be ready for deployment sooner than the other elements of the joint task force and to be so disposed as to be the "first to fight." The danger presented by this practice is that readiness and deployment speed become ends in themselves. This was clearly revealed in the massive and rapid intervention in the Dominican Republic in 1965 when the contingency plans and interservice rivalry appeared to supersede diplomacy. Before the world realized what was happening, the momentum and velocity of the military plans propelled almost 20,000 U.S. soldiers and Marines into the small turbulent republic in an impressive race to test the respective mobility of the Army and the Marines, and to attain overall command of "U.S. Forces Dom. Rep." Only a fraction of the force deployed was needed or justified. A small 1935-model Marine landing force could probably have handled the situation. But the Army airlifted much of the 82nd Airborne Division to the scene, included a lieutenant general, and took charge of the operation.

Simultaneously, in Vietnam during 1965 the four services were racing to build up combat strength in that hapless country. This effort was ostensibly to save South Vietnam from Viet Cong and North Vietnamese aggression. It should also be noted that it was motivated in part by the same old interservice rivalry to demonstrate respective importance and combat effectiveness.

The punitive air strikes immediately following the Tonkin Gulf incident in late 1964 revealed the readiness of naval air forces to bomb North Vietnam. (It now appears that the Navy actually had attack plans ready even before the alleged incident took place!) So by early 1965 the Navy carrier people and the Air Force initiated a contest of comparative strikes, sorties, tonnages dropped, "Killed by Air" claims, and target grabbing which continued up to the 1968 bombing pause. Much of the reporting on air action has consisted of misleading data or propaganda to serve Air Force and Navy purposes. In fact, it became increasingly apparent that the

U.S. bombing effort in both North and South Vietnam has been one of the most wasteful and expensive hoaxes ever to be put over on the American people. Tactical and close air support of ground operations is essential, but air power use in general has to a large degree been a contest for the operations planners, "fine experience" for young pilots, and opportunity for career officers.

The highly trained professional and aggressive career officers of the Army and Marine Corps played a similar game. Prior to the decision to send combat units to South Vietnam in early 1965, both services were striving to increase their involvement. The Army already had over 16,000 military aid personnel serving in South Vietnam in the military advisor role, in training missions, logistic services, supporting helicopter companies, and in Special Forces teams. This investment of men and matériel justified a requirement for additional U.S. combat units to provide local security and to help protect our growing commitment of aid to the South Vietnam regime.

There were also top-ranking Army officers who wanted to project Army ground combat units into the Vietnam struggle for a variety of other reasons; to test plans and new equipment, to test the new air-mobile theories and tactics, to try the tactics and techniques of counterinsurgency, and to gain combat experience for young officers and noncommissioned officers. It also appeared to be a case of the military's duty to stop "Communist aggression" in Vietnam.

The Marines had somewhat similar motivations, the least of which was any real concern about the political or social problems of the Vietnamese people. In early 1965 there was a shooting war going on and the Marines were being left out of it, contrary to all their traditions. The Army's military advisory people were hogging American participation—except for a Marine Corps transport helicopter squadron at Danang which was helping the Army of the Republic of Vietnam. For several years young Marine officers had been going to South Vietnam from the 3rd Marine Division on Okinawa for short tours of "on-the-job training" with the small South Vietnam Marine Corps. There was a growing concern, however, among some senior Marines that the Corps should get involved on a larger scale and be the "first to fight" in keeping with the Corps's traditions. This would help justify the Corps's continued existence, which many Marines seem to consider to be in constant jeopardy.

The Corps had also spent several years exploring the theories of counterinsurgency and as early as 1961 had developed an elaborate lecture-demonstration called OPERATION CORMORANT, for school and Marine Corps promotion purposes, which depicted the Marines conducting a large-scale amphibious operation on the coast of Vietnam and thereby helping resolve a hypothetical aggressor-insurgency problem. As always it was important to Marine planners and doctrinaires to apply an amphibious operation to the Vietnam situation and provide justification for this special Marine functional responsibility. So Marine planners were seeking an acceptable excuse to thrust a landing force over the beaches of Vietnam when the Viet Cong attacked the U.S. Army Special Forces camp at Pleiku in February, 1965. It was considered unacceptable aggression, and the President was thereby prompted to put U.S. ground combat units into the war. Elements of the 3rd Marine Division at Okinawa were already aboard ship and eager to go, for the Marines also intended to get to Vietnam before their neighbor on Okinawa, the Army's 173rd Airborne Brigade, arrived. (Actually the initial Marine unit to deploy was an airlifted anticraft missile battalion which arrived to protect the Danang air base.) With these initial deployments the Army-Marine race to build forces in Vietnam began in earnest and did not slow down until both became overextended, overcommitted, and depleted at home.

For years up to 1964 the chiefs of the armed services, of whom the author was then one, deemed it unnecessary and unwise for U.S. forces to become involved in any ground war in Southeast Asia. In 1964 there were changes in the composition of the Joint Chiefs of Staff, and in a matter of a few months the Johnson Administration, encouraged by the aggressive military, hastened into what has become the quagmire of Vietnam. The intention at the time was that the war effort be kept small and "limited." But as the momentum and involvement built up, the military leaders rationalized a case that this was not a limited-objective exercise, but was a proper war in defense of the United States against "Communist aggression" and in honor of our area commitments.

The battle successes and heroic exploits of America's fine young fighting men have added to the military's traditions which extol service, bravery, and sacrifice, and so it has somehow become unpatriotic to question our military strategy and tactics or the motives of military leaders. Actually, however, the military commanders have directed the war in Vietnam, they have managed the details of its conduct; and more than most civilian officials, the top military planners were initially ready to become involved in Vietnam combat and have the opportunity to practice their trade. It has been popular to blame the civilian administration for the conduct and failures of the war rather than to question the motives of the military. But some of the generals and admirals are by no means without responsibility for the Vietnam miscalculations.

Some of the credibility difficulties experienced by the Johnson Administration over its war situation reports and Vietnam policy can also be blamed in part upon the military advisors. By its very nature most military activity falls under various degrees of security classification. Much that the military plans or does must be kept from the enemy. Thus the military is indoctrinated to be secretive, devious, and misleading in its plans and operations. It does not, however, always confine its security restrictions to purely military operations. Each of the services and all of the major commands practice techniques of controlling the news and the release of self-serving propaganda: in "the interests of national defense," to make the service look good, to cover up mistakes, to build up and publicize a distinguished military personality, or to win a round in the continuous gamesmanship of the interservice contest. If the Johnson Administration suffered from lack of credibility in its reporting of the war, the truth would reveal that much of the hocus-pocus stemmed from schemers in the military services, both at home and abroad.

Our militaristic culture was born of the necessities of World War II, nurtured by the Korean War, and became an accepted aspect of American life during the years of cold war emergencies and real or imagined threats from the Communist bloc. Both the philosophy and the institutions of militarism grew during these years because of the momentum of their own dynamism, the vigor of their ideas, their large size and scope, and because of the dedicated concentration of the emergent military leaders upon their doctrinal objectives. The dynamism of the defense establishment and its culture is also inspired and stimulated by vast amounts of money, by the new creations of military research and matériel development, and by the concepts of the Defense Department-supported "think factories." These latter are extravagantly funded civilian organizations of scientists, analysts, and retired military strategists who feed new militaristic philosophies into the Defense Department to help broaden the views of the single service doctrinaires, to create fresh policies and new requirements for ever larger, more expensive defense forces.

Somewhat like a religion, the basic appeals of anti-Communism, national defense, and patriotism provide the foundation for a powerful creed upon which the defense establishment can build, grow, and justify its cost. More so than many large bureaucratic organizations, the defense establishment now devotes a large share of its efforts to self-perpetuation, to justifying its organizations, to preaching its doctrines, and to self-maintenance and management. Warfare becomes an extension of war games and field tests. War justifies the existence of the establishment, provides experience for the military novice and challenges for the senior officer. Wars and emergencies put the military and their leaders on the front pages and give status and prestige to the professionals. Wars add to the military traditions, the self-nourishment of heroic deeds, and provide a new crop of military leaders who become the rededicated disciples of the code of service and military action. Being recognized public figures in a nation always seeking folk heroes, the military leaders have been largely exempt from the criticism experienced by the more plebeian politician. Flag officers are considered "experts," and their views are often accepted by press and Congress as the gospel. In turn, the distinguished military leader feels obliged not only to perpetuate loyally the doctrine of his service but to comply with the stereotyped military characteristics by being tough, aggressive, and firm in his resistance to Communist aggression and his belief in the military solutions to world problems. Standing closely behind these leaders, encouraging and prompting them, are the rich and powerful defense industries. Standing in front, adorned with service caps, ribbons, and lapel emblems, is a nation of veterans—patriotic, belligerent, romantic, and well intentioned, finding a certain sublimation and excitement in their country's latest military venture. Militarism in America is in full bloom and promises a future of vigorous self-pollination—unless the blight of Vietnam reveals that militarism is more a poisonous weed than a glorious blossom.

The opinions contained herein are the private ones of the author and are not to be construed as official or reflecting the views of the Navy Department or the naval service at large.

For Discussion

1. What were the American attitudes toward the role of the military before World War II?
2. How did World War II and its aftermath contribute to our development as a militaristic culture?
3. In what ways do the various service organizations exert a martial influence?
4. What arguments by the military does Shoup anticipate? What are his answers?
5. What basic motivations does Shoup attribute to the military? How do they differ from civilian motivations?
6. What characteristics of the military foster its increasing influence in government?
7. How does the military view communism? What are the implications of this view? (Also see Goldwater and Wallace.)
8. State Shoup's position on Vietnam. (Also see Wald.)
9. What part does the military play in the credibility gap?
10. What evidence does Shoup offer in support of Eisenhower's warning of a military-industrial complex? (Also see Wald and Ridgeway.)
11. What arguments are given most weight by the authority of Shoup's position?

GERALD DWORKIN

The Hippies:
Permanent Revolution?

Gerald Dworkin, an assistant professor of philosophy at the Massachusetts Institute of Technology, received his Ph.D. from the University of California at Berkeley. In writing about the Hippies, Dworkin is exploring a phenomenon which emerged on the American scene in 1966 and found its most publicized home in the Haight-Ashbury district of San Francisco. Preaching altruism, mysticism, honesty, joy, and nonviolence, the Hippie movement has been called just another expression of youthful romanticism destined to be completely absorbed into the mainstream of American culture. Dworkin suggests otherwise.

> You know, on the waterfront, the richest longshoremen are all ex-Communists. Actually from my own experience, I would say that the Communist Party in the United States is a vehicle for transforming true believers into successful real estate dealers.
>
> —*Eric Hoffer*

The Hippies are merely the latest in a continuous series of revolts by a younger generation against its fathers, both literal and symbolic. The process has become so much a natural development that it no longer occasions surprise—although always some resentment. It is assumed that the young will sow their wild oats and mature into respectability by middle age. Generational revolts—political, moral, artistic, sexual—all come to an end.

I want to suggest that the Hippies really *are* different, that there are reasons for supposing that this revolt may be permanent in a way all other revolts have not been. I shall indicate reasons which support this conclusion but I am not going to try and evelute the data in any systematic way. I neither ran experiments nor made any observation that is beyond the competence of

Reprinted by permission of *Dissent* and the author.

anyone willing to spend some time with Hippies, talking and listening with a sympathetic ear. My own experience and some of the data I have are drawn from the Haight-Ashbury and Berkeley communities.

Most serious as opposed to "plastic" Hippies have now left the Haight, moving to other parts of San Francisco or what promises to be the most interesting new development—to rural communes. Still, I think the points I make are generally true of the Hippie culture, and local variations will not be important.

What, then, distinguishes the Hippies from the generation of Communists who now teach conservative sociology in the academic establishment or make reactionary foreign policy in Foggy Bottom? Why won't they fade into insignificance like the Beats or become insurance salesmen like the Bohemians of the 20's? Why are these youths different from all other youth?

No one can understand what it means to be a Hippie without understanding the decisive role of drugs. Every culture has its rituals, its own way of establishing group identity, and for the Hippie world it is dropping acid. The use of pot will not distinguish the Hippie from the non-Hippie. Pot is too respectable, too middleclass. Pot is euphoric, acid explosive. Pot is safe (everyone knows this even if it's not news fit to print); acid is potentially dangerous. Pot makes you happy; acid blows your mind. And it is this last bit which is significant for my hypothesis. It is at least possible—we don't know enough to say probable—that the long-range effects of regular use of psychedelics will make it impossible to live as the American way of life demands. There is a good deal of loose talk about changes in consciousness induced by the regular taking of psychedelics; still, the conception is not to be dismissed lightly. There is some evidence coming in on the nature of the physiological changes that take place—both in genetic and brain structure. Some of it is hysterical, or at least this is true of the publicity attached to the research reports. Still it is not unlikely that there will soon be hard data on the possible physiological effects of LSD and other hallucenogenics.

Ultimately, however, the psychological changes will be more important. It seems improbable that a Hippie who has taken a hundred trips could settle down to be a used-car salesman. Whether or not they have found God—as many claim—there do seem to be important changes in values associated with the taking of these drugs. "Head" drugs are different from "body" drugs. We know that doctors, who carry on normal lives in all other respects, form one of the largest groups of morphine addicts. As long as they get their daily dose they can function efficiently. But it is significant that morphine addicts have no ideology. Their world isn't changed as a result of their use of drugs. The world of the Hippie is a different world—more mystical, more enthusiastic. It is surrounded by music of a special kind, by social relationships of a unique character, by values antithetical to the dominant morality.

Clearly it is a complicated question to decide which came first—the drugs or the rejection of bourgeois society. All I am suggesting is that the emphasis on the use of psychedelics by the Hippies makes them different from other generational revolts and that the long-range effects, both psychological and physiological, may make it difficult for the Hippies to be re-absorbed into the mainstream of American life.

Every generational revolt involves a rejection of a larger or smaller part of the dominant values of the society. That is what makes it a revolt and not a fad. But the Hippies are involved in a more radical rejection than other rebels have been. Compare the Hippies with any of the radical political sects of the 30's. Surely, it might be claimed, the very notion of a political radical involves a basic break with the fundamental tenets of the powers-that-be. What more could a Hippie do than attack the profit motive, private property, the business ethic? Yet even while, say, a Communist was denouncing his society, he accepted values that were essential to the society. If he was a good party member, he attended meetings faithfully and attended them on time; he accepted party discipline. He listened to his leaders, accepted responsibility for selling a certain number of *Daily Workers* each week, for raising a given quota of money for the fund drive, etc.

The values and mode of life of the Hippie run counter to all this. He doesn't raise money: he burns it. He doesn't accept leadership: each individual is his own trip leader. The thought of attending a meeting is enough to turn him off completely.

(The Yippies who might be thought to be a counter-example are not really. I attended a conference of the New Left in Chicago last spring which met to decide what kind of political action to take at the Democratic convention. The Yippies were there in full force—Krasner, Hoffman, Rubin—and spent most of the time denouncing the proceedings as bullshit and calling for a demonstration of love and acid-rock. Still, even this degree of politicization represents an interesting change from the view expressed a year ago that the only power is flower-power.)

Very crudely my point could be put as follows: It's not a very large step to go from being a labor organizer to being a personnel manager for IBM. If one ran a mimeograph machine for the Socialist Worker's party, one could run a Xerox machine for the local insurance company.

Naturally, there is an ideological shift which has to come first and there are many persons who remain faithful to their early ideological commitments—although many more have abandoned them. What is essential for my argument is the relative ease or difficulty of abandoning one's youthful commitments, and I am arguing that in many respects it's going to be harder for a Hippie to "drop in."

Consider also, the radical break made by the Hippies in their attempt to break down traditional conceptions of sexual identity. Previous revolts took the form of calling for extensions of traditional sexual paths—free love, communal marriages. The Hippies have gone beyond that. Their sex is androgynous; their beauty ideal neither clearly defined as masculine or feminine. It is not so much a homosexual emphasis (although a recent Haight-Ashbury survey reports 37 per cent of the males and 24 per cent of the females as having engaged in some form of homosexual activity) as a pan-sexualism. The long hair is an attempt to defy the traditional ways of classifying individuals on the basis of superficial characteristics, and straight people are aware of this, reserving some of their choicest venom for this part of the Hippie life-style.

There is another fact that is revelant to the question of permanence. All previous generational breaks took place at a fairly late stage in the maturation process. The most usual time was late adolescence and the beginning of college life. The exact age varies—with the Beats it was a bit later, with many radical youths a bit earlier. But in all these cases the individuals involved were fully acculturated into the dominant mores of the society. What is significant about the Hippies is that the break is taking place at a much younger age. The teenie-boppers are a growing phenomenon and it is not uncommon to find eleven-year-olds who have left their family and are living in some kind of communal setup. This generation is never fully acculturated. The whole notion of dating, for example, strikes these kids as weird. It is easier for them to ignore the role of money in our society for the very good reason that they have never been entrusted with it or the responsibilities connected with it. It is usually during the teen-age years that many of the attitudes connected with making a living, caring about material possessions, looking to the products of mass culture for one's idols, are developed. By circircumventing these routes, by having just that much less time for patterns to be built in, the Hippies are provided with just that much more freedom to ignore conventional paths.

Another fairly important development, still in too early a stage to be assessed fully, is what the sociologists would call the "breakdown of the nuclear family and a return to the extended family." What this means in English is that the typical Hippie household is not two parents and 2.5 children, but rather a heterogeneous grouping of six or eight people, some of them, perhaps, being children, linked to each other by ties which are in many ways family-like. Important decisions are made corporately, possessions are shared, children are cared for by whoever is around and in good condition, sexual partners are not clearly demarcated. For many teen-age Hippies, this represents the first family structure that they identify with and which provides a model for living that is greatly at variance with the standard models of the society.

How important these anthropological facts are, just how much they *are* facts, would require empirical investigation; but I think they are significant.

Finally, there is what might be called the Marxist angle. Any society must meet certain basic economic requirements, must find ways of wresting food, shelter, etc. from its environment. Previous rebels have had to return to the fold because they found no way of sustaining themselves outside the market economy. Their efforts at being self-sustaining flopped. Attempts, such as those of the Beats, to compromise by working on a part-time basis were usually not stable. I think the Hippies can make it economically for a number of reasons, the main one being that this is a very affluent society and it is welfare oriented. It is not prepared to see any substantial proportion of its youth die of starvation or illness—particularly if the youth is middle-class and white. And statistically the Hippies are overwhelmingly WASPS; one survey shows 1 per cent Negro, 3 per cent Jews. The parents of the Hippies are not about to cut them off from support no matter how long they maintain their break. Unlike working-class parents who at some point will just give up, the checks from middle-class poppa will flow eternally.

Second, it is a good bet that some time in the near future we will see some form of guaranteed income at least on a subsistence level. But even if this didn't pan out, there are the indigenous ways of making money—pan-handling, pushing, selling Hippie newspapers, etc. (Note on pan-handling: I followed a very Hippie-looking chick down Telegraph Avenue in Berkeley, who confined her pan-handling, oddly enough, only to fellow Hippies—some kind of queer principle at work there—and did amazingly well. I wasn't close enough to make an accurate check, but it looked like about a buck and a half in four blocks.)

For more sophisticated types, there is access to the increasing commercialization of Hippie clothing, music, art work, etc. But this may only be a fad and if they are to last, Hippies will have to fall back on the other sources I mentioned. Remember: Hippies need very little money. One estimate I heard from a girl who was living with seven other people in the Haight was $48 a month. If this seems like very little, consider that there are a number of free goods and services available to Hippies. And what might be a major expense—entertainment—is minor for the Hippies. As one nymphet observed: "We fuck for fun." This doesn't quite exhaust the resources, but drugs are fairly inexpensive. (A new one is introduced almost every week which brings free samples for market promotion.) And Hippies do not buy books. They don't even steal them; they are a fairly non-literate breed. Music is the basic staple of culture and is enjoyed communally, hence economically.

What I have been arguing is that in all the dimensions—biological, physiological, psychological, sociological, economic—the breaks are so far-reaching that it will be much more difficult for Hippies to backslide. Compare for example an ex-bohemian or ex-radical father explaining to his children why he now works as an advertising executive or stockbroker and the kinds of rationalization available to him (maturity, responsibility for a growing family, you can't change the system, duped) with those either necessary or available to a Hippie drop-out.

There are objections that could be raised to each of my arguments. For example: to the economic point—when they're 35 their parents will be dead or stop supporting them. Then they'll have to get a regular job. To the physiological argument about drugs—these effects are not long-term. Or perhaps they only produce drastic value shifts in conjunction with a psychological "set" that only takes place at the time of adolescence. And there is no doubt that with the commercialization of the Hippie—particularly in the area of fashion—some Hippies may be able to "do their thing" and "make it" at the same time. Still I think the kinds of considerations I have advanced should make one cautious about the inevitability of a return to the womb of the "Great Society." It may be later than we thought.

For Discussion

1. How does the essay develop the question mark in the title?
2. In what way does Dworkin see drugs as exercising a significant influence on the Hippie revolution?
3. What, according to Dworkin, are the values and mode of life of the Hippies? (For comparison, see Thoreau and Nietzsche.)
4. Analyze Hippie appearance as a reflection of an attitude toward sex.
5. In your opinion, what are the advantages and disadvantages of the "extended family" as opposed to the "nuclear family"?
6. How does Dworkin manage to cover such a large subject in so brief an article? Look at the opening and closing paragraphs.
7. What considerations may the author have overlooked or underestimated in judging the permanence of the Hippie revolution?
8. Why might Dworkin's tone make it difficult to see this article as dissent?

JOEL FORT

Pot: A Rational Approach

Dr. Fort is a leading medical authority in the field of psychopharmacology and author of *The Pleasure Seekers: The Drug Crisis* and *Youth and Society*. Formerly a consultant on drug abuse for the UN World Health Organization, he is a member of the faculty of the School of Social Welfare at the University of California, Berkeley, and the Department of Biology, San Francisco State College, and is Co-Director of the National Sex and Drug Forum in San Francisco. In his popular weekly NET-TV series, he discusses with characteristic frankness a variety of subjects, including alcoholism, sexual anxiety, insomnia, and drug abuse.

There are an estimated 10,000,000 Americans who smoke marijuana either regularly or occasionally, and they have very obvious reasons for wishing that pot were treated more sensibly by the law. As one of the 190,000,000 who have never smoked marijuana, I also favor the removal of grass from the criminal laws, but for less personal reasons. It is my considered opinion, after studying drug use and drug laws in 30 nations and dealing with drug-abuse problems professionally for 15 years, that the present marijuana statutes in America not only are bad laws for the offending minority but are bad for the vast majority of us who never have lit a marijuana cigarette and never will.

That some changes in these laws are coming in the near future is virtually certain, but it is not at all sure that the changes will be improvements.

On May 19, 1969, the U.S. Supreme Court, in an 8–0 vote, declared that the Marijuana Tax Act of 1937 was unconstitutional. This decision delighted the defendant, Timothy Leary, and was no surprise at all to lawyers who specialize in the fine points of constitutional law. It had long been recognized that the Marijuana Tax Act was "vulnerable"—a polite term meaning that the law had been hastily drawn, rashly considered and rail-roaded through Congress in a mood of old-maidish terror that spent no time on the niceties of the Bill of Rights, scientific fact or common sense.

Celebrations by marijuanaphiles and lamentations by marijuanaphobes, however, are both premature. The Court, while throwing out this one inept piece of legislation, specifically declared that Congress has the right to pass laws governing the use, sale and possession of this drug (provided these laws stay within the perimeter of the Constitution).

And, of course, state laws against pot, which are often far harsher than the Federal law, still remain in effect.

There were two defects found by the Supreme Court in the Federal anti-marijuana law—a section that requires the suspect to pay a tax on the drug, thus incriminating himself, in violation of the Fifth Amendment; and a section that assumes (rather than requiring proof) that a person with foreign-grown marijuana in his possession knows it is smuggled. These provisions were perversions of traditional American jurisprudence, no less than the remaining parts of the law that are bound to fall when challenged before the Supreme Court. These forthcoming decisions will, inevitably, affect the antimarijuana laws of the individual states as well. However, the striking down of the old laws does not guarantee that the new ones will be more enlightened; it merely invites more carefully drawn statutes that are less vulnerable to judicial review. In fact, in a message to Congress, President Nixon specifically demanded harsher penalties for marijuana convictions. But every sane and fair-minded person must be seriously concerned that the new laws are more just and more in harmony with known fact than the old ones. In my opinion, such new laws must treat marijuana no more harshly than alcohol is presently treated.

It is ironic that our present pot laws are upheld chiefly by the older generation, and flouted and condemned by the young; for it is the senior generation that should understand the issue most clearly, having lived through the era of alcohol prohibition. They saw with their own eyes that the entire nation—not just the drinkers and the sellers of liquor—suffered violent moral and mental harm from that particular outbreak of armed and rampant puritanism. They should certainly remember that attempts to legislate morality result only in widespread disrespect for law, new markets and new profits for gangsters, increased violence and such wholesale bribery and corruption that the Government itself becomes a greater object of contempt than the criminal class. Above all, they should be able to see the parallel between the lawless Twenties and the anarchic Sixties and realize that both were produced by bad laws—laws that had no right to exist in the first place.

"Bad law," it has been said, "is the worst form of tyranny." An open tyranny breeds open rebellion, and the issues are clear-cut; bad law, in an otherwise democratic nation, provokes a kind of cultural nihilism in which good and evil become hopelessly confused and the rebel, instead of formulating a single precise program, takes a perverse delight in anything and everything that will shock, startle, perplex, anger, baffle and offend the establishment. Thus it was during alcohol prohibition and thus it is under marijuana prohibition. The parallel is not obvious only because there were already millions of whiskey drinkers when the Volstead Act became law in 1919, leading to immediate flouting of "law and order" by vast hordes—whereas the use of marijuana did not become extensive until the early 1950s, more than 13 years after the Government banned pot in 1937. But the results, despite the delay, are the same: We have bred a generation of psychological rebels.

Banning marijuana not only perpetuates the rebelliousness of the young but it also establishes a frightening precedent, under which puritanical bias is more important to our legislators than experimentally determined fact—something every scientist must dread. Dr. Philip Handler, board chairman of the National Science Foundation, bluntly told a House subcommittee investigating drug laws, "It is our puritan ethics . . . rather than science" that say we should not smoke marijuana.

Consider the most recent study of the effects of marijuana, conducted under careful laboratory conditions and reported in *Science*. This is the research performed by Drs. Norman E. Zinberg and Andrew T. Weil at Boston University in 1968. This study was "double-blind"; that is, neither the subjects nor the researchers knew, during a given session, whether the product being smoked was real marijuana (from the female Cannabis plant) or an inactive placebo (from the male Cannabis plant). Thus, both suggestibility by the subjects and bias by the experimenters were kept to the scientific minimum. The results were:

1. Marijuana causes a moderate increase in heartbeat rate, some redness of the eyes and virtually no other physical effects. Contrary to the belief of both users and policemen, pot does not dilate the pupils—this myth apparently derives from the tradition of smoking Cannabis in a darkened room; it is the darkness that dilates the pupils.

2. Pot does not affect the blood-sugar level, as alcohol does, nor cause abnormal reactions of the involuntary muscles, as LSD often does, nor produce any effects likely to be somatically damaging. In the words of Zinberg and Weil, "The significance of this near absence of physical effects is twofold. First, it demonstrates once again the uniqueness of hemp among psychoactive drugs, most of which strongly affect the body as well as the mind. . . . Second, it makes it unlikely that marijuana has any seriously detrimental physical effects in either short-term or long-term usage."

3. As sociologist Howard Becker pointed out long ago, on the basis of interviews with users, the marijuana "high" is a learned experience. Subjects who had never had Cannabis before simply did not get a "buzz" and re-

ported very minimal subjective reactions, even while physically "loaded" with very high doses, while experienced users were easily turned on.

4. The hypothesis about "set and setting" strongly influencing drug reactions was confirmed. The pharmacological properties of a psychoactive drug are only one factor in a subject's response; equally important—perhaps more important—are the set (his expectations and personality type) and the setting (the total emotional mood of the environment and persons in it).

5. Both inexperienced subjects and longtime users did equally well on some tests for concentration and mental stability, even while they were on very high doses. On tests requiring a higher ability to focus attention, the inexperienced users did show some temporary mental impairment, but the veterans sailed right on, as if they were not high at all. In short, experienced potheads do not have even a *temporary* lowering of the intelligence while they are high, much less a permanent mental impairment.

6. On some tests, the experienced users scored even higher while stoned than they did when tested without any drug.

7. Not only alcohol but even tobacco has more adverse effects on the body than marijuana does.

As Zinberg and Weil noted sardonically in a later article in *The New York Times Magazine,* there is a vicious circle operating in relation to marijuana: "Administrators of scientific and Government institutions feel that marijuana is dangerous. Because it is dangerous, they are reluctant to allow [research] to be done on it. Because no work is done, people continue to think of it as dangerous. We hope that our own study has significantly weakened this trend."

One slight sign that the trend may have been weakened was the appearance last June of a study by the Bureau of Motor Vehicles in the state of Washington concerning the effects of Cannabis on driving ability. Using driving-traffic simulators, not only did the study find that marijuana has less adverse effect on driving ability than alcohol—which many investigators have long suspected—but also, as in the Boston study, the evidence indicated that the only detrimental effect is on inexperienced users. Veteran potheads behave behind the wheel as if they were not drugged at all.

In short, we seem to have a drug here that makes many users very euphoric and happy—high—without doing any of the damage done by alcohol, narcotics, barbiturates, amphetamines or even tobacco.

But we didn't have to wait until 1968 to learn that pot is relatively harmless. Some research has been done in the past, in spite of the vicious circle mentioned by Zinberg and Weil. As far back as 1942, the mayor of New York City, Fiorello La Guardia, alarmed by sensational press stories about "the killer drug, marijuana" that was allegedly driving people to rape and murder, appointed a commission to investigate the pot problem in his city. The commission was made up of 31 eminent physicians, psychiatrists, psychologists, etc., and six officers from the city's narcotics bureau. If there was any bias in that study, it must have been directed against marijuana, considering the presence of the narcotics officers, not to mention psychiatrists and M.D.'s, who were then, as now, rather conservative groups. Nevertheless, after two years of hard study, including psychological and medical examinations of users, electroencephalograms to examine for brain damage, sociological digging into the behavior patterns associated with marijuana use and intelligence tests on confirmed potheads, the commission concluded:

> Those who have been smoking marijuana for a period of years showed no mental or physical deterioration which may be attributed to the drug. . . . Marijuana is not a drug of addiction, comparable to morphine. . . . Marijuana does not lead to morphine or heroin or cocaine addiction. . . . Marijuana is not the determining factor in the commission of major crimes. . . . The publicity concerning the catastrophic effects of marijuana smoking in New York City is unfounded.

Even earlier, a study of marijuana use in the Panama Canal Zone was undertaken by a notably conservative body, the United States Army. Published in 1925, the study concluded, "There is no evidence that marijuana as grown here is a habit-forming drug" and that "Delinquencies due to marijuana smoking which result in trial by military court are negligible in number when compared with delinquencies resulting from the use of alcoholic drinks which also may be classed as stimulants or intoxicants."

What may be the classic study in the whole field goes back further: to the 1893–1894 report of the seven-member Indian Hemp Drug Commission that received evidence from 1193 witnesses from all regions of the country (then including Burma and Pakistan), professionals and laymen, Indians and British, most of whom were required to answer in writing seven comprehensive questions covering most aspects of the subject. The commission found that there was no connection between the use of marijuana and "social and moral evils" such as crime, violence or bad character. It also concluded that occasional and moderate use may be beneficial; that moderate use is attended by no injurious physical, mental or other effects; and that moderate use is the rule: "It has been the most striking feature of this inquiry to find how little the effects of hemp drugs have intruded themselves on observation. The large numbers of witnesses of all classes who profess never to have seen them, the very few witnesses who could so recall a case to give any definite account of it and the manner in which a large proportion of these cases broke down on the first attempt to examine them are facts which combine to show most clearly how little injury society has hitherto sustained from hemp drugs." This conclusion is all the more remarkable when one realizes that the pattern of use in India included far more potent forms and doses of Cannabis than are presently used in the United States. The commission, in its conclusion, stated:

> Total prohibition of the hemp drugs is neither necessary nor expedient in consideration of their ascertained effects, of the prevalence of the habit of using them, of the social or religious feelings on the subject and of the possibility of its driving the consumers to have recourse to other stimulants [alcohol] or narcotics which may be more deleterious.

Ever since there have been attempts to study marijuana scientifically, every major investigation has arrived at, substantially, the same conclusions, and these directly contradict the mythology of the Federal Bureau of Narcotics. In contrast with the above facts, consider the following advertisement, circulated before the passage of the 1937 Federal anti-marijuana law:

> Beware! Young and Old—People in All Walks of Life! This [picture of a marijuana cigarette] may be handed you by the *friendly stranger*. It contains the Killer Drug "Marijuana"—a powerful narcotic in which lurks *Murder! Insanity! Death!*

Such propaganda was widely disseminated in the mid-1930s, and it was responsible for stampeding Congress into the passage of a law unique in all American history in the extent to which it is based on sheer ignorance and misinformation.

Few people realize how recent anti-marijuana legislation is. Pot was widely used as a folk medicine in the 19th Century. Its recreational use in this country began in the early 1900s with Mexican laborers in the Southwest, spread to Mexican Americans and Negroes in the South and then the North, and then moved from rural to urban areas. In terms of public reaction and social policy, little attention was paid to pot until the mid-1930s (although some generally unenforced state laws existed before then). At that time, a group of former alcohol-prohibition agents headed by Harry J. Anslinger, who became head of the Federal Bureau of Narcotics, began issuing statements to the public (via a cooperative press) claiming that marijuana caused crime, violence, assassination, insanity, release of anti-social inhibitions, mental deterioration and numerous other onerous activities.

In what became a model for future Federal and state legislative action on marijuana, Congressional hearings were held in 1937 on the Marijuana Tax Act. No medical, scientific or sociological evidence was sought or heard; no alternatives to criminalizing users and sellers were considered; and the major attention was given to the oilseed, birdseed and paint industries' need for unrestrained access to the hemp plant from which marijuana comes. A U.S. Treasury Department witness began his testimony by stating flatly that "Marijuana is being used extensively by high school children in cigarettes with deadly effect," and went on to introduce as further "evidence" an editorial from a Washington newspaper supposedly quoting the American Medical Association as having stated in its journal that marijuana use was one of the problems of greatest menace in the United States. Fortunately for historical analysis, a Dr. Woodward, serving as legislative counsel for the American Medical Association, was present to point out that the statement in question was by Anslinger and had only been reported in the A.M.A. journal.

Dr. Woodward deserves a posthumous accolade for his singlehanded heroic efforts to introduce reason and sanity to the hearing. Most importantly, the doctor (who was also a lawyer) criticized the Congressmen for proposing a law that would interfere with future medical uses of Cannabis and pointed out that no one from the Bureau of Prisons had been produced to show the number of prisoners "addicted" to marijuana, no one from the Children's Bureau or Office of Education to show the nature and extent of the "habit" among children and no one from the Division of Mental Hygiene or the Division of Pharmacology of the Public Health Service to give "direct and primary evidence rather than indirect and hearsay evidence." Saying that he assumed it was true that a certain amount of "narcotic addiction" existed, since "the newspapers have called attention to it so prominently that there must be some grounds for their statements," he concluded that the particular type of statute under consideration was neither necessary nor desirable. The Congressmen totally ignored the content of Dr. Woodward's testimony and attacked his character, qualifications, experience and relationship to the American Medical Association, all of which were impeccable. He was then forced to admit that he could not say with certainty that no problem existed. Finally, his testimony was brought to a halt with the warning, "You are not cooperative in this. If you want to advise us on legislation, you ought to come here with some constructive proposals rather than criticism, rather than trying to throw obstacles in the way of something that the Federal Government is trying to do."

A similar but shorter hearing was held in the Senate, where Anslinger presented anecdotal "evidence" that marijuana caused murder, rape and insanity.

Thus, the Marijuana Tax Act of 1937 was passed—and out of it grew a welter of state laws that were, in many cases, even more hastily ill conceived.

The present Federal laws impose a two-to-ten-year sentence for a first conviction for possessing even a small amount of marijuana, five to twenty years for a second conviction and ten to forty for a third. If Congress is not forced to recognize scientific fact and basic civil liberties, these penalties will be retained when the new Federal law is written without the sections declared invalid in the Leary case. The usual discretion that judges are given to grant probation or suspended sentences for real crimes is taken from them by this (and state) law as is the opportunity for parole. For sale or "dissemination," no matter how small the quantity of marijuana involved, and even if the dissemination is a gift between friends, the Federal penalty for first-offense conviction is five to twenty years; for a second offense, it's ten to forty.

The state laws, as I stated, are even hairier. Here are two real, and recent, cases: In Texas, Richard Dorsey, a shoe-shine-stand operator in a bowling alley, sold a matchbox full of marijuana (considerably less than an ounce) to a Dallas undercover policeman, for five dollars. His sentence: 50 years.

In Michigan, for selling five dollars' worth of grass to another police agent, Larry Belcher was sentenced to 20 to 30 years in prison. This case is worth noting as an example of how the marijuana laws actually function in many instances. Belcher is the only individual in Grand Traverse County to receive this sentence in the past two years; 25 other marijuana arrestees were all placed on probation within that time. Belcher, it appears, was the author of a column called "Dope-O-Scope" in a local underground newspaper and had presented there some of the same scientific facts incorporated into this article. People who publicly oppose the marijuana laws and marijuana mythology of our narcotics police have an unusually high arrest record.

There is no consistency in these laws from state to state. Until 1968, South Dakota had the nation's lowest penalty for first-offense possession—90 days (it has since been raised to two to five years); however, if you crossed the state line to North Dakota, the picture changed abruptly. North Dakota had (and still has) the nation's highest penalty for first-offense possession— 99 years at hard labor. In New York state, in spite of the revelatory work of the La Guardia commission, the penalties have increased since the Forties. Today, in that state, selling or transferring marijuana to anyone under 21 carries a penalty of one to 25 years, even if the transfer is by somebody who is also under 21 and is a gift to a friend. (The state legislature recently tried to raise this penalty to 15 years to life, but Governor Rockefeller vetoed the bill.) In Louisiana, a minor selling to a minor is subject to five to fifteen years' imprisonment, while an adult selling to a minor may receive the death penalty. Finally, in Georgia, the penalty for a first conviction for selling to a minor is life imprisonment. If the offender is paroled or his sentence suspended, and he is convicted again, he can be sentenced to death.

The barbarity of such penalties in relation to pot's relative harmlessness is even beginning to be recognized in Washington, despite incessant and quite unscientific efforts to maintain the old mythology, emanating from the Federal Bureau of Narcotics. In 1963, President Kennedy's Advisory Commission on Narcotic and Drug Abuse called into question some of the prevailing beliefs about marijuana and recommended lighter sentences for possession. In 1967, President Johnson's Commission on Law Enforcement and the Administration of Justice took a similar view, recommending more flexible penalties; more significantly, it stated that marijuana has virtually nothing in common with true narcotics or opiates—the first time that fact was publicly admitted by a U.S. Government agency. And in 1967, Dr. James Goddard, while commissioner of the U.S. Food and Drug Administration, was quoted as saying that it would disturb him less if his teenage daughter smoked one marijuana cigarette than if she drank an alcoholic beverage. (Faced with a predictable outcry from conservatives in Congress, Goddard said he had been misquoted—but quite honestly added that the known facts did not support the opinion that marijuana is more dangerous than alcohol.)

Not only is marijuana comparatively harmless on the face of all the evidence but there are even reasons to believe it may be beneficial in some cases. In many countries, Cannabis has been used medicinally for as long as 5000 years and is regarded as a sovereign remedy for a variety of ills. There are references to medicinal uses of marijuana in American medical journals (mostly of the 19th Century) where doctors reported it as useful as an analgesic, appetite stimulant, anti-spasmodic, anti-depressant, tranquilizer, anti-asthmatic, topical anesthetic, childbirth analgesic and antibiotic. My own investigations in areas of the world where this folk medicine still flourishes and my study of 20th Century scientific literature lead me to believe that marijuana would be useful for treating depression, loss of appetite, high blood pressure, anxiety and migraine.

An English psychiatrist who employed marijuana in the therapy of depressive patients, Dr. George T. Stockings, concluded that it "might be more effective than any tranquilizer now in use." Dr. Robert Walton of the University of Mississippi has also suggested its use for certain gynecological and menstrual problems and in easing childbirth. We should not let lingering puritanical prejudices prevent us from investigating these areas further. As Dr. Tod Mikuriya, a psychiatrist formerly associated with the National Institute of Mental Health, notes, "The fact that a drug has a recreational history should not blind us to its possible other uses. Morton was the first to use ether publicly for anesthesia after observing medical students at 'ether frolics' in 1846." While such speculations about the benefits of pot must await further research before a final answer is given, there can be no doubt that a grave injustice has been suffered by those currently in prison because of laws passed when the drug was believed to incite crime and madness.

Even the Federal Bureau of Narcotics and its propagandists have largely given up the "steppingstone theory" (that marijuana smoking leads to use of addictive drugs) and the "degeneracy theory" (that it leads to crime or "bad character"). They have recently rallied around the oldest, and most discredited, canard of all—the legend that marijuana causes insanity. To shore up this crumbling myth, they cite recent research at the Addiction Research Center in Lexington, Kentucky, where 30 former opiate addicts were given high doses of synthetic THC (the active ingredient in marijuana) or concentrated Cannabis extract. Most of the subjects showed marked perceptual changes, which the experimenter chose to describe as "hallucinations" and "psychotic reactions." This, of course, merely confirms a basic axiom of pharmacology; i.e., with increasing doses of any drug, different and more dangerous responses will occur; you could obtain some spectacularly adverse reactions with horse doctors' doses of aspirin, coffee or even orange juice. (With ordinary doses of THC or marijuana, the subjects experienced the same "high" found in normal, social marijuana smoking.)

A more serious defect in this research lies in the loaded terminology with which the experimenter, Dr. Harris Isbell, reported his results. Psychiatrist Thomas Szasz, a crusader for reform in the mental-health field, points out that a "psychotic reaction" is not something *in* an individual, Mr. A, like cancer; rather, it is a label that a second individual, Mr. B (more often, Dr. B), pins on Mr. A. The *fact* is that the subjects experienced perceptual changes; it is not a fact but merely an *opinion* whether one wants to call these changes "consciousness expansion" and "transcendence of the ego" (with Timothy Leary) or "hallucinations" and "psychotic reactions" (with Dr. Isbell).

Sociologist Howard Becker—the observer who first noted the effect of "learning" on the marijuana experience—has researched medical literature from the early 1930s to the present in search of reported cases of "marijuana psychosis." He found none after 1940, a remarkable fact, considering the pyramiding acceleration of marijuana use during the Forties, Fifties and Sixties. Becker concluded that persons who were diagnosed as "marijuana psychotics" in the Thirties were simply anxious and disoriented because they hadn't learned yet how to use the drug. Dr. Isbell's subjects, almost certainly, were not advised about the effects of the drugs; and his experiment is really just another proof of the effect of "set and setting" as well as high doses on drug experience.

A 1946 study examined 310 persons who had been using marijuana for an average of seven years each. There was no record of mental-hospital commitment among any of them.

The marijuanaphobes also cite studies from the Near East to prove that marijuana is associated with psychosis. In the first place, many of the people in these studies smoked hashish, not marijuana; and while hashish is derived from the same plant, Cannabis sativa, it is otherwise a considerably stronger form of the drug. One might compare the two Cannabis drugs with two alcohol drugs as follows: Smoking a pipe of hashish is equivalent to drinking a fifth of vodka; smoking the same pipe of marijuana is about like drinking a bottle of beer. However, the studies themselves do not deserve such careful rebuttal; they are scientifically worthless. They prove only that, in countries where most of the population regularly use Cannabis, many of the patients in mental hospitals also have a history of Cannabis use. Usually the proportion of users in the institution is less than that in the general population, leading to a possible conclusion that it is psychologically beneficial. In fact, however, there are no scientifically valid statistics or records kept at these facilities. The testimony turns out, on examination, to be impressionistic and anecdotal rather than scientific and precise. The diagnosis of psychosis and its attribution to Cannabis is often made by a ward attendant. In short, we are faced with the kind of "evidence" that the Indian Hemp Drug Commission discarded in 1893. I have visited the mental hospitals of several of the countries involved in the "Cannabis psychosis" and none of the record keeping involved meets the minimum requirements demanded of freshman scientific reports in American colleges.

Perhaps the last bastion of marijuanaphobia is the argument by uncertainty. "Who knows?" this line goes. "Maybe, in the future, marijuana might be discovered, by further research, to have dangerous side effects that haven't been noted yet." This argument, of course, is unanswerable; but it applies equally well to such diverse objects as diet pills and bubble gum. One cannot prove that the future will not discover new things; but does such a fact—science's lack of clairvoyance—justify our present marijuana laws? It clearly does not. No drug, including marijuana, will ever be found to be totally harmless; and no drug, particularly marijuana, will ever be found to be as dangerous as the hydrogen bomb (once claimed by Anslinger). Social policy should not be determined by this anyway. The possible risks should be dealt with by education. What is unacceptable is locking a man up for 99 years for possessing something of far less proven danger than tobacco, alcohol, automobiles and guns.

Instead of decreasing marijuana usage, our present laws have created the contempt for Government about which I spoke earlier. In addition to continuing to disobey the law, hordes of young people have begun to flout it publicly. There have been smoke-ins—masses who gather in a public park, where those in the inner core of the group light up, while the outer perimeter obstruct and slow down the police until the evidence is consumed—at Berkeley, in Boston and elsewhere. Planting marijuana in conspicuous places has become a fad; among the notable seedings have been the center strip of Park Avenue in New York City, the lawn in front of a police station in ultrarespectable Westchester County, the UN Building and (twice recently) in front of the state capitol in Austin, Texas.

But the American marijuana tragedy is even worse than I have indicated. Like other crimes-without-victims, pot smoking is a private activity and involves no harm to anyone else. Remember: The police do not have to engage in cloak-and-dagger activities to find out if there have been any banks or grocery stores robbed lately—the bankers and store owners (the victims) call them immediately. But since there is no victim in the "crime" of smoking marijuana, nobody is going to call the police to report it—except, very rarely, a neighbor who finds the evidence. Hence, the entire apparatus of the police state comes into existence as soon as we attempt to enforce anti-grass legislation; and by the nature of such legislation, totalitarian results must ensue. We cannot police the private lives of the citizenry without invading their privacy; this is an axiom.

That a man's home is his castle has long been a basic principle of Anglo-American jurisprudence, and some of us can still recall the near poetry of the great oration by William Pitt in which he says, "The poorest man may in his cottage bid defiance to the force of the Crown. It may be frail, its roof may shake; the wind may blow through it; the storms may enter; the rain may enter; but the King of England cannot enter—all his forces dare not cross the threshold of the ruined tenement!" This principle goes back to the Magna Charta and is firmly entrenched in the Fourth Amendment to our own Constitution, guaranteeing the people "the right . . . to be secure in their persons, houses, papers and effects, against unreasonable searches and seizures."

This libertarian tradition is a great hindrance to the police when they attempt to enforce sumptuary laws—laws concerning the private morals of the citizens. And, in fact, the enforcement of the marijuana law requires pernicious police behavior.

For instance, the *Chicago Sun-Times* told, in 1967, how the police of that city obtain search warrants for use in legalizing raids that otherwise would be mere "fishing expeditions"—intolerable to any American court. In dealing with the organized-crime cartel usually called "the Syndicate," the police have obtained from the courts the right to use what are called "blank warrants"—warrants in which the witness who alleges he has seen the crime is permitted to sign a false name. This is supposedly necessary to protect informers against the wrath of the reputedly all-seeing and all-powerful Syndicate. Once this dangerous precedent was set, the police began applying it to marijuana users as well. As the *Sun-Times* noted:

> Those methods are dubious. . . . We refer to the method of obtaining search warrants. The informer signs a search-warrant complaint, with an assumed name, alleging perhaps that he bought illicit drugs from a certain person, at a certain place. The police do not have to disclose the name of the informer or the time when the drugs were bought. There is also a device known as constructive possession: The police can arrest anybody found in the vicinity of prohibited drugs, whether he's an innocent visitor or the real culprit. The frame-up is easy. Plant the drugs, get the search

warrant, grab everybody in sight. It could happen to you and you'd never have the right to face your accuser.

William Braden, a *Sun-Times* reporter, also uncovered one informer, a heroin addict, who admitted signing dozens of such warrants without the names of the accused on them. The narcotics squad could then type in the name of any individual whose apartment they wanted to raid and it would be perfectly "legal" in form—but a terrifying distance in spirit from the actual meaning of the Constitution. Such raids, of course, violate the Sixth Amendment—guaranteeing the right "to be confronted with the witness" against you—as well as the Fourth (no "unreasonable searches"); and they occur everywhere in the nation.

Most of us never hear of such things, because reporters routinely print the police version of the raid, without interviewing the arrested "dope fiends." It is also standard practice for the police to multiply the quantity of drugs seized in such a raid by a factor of two (and the price by a factor of ten) when giving the news to the press. This makes for impressive headlines; it also contributes to the growing tendency toward "trial by newspaper," which worries civil libertarians.

Some types of entrapment are regarded as legal in America today—although some still are not. In my own opinion, *all* forms of entrapment are profoundly immoral, whether technically legal or illegal; but my opinion is, perhaps, immaterial. The results of this practice, however, are truly deplorable from the point of view of anyone who has any lingering affection for the spirit of the Bill of Rights.

Here is a specific case: John Sinclair, a poet, leader of the Ann Arbor hippie community and manager of a rock group called MC-5, became friendly, around October 1966, with Vahan Kapagian and Jane Mumford, who presented themselves to him as members of the hippie-artist-mystic subculture that exists in all of our large cities. Over a period of two months, they worked to secure his confidence and friendship and several times asked him to get them some marijuana. Finally, on December 22, Sinclair, apparently feeling that he could now trust them, gave two marijuana cigarettes to Miss Mumford—one for her and one for Kapagian. He was immediately arrested; his "friends" were police undercover agents.

Sinclair has been convicted of both "possessing" and "dispensing" marijuana and faces a minimum of 20 years under each statute, and a maximum of life for the sale. If his appeal is not upheld, the very smallest sentence he could receive is 40 years. As his lawyers pointed out in his appeal, "The minimum sentence to which [Sinclair] is subject to imprisonment is 20 times greater than the minimum to which a person may be imprisoned [in Michigan] for such crimes as rape, robbery, arson, kidnaping or second-degree murder. It is more than 20 times greater than the minimum sentence of imprisonment for any other offense in Michigan law, except first-degree murder."

That illegal wire tapping has also been widely used by the narcotics police was an open secret for years; now it is no secret at all—and not illegal, either. The 1968 Omnibus Crime Bill authorizes such wire tapping for suspected marijuana users. Since this usage has spread to all classes and all educational levels, such suspicion can be directed at virtually anyone (after all, the nephew and the brother of one of President Nixon's closest friends were recently busted on pot charges): thus, almost any American can now have his phone tapped legally. Considering the elastic interpretation police usually give to such Congressional authorization, an anonymous tip by any crank in your neighborhood would probably be enough to get a tap on your phone by tomorrow morning. Why not? As *Chicago Daily News* columnist Mike Royko recently wrote, "There is a democratic principle in injustice. If enough people support it, they'll all get it."

With the doctrine of "constructive possession," anyone who has a pot-smoking friend is subject to marijuana laws if he walks into the friend's house at the wrong time. In California two years ago, a woman was sentenced to sterilization for being in the same room with a man who was smoking grass. The fact that a higher court overturned this sentence does not lessen its frightening implications.

And a new wrinkle has been added. According to a story in the *San Francisco Chronicle* last June 20, the Government is planning "an unpleasant surprise for marijuana smokers—'sick pot.' " The article goes on to explain how an unspecified chemical can be sprayed on Mexican marijuana fields from a helicopter, whereupon "just a puff or two produces uncontrollable vomiting that not even the most dedicated smoker could ignore."

This, I submit, could have come from the morbid fantasy of Kafka, Burroughs or Orwell. The Government, in its holy war against a relatively harmless drug, is deliberately creating a very harmful drug. Nor is the *Chronicle* story something dreamed up by a sensation-mongering reporter. A call to the Justice Department in Washington has confirmed that this plan has been discussed and may go into operation in the near future.

Consider, now, the actual social background in which this crusade against Cannabis is being waged. America is not the Victorian garden it pretends to be; we are, in fact, a drug-prone nation. Parents and other adults after whom children model their own behavior teach them that every time one relates to other human beings, whether at a wedding or at a funeral, and every time one has a pain, problem or trouble, it is necessary or desirable to pop a pill, drink a cocktail or smoke a cigarette. The alcohol, tobacco and over-the-counter pseudo-"sedative" industries jointly spend more than $2,000,000 a day in the United States alone to promote as much drug use as possible.

The average "straight" adult consumes three to five mind-altering drugs a day, beginning with the stimulant caffeine in coffee, tea or Coca-Cola, going on to include alcohol and nicotine, often a tranquilizer, not uncommonly a sleeping pill at night and sometimes an amphetamine the next morning to overcome the effects of the sedative taken the evening before.

We have 80,000,000 users of alcohol in this country, including 6,000,-000 alcoholics; 50,000,000 users of tobacco cigarettes; 25,000,000 to 30,000,-000 users of sedatives, stimulants and tranquilizers; and hundreds of thousands of users of consciousness alterers that range from heroin and LSD to cough syrup, glue, nutmeg and catnip—all in addition to marijuana use.

Drs. Manheimer and Mellinger, surveying California adults over 21, found that 51 percent had at some time used sedatives, stimulants or tranquilizers (17 percent had taken these drugs frequently) and 13 percent had at some time used marijuana.

Further underlining the extent of use of the prescription drugs is the estimate from the National Prescription Audit that 175,000,000 prescriptions for sedatives, stimulants and tranquilizers, were filled in 1968. Also enough barbiturates (Nembutal, Seconal, phenobarbital) alone are manufactured to provide 25 to 30 average doses per year for every man, woman and child in this country.

In the light of this total drug picture, the persecution of potheads seems to be a species of what anthropologists call "scapegoatism"—the selection of one minority group to be punished for the sins of the whole population, whose guilt is vicariously extirpated in the punishment of the symbolic sacrificial victims.

Meanwhile, my criticisms—and those of increasing numbers of writers, scientific and popular—continue to bounce off the iron walls of prejudice that seem to surround Congress and state legislatures. It is quite possible that our new, post-Leary pot laws will be as bad as the old ones. If there is any improvement, it is likely to come, once again, from the courts.

Several legal challenges to our anti-pot mania are, in fact, working their way upward toward the Supreme Court, and the issues they raise are potentially even more significant than those involved in the Leary case.

First is the challenge raised by attorney Joseph Oteri in his defense of two Boston University students. Oteri's case cites the equal-protection clause of the Constitution—grass is less harmful than booze, so you can't outlaw one without the other. He also argues that the marijuana statute is irrational and arbitrary and an invalid exercise of police power because pot is harmless and wrongly defined as a narcotic, when it is, technically, not a narcotic. This is not mere hairsplitting. It is impossible, under law, to hang a man for murder if his actual crime was stealing hubcaps; it should be equally impossible to convict him of "possession of a narcotic" if he was not in possession of a narcotic but of a drug belonging to an entirely different chemical family.

And marijuana, decidedly, is not a narcotic—although just what it should be called is something of a mystery. The tendency these days is to call it a "mild psychedelic," with the emphasis on mild; this is encouraged both by the Tim Leary crowd—to whom psychedelic is a good word, denoting peace, ecstasy, non-violent revolution, union with God and the end of all neurotic hang-ups of Western man—and by those to whom psychedelic is a monster word denoting hallucinations, insanity, suicide and chaos. I doubt the psychedelic label very much and think it is as off base as narcotic. Since marijuana has very little in common with LSD and the true psychedelics, but much in common with alcohol and other sedatives, and a certain similarity also to amphetamine and other stimulants, I prefer to call it a sedative-stimulant as it is classified by Dr. Frederick Meyers, who also notes its resemblance to laughing gas (nitrous oxide). Dr. Leo Holloster finds enough resemblance to LSD to call it a sedative-hypnotic-psychedelic. *Goodman and Gilman*, the orthodox pharmacological reference, dodges the issue entirely by listing marijuana as a "miscellaneous" drug. In any case, it is not a narcotic, and anyone arrested for having a narcotic in his possession when he actually has marijuana definitely is being charged with a crime he hasn't commited.

A second challenge, raised by Oteri and also being pressed by two Michigan attorneys, is based on the prohibition of "cruel and unusual punishments" in the Eighth Amendment. The courts have held, in the past, that a law can be struck down if the punishments it requires are cruel and unusual in comparison with the penalties in the same state for similar or related crimes. For instance, the statute against chicken stealing was made quite harsh in the early days of Oklahoma, apparently because the offense was common and provoked great public indignation. As a result, a man named Skinner was threatened with the punishment of sterilization under one section of this law. He appealed to the Supreme Court, which struck down the Oklahoma statute because similarly harsh penalties were not provided for other forms of theft. Obviously, in the states where the penalty for possession of marijuana is higher than the penalty for armed robbery, rape, second-degree murder, etc., the law is vulnerable to legal attack as cruel and unusual.

There is also the "zone of privacy" argument, originally stated in the Connecticut birth-control decision and more recently invoked by the Kentucky supreme court, in striking down a local (Barbourville, Kentucky) ordinance making it a crime to smoke *tobacco* cigarettes. The court ruled that "The city . . . may not unreasonably interfere with the right of the citizen to determine for himself such personal matters." The zone of privacy was also cited by the U.S. Supreme Court in invalidating the Georgia law against possession (not sale) of pornography.

The drug police and their legislative allies have been experimenting with our liberties for a long time now. The Leary decision, however, shows that it is not too late to reverse the trend, and the issues raised by the constitutional questions discussed above show how the erosion of our liberties can, indeed, be reversed.

A compelling medical, sociological and philosophical case exists for the full legalization of marijuana, particularly if legalization is the only alternative to the present criminalization of users. But an even more substantial case exists for ending all criminal penalties for possession or use of the drug, while still exercising some caution. I would recommend, for example, that to prevent the sale of dangerously adulterated forms of the drug, marijuana be produced under Federal supervision, as alcohol is. Futhermore, sellers of the drug should be licensed, and they should be prohibited from selling to minors. If there are infractions of these laws, the penalties should be directed at the seller, not the user. I would also strongly recommend that all advertising and promotion of marijuana be prohibited, and that packages of the drug carry the warning: CAUTION: MARIJUANA MAY BE HARMFUL TO YOUR HEALTH.

If marijuana were to be legalized, what would happen? According to the marijuanaphobes, the weed will spread into every American home; people will become lazy and sluggish, sit around all day in a drugged stupor and talk philosophy when they talk at all; we will sink into the "backward" state of the Near Eastern and Asian nations.

There are good, hard scientific reasons for doubting this gloomy prognostication.

1. Most Americans have already found their drug of choice—alcohol—and there is more conditioning involved in such preferences than most people realize. The average American heads straight for the bar when he feels the impulse to relax; a change in the laws will not change this conditioned reflex. When the Catholic Church allowed its members to eat meat on Friday, the majority went right on following the conditioned channel that told them, "Friday is fish day."

2. Of the small minority that will try pot (after it is legalized) in search of a new kick, most will be vastly disappointed, since (a) it doesn't live up to its sensational publicity, largely given to it by the Federal Narcotics Bureau; and (b) the "high" depends, as we have indicated, not only on set and setting but, unlike alcohol, on learning.

This involves conditioning and the relationship of the actual chemistry of the two drugs to the total *Gestalt* of our culture. What pot actually does—outside mythology—is produce a state midway between euphoria and drowsiness, like a mild alcohol high; accelerate and sharpen the thoughts (at least in the subjective impression of the user), like amphetamine; and intensify sound and color perception, although not nearly as much as a true psychedelic. It can also enhance sexual experience, but not create it—contrary to Mr. Anslinger, pot is not an aphrodisiac. It is, in short, the drug of preference for creative and contemplative types—or, at least, people with a certain streak of that tendency in their personality. Alcohol, on the other hand, depresses the forebrain, relaxes inhibitions, produces euphoria and drowsiness and, while depleting some functions, such as speech and walking, does not draw one into the mixture of sensuality and introspection created by pot. It is the drug of preference for aggressive and extroverted types. Therefore, the picture of pot spreading everywhere and changing our culture is sociologically putting the cart before the horse; our society would first have to change basically before pot could spread everywhere.

3. Even if, against all likelihood, marijuana were to sweep the country, this would not have dire consequences. Marijuana has no specifically anti-machine property in it; it would not make our technology go away, like a wave of an evil sorcerer's wand. Nor does it dull the mental faculties, as we have seen in reviewing the scientific evidence. (I might add, here, that the highest honor students at certain Ivy League colleges are frequently pot users, and one study at Yale found more marijuana smokers at the top of the class than at the bottom.)

4. Finally, the whole specter of America sinking into backwardness due to pot is based upon totally false anthropological concepts. The Near East is not tribal, preindustrial, superstitious, and so forth, merely because Mohammed banned alcohol in the Koran but forgot to exclude Cannabis drugs also; a whole complex of historical and cultural factors is involved, not the least of which is the continuous intervention of Western imperialism from the Crusades onward. Other factors are the rigid structure of the Islamic religion and the lack of a scientific minority that can effectively challenge these dogmas; the Western world was equally backward—please note—when the Christian religion was not open to scientific dissent and criticism. Backwardness is a relative concept, and, although pot has been used in the Arabic countries for millenniums, they have several times been ahead of the West in basic science (the most famous example being their invention of algebra). The populations of these nations are not "lazy" due to marijuana nor to any other cause; they are merely underemployed by a feudalistic economic system. The ones lucky enough to find work usually toil for longer hours, in a hotter sun, than most Americans would find bearable.

Thus, treating marijuana in a sane and rational way presents no threat to our society, whereas continuing the present hysteria will alienate increasing numbers of the young while accelerating the drift toward a police state. I take no pleasure in the spread of even so mild a drug as marijuana, and I am sure (personally, not scientifically) that in a truly open, libertarian and decent society, nobody would be inclined to any kind of drug use. While I agree with the psychedelic generation about the absurdity and injustice of our criminal laws relating to drugs, I am not an apostle of the "turn on, tune in, drop out" mystique. I recognize that drugs can be an evasion of responsibility, and that there is no simple chemical solution to all the psychic, social and political problems of our time. My own program would be: Turn on to the life around you, tune in to knowledge and feeling, and drop *in* to changing the world for the better. If that course could prevail, the adventurous young, no longer haunted by the anxiety and *anomie* of the present system, would probably discover that love, comradeship, music, the arts, sex, meaningful work, alertness, self-discipline, real education (which is a life-long task) and plain hard thought are bigger, better and more permanent highs than any chemical can produce.

But, meanwhile, I must protest—I will continue to protest—against the bureaucrat who stands with cocktail in one hand and cigarette in the other and cries out that the innocent recreation of pot smoking is the major problem facing our society, one that can be solved only by raising the penalty to castration for the first offense and death for the second. He would be doing the young people—and all the rest of us—a true favor if he forgot about marijuana for a while and thought, a few minutes a day, about such real problems as racism, poverty, starvation, air pollution and our stumbling progress toward World War Three and the end of life on earth.

It is an irony of our time that our beloved George Washington would be a criminal today, for he grew hemp at Mount Vernon, and his diary entries, dealing specifically with separating the female plants from the male before pollination, show that he was not harvesting it for rope. The segregation of the plants by sex is only necessary if you intend to extract "the killer drug, marijuana" from the female plant.

Of course, we have no absolute evidence that George turned on. More likely, he was using marijuana as many Americans in that age used it; as a medicine for bronchitis, chest colds and other respiratory ailments. (Pot's euphoric qualities were not well known outside the East in those days.) But can you imagine General Washington trying to explain to an agent of the Federal Narcotics Bureau, "I was only smoking it to clear up my lumbago"? It would never work; he would land in prison, perhaps for as long as 40 years. He would be sharing the same cruel fate as several thousand other harmless Americans today. As it says in the book of *Job*, "From the dust the dying groan, and the souls of the wounded cry out."

For Discussion

1. How does the marijuana "high" differ from that publicized by the FBI, police, and other groups?
2. Discuss the disparity between age groups in their reactions to marijuana.
3. Fort states that "attempts to legislate morality result only in widespread

disrespect for law." In what sense is he using the word *morality?* In what sense do all laws attempt to legislate morality?

4. Identify the three issues which form a legal basis for challenging the anti-pot laws. Which ones are treated elsewhere in the essay?

5. Fort provides examples to support his statement that enforcement of the marijuana laws requires "pernicious" behavior by the police. Cite some examples of such behavior by either the police or the government about which you know or have read.

6. To what extent do you think Fort is justified in claiming that pot laws have bred a generation of rebels? What other factors may have been responsible?

7. In what ways does Fort argue that America is a drug culture?

8. The author refers to the Puritan ethic and prejudices. What meaning does this have for you?

9. Where does Fort stand in relation to drug advocacy? What is his position regarding the "turn-on, tune-in, drop-out" mystique?

10. What unresolved questions about marijuana does the article raise for you? What issues are not discussed?

11. How are the method of development and the tone of this article appropriate to *The Discursive NO?* How is the tone modified in the last three paragraphs?

THE REFLECTIVE NO

> *J always as J admit seem to be talking but talking can be a way of listening that is if one has the profound need of hearing and seeing what every one is telling.*
>
> GERTRUDE STEIN
> "The Gradual Making of
> *The Making of Americans*"

Of the four "voices" in The Rhetoric of No, the reflective is the most personal, and for this reason the most difficult to define. However, if we compare it to the impassioned and discursive voices, we see that it has its own distinctive and identifiable qualities—qualities found in some of the most effective writing.

An essential difference is in the author's relationship to his reader. The impassioned writer reaches out to the reader principally with his feeling; the discursive writer reaches out to the reader with his subject, trusting him to perceive its validity. But unlike both of these, the reflective writer reaches out to his reader only incidentally. His primary interest is in *what his subject means to him.* As Gertrude Stein suggests, his talking is "a way of listening" to himself, a way of exploring his own opinions and feelings. Thus the reader becomes an extension of the writer, a kind of alter-ego listening in to what is being thought.

This is not to say that the reflective writer is unconscious of his reader but rather that his writing stems more from a need to formulate, for himself, the substance of his subject than from a desire to condemn, judge, or convert others. He is impelled to express himself even when he feels that what he is saying will

249

cause no change in the world. He may explain himself (as in King's "Letter from Birmingham Jail") or advise others (as in Tolstoy's "Advice to a Draftee"), but his real purpose is to give outward expression to his inner thoughts and feelings.

When an author expresses himself reflectively, therefore, he is writing about a subject which deeply and personally involves him. His tone reveals a feeling of intimacy with his subject— a quiet, familiar concern instead of either an impassioned or impersonal one. His attitude toward his subject remains relatively calm; he doesn't shout or demand, accuse or command. He doesn't necessarily try to arrange his argument in a formally logical way to be analyzed or evaluated. Even when he is writing to a particular person (in a letter, for example), his main interest is in *sharing*, rather than *presenting* his argument. If the reader listens, fine; but if not, no matter. The author has accomplished his purpose by articulating his subject for its own sake.

The Reflective NO contains a variety of writers who express their dissent in various styles and forms—letters, journals, essays, articles. They all speak in a similar voice, inviting us to share with them the working out of their ideas.

HENRY DAVID THOREAU

On the Duty of Civil Disobedience

Born in 1817 in Concord, Massachusetts, and educated at Harvard College, Henry David Thoreau spent most of his life in and around Concord, teaching for a brief time but preferring the freedom of manual labor to the academic life while he continued to write. Pre-eminent as a nature writer (notably *Walden*), Thoreau has gained increasing prestige with the years. His emphasis on simplicity, his nonconformity, and his dedication to a life of high principle have influenced countless thinkers and writers as diverse as Hemingway and Gandhi, Henry Miller and Martin Luther King, Jr. His friend and mentor, Emerson, delivering his obituary address in 1862 said, "His soul was made for the noblest society." The essay which follows, first published in 1849, has become a world classic.

I heartily accept the motto,—"That government is best which governs least;" and I should like to see it acted up to more rapidly and systematically. Carried out, it finally amounts to this, which also I believe,—"That government is best which governs not at all;" and when men are prepared for it, that will be the kind of government which they will have. Government is at best but an expedient; but most governments are usually, and all governments are sometimes, inexpedient. The objections which have been brought against a standing army, and they are many and weighty, and deserve to prevail, may also at last be brought against a standing government. The standing army is only an arm of the standing government. The government itself, which is only the mode which the people have chosen to execute their will, is equally liable to be abused and perverted before the people can act through it. Witness the present Mexican war, the work of comparatively a few individuals using the standing government as their tool; for, in the outset, the people would not have consented to this measure.

This American government—what is it but a tradition, though a recent one, endeavoring to transmit itself unimpaired to posterity, but each instant losing some of its integrity? It has not the vitality and force of a single living man; for a single man can bend it to his will. It is a sort of wooden gun to the people themselves. But it is not the less necessary for this; for the people must have some complicated machinery or other, and hear its din, to satisfy that idea of government which they have. Governments show thus how successfully men can be imposed on, even impose on themselves, for their own advantage. It is excellent, we must all allow. Yet this government never of itself furthered any enterprise, but by the alacrity with which it got out of its way. It does not keep the country free. It does not settle the West. It does not educate. The character inherent in the American people has done all that has been accomplished; and it would have done somewhat more, if the government had not sometimes got in its way. For government is an expedient by which men would fain succeed in letting one another alone; and, as has been said, when it is most expedient, the governed are most let alone by it. Trade and commerce, if they were not made of India-rubber, would never manage to bounce over the obstacles which legislators are continually putting in their way; and, if one were to judge these men wholly by the effects of their actions and not partly by their intentions, they would deserve to be classed and punished with those mischievous persons who put obstructions on the railroads.

But, to speak practically and as a citizen, unlike those who call themselves no-government men, I ask for, not at once no government, but at once a better government. Let every man make known what kind of government would command his respect, and that will be one step toward obtaining it.

After all, the practical reason why, when the power is once in the hands of the people, a majority are permitted, and for a long period continue, to rule is not because they are most likely to be in the right, nor because this seems fairest to the minority, but because they are physically the strongest. But a government in which the majority rule in all cases cannot be based on justice, even as far as men understand it. Can there not be a government in which majorities do not virtually decide right and wrong, but conscience? —in which majorities decide only those questions to which the rule of expediency is applicable? Must the citizen ever for a moment, or in the least degree, resign his conscience to the legislator? Why has every man a conscience, then? I think that we should be men first, and subjects afterward. It is not desirable to cultivate a respect for the law, so much as for the right. The only obligation which I have a right to assume is to do at any time what I think right. It is truly enough said, that a corporation has no conscience; but a corporation of conscientious men is a corporation *with* a conscience. Law never made men a whit more just; and, by means of their respect for it, even the well-disposed are daily made the agents of injustice. A common and natural result of an undue respect for law is, that you may see a file of soldiers, colonel, captain, corporal, privates, powder-monkeys, and all, marching in admirable order over hill and dale to the wars, against their wills, ay, against their common sense and consciences, which makes it very steep marching indeed, and produces a palpitation of the heart. They have no doubt that it is a damnable business in which they are concerned; they are all peaceably inclined. Now, what are they? Men at all? or small movable forts and magazines, at the service of some unscrupulous man in power? Visit the Navy-Yard, and behold a marine, such a man as an American government can make, or such as it can make a man with its black arts,—a mere shadow and reminiscence of humanity, a man laid out alive and standing, and already, as one may say, buried under arms with funeral accompaniments, though it may be,—

> "Not a drum was heard, not a funeral note,
>   As his corse to the rampart we hurried;
> Not a soldier discharged his farewell shot
>   O'er the grave where our hero we buried."

The mass of men serve the state thus, not as men mainly, but as machines, with their bodies. They are the standing army, and the militia, jailers, constables, posse comitatus, etc. In most cases there is no free exercise whatever of the judgment or of the moral sense; but they put themselves on a level with wood and earth and stones; and wooden men can perhaps be manufactured that will serve the purpose as well. Such command no more respect than men of straw or a lump of dirt. They have the same sort of worth only as horses and dogs. Yet such as these even are commonly esteemed good citizens. Others—as most legislators, politicians, lawyers, ministers, and office-holders—serve the state chiefly with their heads; and, as they rarely make any moral distinctions, they are as likely to serve the Devil, without *intending* it, as God. A very few, as heroes, patriots, martyrs, reformers in the great sense, and *men*, serve the state with their consciences also, and so necessarily resist it for the most part; and they are commonly treated as enemies by it. A wise man will only be useful as a man, and will not submit to be "clay," and "stop a hole to keep the wind away," but leave that office to his dust at least:—

> "I am too high-born to be propertied,
> To be a secondary at control,
> Or useful serving-man and instrument
> To any sovereign state throughout the world."

He who gives himself entirely to his fellow-men appears to them useless and selfish; but he who gives himself partially to them is pronounced a benefactor and philanthropist.

How does it become a man to behave toward this American government to-day? I answer, that he cannot without disgrace be associated with it. I cannot for an instant recognize that political organization as *my* government which is the *slave's* government also.

All men recognize the right of revolution; that is, the right to refuse allegiance to, and to resist, the government, when its tyranny or its inefficiency are great and unendurable. But almost all say that such is not the case now. But such was the case, they think, in the Revolution of '75. If one were to tell me that this was a bad government because it taxed certain foreign commodities brought to its ports, it is most probable that I should not make an ado about it, for I can do without them. All machines have their friction; and possibly this does enough good to counterbalance the evil. At any rate, it is a great evil to make a stir about it. But when the friction comes to have its machine, and oppression and robbery are organized, I say, let us not have such a machine any longer. In other words, when a sixth of the population of a nation which has undertaken to be the refuge of liberty are slaves, and a whole country is unjustly overrun and conquered by a foreign army, and subjected to military law, I think that it is not too soon for honest men to rebel and revolutionize. What makes this duty the more urgent is the fact that the country so overrun is not our own, but ours is the invading army.

Paley, a common authority with many on moral questions, in his chapter on the "Duty of Submission to Civil Government," resolves all civil obligation into expediency; and he proceeds to say, "that so long as the interest of the whole society requires it, that is, so long as the established government cannot be resisted or changed without public inconveniency, it is the will of God that the established government be obeyed, and no longer. . . . This principle being admitted, the justice of every particular case of resistance is reduced to a computation of the quantity of the danger and grievance on the one side, and of the probability and expense of redressing it on the other." Of this, he says, every man shall judge for himself. But Paley appears never to have contemplated those cases to which the rule of expediency does not apply, in which a people, as well as an individual, must do justice, cost what it may. If I have unjustly wrested a plank from a drowning man, I must restore it to him though I drown myself. This, according to Paley, would be inconvenient. But he that would save his life, in such a case, shall lose it. This people must cease to hold slaves, and to make war on Mexico, though it cost them their existence as a people.

In their practice, nations agree with Paley; but does any one think that Massachusetts does exactly what is right at the present crisis?

"A drab of state, a cloth-o'-silver slut,
To have her train borne up, and her soul trail in the dirt."

Practically speaking, the opponents to a reform in Massachusetts are not a hundred thousand politicians at the South, but a hundred thousand merchants and farmers here, who are more interested in commerce and agriculture than they are in humanity, and are not prepared to do justice to the slave and to Mexico, *cost what it may*. I quarrel not with far-off foes, but with those who, near at home, coöperate with, and do the bidding of, those far away, and without whom the latter would be harmless. We are accustomed to say, that the mass of men are unprepared; but improvement is slow, because the few are not materially wiser or better than the many. It is not so important that many should be as good as you, as that there be some absolute goodness somewhere; for that will leaven the whole lump. There are thousands who are *in opinion* opposed to slavery and to the war, who yet in effect do nothing to put an end to them; who, esteeming themselves children of Washington and Franklin, sit down with their hands in their pockets, and say that they know not what to do, and do nothing; who even postpone the question of freedom to the question of free-trade, and quietly read the prices-current along with the latest advices from Mexico, after dinner, and, it may be, fall asleep over them both. What is the price-current of an honest man and patriot to-day? They hesitate, and they regret, and sometimes they petition; but they do nothing in earnest and with effect. They will wait, well disposed, for others to remedy the evil, that they may no longer have it to regret. At most, they give only a cheap vote, and a feeble countenance and Godspeed, to the right, as it goes by them. There are nine hundred and ninety-nine patrons of virtue to one virtuous man. But it is easier to deal with the real possessor of a thing than with the temporary guardian of it.

All voting is a sort of gaming, like checkers or backgammon, with a slight moral tinge to it, a playing with right and wrong, with moral questions; and betting naturally accompanies it. The character of the voters is not staked. I cast my vote, perchance, as I think right; but I am not vitally concerned that that right should prevail. I am willing to leave it to the majority. Its obligation, therefore, never exceeds that of expediency. Even voting *for the right* is *doing* nothing for it. It is only expressing to men feebly your desire that it should prevail. A wise man will not leave the right to the mercy of chance, nor wish it to prevail through the power of the majority. There is but little virtue in the action of masses of men. When the majority shall at length vote for the abolition of slavery, it will be because they are indifferent to slavery, or because there is but little slavery left to be abolished by their vote. *They* will then be the only slaves. Only *his* vote can hasten the abolition of slavery who asserts his own freedom by his vote.

I hear of a convention to be held at Baltimore, or elsewhere, for the selection of a candidate for the Presidency, made up chiefly of editors, and men who are politicians by profession; but I think, what is it to any independent, intelligent, and respectable man what decision they may come to? Shall we not have the advantage of his wisdom and honesty, nevertheless? Can we not count upon some independent votes? Are there not many individuals in the country who do not attend conventions? But no: I find that the respectable man, so called, has immediately drifted from his position, and despairs of his country, when his country has more reason to despair of him. He forthwith adopts one of the candidates thus selected as the only *available* one, thus proving that he is himself *available* for any purposes of the demagogue. His vote is of no more worth than that of any unprincipled foreigner or hireling native, who may have been bought. O for a man who is a *man*, and, as my neighbor says, has a bone in his back which you cannot pass your hand through! Our statistics are at fault: the population has been returned too large. How many *men* are there to a square thousand miles in this country? Hardly one. Does not America offer any inducement for men to settle here? The American has dwindled into an Odd Fellow,—one who may be known by the development of his organ of gregariousness, and a manifest lack of intellect and cheerful self-reliance; whose first and chief concern, on coming into the world, is to see that the Almshouses are in good repair; and, before yet he has lawfully donned the virile garb, to collect a fund for the support of the widows and orphans that may be; who, in short, ventures to live only by the aid of the Mutual Insurance company, which has promised to bury him decently.

It is not a man's duty, as a matter of course, to devote himself to the eradication of any, even the most enormous wrong; he may still properly have other concerns to engage him; but it is his duty, at least, to wash his hands of it, and, if he gives it no thought longer, not to give it practically his support. If I devote myself to other pursuits and contemplations, I must first see, at least, that I do not pursue them sitting upon another man's shoulders. I must get off him first, that he may pursue his contemplations too. See what gross inconsistency is tolerated. I have heard some of my townsmen say, "I should like to have them order me out to help put down an insurrection of the slaves, or to march to Mexico;—see if I would go;" and yet these very men have each, directly by their allegiance, and so indirectly, at least, by their money, furnished a substitute. The soldier is applauded who refuses to serve in an unjust war by those who do not refuse to sustain the unjust government which makes the war; is applauded by those whose own act and authority he disregards and sets at naught; as if the state were penitent to that degree that it hired one to scourge it while it sinned, but not to that degree that it left off sinning for a moment. Thus, under the name of Order and Civil Government, we are all made at last to pay homage to and support our own meanness. After the first blush of sin comes its indifference; and from immoral it becomes, as it were, *un*moral, and not quite unnecessary to that life which we have made.

The broadest and most prevalent error requires the most disinterested virtue to sustain it. The slight reproach to which the virtue of patriotism is commonly liable, the noble are most likely to incur. Those who, while they disapprove of the character and measures of a government, yield to it their allegiance and support are undoubtedly its most conscientious supporters, and so frequently the most serious obstacles to reform. Some are petitioning the state to dissolve the Union, to disregard the requisitions of the President. Why do they not dissolve it themselves,—the union between themselves and the state,—and refuse to pay their quota into its treasury? Do not they stand in the same relation to the state that the state does to the Union? And have not the same reasons prevented the state from resisting the Union which have prevented them from resisting the state?

How can a man be satisfied to entertain an opinion merely, and enjoy *it*? Is there any enjoyment in it, if his opinion is that he is aggrieved? If you are cheated out of a single dollar by your neighbor, you do not rest satisfied with knowing that you are cheated, or with saying that you are cheated, or even with petitioning him to pay you your due; but you take effectual steps at once to obtain the full amount, and see that you are never cheated again. Action from principle, the perception and the performance of right, changes things and relations; it is essentially revolutionary, and does not consist wholly with anything which was. It not only divides states and churches, it divides families; ay, it divides the *individual,* separating the diabolical in him from the divine.

Unjust laws exist: shall we be content to obey them, or shall we endeavor to amend them, and obey them until we have succeeded, or shall we transgress them at once? Men generally, under such a government as this, think that they ought to wait until they have persuaded the majority to alter them. They think that, if they should resist, the remedy would be worse than the evil. But it is the fault of the government itself that the remedy *is* worse than the evil. *It* makes it worse. Why is it not more apt to anticipate and provide for reform? Why does it not cherish its wise minority? Why does it cry and resist before it is hurt? Why does it not encourage its citizens to be on the alert to point out its faults, and *do* better than it would have them? Why does it always crucify Christ, and excommunicate Copernicus and Luther, and pronounce Washington and Franklin rebels?

One would think, that a deliberate and practical denial of its authority was the only offense never contemplated by government; else, why has it not assigned its definite, its suitable and proportionate penalty? If a man who has no property refuses but once to earn nine shillings for the state, he is put in prison for a period unlimited by any law that I know, and determined only by the discretion of those who placed him there; but if he should steal ninety times nine shillings from the state, he is soon permitted to go at large again.

If the injustice is part of the necessary friction of the machine of government, let it go, let it go: perchance it will wear smooth,—certainly the machine will wear out. If the injustice has a spring, or a pulley, or a rope, or a crank, exclusively for itself, then perhaps you may consider whether the remedy will not be worse than the evil; but if it is of such a nature that it requires you to be the agent of injustice to another, then, I say, break the law. Let your life be a counter friction to stop the machine. What I have to do is to see, at any rate, that I do not lend myself to the wrong which I condemn.

As for adopting the ways which the state has provided for remedying the evil, I know not of such ways. They take too much time, and a man's life will be gone. I have other affairs to attend to. I came into this world, not chiefly to make this a good place to live in, but to live in it, be it good or bad. A man has not everything to do, but something; and because he cannot do *everything*, it is not necessary that he should do *something* wrong. It is not my business to be petitioning the Governor or the Legislature any more than it is theirs to petition me; and if they should not hear my petition, what should I do then? But in this case the state has provided no way: its very Constitution is the evil. This may seem to be harsh and stubborn and unconciliatory; but it is to treat with the utmost kindness and consideration the only spirit that can appreciate or deserves it. So is all change for the better, like birth and death, which convulse the body.

I do not hesitate to say, that those who call themselves Abolitionists should at once effectually withdraw their support, both in person and property, from the government of Massachusetts, and not wait till they constitute a majority of one, before they suffer the right to prevail through them. I think that it is enough if they have God on their side, without waiting for that other one. Moreover, any man more right than his neighbors constitutes a majority of one already.

I meet this American government, or its representative, the state government, directly, and face to face, once a year—no more—in the person of its tax-gatherer; this is the only mode in which a man situated as I am necessarily meets it; and it then says distinctly, Recognize me; and the simplest, the most effectual, and, in the present posture of affairs, the indispensablest mode of treating with it on this head, of expressing your little satisfaction with and love for it, is to deny it then. My civil neighbor, the tax-gatherer, is the very man I have to deal with,—for it is, after all, with men and not with parchment that I quarrel,—and he has voluntarily chosen to be an agent of the government. How shall he ever know well what he is and does as an officer of the government, or as a man, until he is obliged to consider whether he shall treat me, his neighbor, for whom he has respect, as a neighbor and well-disposed man, or as a maniac and disturber of the peace, and see if he can get over this obstruction to his neighborliness without a ruder and more impetuous thought or speech corresponding with his action. I know this well, that if one thousand, if one hundred, if ten men whom I could name,—if ten *honest* men only,—ay, if *one* HONEST man, in this State of Massachusetts, *ceasing to hold slaves,* were actually to withdraw from this copartnership, and be locked up in the county jail therefor, it would be the abolition of slavery in America. For it matters not how small the beginning may seem to be: what is once well done is done forever. But we love better to talk about it: that we say is our mission. Reform keeps many scores of newspapers in its service, but not one man. If my esteemed neighbor, the State's ambassador, who will devote his days to the settlement of the question of human rights in the Council Chamber, instead of being threatened with the prisons of Carolina, were to sit down the prisoner of Massachusetts, that State which is so anxious to foist the sin of slavery upon her sister,—though at present she can discover only an act of inhospitality to be the ground of a quarrel with her,— the Legislature would not wholly waive the subject the following winter.

Under a government which imprisons any unjustly, the true place for a just man is also a prison. The proper place to-day, the only place which Massachusetts has provided for her freer and less desponding spirits, is in her prisons, to be put out and locked out of the State by her own act, as they have already put themselves out by their principles. It is there that the fugitive slave, and the Mexican prisoner on parole, and the Indian come to plead the wrongs of his race should find them; on that separate, but more free and honorable ground, where the State places those who are not *with* her, but *against* her,—the only house in a slave State in which a free man can abide with honor. If any think that their influence would be lost there, and their voices no longer afflict the ear of the State, that they would not be as an enemy within its walls, they do not know by how much truth is stronger than error, nor how much more eloquently and effectively he can combat injustice who has experienced a little in his own person. Cast your whole vote, not a strip of paper merely, but your whole influence. A minority is powerless while it conforms to the majority; it is not even a minority then; but it is irresistible when it clogs by its whole weight. If the alternative is to keep all just men in prison, or give up war and slavery, the State will not hesitate which to choose. If a thousand men were not to pay their tax-bills this year, that would not be a violent and bloody measure, as it would be to pay them, and enable the State to commit violence and shed innocent blood. This is, in fact, the definition of a peaceable revolution, if any such is possible. If the tax-gatherer, or any other public officer, asks me, as one has done, "But what shall I do?" my answer is, "If you really wish to do anything, resign your office." When the subject has refused allegiance, and the officer has resigned his office, then the revolution is accomplished. But even suppose blood should flow. Is there not a sort of blood shed when the conscience is wounded? Through this wound a man's real manhood and immortality flow out, and he bleeds to an everlasting death. I see this blood flowing now.

. . .

Some years ago, the State met me in behalf of the Church, and commanded me to pay a certain sum toward the support of a clergyman whose preaching my father attended, but never I myself. "Pay," it said, "or be locked up in the jail." I declined to pay. But, unfortunately, another man saw fit to pay it. I did not see why the schoolmaster should be taxed to support the priest, and not the priest the schoolmaster; for I was not the State's schoolmaster, but I supported myself by voluntary subscription. I did not see why the lyceum should not present its tax-bill, and have the State to back its demand, as well as the Church. However, at the request of the selectmen, I condescended to make some such statement as this in writing:—"Know all men by these presents, that I, Henry Thoreau, do not wish to be regarded as a member of any incorporated society which I have not joined." This I gave to the town clerk; and he has it. The State, having thus learned that I did not wish to be regarded as a member of that church, has never made a like demand on me since; though it said that it must adhere to its original presumption that time. If I had known how to name them, I should then have signed off in detail from all the societies which I never signed on to; but I did not know where to find a complete list.

I have paid no poll-tax for six years. I was put into a jail once on this account, for one night; and, as I stood considering the walls of solid stone, two or three feet thick, the door of wood and iron, a foot thick, and the iron grating which strained the light, I could not help being struck with the foolishness of that institution which treated me as if I were mere flesh and blood and bones, to be locked up. I wondered that it should have concluded at length that this was the best use it could put me to, and had never thought to avail itself of my services in some way. I saw that, if there was a wall of stone between me and my townsmen, there was a still more difficult one to climb or break through before they could get to be as free as I was. I did not for a moment feel confined, and the walls seemed a great waste of stone and mortar. I felt as if I alone of all my townsmen had paid my tax. They plainly did not know how to treat me, but behaved like persons who are underbred. In every threat and in every compliment there was a blunder; for they thought that my chief desire was to stand the other side of that stone wall. I could not but smile to see how industriously they locked the door on my meditations, which followed them out again without let or hindrance, and *they* were really all that was dangerous. As they could not reach me, they had resolved to punish my body; just as boys, if they cannot come at some person against whom they have a spite, will abuse his dog. I saw that the State was half-witted, that it was timid as a lone woman with her silver spoons, and that it did not know its friends from its foes, and I lost all my remaining respect for it, and pitied it.

Thus the State never intentionally confronts a man's sense, intellectual or moral, but only his body, his senses. It is not armed with superior wit or honesty, but with superior physical strength. I was not born to be forced. I will breathe after my own fashion. Let us see who is the strongest. What force has a multitude? They only can force me who obey a higher law than I. They force me to become like themselves. I do not hear of *men* being *forced* to live this way or that by masses of men. What sort of life were that to live? When I meet a government which says to me, "Your money or your life," why should I be in haste to give it my money? It may be in a great strait, and not know what to do: I cannot help that. It must help itself; do as I do. It is not worth the while to snivel about it. I am not responsible for the successful working of the machinery of society. I am not the son of the engineer. I perceive that, when an acorn and a chestnut fall side by side, the one does not remain inert to make way for the other, but both obey their own laws, and spring and grow and flourish as best they can, till one, perchance, overshadows and destroys the other. If a plant cannot live according to its nature, it dies; and so a man.

. . .

When I came out of prison,—for some one interfered, and paid that tax—I did not perceive that great changes had taken place on the common, such as he observed who went in a youth and emerged a tottering and gray-headed man; and yet a change had to my eyes come over the scene,— the town, and State, and country,—greater than any that mere time could effect. I saw yet more distinctly the State in which I lived. I saw to what extent the people among whom I lived could be trusted as good neighbors and friends; that their friendship was for summer weather only; that they did not greatly propose to do right; that they were a distinct race from me by their prejudices and superstitions, as the Chinamen and Malays are; that in their sacrifices to humanity they ran no risks, not even to their property; that after all they were not so noble but they treated the thief as he had treated them, and hoped, by a certain outward observance and a few prayers, and by walking in a particular straight though useless path from time to time, to save their souls. This may be to judge my neighbors harshly; for I believe that many of them are not aware that they have such an institution as the jail in their village.

It was formerly the custom in our village, when a poor debtor came out of jail, for his acquaintances to salute him, looking through their fingers, which were crossed to represent the grating of a jail window, "How do ye do?" My neighbors did not thus salute me, but first looked at me, and then at one another, as if I had returned from a long journey. I was put into jail as I was going to the shoemaker's to get a shoe which was mended. When I was let out the next morning, I proceeded to finish my errand, and, having put on my mended shoe, joined a huckleberry party, who were impatient to put themselves under my conduct; and in half an hour,—for the horse was soon tackled,—was in the midst of a huckleberry field, on one of our highest hills, two miles off, and then the State was nowhere to be seen.

. . .

I have never declined paying the highway tax, because I am as desirous of being a good neighbor as I am of being a bad subject; and as for supporting schools, I am doing my part to educate my fellow-countrymen now. It is for no particular item in the tax-bill that I refuse to pay it. I simply wish to refuse allegiance to the State, to withdraw and stand aloof from it effectually. I do not care to trace the course of my dollar, if I could, till it buys a man or a musket to shoot one with,—the dollar is innocent—but I am concerned to trace the effects of my allegiance. In fact, I quietly declare war with the State, after my fashion, though I will still make what use and get what advantage of her I can, as is usual in such cases.

. . .

I do not wish to quarrel with any man or nation. I do not wish to split hairs, to make fine distinctions, or set myself up as better than my neighbors. I seek rather, I may say, even an excuse for conforming to the laws of the land. I am but too ready to conform to them. Indeed, I have reason to suspect myself on this head; and each year, as the taxgatherer comes round, I find myself disposed to review the acts and position of the general and State governments, and the spirit of the people, to discover a pretext for conformity.

> "We must affect our country as our parents,
> And if at any time we alienate
> Our love or industry from doing it honor,
> We must respect effects and teach the soul
> Matter of conscience and religion,
> And not desire of rule or benefit."

I believe that the State will soon be able to take all my work of this sort out of my hands, and then I shall be no better a patriot than my fellow-countrymen. Seen from a lower point of view, the Constitution, with all its faults, is very good; the law and the courts are very respectable; even this State and this American government are, in many respects, very admirable, and rare things, to be thankful for, such as a great many have described them; but seen from a point of view a little higher, they are what I have described them; seen from a higher still, and the highest, who shall say what they are, or that they are worth looking at or thinking of at all?

However, the government does not concern me much, and I shall bestow the fewest possible thoughts on it. It is not many moments that I live under a government, even in this world. If a man is thought-free, fancy-free, imagination-free, that which *is not* never for a long time appearing *to be* to him, unwise rulers or reformers cannot fatally interrupt him.

. . .

The authority of government, even such as I am willing to submit to, —for I will cheerfully obey those who know and can do better than I, and in many things even those who neither know nor can do so well,— is still an impure one: to be strictly just, it must have the sanction and consent of the governed. It can have no pure right over my person and property but what I concede to it. The progress from an absolute to a limited monarchy, from a limited monarchy to a democracy, is a progress toward a true respect for the individual. Even the Chinese philosopher was wise enough to regard the individual as the basis of the empire. Is a democracy, such as we know it, the last improvement possible in government? Is it not possible to take a step further towards recognizing and organizing the rights of man? There will never be a really free and enlightened State until the State comes to recognize the individual as a higher and independent power, from which all its own power and authority are derived, and treats him accordingly. I please myself with imagining a State at last which can afford to be just to all men, and to treat the individual with respect as a neighbor; which even would not think it inconsistent with its own repose if a few were to live aloof from it, not meddling with it, nor embraced by it, who fulfilled all the duties of neighbors and fellow-men. A State which bore this kind of fruit, and suffered it to drop off as fast as it ripened, would prepare the way for a still more perfect and glorious State, which also I have imagined, but not yet anywhere seen.

For Discussion

1. What situations prompted Thoreau to declare that a man could not without disgrace be associated with the American government?
2. Does Thoreau's idea of the function of government make him an anarchist?

3. What is Thoreau's objection to working through government to remedy unjust laws?

4. Are Thoreau's objections to rule by majority valid today? How can a "wise minority" make its power felt?

5. What is the difference between Thoreau's "The only obligation which I have a right to assume is to do at any time what I think right" and ". . . to do my own thing"? (Also see Camus on rebellion and the educated man.)

6. Discuss the "patron of virtue" and the "Oddfellow" today.

7. How do the following quotations apply today?

   a) "All voting is a sort of gaming, like checkers or backgammon, with a slight moral tinge to it, a playing with right and wrong, with moral questions; and betting naturally accompanies it."

   b) "If I devote myself to other pursuits and contemplations, I must first see, at least, that I do not pursue them sitting upon another man's shoulders."

   c) "Let your life be a counter friction to stop the machine."

   d) "So is all change for the better, like birth and death, which convulse the body."

   e) "Under a government which imprisons any unjustly, the true place for a just man is also a prison."

   f) "Absolutely speaking, the more money, the less virtue; . . ."

   g) "I am as desirous of being a good neighbor as I am of being a bad subject; . . ."

8. What is the basic concept of man underlying Thoreau's social and political ideas?

9. Discuss Thoreau's metaphorical use of the term *machine*.

10. What in this essay makes Thoreau's voice primarily reflective? Where is he also impassioned, discursive, and ironic?

LEO TOLSTOY

Advice to a Draftee

Leo Tolstoy, a Russian nobleman born in 1828, began to write fiction while serving as an artillery officer in the Crimean War. He became one of Russia's greatest novelists (*Anna Karenina* and *War and Peace*) as well as an important religious thinker. His religious beliefs caused him to renounce the world and his material possessions and to live the life.of a Christian ascetic until his death in 1910. The following letter was written to a young Hessian named Ernst Schramm in 1899, when the Hessian army was a peacetime army and the penalty for evading conscription was death. The letter was forwarded from Darmstadt to Bavaria, which suggests that Schramm left the country rather than be conscripted.

In my last letter I answered your question as well as I could. It is not only Christians but all just people who must refuse to become soldiers—that is, to be ready on another's command (for this is what a soldier's duty actually consists of) to kill all those one is ordered to kill. The question as you state it—which is more useful, to become a good teacher or to suffer for rejecting conscription—is falsely stated. The question is falsely stated because it is wrong for us to determine our actions according to their results, to view actions merely as useful or destructive. In the choice of our actions we can be led by their advantages or disadvantages only when the actions themselves are not opposed to the demands of morality.

We can stay home, go abroad, or concern ourselves with farming or science according to what we find useful for ourselves or others; for neither in domestic life, foreign travel, farming, nor science is there anything immoral. But under no circumstance can we inflict violence on people, torture or kill them because we think such acts could be of use to us or to others. We cannot and may not do such things, especially because we

Translated by Rodney Dennis. Reprinted by permission of Houghton Library, Harvard University.

can never be sure of the results of our actions. Often actions which seem the most advantageous of all turn out in fact to be destructive; and the reverse is also true.

The question should not be stated: which is more useful, to be a good teacher or to go to jail for refusing conscription? but rather: what should a man do who has been called upon for military service—that is, called upon to kill or to prepare himself to kill?

And to this question, for a person who understands the true meaning of military service and who wants to be moral, there is only one clear and incontrovertible answer: such a person must refuse to take part in military service no matter what consequences this refusal may have. It may seem to us that this refusal could be futile or even harmful, and that it would be a far more useful thing, after serving one's time, to become a good village teacher. But in the same way, Christ could have judged it more useful for himself to be a good carpenter and submit to all the principles of the Pharisees than to die in obscurity as he did, repudiated and forgotten by everyone.

Moral acts are distinguished from all other acts by the fact that they operate independently of any predictable advantage to ourselves or to others. No matter how dangerous the situation may be of a man who finds himself in the power of robbers who demand that he take part in plundering, murder, and rape, a moral person cannot take part. Is not military service the same thing? Is one not required to agree to the deaths of all those one is commanded to kill?

But how can one refuse to do what everyone does, what everyone finds unavoidable and necessary? Or, must one do what no one does and what everyone considers unnecessary or even stupid and bad? No matter how strange it sounds, this strange argument is the main one offered against those moral acts which in our times face you and every other person called up for military service. But this argument is even more incorrect than the one which would make a moral action dependent upon considerations of advantage.

If I, finding myself in a crowd of running people, run with the crowd without knowing where, it is obvious that I have given myself up to mass hysteria; but if by chance I should push my way to the front, or be gifted with sharper sight than the others, or receive information that this crowd was racing to attack human beings and toward its own corruption, would I really not stop and tell the people what might rescue them? Would I go on running and do these things which I knew to be bad and corrupt? This is the situation of every individual called up for military service, if he knows what military service means.

I can well understand that you, a young man full of life, loving and loved by your mother, friends, perhaps a young woman, think with a natural terror about what awaits you if you refuse conscription; and perhaps you will not feel strong enough to bear the consequences of refusal, and knowing your weakness, will submit and become a soldier. I understand completely, and I do not for a moment allow myself to blame you, knowing very well that in your place I might perhaps do the same thing. Only do not say that you did it because it was useful or because everyone does it. If you did it, know that you did wrong.

In every person's life there are moments in which he can know himself, tell himself who he is, whether he is a man who values his human dignity above his life or a weak creature who does not know his dignity and is concerned merely with being useful (chiefly to himself). This is the situation of a man who goes out to defend his honor in a duel or a soldier who goes into battle (although here the concepts of life are wrong). It is the situation of a doctor or a priest called to someone sick with plague, of a man in a burning house or a sinking ship who must decide whether to let the weaker go first or shove them aside and save himself. It is the situation of a man in poverty who accepts or rejects a bribe. And in our times, it is the situation of a man called to military service. For a man who knows its significance, the call to the army is perhaps the only opportunity for him to behave as a morally free creature and fulfill the highest requirement of his life—or else merely to keep his advantage in sight like an animal and thus remain slavishly submissive and servile until humanity becomes degraded and stupid.

For these reasons I answered your question whether one has to refuse to do military service with a categorical "yes"—if you understand the meaning of military service (and if you did not understand it then, you do now) and if you want to behave as a moral person living in our times must.

Please excuse me if these words are harsh. The subject is so important that one cannot be careful enough in expressing oneself so as to avoid false interpretation.

April 7, 1899   LEO TOLSTOY

For Discussion

1. Why does Tolstoy see the draftee's question as "falsely stated"? Put his objection into your own words.
2. Tolstoy takes an absolutist position regarding practical action. How does he relate it to violence?
3. What point does Tolstoy make in using Jesus as an illustration? What do you think of the argument?
4. Examine the "strange argument" in terms of today's draftee.

5. What is the meaning of military service as Tolstoy sees it?
6. What is the actual *advice* which Tolstoy gives the draftee?
7. Tolstoy apologizes for his harsh words. Do you agree that they are harsh? Why or why not?
8. What is Tolstoy's attitude toward the draftee, and how is it revealed?

MOHANDAS K. GANDHI

Passive Resistance

The life of the Mahatma, Mohandas K. Gandhi (1869–1948), is the history of Indian independence, for he devoted his life to the cause of *Swaraj* (home rule) for India. When it was granted, Gandhi sought to unite Hindus and Moslems to form a single country; but he was unsuccessful, and in 1947 India was partitioned into Pakistan and India. He continued to work for religious and social harmony until he was assassinated by a Hindu extremist in 1948. Revered as a saint throughout the world, Gandhi exemplified the virtues he championed—peace, humility, charity, and love. Among his writings, many of which were written in prison, is the following dialogue from a pamphlet printed in 1909. Gandhi addresses his audience as Reader.

READER: Is there any historical evidence as to the success of what you have called soul-force or truth-force? No instance seems to have happened of any nation having risen through soul-force. I still think that the evil-doers will not cease doing evil without physical punishment.

EDITOR: The poet Tulsidas has said: "Of religion, pity (or love) is the root, as egotism of the body. Therefore, we should not abandon pity so long as we are alive." This appears to me to be a scientific truth. I believe in it as much as I believe in two and two being four. The force of love is the same as the force of the soul or truth. We have evidence of its working at every step. The universe would disappear without the existence of that force. But you ask for historical evidence. It is, therefore, necessary to know what history means. The Gujarati equivalent means; "It so happened." If that is the meaning of history, it is possible to give copious evidence. But, if it means the doings of kings and emperors, there can be no evidence of soul-force or passive resistance in such history. You cannot expect silver ore in a tin mine. History, as we know it, is a record of the wars of the world, and so there is a proverb among Englishmen that a

269

nation which has no history, that is, no wars, is a happy nation. How kings played, how they became enemies of one another, how they murdered one another, is found accurately recorded in history, and if this were all that had happened in the world, it would have been ended long ago. If the story of the universe had commenced with wars, not a man would have been found alive today. Those people who have been warred against have disappeared as, for instance, the natives of Australia of whom hardly a man was left alive by the intruders. Mark, please, that these natives did not use soul-force in self-defense, and it does not require much foresight to know that the Australians will share the same fate as their victims. "Those that take the sword shall perish by the sword." With us the proverb is that professional swimmers will find a watery grave.

The fact that there are so many men still alive in the world shows that it is based not on the force of arms but on the force of truth or love. Therefore, the greatest and most unimpeachable evidence of the success of this force is to be found in the fact that, in spite of the wars of the world, it still lives on.

Thousands, indeed tens of thousands, depend for their existence on a very active working of this force. Little quarrels of millions of families in their daily lives disappear before the exercise of this force. Hundreds of nations live in peace. History does not and cannot take note of this fact. History is really a record of every interruption of the even working of the force of love or of the soul. Two brothers quarrel; one of them repents and re-awakens the love that was lying dormant in him; the two again begin to live in peace; nobody takes note of this. But if the two brothers, through the intervention of solicitors or some other reason, take up arms or go to law—which is another form of the exhibition of brute force—their doings would be immediately noticed in the press, they would be the talk of their neighbors and would probably go down to history. And what is true of families and communities is true of nations. There is no reason to believe that there is one law for families and another for nations. History, then, is a record of an interruption of the course of nature. Soul-force, being natural, is not noted in history.

READER: According to what you say, it is plain that instances of this kind of passive resistance are not to be found in history. It is necessary to understand this passive resistance more fully. It will be better, therefore, if you enlarge upon it.

EDITOR: Passive resistance is a method of securing rights by personal suffering; it is the reverse of resistance by arms. When I refuse to do a thing that is repugnant to my conscience, I use soul-force. For instance, the Government of the day has passed a law which is applicable to me. I do not like it. If by using violence I force the Government to repeal the law, I am employing what may be termed body-force. If I do not obey the law and accept the penalty for its breach, I use soul-force. It involves sacrifice of self.

Everybody admits that sacrifice of self is infinitely superior to sacrifice of others. Moreover, if this kind of force is used in a cause that is unjust, only the person using it suffers. He does not make others suffer for his mistakes. Men have before now done many things which were subsequently found to have been wrong. No man can claim that he is absolutely in the right or that a particular thing is wrong because he thinks so, but it is wrong for him so long as that is his deliberate judgment. It is therefore meet that he should not do that which he knows to be wrong, and suffer the consequence whatever it may be. This is the key to the use of soul-force.

READER: You would then disregard laws—this is rank disloyalty. We have always been considered a law-abiding nation. You seem to be going even beyond the extremists. They say that we must obey the laws that have been passed, but that if the laws be bad, we must drive out the law-givers even by force.

EDITOR: Whether I go beyond them or whether I do not is a matter of no consequence to either of us. We simply want to find out what is right and to act accordingly. The real meaning of the statement that we are a law-abiding nation is that we are passive resisters. When we do not like certain laws, we do not break the heads of law-givers but we suffer and do not submit to the laws. That we should obey laws whether good or bad is a new-fangled notion. There was no such thing in former days. The people disregarded those laws they did not like and suffered the penalties for their breach. It is contrary to our manhood if we obey laws repugnant to our conscience. Such teaching is opposed to religion and means slavery. If the Government were to ask us to go about without any clothing, should we do so? If I were a passive resister, I would say to them that I would have nothing to do with their law. But we have so forgotten ourselves and become so compliant that we do not mind any degrading law.

A man who has realized his manhood, who fears only God, will fear no one else. Man-made laws are not necessarily binding on him. Even the Government does not expect any such thing from us. They do not say: "You must do such and such a thing," but they say: "If you do not do it, we will punish you." We are sunk so low that we fancy that it is our duty and our religion to do what the law lays down. If man will only realize that it is unmanly to obey laws that are unjust, no man's tyranny will enslave him. This is the key to self-rule or home-rule.

It is a superstition and ungodly thing to believe that an act of a majority binds a minority. Many examples can be given in which acts of majorities will be found to have been wrong and those of minorities to have been right. All reforms owe their origin to the initiation of minorities in opposition to majorities. If among a band of robbers a knowledge of robbing is obligatory, is a pious man to accept the obligation? So long as the superstition that men should obey unjust laws exists, so long will their slavery exist. And a passive resister alone can remove such a superstition.

To use brute-force, to use gunpowder, is contrary to passive resistance, for it means that we want our opponent to do by force that which we desire but he does not. And if such a use of force is justifiable, surely he is entitled to do likewise by us. And so we should never come to an agreement. We may simply fancy, like the blind horse moving in a circle round a mill, that we are making progress. Those who believe that they are not bound to obey laws which are repugnant to their conscience have only the remedy of passive resistance open to them. Any other must lead to disaster.

READER: From what you say I deduce that passive resistance is a splendid weapon of the weak, but that when they are strong they may take up arms.

EDITOR: This is a gross ignorance. Passive resistance, that is, soul-force, is matchless. It is superior to the force of arms. How, then, can it be considered only a weapon of the weak? Physical-force men are strangers to the courage that is requisite in a passive resister. Do you believe that a coward can ever disobey a law that he dislikes? Extremists are considered to be advocates of brute force. Why do they, then, talk about obeying laws? I do not blame them. They can say nothing else. When they succeed in driving out the English and they themselves become governors, they will want you and me to obey their laws. And that is a fitting thing for their constitution. But a passive resister will say he will not obey a law that is against his conscience, even though he may be blown to pieces at the mouth of a cannon.

What do you think? Wherein is courage required—in blowing others to pieces from behind a cannon, or with a smiling face to approach a cannon and be blown to pieces? Who is the true warrior—he who keeps death always as a bosom-friend, or he who controls the death of others? Believe me that a man devoid of courage and manhood can never be a passive resister.

This, however, I will admit: that even a man weak in body is capable of offering this resistance. One man can offer it just as well as millions. Both men and women can indulge in it. It does not require the training of an army; it needs no jiu-jitsu. Control over the mind is alone necessary, and when that is attained, man is free like the king of the forest and his very glance withers the enemy.

Passive resistance is an all-sided sword, it can be used anyhow; it blesses him who uses it and him against whom it is used. Without drawing a drop of blood it produces far-reaching results. It never rusts and cannot be stolen. Competition between passive resisters does not exhaust. The sword of passive resistance does not require a scabbard. It is strange indeed that you should consider such a weapon to be a weapon merely of the weak. . . .

READER: From what you say, then, it would appear that it is not a small thing to become a passive resister, and, if that is so, I should like you to explain how a man may become one.

EDITOR: To become a passive resister is easy enough but it is also equally difficult. I have known a lad of fourteen years become a passive resister; I have known also sick people do likewise; and I have also known physically strong and otherwise happy people unable to take up passive resistance. After a great deal of experience it seems to me that those who want to become passive resisters for the service of the country have to observe perfect chastity, adopt poverty, follow truth, and cultivate fearlessness.

. . .

Just as there is necessity for chastity, so is there for poverty. Pecuniary ambition and passive resistance cannot go well together. Those who have money are not expected to throw it away, but they are expected to be indifferent about it. They must be prepared to lose every penny rather than give up passive resistance.

Passive resistance has been described in the course of our discussion as truth-force. Truth, therefore, has necessarily to be followed and that at any cost. In this connection, academic questions such as whether a man may not lie in order to save a life, etc., arise, but these questions occur only to those who wish to justify lying. Those who want to follow truth every time are not placed in such a quandary; and if they are, they are still saved from a false position.

Passive resistance cannot proceed a step without fearlessness. Those alone can follow the path of passive resistance who are free from fear, whether as to their possessions, false honor, their relatives, the government, bodily injuries or death.

These observances are not to be abandoned in the belief that they are difficult. Nature has implanted in the human breast ability to cope with any difficulty or suffering that may come to man unprovoked. These qualities are worth having, even for those who do not wish to serve the country. Let there be no mistake, as those who want to train themselves in the use of arms are also obliged to have these qualities more or less. Everybody does not become a warrior for the wish. A would-be warrior will have to observe chastity and to be satisfied with poverty as his lot. A warrior without fearlessness cannot be conceived of. It may be thought that he would not need to be exactly truthful, but that quality follows real fearlessness. When a man abandons truth, he does so owing to fear in some shape or form. The above four attributes, then, need not frighten anyone.

It may be as well here to note that a physical-force man has to have many other useless qualities which a passive resister never needs. And you will find that whatever extra effort a swordsman needs is due to lack of fearlessness. If he is an embodiment of the latter, the sword will drop from his hand that very moment. He does not need its support. One who is free from hatred requires no sword. A man with a stick suddenly came face to face with a lion and instinctively raised his weapon in self-defense. The man saw that he had only prated about fearlessness when there was none in him. That moment he dropped the stick and found himself free from all fear.

For Discussion

1. What is "soul-force" or "truth-force"? How does the life of man support it? The history of man ignore it?
2. Discuss Gandhi's explanation of passive resistance. How does it relate to soul-force?
3. How does Gandhi's concept of civil disobedience function within the framework of government? (Also see Thoreau and Brown.)
4. Contrast passive resistance and brute force as methods of protest. Cite examples of each in current situations.
5. Discuss the implications of the following statements as applied to contemporary society:
    a) "All reforms owe their origin to the initiation of minorities in opposition to majorities."
    b) "When a man abandons truth he does so owing to fear in some shape or form."
    c) "One who is free from hatred requires no sword."
6. Examine Gandhi's rationale for the four qualities needed by the person who resists passively. Do you agree? Explain.
7. How appropriate is the metaphor of the sword? How effective?
8. In what sense is this essay reflective?

D. H. LAWRENCE

Sex versus Loveliness

David Herbert Lawrence, born in England in 1885, completed an enormous body of work—novels, short stories, poetry, travel writings, and literary criticism—before his death from tuberculosis in 1930. Always a nonconformist, Lawrence was highly criticized for his unconventional private life as well as for his frank treatment of love and sex in his novels, particularly *Sons and Lovers, The Rainbow, Women in Love,* and *Lady Chatterly's Lover.* Because his books were banned on charges of obscenity, Lawrence experienced financial difficulties which, along with his hatred of English industrialism and his poor health, prompted him to live abroad. He lived in various exotic places throughout the world, at one time settling in Taos, New Mexico, where his interest in primitive cultures found stimulus and where a shrine commemorates him.

It is a pity that *sex* is such an ugly little word. An ugly little word, and really almost incomprehensible. What *is* sex, after all? The more we think about it the less we know.

Science says it is an instinct; but what is an instinct? Apparently an instinct is an old, old habit that has become ingrained. But a habit, however old, has to have a beginning. And there is really no beginning to sex. Where life is, there it is. So sex is no "habit" that has been formed.

Again, they talk of sex as an appetite, like hunger. An appetite; but for what? An appetite for propagation? It is rather absurd. They say a peacock puts on all his fine feathers to dazzle the peahen into letting him satisfy his appetite for propagation. But why should the peahen not put on fine feathers, to dazzle the peacock, and satisfy *her* desire for propagation? She has surely quite as great a desire for eggs and chickens as he has. We cannot believe that her sex-urge is so weak that she needs all that blue splendour of feathers to rouse her. Not at all.

As for me, I never even saw a peahen so much as look at her lord's bronze and blue glory. I don't believe she ever sees it. I don't believe for a moment that she knows the difference between bronze, blue, brown or green.

If I had ever seen a peahen gazing with rapt attention on her lord's flamboyancy, I might believe that he had put on all those feathers just to "attract" her. But she never looks at him. Only she seems to get a little perky when he shudders all his quills at her, like a storm in the trees. Then she does seem to notice, just casually, his presence.

These theories of sex are amazing. A peacock puts on his glory for the sake of a wall-eyed peahen who never looks at him. Imagine a scientist being so naïve as to credit the peahen with a profound, dynamic appreciation of a peacock's colour and pattern. Oh, highly aesthetic peahen!

And a nightingale sings to attract his female. Which is mighty curious, seeing he sings his best when courtship and honeymoon are over and the female is no longer concerned with him at all, but with the young. Well, then, if he doesn't sing to attract her, he must sing to distract her and amuse her while she's sitting.

How delightful, how naïve theories are! But there is a hidden will behind them all. There is a hidden will behind all theories of sex, implacable. And that is the will to deny, to wipe out the mystery of beauty.

Because beauty is a mystery. You can neither eat it nor make flannel out of it. Well, then, says science, it is just a trick to catch the female and induce her to propagate. How naïve! As if the female needed inducing. She will propagate in the dark, even—so where, then, is the beauty trick?

Science has a mysterious hatred of beauty, because it doesn't fit in the cause-and-effect chain. And society has a mysterious hatred of sex, because it perpetually interferes with the nice money-making schemes of social man. So the two hatreds made a combine, and sex and beauty are mere propagation appetite.

Now sex and beauty are one thing, like flame and fire. If you hate sex you hate beauty. If you love *living* beauty, you have a reverence for sex. Of course you can love old, dead beauty and hate sex. But to love living beauty you must have a reverence for sex.

Sex and beauty are inseparable, like life and consciousness. And the intelligence which goes with sex and beauty, and arises out of sex and beauty, is intuition. The great disaster of our civilization is the morbid hatred of sex. What, for example, could show a more poisoned hatred of sex than Freudian psycho-analysis?—which carries with it a morbid fear of beauty, "alive" beauty, and which causes the atrophy of our intuitive faculty and our intuitive self.

The deep psychic disease of modern men and women is the diseased, atrophied condition of the intuitive faculties. There is a whole world of life that we might know and enjoy by intuition, and by intuition alone. This is denied us, because we deny sex and beauty, the source of the intuitive life and of the insouciance which is so lovely in free animals and in plants.

Sex is the root of which intuition is the foliage and beauty the flower. Why is a woman lovely, if ever, in her twenties? It is the time when sex rises softly to her face, as a rose to the top of a rose bush.

And the appeal is the appeal of beauty. We deny it wherever we can. We try to make the beauty as shallow and trashy as possible. But, first and foremost, sex appeal is the appeal of beauty.

Now beauty is a thing about which we are so uneducated we can hardly speak of it. We try to pretend it is a fixed arrangement: straight nose, large eyes, etc. We think a lovely woman must look like Lilian Gish, a handsome man must look like Rudolph Valentino. So we *think*.

In actual life we behave quite differently. We say: "She's quite beautiful, but I don't care for her." Which shows we are using the word *beautiful* all wrong. We should say: "She has the stereotyped attributes of beauty, but she is not beautiful to me."

Beauty is an *experience*, nothing else. It is not a fixed pattern or an arrangement of features. It is something *felt*, a glow or a communicated sense of fineness. What ails us is that our sense of beauty is so bruised and blunted, we miss all the best.

But to stick to the films—there is a greater essential beauty in Charlie Chaplin's odd face than ever there was in Valentino's. There is a bit of true beauty in Chaplin's brows and eyes, a gleam of something pure.

But our sense of beauty is so bruised and clumsy, we don't see it, and don't know it when we do see it. We can only see the blatantly obvious, like the so-called beauty of Rudolph Valentino, which only pleases because it satisfies some ready-made notion of handsomeness.

But the plainest person can look beautiful, can *be* beautiful. It only needs the fire of sex to rise delicately to change an ugly face to a lovely one. That is really sex appeal: the communicating of a sense of beauty.

And in the reverse way, no one can be quite so repellent as a really pretty woman. That is, since beauty is a question of experience, not of concrete form, no one can be as acutely ugly as a really pretty woman. When the sex-glow is missing, and she moves in ugly coldness, how hideous she seems, and all the worse for her externals of prettiness.

What sex is, we don't know, but it must be some sort of fire. For it always communicates a sense of warmth, of glow. And when the glow becomes a pure shine, then we feel the sense of beauty.

But the communicating of the warmth, the glow of sex, is true sex appeal. We all have the fire of sex slumbering or burning inside us. If we live to be ninety, it is still there. Or, if it dies, we become one of those ghastly living corpses which are unfortunately becoming more numerous in the world.

Nothing is more ugly than a human being in whom the fire of sex has gone out. You get a nasty clayey creature whom everybody wants to avoid.

But while we are fully alive, the fire of sex smoulders or burns in us. In youth it flickers and shines; in age it glows softer and stiller, but there it is. We have some control over it; but only partial control. That is why society hates it.

While ever it lives, the fire of sex, which is the source of beauty and anger, burns in us beyond our understanding. Like actual fire, while it lives it will burn our fingers if we touch it carelessly. And so social man, who only wants to be "safe," hates the fire of sex.

Luckily, not many men succeed in being merely social men. The fire of the old Adam smoulders. And one of the qualities of fire is that it calls to fire. Sex-fire here kindles sex-fire there. It may only rouse the smoulder into a soft glow. It may call up a sharp flicker. Or rouse a flame; and then flame leans to flame, and starts a blaze.

Whenever the sex-fire glows through, it will kindle an answer somewhere or other. It may only kindle a sense of warmth and optimism. Then you say: "I like that girl; she's a real good sort." It may kindle a glow that makes the world look kindlier, and life feel better. Then you say: "She's an attractive woman. I like her."

Or she may rouse a flame that lights up her own face first, before it lights up the universe. Then you say: "She's a lovely woman. She looks lovely to me."

It takes a rare woman to rouse a real sense of loveliness. It is not that a woman is born beautiful. We say that to escape our own poor, bruised, clumsy understanding of beauty. There have been thousands and thousands of women quite as good-looking as Diane de Poitiers, or Mrs. Langtry, or any of the famous ones. There are today thousands and thousands of superbly good-looking women. But oh, how few lovely women!

And why? Because of the failure of their sex appeal. A good-looking woman becomes lovely when the fire of sex rouses pure and fine in her and flickers through her face and touches the fire in me.

Then she becomes a lovely woman to me, then she is in the living flesh a lovely woman: not a mere photograph of one. And how lovely a lovely woman! But, alas! how rare! How bitterly rare in a world full of unusually handsome girls and women!

Handsome, good-looking, but not lovely, not beautiful. Handsome and good-looking women are the women with good features and the right hair. But a lovely woman is an experience. It is a question of communicated fire. It is a question of sex appeal in our poor, dilapidated modern phraseology. Sex appeal applied to Diane de Poitiers, or even, in the lovely hours, to one's wife—why, it is a libel and a slander in itself. Nowadays, however, instead of the fire of loveliness, it is sex appeal. The two are the same thing, I suppose, but on vastly different levels.

The business man's pretty and devoted secretary is still chiefly valuable because of her sex appeal. Which does not imply "immoral relations" in the slightest.

Even today a girl with a bit of generosity likes to feel she is helping a man if the man will take her help. And this desire that he shall take her help is her sex appeal. It is the genuine fire, if of a very mediocre heat.

Still, it serves to keep the world of "business" alive. Probably, but for the introduction of the lady secretary into the business man's office, the business man would have collapsed entirely by now. She calls up the sacred fire in her and she communicates it to her boss. He feels an added flow of energy and optimism, and—business flourishes.

There is, of course, the other side of sex appeal. It can be the destruction of the one appealed to. When a woman starts using her sex appeal to her own advantage it is usually a bad moment for some poor devil. But this side of sex appeal has been overworked lately, so it is not nearly as dangerous as it was.

The sex-appealing courtesans who ruined so many men in Balzac no longer find it smooth running. Men have grown canny. They fight shy even of the emotional vamp. In fact, men are inclined to think they smell a rat the moment they feel the touch of feminine sex appeal today.

Which is a pity, for sex appeal is only a dirty name for a bit of life-flame. No man works so well and so successfully as when some woman has kindled a little fire in his veins. No woman does her housework with real joy unless she is in love—and a woman may go on being quietly in love for fifty years almost without knowing it.

If only our civilization had taught us how to let sex appeal flow properly and subtly, how to keep the fire of sex clear and alive, flickering or glowing or blazing in all its varying degrees of strength and communication, we might, all of us, have lived all our lives in love, which means we should be kindled and full of zest in all kinds of ways and for all kinds of things. . . .

Whereas, what a lot of dead ash there is in life now.

For Discussion

1. What theories regarding sex does Lawrence reject? What are his arguments?
2. Explain what Lawrence means by the word "mystery."
3. What is the relationship among sex, beauty, and intuition?

4. Discuss Lawrence's concept of beauty. Who determines what is beautiful?
5. Suggest modern counterparts to Valentino, Gish, and Chaplin.
6. What is the current connotation of sex appeal? What is Lawrence's definition?
7. According to Lawrence, why does society hate sex?
8. How accurate is Lawrence's idea that our sense of beauty is "bruised and blunted"?
9. What recurring metaphor dominates this essay?
10. Examine the tone of the last two paragraphs. What attitude does it reveal toward sex? Toward people? Toward life?

NORBERT WIENER

A Scientist Rebels

Norbert Wiener (1890-1964) was a child prodigy. Receiving his Ph.D. from Harvard University at the age of eighteen, he began a forty-two year career in mathematics at the Massachusetts Institute of Technology in 1919. His *Cybernetics,* published in 1948, introduced a new branch of science to the world—and a new word to the language. Concerned that computers be carefully controlled so as not to devalue human intellect, he became the "watchdog" as well as the "father" of automation. Although he designed aiming devices for antiaircraft guns during World War II, he refused to apply the new science to weapons research. The letter reprinted below, addressed to a research scientist of an aircraft corporation, clearly establishes his position.

SIR:—

I have received from you a note in which you state that you are engaged in a project concerning controlled missiles, and in which you request a copy of a paper which I wrote for the National Defense Research Committee during the war.

As the paper is the property of a government organization, you are of course at complete liberty to turn to that government organization for such information as I could give you. If it is out of print as you say, and they desire to make it available for you, there are doubtless proper avenues of approach to them.

When, however, you turn to me for information concerning controlled missiles, there are several considerations which determine my reply. In the past, the comity of scholars has made it a custom to furnish scientific information to any person seriously seeking it. However, we must face these facts: The policy of the government itself during and after the war, say in the bombing of Hiroshima and Nagasaki, has made it clear that to provide scientific information is not a necessarily innocent act, and may entail the gravest consequences. One therefore cannot escape reconsidering the established custom of the scientist to give information to every person who may inquire of him. The interchange of ideas which is one of the great traditions of science must of course receive certain limitations when the scientist becomes an arbiter of life and death.

For the sake, however, of the scientist and the public, these limitations should be as intelligent as possible. The measures taken during the war by our military agencies, in restricting the free intercourse among scientists on related projects or even on the same project, have gone so far that it is clear that if continued in time of peace this policy will lead to the total irresponsibility of the scientist, and ultimately to the death of science. Both of these are disastrous for our civilization, and entail grave and immediate peril for the public.

I realize, of course, that I am acting as the censor of my own ideas, and it may sound arbitrary, but I will not accept a censorship in which I do not participate. The experience of the scientists who have worked on the atomic bomb has indicated that in any investigation of this kind the scientist ends by putting unlimited powers in the hands of the people whom he is least inclined to trust with their use. It is perfectly clear also that to disseminate information about a weapon in the present state of our civilization is to make it practically certain that that weapon will be used. In that respect the controlled missile represents the still imperfect supplement to the atom bomb and to bacterial warfare.

The practical use of guided missiles can only be to kill foreign civilians indiscriminately, and it furnishes no protection whatsoever to civilians in this country. I cannot conceive a situation in which such weapons can produce any effect other than extending the kamikaze way of fighting to whole nations. Their possession can do nothing but endanger us by encouraging the tragic insolence of the military mind.

If therefore I do not desire to participate in the bombing or poisoning of defenseless peoples—and I most certainly do not—I must take a serious responsibility as to those to whom I disclose my scientific ideas. Since it is obvious that with sufficient effort you can obtain my material, even though it is out of print, I can only protest pro forma in refusing to give you any information concerning my past work. However, I rejoice at the fact that my material is not readily available, inasmuch as it gives me the opportunity to raise this serious moral issue. I do not expect to publish any future work of mine which may do damage in the hands of irresponsible militarists.

I am taking the liberty of calling this letter to the attention of other people in scientific work. I believe it is only proper that they should know of it in order to make their own independent decisions, if similar situations should confront them.

For Discussion

1. What situation prompted the writing of this letter?
2. Explain the relationship between political policy and science.
3. What dangers does Wiener see in both the restrictions against free intercourse among scientists and the open dissemination of scientific information?
4. Discuss the "tragic insolence of the military mind." (Also see Shoup.)
5. Explain what the writer means by the practical use of guided missiles. Discuss other possible uses.
6. What does Wiener say about publishing his future work as a scientist? What evidence can you cite that he is not alone in his position?
7. In your opinion, what is the moral responsibility of the scientist?

ALBERT CAMUS

The Rebel

An Algerian by birth and education, Albert Camus began his career as an actor and theatrical manager, then worked as a journalist in Algeria and Paris during the late 1930's. He joined the French Resistance movement in World War II and wrote for the underground newspaper *Combat*. Between the years 1942–1947, Camus' novels, *The Stranger* and *The Plague*; his plays, *Caligula* and *The Misunderstanding*; and his philosophical treatise, "The Myth of Sisyphus," created for him an extraordinary following, both in France and throughout the world. Publication of *The Rebel* in 1951, of which the following essay is the opening chapter, and *The Exile and the Kingdom* in 1957 enhanced his position as a leading existential and political philosopher. In 1957 he was awarded the Nobel Prize for Literature. Camus was only forty-six, at the height of his creative power, when he was killed in an automobile accident in 1960.

What is a rebel? A man who says no, but whose refusal does not imply a renunciation. He is also a man who says yes, from the moment he makes his first gesture of rebellion. A slave who has taken orders all his life suddenly decides that he cannot obey some new command. What does he mean by saying "no"?

He means, for example, that "this has been going on too long," "up to this point yes, beyond it no," "you are going too far," or, again, "there is a limit beyond which you shall not go." In other words, his no affirms the existence of a borderline. The same concept is to be found in the rebel's feeling that the other person "is exaggerating," that he is exerting his authority beyond a limit where he begins to infringe on the rights of others. Thus the movement of rebellion is founded simultaneously on the categorical rejection of an intrusion that is considered intolerable and on the confused conviction of an absolute right which, in the rebel's mind, is more precisely the impression that he "has the right to. . . ." Rebellion cannot exist without the feeling that, somewhere and somehow, one is right. It is in this way that the rebel slave says yes and no simultaneously. He affirms that there are limits and also that he suspects—and wishes to preserve—the existence of certain things on this side of the borderline. He demonstrates, with obstinacy, that there is something in him which "is worth while . . ." and which must be taken into consideration. In a certain way, he confronts an order of things which oppresses him with the insistence on a kind of right not to be oppressed beyond the limit that he can tolerate.

In every act of rebellion, the rebel simultaneously experiences a feeling of revulsion at the infringement of his rights and a complete and spontaneous loyalty to certain aspects of himself. Thus he implicitly brings into play a standard of values so far from being gratuitous that he is prepared to support it no matter what the risks. Up to this point he has at least remained silent and has abandoned himself to the form of despair in which a condition is accepted even though it is considered unjust. To remain silent is to give the impression that one has no opinions, that one wants nothing, and in certain cases it really amounts to wanting nothing. Despair, like the absurd, has opinions and desires about everything in general and nothing in particular. Silence expresses this attitude very well. But from the moment that the rebel finds his voice—even though he says nothing but "no"—he begins to desire and to judge. The rebel, in the etymological sense, does a complete turnabout. He acted under the lash of his master's whip. Suddenly he turns and faces him. He opposes what is preferable to what is not. Not every value entails rebellion, but every act of rebellion tacitly invokes a value. Or is it really a question of values?

Awareness, no matter how confused it may be, develops from every act of rebellion: the sudden, dazzling perception that there is something in man with which he can identify himself, even if only for a moment. Up to now this identification was never really experienced. Before he rebelled, the slave accepted all the demands made upon him. Very often he even took orders, without reacting against them, which were far more conducive to insurrection than the one at which he balks. He accepted them patiently, though he may have protested inwardly, but in that he remained silent he was more concerned with his own immediate interests than as yet aware of his own rights. But with loss of patience—with impatience—a reaction begins which can extend to everything that he previously accepted, and which is almost always retroactive. The very moment the slave refuses to obey the humiliating orders of his master, he simultaneously rejects the condition of slavery. The act of rebellion carries him far beyond the point he had reached by simply refusing. He exceeds the bounds that he fixed for his antagonists, and now demands to be treated as an equal. What was at first the man's obstinate resistance now becomes the whole man, who is identified with and summed up in this resistance. The part of himself that he wanted to be respected he proceeds to place above everything else and proclaims it preferable to everything, even to life itself. It becomes for him the supreme good. Having up to now been willing to compromise, the slave suddenly adopts ("because this is how it must be . . .") an attitude of All or Nothing. With rebellion, awareness is born.

But we can see that the knowledge gained is, at the same time, of an "all" that is still rather obscure and of a "nothing" that proclaims the possibility of sacrificing the rebel to this "All." The rebel himself wants to be "all"—to identify himself completely with this good of which he has suddenly become aware and by which he wants to be personally recognized and acknowledged—or "nothing"; in other words, to be completely destroyed by the force that dominates him. As a last resort, he is willing to accept the final defeat, which is death, rather than be deprived of the personal sacrament that he would call, for example, freedom. Better to die on one's feet than to live on one's knees.

Values, according to good authorities, "most often represent a transition from facts to rights, from what is desired to what is desirable (usually through the intermediary of what is generally considered desirable)."[1] The transition from facts to rights is manifest, as we have seen, in rebellion. So is the transition from "this must be" to "this is how I should like things to be," and even more so, perhaps, the idea of the sublimation of the individual in a henceforth universal good. The sudden appearance of the concept of "All or Nothing" demonstrates that rebellion, contrary to current opinion, and though it springs from everything that is most strictly individualistic in man, questions the very idea of the individual. If the individual, in fact, accepts death and happens to die as a consequence of his act of rebellion, he demonstrates by doing so that he is willing to sacrifice himself for the sake of a common good which he considers more important than his own destiny. If he prefers the risk of death to the negation of the rights that he defends, it is because he considers these rights more important than himself. Therefore he is acting in the name of certain values which are still indeterminate but which he feels are common to himself and to all men. We see that the affirmation implicit in every act of rebellion is extended to something that transcends the individual in so far as it withdraws him from his supposed solitude and provides him with a reason to act. But it is already worth noting that this concept of values as pre-existent to any kind of action contradicts the purely historical philosophies, in which values are acquired (if they are ever acquired) after the action has been completed. Analysis of rebellion leads at least to the suspicion that, contrary to the postulates of

[1] Lalande: *Vocabulaire philosophique.*

contemporary thought, a human nature does exist, as the Greeks believed. Why rebel if there is nothing permanent in oneself worth preserving? It is for the sake of everyone in the world that the slave asserts himself when he comes to the conclusion that a command has infringed on something in him which does not belong to him alone, but which is common ground where all men—even the man who insults and oppresses him—have a natural community.[2]

Two observations will support this argument. First, we can see that an act of rebellion is not, essentially, an egoistic act. Of course, it can have egoistic motives. But one can rebel equally well against lies as against oppression. Moreover, the rebel—once he has accepted the motives and at the moment of his greatest impetus—preserves nothing in that he risks everything. He demands respect for himself, of course, but only in so far as he identifies himself with a natural community.

Then we note that rebellion does not arise only, and necessarily, among the oppressed, but that it can also be caused by the mere spectacle of oppression of which someone else is the victim. In such cases there is a feeling of identification with another individual. And it must be pointed out that this is not a question of psychological identification—a mere subterfuge by which the individual imagines that it is he himself who has been offended. On the contrary, it can often happen that we cannot bear to see offenses done to others which we ourselves have accepted without rebelling. The suicides of the Russian terrorists in Siberia as a protest against their comrades' being whipped is a case in point. Nor is it a question of the feeling of a community of interests. Injustices done to men whom we consider enemies can, actually, be profoundly repugnant to us. There is only identification of one's destiny with that of others and a choice of sides. Therefore the individual is not, in himself alone, the embodiment of the values he wishes to defend. It needs all humanity, at least, to comprise them. When he rebels, a man identifies himself with other men and so surpasses himself, and from this point of view human solidarity is metaphysical. But for the moment we are only talking of the kind of solidarity that is born in chains.

It would be possible for us to define the positive aspect of the values implicit in every act of rebellion by comparing them with a completely negative concept like that of resentment as defined by Scheler. Rebellion is, in fact, much more than pursuit of a claim, in the strongest sense of the word. Resentment is very well defined by Scheler as an autointoxication—the evil secretion, in a sealed vessel, of prolonged impotence. Rebellion, on the contrary, breaks the seal and allows the whole being to come into play.

[2] The community of victims is the same as that which unites victim and executioner. But the executioner does not know this.

It liberates stagnant waters and turns them into a raging torrent. Scheler himself emphasizes the passive aspect of resentment and remarks on the prominent place it occupies in the psychology of women who are dedicated to desire and possession. The fountainhead of rebellion, on the contrary, is the principle of superabundant activity and energy. Scheler is also right in saying that resentment is always highly colored by envy. But one envies what one does not have, while the rebel's aim is to defend what he is. He does not merely claim some good that he does not possess or of which he was deprived. His aim is to claim recognition for something which he has and which has already been recognized by him, in almost every case, as more important than anything of which he could be envious. Rebellion is not realistic. According to Scheler, resentment always turns into either unscrupulous ambition or bitterness, depending on whether it is implanted in a strong person or a weak one. But in both cases it is a question of wanting to be something other than what one is. Resentment is always resentment against oneself. The rebel, on the contrary, from his very first step, refuses to allow anyone to touch what he is. He is fighting for the integrity of one part of his being. He does not try, primarily, to conquer, but simply to impose.

Finally, it would seem that resentment takes delight, in advance, in the pain that it would like the object of its envy to feel. Nietzsche and Scheler are right in seeing an excellent example of this in the passage where Tertullian informs his readers that one of the greatest sources of happiness among the blessed will be the spectacle of the Roman emperors consumed in the fires of hell. This kind of happiness is also experienced by the decent people who go to watch executions. The rebel, on the contrary, limits himself, as a matter of principle, to refusing to be humiliated without asking that others should be. He will even accept pain provided his integrity is respected.

It is therefore hard to understand why Scheler completely identifies the spirit of rebellion with resentment. His criticism of the resentment to be found in humanitarianism (which he treats as the non-Christian form of love for mankind) could perhaps be applied to certain indeterminate forms of humanitarian idealism, or to the techniques of terror. But it rings false in relation to man's rebellion against his condition—the movement that enlists the individual in the defense of a dignity common to all men. Scheler wants to demonstrate that humanitarian feelings are always accompanied by a hatred of the world. Humanity is loved in general in order to avoid having to love anybody in particular. This is correct, in some cases, and it is easier to understand Scheler when we realize that for him humanitarianism is represented by Bentham and Rousseau. But man's love for man can be born of other things than a mathematical calculation of the resultant rewards or a theoretical confidence in human nature. In face of the utilitarians, and of Emile's preceptor, there is, for example, the kind of logic, embodied by Dostoievsky in Ivan Karamazov, which progresses from an act of rebellion to metaphysical insurrection. Scheler is aware of this and sums up the concept in the following manner: "There is not enough love in the world to squander it on anything but human beings." Even if this proposition were true, the appalling despair that it implies would merit anything but contempt. In fact, it misunderstands the tortured character of Karamazov's rebellion. Ivan's drama, on the contrary, arises from the fact that there is too much love without an object. This love finding no outlet and God being denied, it is then decided to lavish it on human beings as a generous act of complicity.

Nevertheless, in the act of rebellion as we have envisaged it up to now, an abstract ideal is not chosen through lack of feeling and in pursuit of a sterile demand. We insist that the part of man which cannot be reduced to mere ideas should be taken into consideration—the passionate side of his nature that serves no other purpose than to be part of the act of living. Does this imply that no rebellion is motivated by resentment? No, and we know it only too well in this age of malice. But we must consider the idea of rebellion in its widest sense on pain of betraying it; and in its widest sense rebellion goes far beyond resentment. When Heathcliff, in *Wuthering Heights,* says that he puts his love above God and would willingly go to hell in order to be reunited with the woman he loves, he is prompted not only by youth and humiliation but by the consuming experience of a whole lifetime. The same emotion causes Eckart, in a surprising fit of heresy, to say that he prefers hell with Jesus to heaven without Him. This is the very essence of love. Contrary to Scheler, it would therefore be impossible to overemphasize the passionate affirmation that underlies the act of rebellion and distinguishes it from resentment. Rebellion, though apparently negative, since it creates nothing, is profoundly positive in that it reveals the part of man which must always be defended.

But, to sum up, are not rebellion and the values that it implies relative? Reasons for rebellion do seem to change, in fact, with periods and civilizations. It is obvious that a Hindu pariah, an Inca warrior, a primitive native of central Africa, and a member of one of the first Christian communities had not at all the same ideas about rebellion. We could even assert, with considerable assurance, that the idea of rebellion has no meaning in these particular cases. However, a Greek slave, a serf, a *condottiere* of the Renaissance, a Parisian bourgeois during the Regency, a Russian intellectual at the beginning of the twentieth century, and a contemporary worker would undoubtedly agree that rebellion is legitimate, even if they differed about the reasons for it. In other words, the problem of rebellion seems to assume a precise meaning only within the confines of

Western thought. It is possible to be even more explicit by remarking, like Scheler, that the spirit of rebellion finds few means of expression in societies where inequalities are very great (the Hindu caste system) or, again, in those where there is absolute equality (certain primitive societies). The spirit of rebellion can exist only in a society where a theoretical equality conceals great factual inequalities. The problem of rebellion, therefore, has no meaning except within our own Western society. One might be tempted to affirm that it is relative to the development of individualism if the preceding remarks had not put us on our guard against this conclusion.

On the basis of the evidence, the only conclusion that can be drawn from Scheler's remark is that, thanks to the theory of political freedom, there is, in the very heart of our society, an increasing awareness in man of the idea of man and, thanks to the application of this theory of freedom, a corresponding dissatisfaction. Actual freedom has not increased in proportion to man's awareness of it. We can only deduce from this observation that rebellion is the act of an educated man who is aware of his own rights. But there is nothing which justifies us in saying that it is only a question of individual rights. Because of the sense of solidarity we have already pointed out, it would rather seem that what is at stake is humanity's gradually increasing self-awareness as it pursues its course. In fact, for the Inca and the pariah the problem never arises, because for them it had been solved by a tradition, even before they had had time to raise it—the answer being that tradition is sacred. If in a world where things are held sacred the problem of rebellion does not arise, it is because no real problems are to be found in such a world, all the answers having been given simultaneously. Metaphysic is replaced by myth. There are no more questions, only eternal answers and commentaries, which may be metaphysical. But before man accepts the sacred world and in order that he should be able to accept it—or before he escapes from it and in order that he should be able to escape from it—there is always a period of soul-searching and rebellion. The rebel is a man who is on the point of accepting or rejecting the sacred and determined on laying claim to a human situation in which all the answers are human—in other words, formulated in reasonable terms. From this moment every question, every word, is an act of rebellion while in the sacred world every word is an act of grace. It would be possible to demonstrate in this manner that only two possible worlds can exist for the human mind: the sacred (or, to speak in Christian terms, the world of grace[3]) and the world of rebellion. The disappearance of one is equivalent to the appear-

---

[3] There is, of course, an act of metaphysical rebellion at the beginning of Christianity, but the resurrection of Christ and the annunciation of the kingdom of heaven interpreted as a promise of eternal life are the answers that render it futile.

ance of the other, despite the fact that this appearance can take place in disconcerting forms. There again we rediscover the *All or Nothing.* The present interest of the problem of rebellion only springs from the fact that nowadays whole societies have wanted to discard the sacred. We live in an unsacrosanct moment in history. Insurrection is certainly not the sum total of human experience. But history today, with all its storm and strife, compels us to say that rebellion is one of the essential dimensions of man. It is our historic reality. Unless we choose to ignore reality, we must find our values in it. Is it possible to find a rule of conduct outside the realm of religion and its absolute values? That is the question raised by rebellion.

We have already noted the confused values that are called into play by incipient rebellion. Now we must inquire if these values are to be found again in contemporary forms of rebellious thought and action, and if they are, we must specify their content. But, before going any farther, let us note that the basis of these values is rebellion itself. Man's solidarity is founded upon rebellion, and rebellion, in its turn, can only find its justification in this solidarity. We have, then, the right to say that any rebellion which claims the right to deny or destroy this solidarity loses simultaneously its right to be called rebellion and becomes in reality an acquiescence in murder. In the same way, this solidarity, except in so far as religion is concerned, comes to life only on the level of rebellion. And so the real drama of revolutionary thought is announced. In order to exist, man must rebel, but rebellion must respect the limit it discovers in itself—a limit where minds meet and, in meeting, begin to exist. Rebellious thought, therefore, cannot dispense with memory: it is a perpetual state of tension. In studying its actions and its results, we shall have to say, each time, whether it remains faithful to its noble promise or if, through indolence or folly, it forgets its original purpose and plunges into a mire of tyranny or servitude.

Meanwhile, we can sum up the initial progress that the spirit of rebellion provokes in a mind that is originally imbued with the absurdity and apparent sterility of the world. In absurdist experience, suffering is individual. But from the moment when a movement of rebellion begins, suffering is seen as a collective experience. Therefore the first progressive step for a mind overwhelmed by the strangeness of things is to realize that this feeling of strangeness is shared with all men and that human reality, in its entirety, suffers from the distance which separates it from the rest of the universe. The malady experienced by a single man becomes a mass plague. In our daily trials rebellion plays the same role as does the "cogito" in the realm of thought: it is the first piece of evidence. But this evidence lures the individual from his solitude. It founds its first value on the whole human race. I rebel—therefore we exist.

For Discussion

1. How does Camus relate *despair* and *silence?* *Rebellion* and *awareness?*
2. According to Camus, how do *resentment* and *rebellion* differ?
3. How does Camus argue that rebellion is affirmative?
4. Why does Camus say that the "spirit of rebellion" applies only to Western society? Do you agree?
5. How does Camus respond to the common belief that one should rebel against an injustice only when one has a solution? In this regard discuss current rebellion on the part of students, blacks, and other groups.
6. By what reasoning does Camus reach the conclusion that "every act of rebellion tacitly invokes a value"?
7. Camus is very abstract in describing the proper limits of rebellion. In your opinion, what should these limits be?
8. Camus, like Sartre and other existentialists, is involved with "the absurd." After reading this essay, what is your understanding of the term?
9. "I rebel; therefore we exist" is a modern descendant of Descartes' "I think; therefore I am" and Rousseau's "I feel; therefore I am." Discuss the implications of each of these statements.

RACHEL CARSON

Silent Spring

Rachel L. Carson (1907–1964) did her graduate work in biology at Johns Hopkins and the Marine Biological Laboratory at Woods Hole, Massachusetts, and taught biology at Johns Hopkins and the University of Maryland. Author of *The Sea Around Us* and *The Edge of the Sea,* she reveals a skill with language that equals her professional standing in science. Underlying all her work is a basic interest in the relation of life to its environment, an interest which caused her to spend four and one-half years gathering data from all over America, and other parts of the world, on the effects of pesticides now in general use. The result was *Silent Spring,* from which the following selections are taken.

a fable for tomorrow

There was once a town in the heart of America where all life seemed to live in harmony with its surroundings. The town lay in the midst of a checkerboard of prosperous farms, with fields of grain and hillsides of orchards where, in spring, white clouds of bloom drifted above the green fields. In autumn, oak and maple and birch set up a blaze of color that flamed and flickered across a backdrop of pines. Then foxes barked in the hills and deer silently crossed the fields, half hidden in the mists of the fall mornings.

Along the roads, laurel, viburnum and alder, great ferns and wildflowers delighted the traveler's eye through much of the year. Even in winter the roadsides were places of beauty, where countless birds came to feed on the berries and on the seed heads of the dried weeds rising above the snow. The countryside was, in fact, famous for the abundance and variety of its bird life, and when the flood of migrants was pouring through in spring and fall people traveled from great distances to observe them. Others came to fish the streams, which flowed clear and cold out of the hills and contained shady pools where trout lay. So it had been from the days many years ago when the first settlers raised their houses, sank their wells, and built their barns.

Then a strange blight crept over the area and everything began to change. Some evil spell had settled on the community: mysterious maladies swept the flocks of chickens; the cattle and sheep sickened and died. Everywhere was a shadow of death. The farmers spoke of much illness among their families. In the town the doctors had become more and more puzzled by new kinds of sickness appearing among their patients. There had been several sudden and unexplained deaths, not only among adults but even among children, who would be stricken suddenly while at play and die within a few hours.

There was a strange stillness. The birds, for example—where had they gone? Many people spoke of them, puzzled and disturbed. The feeding stations in the backyards were deserted. The few birds seen anywhere were moribund; they trembled violently and could not fly. It was a spring without voices. On the mornings that had once throbbed with the dawn chorus of robins, catbirds, doves, jays, wrens, and scores of other bird voices there was now no sound; only silence lay over the fields and woods and marsh.

On the farms the hens brooded, but no chicks hatched. The farmers complained that they were unable to raise any pigs—the litters were small and the young survived only a few days. The apple trees were coming into bloom but no bees droned among the blossoms, so there was no pollination and there would be no fruit.

The roadsides, once so attractive, were now lined with browned and withered vegetation as though swept by fire. These, too, were silent, deserted by all living things. Even the streams were now lifeless. Anglers no longer visited them, for all the fish had died.

In the gutters under the eaves and between the shingles of the roofs, a white granular powder still showed a few patches; some weeks before it had fallen like snow upon the roofs and the lawns, the fields and streams.

No witchcraft, no enemy action had silenced the rebirth of new life in this stricken world. The people had done it themselves.

This town does not actually exist, but it might easily have a thousand counterparts in America or elsewhere in the world. I know of no community that has experienced all the misfortunes I describe. Yet every one of these disasters has actually happened somewhere, and many real communities have already suffered a substantial number of them. A grim specter has crept upon us almost unnoticed, and this imagined tragedy may easily become a stark reality we all shall know.

What has already silenced the voices of spring in countless towns in America? This book is an attempt to explain.

the obligation to endure

The history of life on earth has been a history of interaction between living things and their surroundings. To a large extent, the physical form and the habits of the earth's vegetation and its animal life have been molded by the environment. Considering the whole span of earthly time, the opposite effect, in which life actually modifies its surroundings, has been relatively slight. Only within the moment of time represented by the present century has one species—man—acquired significant power to alter the nature of his world.

During the past quarter century this power has not only increased to one of disturbing magnitude but it has changed in character. The most alarming of all man's assaults upon the environment is the contamination of air, earth, rivers, and sea with dangerous and even lethal materials. This pollution is for the most part irrecoverable; the chain of evil it initiates not only in the world that must support life but in living tissues is for the most part irreversible. In this now universal contamination of the environment, chemicals are the sinister and little-recognized partners of radiation in changing the very nature of the world—the very nature of its life. Strontium 90, released through nuclear explosions into the air, comes to earth in rain or drifts down as fallout, lodges in soil, enters into the grass or corn or wheat grown there, and in time takes up its abode in the bones of a human being, there to remain until his death. Similarly, chemicals sprayed on croplands or forests or gardens lie long in soil, entering into living organisms, passing from one to another in a chain of poisoning and death. Or they pass mysteriously by underground streams until they emerge and, through the alchemy of air and sunlight, combine into new forms that kill vegetation, sicken cattle, and work unknown harm on those who drink from once pure wells. As Albert Schweitzer has said, "Man can hardly even recognize the devils of his own creation."

It took hundreds of millions of years to produce the life that now inhabits the earth—eons of time in which that developing and evolving and diversifying life reached a state of adjustment and balance with its surroundings. The environment, rigorously shaping and directing the life it supported, contained elements that were hostile as well as supporting. Certain rocks gave out dangerous radiation; even within the light of the sun, from which all life draws its energy, there were short-wave radiations with power to injure. Given time—time not in years but in millennia—life adjusts, and a balance has been reached. For time is the essential ingredient, but in the modern world there is no time.

The rapidity of change and the speed with which new situations are created follow the impetuous and heedless pace of man rather than the deliberate pace of nature. Radiation is no longer merely the background radiation of rocks, the bombardment of cosmic rays, the ultraviolet of the sun that have existed before there was any life on earth; radiation is now the unnatural creation of man's tampering with the atom. The chemicals to which life is asked to make its adjustment are no longer merely the calcium and silica and copper and all the rest of the minerals washed out of the rocks and carried in rivers to the sea; they are the synthetic creations of man's inventive mind, brewed in his laboratories, and having no counterparts in nature.

To adjust to these chemicals would require time on the scale that is nature's; it would require not merely the years of a man's life but the life of generations. And even this, were it by some miracle possible, would be futile, for the new chemicals come from our laboratories in an endless stream; almost five hundred annually find their way into actual use in the United States alone. The figure is staggering and its implications are not easily grasped—500 new chemicals to which the bodies of men and animals are required somehow to adapt each year, chemicals totally outside the limits of biologic experience.

Among them are many that are used in man's war against nature. Since the mid-1940's over 200 basic chemicals have been created for use in killing insects, weeds, rodents, and other organisms described in the modern vernacular as "pests"; and they are sold under several thousand different brand names.

These sprays, dusts, and aerosols are now applied almost universally to farms, gardens, forests, and homes—nonselective chemicals that have the power to kill every insect, the "good" and the "bad," to still the song of birds and the leaping of fish in the streams, to coat the leaves with a deadly film, and to linger on in soil—all this though the intended target may be only a few weeds or insects. Can anyone believe it is possible to lay down such a barrage of poisons on the surface of the earth without making it unfit for all life? They should not be called "insecticides," but "biocides."

The whole process of spraying seems caught up in an endless spiral. Since DDT was released for civilian use, a process of escalation has been going on in which ever more toxic materials must be found. This has happened because insects, in a triumphant vindication of Darwin's principle of the survival of the fittest, have evolved super races immune to the particular insecticide used, hence a deadlier one has always to be developed— and then a deadlier one than that. It has happened also because . . . destructive insects often undergo a "flareback," or resurgence, after spraying, in numbers greater than before. Thus the chemical war is never won, and all life is caught in its violent crossfire.

Along with the possibility of the extinction of mankind by nuclear war, the central problem of our age has therefore become the contamination of man's total environment with such substances of incredible potential for harm—substances that accumulate in the tissues of plants and animals and even penetrate the germ cells to shatter or alter the very material of heredity upon which the shape of the future depends.

Some would-be architects of our future look toward a time when it will be possible to alter the human germ plasm by design. But we may easily be doing so now by inadvertence, for many chemicals, like radiation, bring about gene mutations. It is ironic to think that man might determine his own future by something so seemingly trivial as the choice of an insect spray.

All this has been risked—for what? Future historians may well be amazed by our distorted sense of proportion. How could intelligent beings seek to control a few unwanted species by a method that contaminated the entire environment and brought the threat of disease and death even to their own kind? Yet this is precisely what we have done. We have done it, moreover, for reasons that collapse the moment we examine them. We are told that the enormous and expanding use of pesticides is necessary to maintain farm production. Yet is our real problem not one of *overproduction*? Our farms, despite measures to remove acreages from production and to pay farmers *not* to produce, have yielded such a staggering excess of crops that the American taxpayer in 1962 is paying out more than one billion dollars a year as the total carrying cost of the surplus-food storage program. And is the situation helped when one branch of the Agriculture Department tries to reduce production while another states, as it did in 1958, "It is believed generally that reduction of crop acreages under provisions of the Soil Bank will stimulate interest in use of chemicals to obtain maximum production on the land retained in crops."

All this is not say there is no insect problem and no need of control. I am saying, rather, that control must be geared to realities, not to mythical situations, and that the methods employed must be such that they do not destroy us along with the insects.

The problem whose attempted solution has brought such a train of disaster in its wake is an accompaniment of our modern way of life. Long before the age of man, insects inhabited the earth—a group of extraordinarily varied and adaptable beings. Over the course of time since man's advent, a small percentage of the more than half a million species of insects have come into conflict with human welfare in two principal ways: as competitors for the food supply and as carriers of human disease.

Disease-carrying insects become important where human beings are crowded together, especially under conditions where sanitation is poor, as in time of natural disaster or war or in situations of extreme poverty and deprivation. Then control of some sort becomes necessary. It is a sobering fact, however, as we shall presently see, that the method of massive chemical control has had only limited success, and also threatens to worsen the very conditions it is intended to curb.

Under primitive agricultural conditions the farmer had few insect problems. These arose with the intensification of agriculture—the devotion of immense acreages to a single crop. Such a system set the stage for explosive increases in specific insect populations. Single-crop farming does not take advantage of the principles by which nature works; it is agriculture as an engineer might conceive it to be. Nature has introduced great variety into the landscape, but man has displayed a passion for simplifying it. Thus he undoes the built-in checks and balances by which nature holds the species within bounds. One important natural check is a limit on the amount of suitable habitat for each species. Obviously then, an insect that lives on wheat can build up its population to much higher levels on a farm devoted to wheat than on one in which wheat is intermingled with other crops to which the insect is not adapted.

The same thing happens in other situations. A generation or more ago, the towns of large areas of the United States lined their streets with the noble elm tree. Now the beauty they hopefully created is threatened with complete destruction as disease sweeps through the elms, carried by a beetle that would have only limited chance to build up large populations and to spread from tree to tree if the elms were only occasional trees in a richly diversified planting.

Another factor in the modern insect problem is one that must be viewed against a background of geologic and human history: the spreading of thousands of different kinds of organisms from their native homes to invade new territories. This worldwide migration has been studied and graphically described by the British ecologist Charles Elton in his recent book *The Ecology of Invasions*. During the Cretaceous Period, some hundred million years ago, flooding seas cut many land bridges between continents and living things found themselves confined in what Elton calls "colossal separate nature reserves." There, isolated from others of their kind, they developed many new species. When some of the land masses were joined again, about 15 millions years ago, these species began to move out into new territories— a movement that is not only still in progress but is now receiving considerable assistance from man.

The importation of plants is the primary agent in the modern spread of species, for animals have almost invariably gone along with the plants, quarantine being a comparatively recent and not completely effective innovation. The United States Office of Plant Introduction alone has introduced almost 200,000 species and varieties of plants from all over the world. Nearly half of the 180 or so major insect enemies of plants in the United States are accidental imports from abroad, and most of them have come as hitch-hikers on plants.

In new territory, out of reach of the restraining hand of the natural enemies that kept down its numbers in its native land, an invading plant or animal is able to become enormously abundant. Thus it is no accident that our most troublesome insects are introduced species.

These invasions, both the naturally occurring and those dependent on human assistance, are likely to continue indefinitely. Quarantine and massive chemical campaigns are only extremely expensive ways of buying time. We are faced, according to Dr. Elton, "with a life-and-death need not just to find new technological means of suppressing this plant or that animal"; instead we need the basic knowledge of animal populations and their relations to their surroundings that will "promote an even balance and damp down the explosive power of outbreaks and new invasions."

Much of the necessary knowledge is now available but we do not use it. We train ecologists in our universities and even employ them in our governmental agencies but we seldom take their advice. We allow the chemical death rain to fall as though there were no alternative, whereas in fact there are many, and our ingenuity could soon discover many more if given opportunity.

Have we fallen into a mesmerized state that makes us accept as inevitable that which is inferior or detrimental, as though having lost the will or the vision to demand that which is good? Such thinking, in the words of the ecologist Paul Shepard, "idealizes life with only its head out of water, inches above the limits of toleration of the corruption of its own environment . . . Why should we tolerate a diet of weak poisons, a home in insipid surroundings, a circle of acquaintances who are not quite our enemies, the noise of motors with just enough relief to prevent insanity? Who would want to live in a world which is just not quite fatal?"

Yet such a world is pressed upon us. The crusade to create a chemically sterile, insect-free world seems to have engendered a fanatic zeal on the part of many specialists and most of the so-called control agencies. On every hand there is evidence that those engaged in spraying operations exercise a ruthless power. "The regulatory entomologists . . . function as prosecutor, judge and jury, tax assessor and collector and sheriff to enforce their own orders," said Connecticut entomologist Neely Turner. The most flagrant abuses go unchecked in both state and federal agencies.

It is not my contention that chemical insecticides must never be used. I do contend that we have put poisonous and biologically potent chemicals indiscriminately into the hands of persons largely or wholly ignorant of their potentials for harm. We have subjected enormous numbers of people to contact with these poisons, without their consent and often without their knowledge. If the Bill of Rights contains no guarantee that a citizen shall be secure against lethal poisons distributed either by private individuals or by public officials, it is surely only because our forefathers, despite their considerable wisdom and foresight, could conceive of no such problem.

I contend, furthermore, that we have allowed these chemicals to be used with little or no advance investigation of their effect on soil, water, wildlife, and man himself. Future generations are unlikely to condone our lack of prudent concern for the integrity of the natural world that supports all life.

There is still very limited awareness of the nature of the threat. This is an era of specialists, each of whom sees his own problem and is unaware of or intolerant of the larger frame into which it fits. It is also an era dominated by industry, in which the right to make a dollar at whatever cost is seldom challenged. When the public protests, confronted with some obvious evidence of damaging results of pesticide applications, it is fed little tranquilizing pills of half truth. We urgently need an end to these false assurances, to the sugar coating of unpalatable facts. It is the public that is being asked to assume the risks that the insect controllers calculate. The public must decide whether it wishes to continue on the present road, and it can do so only when in full possession of the facts. In the words of Jean Rostand, "The obligation to endure gives us the right to know."

For Discussion

1. How does the fable set the mood for the chapter which follows it? What frame of mind does it create in the reader?
2. Why is time the essential ingredient for life? Explain fully.
3. How have agricultural practices threatened the balance of nature?
4. What evidence does Carson present to prove that man's so-called progress has, in fact, been destructive? What recent examples can you offer which point to man's irresponsibility?
5. Underlying Carson's presentation is an implicit philosophy of nature and man's position in it. What is it?
6. What general solutions does Carson suggest? What specific steps or additional recommendations can you make?
7. How strong is the author's argument that our civil rights are being abrogated by the indiscriminate use of chemicals?
8. In "The Obligation to Endure," find examples in which the connotations of the words affect the argument.
9. The author presents her argument logically. Why, then, isn't this selection in *The Discursive NO?*

JAMES BALDWIN

My Dungeon Shook

letter to my nephew on the one hundredth anniversary of the emancipation

Author-essayist-playwright James Baldwin, born in Harlem in 1924, grew up in the ghetto and lived and worked in Greenwich Village until a Rosenwald Fellowship enabled him to go to Paris to write. He remained abroad until 1957, writing his first two novels, *Go Tell It on the Mountain* (1952) and *Giovanni's Room* (1956), as well as the essays published as *Notes of a Native Son* (1955), wherein he introduced his theme of the Negro as "the conscience of the country." *Nobody Knows My Name* followed in 1961. Upon publication of *Another Country* (1962), the racial situation in the United States had created the need for a black artist-spokesman, a position in which Baldwin found himself. His most recent collection, *The Fire Next Time* (1962), contains the following essay.

DEAR JAMES:

I have begun this letter five times and torn it up five times. I keep seeing your face, which is also the face of your father and my brother. Like him, you are tough, dark, vulnerable, moody—with a very definite tendency to sound truculent because you want no one to think you are soft. You may be like your grandfather in this, I don't know, but certainly both you and your father resemble him very much physically. Well, he is dead, he never saw you, and he had a terrible life; he was defeated long before he died because, at the bottom of his heart, he really believed what white people said about him. This is one of the reasons that he became so holy. I am sure that your father has told you something about all that. Neither you nor your father exhibit any tendency towards holiness: you really *are* of another era, part of what happened when the Negro left the land and came into what the late E. Franklin Frazier called "the cities of destruction." You can only be destroyed by believing that you really are what the white world calls a *nigger*. I tell you this because I love you, and please don't you ever forget it.

I have known both of you all your lives, have carried your Daddy in my arms and on my shoulders, kissed and spanked him and watched him learn to walk. I don't know if you've known anybody from that far back; if you've loved anybody that long, first as an infant, then as a child, then as a man, you gain a strange perspective on time and human pain and effort. Other people cannot see what I see whenever I look into your father's face, for behind your father's face as it is today are all those other faces which were his. Let him laugh and I see a cellar your father does not remember and a house he does not remember and I hear in his present laughter his laughter as a child. Let him curse and I remember him falling down the cellar steps, and howling, and I remember, with pain, his tears, which my hand or your grandmother's so easily wiped away. But no one's hand can wipe away those tears he sheds invisibly today, which one hears in his laughter and in his speech and in his songs. I know what the world has done to my brother and how narrowly he has survived it. And I know, which is much worse, and this is the crime of which I accuse my country and my countrymen, and for which neither I nor time nor history will ever forgive them, that they have destroyed and are destroying hundreds of thousands of lives and do not know it and do not want to know it. One can be, indeed one must strive to become, tough and philosophical concerning destruction and death, for this is what most of mankind has been best at since we have heard of man. (But remember: *most* of mankind is not *all* of mankind.) But it is not permissible that the authors of devastation should also be innocent. It is the innocence which constitutes the crime.

Now, my dear namesake, these innocent and well-meaning people, your countrymen, have caused you to be born under conditions not very far removed from those described for us by Charles Dickens in the London of more than a hundred years ago (I hear the chorus of the innocents screaming, "No! This is not true! How *bitter* you are!"—but I am writing this letter to *you*, to try to tell you something about how to handle *them*, for most of them do not yet really know that you exist. I *know* the conditions under which you were born, for I was there. Your countrymen were *not* there, and haven't made it yet. Your grandmother was also there, and no one has ever accused her of being bitter. I suggest that the innocents check with her. She isn't hard to find. Your countrymen don't know that *she* exists, either, though she has been working for them all their lives.)

Well, you were born, here you came, something like fifteen years ago; and though your father and mother and grandmother, looking about the streets through which they were carrying you, staring at the walls into which they brought you, had every reason to be heavyhearted, yet they were not. For here you were, Big James, named for me—you were a big baby, I was not—here you were: to be loved. To be loved, baby, hard, at once, and forever, to strengthen you against the loveless world. Remember that: I know how black it looks today, for you. It looked bad that day, too, yes, we were trembling. We have not stopped trembling yet, but if we had not loved each other none of us would have survived. And now you must survive because we love you, and for the sake of your children and your children's children.

This innocent country set you down in a ghetto in which, in fact, it intended that you should perish. Let me spell out precisely what I mean by that, for the heart of the matter is here, and the root of my dispute with my country. You were born where you were born and faced the future that you faced because you were black and *for no other reason.* The limits of your ambition were, thus, expected to be set forever. You were born into a society which spelled out with brutal clarity, and in as many ways as possible, that you were a worthless human being. You were not expected to aspire to excellence: you were expected to make peace with mediocrity. Wherever you have turned, James, in your short time on this earth, you have been told where you could go and what you could do (and *how* you could do it) and where you could live and whom you could marry. I know your countrymen do not agree with me about this, and I hear them saying, "You exaggerate." They do not know Harlem, and I do. So do you. Take no one's word for anything, including mine— but trust your experience. Know whence you came. If you know whence you came, there is really no limit to where you can go. The details and symbols of your life have been deliberately constructed to make you believe what white people say about you. Please try to remember that what they believe, as well as what they do and cause you to endure, does not testify to your inferiority but to their inhumanity and fear. Please try to be clear, dear James, through the storm which rages about your youthful head today, about the reality which lies behind the words *acceptance* and *integration.* There is no reason for you to try to become like white people and there is no basis whatever for their impertinent assumption that *they* must accept *you.* The really terrible thing, old buddy, is that *you* must accept *them.* And I mean that very seriously. You must accept them and accept them with love. For these innocent people have no other hope. They are, in effect, still trapped in a history which they do not understand; and until they understand it, they cannot be released from it. They have had to believe for many years, and for innumerable reasons, that black men are inferior to white men. Many of them, indeed, know better, but, as you will discover, people find it very difficult to act on what they know. To act is to be committed, and to be committed is to be in danger. In this case, the danger, in the minds of most white Americans, is the loss of their identity. Try to imagine how you would feel if you woke up one morning to find the sun shining and all the stars aflame. You would be frightened because it is out of the order of nature. Any upheaval in the universe is terrifying because it so profoundly attacks one's sense of one's own reality. Well, the black man has functioned in the white man's world as a fixed star, as an immovable pillar: and as he moves out of his place, heaven and earth are shaken to their foundations. You, don't be afraid. I said that it was intended that you should perish in the ghetto, perish by never being allowed to go behind the white man's definitions, by never being allowed to spell your proper name. You have, and many of us have, defeated this intention; and, by a terrible law, a terrible paradox, those innocents who believed that your imprisonment made them safe are losing their grasp of reality. But these men are your brothers—your lost, younger brothers. And if the word *integration* means anything, this is what it means: that we, with love, shall force our brothers to see themselves as they are, to cease fleeing from reality and begin to change it. For this is your home, my friend, do not be driven from it; great men have done great things here, and will again, and we can make America what America must become. It will be hard, James, but you come from sturdy, peasant stock, men who picked cotton and dammed rivers and built railroads, and, in the teeth of the most terrifying odds, achieved an unassailable and monumental dignity. You come from a long line of great poets, some of the greatest poets since Homer. One of them said, *The very time I thought I was lost, My dungeon shook and my chains fell off.*

You know, and I know, that the country is celebrating one hundred years of freedom one hundred years too soon. We cannot be free until they are free. God bless you, James, and Godspeed.

Your uncle,

JAMES

For Discussion

1. This essay is included in Baldwin's *The Fire Next Time,* the title of which is taken from a slave song containing the lines "God gave Noah the rainbow sign/No more water, the fire next time." How does this relate to Baldwin's message?
2. What are Baldwin's feelings toward his father's holiness?
3. What does Baldwin say about the innocence of Americans?
4. Discuss Baldwin's definition of integration.

5. How does each member of Baldwin's family (with the exception of his nephew) represent a typical response to being a Black American? Why does Baldwin make the nephew an exception?

6. In *Soul on Ice* and other writings, Cleaver has expressed strong criticism of Baldwin. From this essay, can you guess why?

7. It has been pointed out that much of Baldwin's style comes from his youthful experience as a preacher. What evidence of this influence can you find? In this regard, read aloud the paragraph beginning "I have known both of you all your life. . . ."

8. Reread selected paragraphs aloud, trying to convey, as closely as possible, what you feel to be Baldwin's tone: his attitude toward his subject and his audience.

MARTIN LUTHER KING, JR.

Letter from Birmingham Jail

A Baptist minister and president of the Southern Leadership Conference, Martin Luther King, Jr. was the acknowledged leader of the civil rights movement in America until his assassination in 1968. An eloquent speaker, Dr. King united blacks and whites by the force of his love and by his dedication to his people. He was honored in his lifetime, receiving the Nobel Prize for Peace in 1964, and in his death became the symbol of black martyrdom. In the months preceding his assassination, Dr. King had moved to a more militant position in regard to racial issues and a highly critical position on United States foreign policy.

April 16, 1963

MY DEAR FELLOW CLERGYMEN:

While confined here in the Birmingham city jail, I came across your recent statement calling my present activities "unwise and untimely." Seldom do I pause to answer criticism of my work and ideas. If I sought to answer all the criticisms that cross my desk, my secretaries would have little time for anything other than such correspondence in the course of the day, and

This response to a published statement by eight fellow clergymen from Alabama (Bishop C. C. J. Carpenter, Bishop Joseph A. Durick, Rabbi Hilton L. Grafman, Bishop Paul Hardin, Bishop Holan B. Harmon, the Reverend George M. Murray, the Reverend Edward V. Ramage and the Reverend Earl Stallings) was composed under somewhat constricting circumstances. Begun on the margins of the newspaper in which the statement appeared while I was in jail, the letter was continued on scraps of writing paper supplied by a friendly Negro trusty, and concluded on a pad my attorneys were eventually permitted to leave me. Although the text remains in substance unaltered, I have indulged in the author's prerogative of polishing it for publication.—MARTIN LUTHER KING, JR.

I would have no time for constructive work. But since I feel that you are men of genuine good will and that your criticisms are sincerely set forth, I want to try to answer your statement in what I hope will be patient and reasonable terms.

I think I should indicate why I am here in Birmingham, since you have been influenced by the view which argues against "outsiders coming in." I have the honor of serving as president of the Southern Christian Leadership Conference, an organization operating in every southern state, with headquarters in Atlanta, Georgia. We have some eighty-five affiliated organizations across the South, and one of them is the Alabama Christian Movement for Human Rights. Frequently we share staff, educational and financial resources with our affiliates. Several months ago the affiliate here in Birmingham asked us to be on call to engage in a nonviolent direct-action program if such were deemed necessary. We readily consented, and when the hour came we lived up to our promise. So I, along with several members of my staff, am here because I was invited here. I am here because I have organizational ties here.

But more basically, I am in Birmingham because injustice is here. Just as the prophets of the eighth century B.C. left their villages and carried their "thus saith the Lord" far beyond the boundaries of their home towns, and just as the Apostle Paul left his village of Tarsus and carried the gospel of Jesus Christ to the far corners of the Greco-Roman world, so am I compelled to carry the gospel of freedom beyond my own home town. Like Paul, I must constantly respond to the Macedonian call for aid.

Moreover, I am cognizant of the interrelatedness of all communities and states. I cannot sit idly by in Atlanta and not be concerned about what happens in Birmingham. Injustice anywhere is a threat to justice everywhere. We are caught in an inescapable network of mutuality, tied in a single garment of destiny. Whatever affects one directly, affects all indirectly. Never again can we afford to live with the narrow, provincial "outside agitator" idea. Anyone who lives inside the United States can never be considered an outsider anywhere within its bounds.

You deplore the demonstrations taking place in Birmingham. But your statement, I am sorry to say, fails to express a similar concern for the conditions that brought about the demonstrations. I am sure that none of you would want to rest content with the superficial kind of social analysis that deals merely with effects and does not grapple with underlying causes. It is unfortunate that demonstrations are taking place in Birmingham, but it is even more unfortunate that the city's white power structure left the Negro community with no alternative.

In any nonviolent campaign there are four basic steps: collection of the facts to determine whether injustices exist; negotiation; self-purification; and direct action. We have gone through all these steps in Birmingham.

There can be no gainsaying the fact that racial injustice engulfs this community. Birmingham is probably the most thoroughly segregated city in the United States. Its ugly record of brutality is widely known. Negroes have experienced grossly unjust treatment in the courts. There have been more unsolved bombings of Negro homes and churches in Birmingham than in any other city in the nation. These are the hard, brutal facts of the case. On the basis of these conditions, Negro leaders sought to negotiate with the city fathers. But the latter consistently refused to engage in good-faith negotiation.

Then, last September, came the opportunity to talk with leaders of Birmingham's economic community. In the course of the negotiations, certain promises were made by the merchants—for example, to remove the stores' humiliating racial signs. On the basis of these promises, the Reverend Fred Shuttlesworth and the leaders of the Alabama Christian Movement for Human Rights agreed to a moratorium on all demonstrations. As the weeks and months went by, we realized that we were the victims of a broken promise. A few signs, briefly removed, returned; the others remained.

As in so many past experiences, our hopes had been blasted, and the shadow of deep disappointment settled upon us. We had no alternative except to prepare for direct action, whereby we would present our very bodies as a means of laying our case before the conscience of the local and the national community. Mindful of the difficulties involved, we decided to undertake a process of self-purification. We began a series of workshops on nonviolence, and we repeatedly asked ourselves: "Are you able to accept blows without retaliating?" "Are you able to endure the ordeal of jail?" We decided to schedule our direct-action program for the Easter season, realizing that except for Christmas, this is the main shopping period of the year. Knowing that a strong economic-withdrawal program would be the by-product of direct action, we felt that this would be the best time to bring pressure to bear on the merchants for the needed change.

Then it occurred to us that Birmingham's mayoral election was coming up in March, and we speedily decided to postpone action until after election day. When we discovered that the Commissioner of Public Safety, Eugene "Bull" Connor, had piled up enough votes to be in the run-off, we decided again to postpone action until the day after the run-off so that the demonstrations could not be used to cloud the issues. Like many others, we waited to see Mr. Connor defeated, and to this end we endured postponement after postponement. Having aided in this community need, we felt that our direct-action program could be delayed no longer.

You may well ask: "Why direct action? Why sit-ins, marches and so forth? Isn't negotiation a better path?" You are quite right in calling for negotiation. Indeed, this is the very purpose of direct action. Nonviolent direct action seeks to create such a crisis and foster such a tension that a community which has constantly refused to negotiate is forced to confront the issue. It seeks so to dramatize the issue that it can no longer be ignored. My citing the creation of tension as part of the work of the nonviolent-resister may sound rather shocking. But I must confess that I am not afraid of the word "tension." I have earnestly opposed violent tension, but there is a type of constructive, nonviolent tension which is necessary for growth. Just as Socrates felt that it was necessary to create a tension in the mind so that individuals could rise from the bondage of myths and half-truths to the unfettered realm of creative analysis and objective appraisal, so must we see the need for nonviolent gadflies to create the kind of tension in society that will help men rise from the dark depths of prejudice and racism to the majestic heights of understanding and brotherhood.

The purpose of our direct-action program is to create a situation so crisis-packed that it will inevitably open the door to negotiation. I therefore concur with you in your call for negotiation. Too long has our beloved Southland been bogged down in a tragic effort to live in monologue rather than dialogue.

One of the basic points in your statement is that the action that I and my associates have taken in Birmingham is untimely. Some have asked: "Why didn't you give the new city administration time to act?" The only answer that I can give to this query is that the new Birmingham administration must be prodded about as much as the outgoing one, before it will act. We are sadly mistaken if we feel that the election of Albert Boutwell as mayor will bring the millennium to Birmingham. While Mr. Boutwell is a much more gentle person than Mr. Connor, they are both segregationists, dedicated to maintenance of the status quo. I have hope that Mr. Boutwell will be reasonable enough to see the futility of massive resistance to desegregation. But he will not see this without pressure from devotees of civil rights. My friends, I must say to you that we have not made a single gain in civil rights without determined legal and nonviolent pressure. Lamentably, it is an historical fact that privileged groups seldom give up their privileges voluntarily. Individuals may see the moral light and voluntarily give up their unjust posture; but, as Reinhold Niebuhr has reminded us, groups tend to be more immoral than individuals.

We know through painful experience that freedom is never voluntarily given by the oppressor; it must be demanded by the oppressed. Frankly, I have yet to engage in a direct-action campaign that was "well timed" in the view of those who have not suffered unduly from the disease of segregation. For years now I have heard the word "Wait!" It rings in the ear of every Negro with piercing familiarity. This "Wait" has almost always meant "Never." We must come to see, with one of our distinguished jurists, that "justice too long delayed is justice denied."

We have waited for more than 340 years for our constitutional and

God-given rights. The nations of Asia and Africa are moving with jetlike speed toward gaining political independence, but we still creep at horse-and-buggy pace toward gaining a cup of coffee at a lunch counter. Perhaps it is easy for those who have never felt the stinging darts of segregation to say, "Wait." But when you have seen vicious mobs lynch your mothers and fathers at will and drown your sisters and brothers at whim; when you have seen hate-filled policemen curse, kick and even kill your black brothers and sisters; when you see the vast majority of your twenty million Negro brothers smothering in an airtight cage of poverty in the midst of an affluent society; when you suddenly find your tongue twisted and your speech stammering as you seek to explain to your six-year-old daughter why she can't go to the public amusement park that has just been advertised on television, and see tears welling up in her eyes when she is told that Funtown is closed to colored children, and see ominous clouds of inferiority beginning to form in her little mental sky, and see her beginning to distort her personality by developing an unconscious bitterness toward white people; when you have to concoct an answer for a five-year-old son who is asking: "Daddy, why do white people treat colored people so mean?"; when you take a cross-country drive and find it necessary to sleep night after night in the uncomfortable corners of your automobile because no motel will accept you; when you are humiliated day in and day out by nagging signs reading "white" and "colored"; when your first name becomes "nigger," your middle name becomes "boy" (however old you are) and your last becomes "John," and your wife and mother are never given the respected title "Mrs."; when you are harried by day and haunted by night by the fact that you are a Negro, living constantly at tiptoe stance, never quite knowing what to expect next, and are plagued with inner fears and outer resentments; when you are forever fighting a degenerating sense of "nobodiness"—then you will understand why we find it difficult to wait. There comes a time when the cup of endurance runs over, and men are no longer willing to be plunged into the abyss of despair. I hope, sirs, you can understand our legitimate and unavoidable impatience.

You express a great deal of anxiety over our willingness to break laws. This is certainly a legitimate concern. Since we so diligently urge people to obey the Supreme Court's decision of 1954 outlawing segregation in the public schools, at first glance it may seem rather paradoxical for us consciously to break laws. One may well ask: "How can you advocate breaking some laws and obeying others?" The answer lies in the fact that there are two types of laws: just and unjust. I would be the first to advocate obeying just laws. One has not only a legal but a moral responsibility to obey just laws. Conversely, one has a moral responsibility to disobey unjust laws. I would agree with St. Augustine that "an unjust law is no law at all."

Now, what is the difference between the two? How does one determine

whether a law is just or unjust? A just law is a man-made code that squares
with the moral law or the law of God. An unjust law is a code that is out of
harmony with the moral law. To put it in the terms of St. Thomas Aquinas:
An unjust law is a human law that is not rooted in eternal law and natural
law. Any law that uplifts human personality is just. Any law that degrades
human personality is unjust. All segregation statutes are unjust because
segregation distorts the soul and damages the personality. It gives the segre-
gator a false sense of superiority and the segregated a false sense of inferiority.
Segregation, to use the terminology of the Jewish philosopher Martin Buber,
substitutes an "I—it" relationship for an "I—thou" relationship and ends up
relegating persons to the status of things. Hence segregation is not only
politically, economically and sociologically unsound, it is morally wrong
and sinful. Paul Tillich has said that sin is separation. Is not segregation
an existential expression of man's tragic separation, his awful estrangement,
his terrible sinfulness? Thus it is that I can urge men to obey the 1954
decision of the Supreme Court, for it is morally right; and I can urge them
to disobey segregation ordinances, for they are morally wrong.

Let us consider a more concrete example of just and unjust laws. An
unjust law is a code that a numerical or power majority group compels a
minority group to obey but does not make binding on itself. This is *difference*
made legal. By the same token, a just law is a code that a majority compels
a minority to follow and that it is willing to follow itself. This is *sameness*
made legal.

Let me give another explanation. A law is unjust if it is inflicted on
a minority that, as a result of being denied the right to vote, had no part
in enacting or devising the law. Who can say that the legislature of Alabama which set up that state's segregation laws was democratically elected?
Throughout Alabama all sorts of devious methods are used to prevent Negroes from becoming registered voters, and there are some counties in which,
even though Negroes constitute a majority of the population, not a single
Negro is registered. Can any law enacted under such circumstances be considered democratically structured?

Sometimes a law is just on its face and unjust in its application. For
instance, I have been arrested on a charge of parading without a permit.
Now, there is nothing wrong in having an ordinance which requires a permit for a parade. But such an ordinance becomes unjust when it is used
to maintain segregation and to deny citizens the First-Amendment privilege
of peaceful assembly and protest.

I hope you are able to see the distinction I am trying to point out.
In no sense do I advocate evading or defying the law, as would the rabid
segregationist. That would lead to anarchy. One who breaks an unjust law
must do so openly, lovingly, and with a willingness to accept the penalty.
I submit that an individual who breaks a law that conscience tells him is

unjust, and who willingly accepts the penalty of imprisonment in order to arouse the conscience of the community over its injustice, is in reality expressing the highest respect for law.

Of course, there is nothing new about this kind of civil disobedience. It was evidenced sublimely in the refusal of Shadrach, Meshach and Abednego to obey the laws of Nebuchadnezzar, on the ground that a higher moral law was at stake. It was practiced superbly by the early Christians, who were willing to face hungry lions and the excruciating pain of chopping blocks rather than submit to certain unjust laws of the Roman Empire. To a degree, academic freedom is a reality today because Socrates practiced civil disobedience. In our own nation, the Boston Tea Party represented a massive act of civil disobedience.

We should never forget that everything Adolf Hitler did in Germany was "legal" and everything the Hungarian freedom fighters did in Hungary was "illegal." It was "illegal" to aid and comfort a Jew in Hitler's Germany. Even so, I am sure that, had I lived in Germany at the time, I would have aided and comforted my Jewish brothers. If today I lived in a Communist country where certain principles dear to the Christian faith are suppressed, I would openly advocate disobeying that country's antireligious laws.

I must make two honest confessions to you, my Christian and Jewish brothers. First, I must confess that over the past few years I have been gravely disappointed with the white moderate. I have almost reached the regrettable conclusion that the Negro's great stumbling block in his stride toward freedom is not the White Citizen's Counciler or the Ku Klux Klanner, but the white moderate, who is more devoted to "order" than to justice; who prefers a negative peace which is the absence of tension to a positive peace which is the presence of justice; who constantly says: "I agree with you in the goal you seek, but I cannot agree with your methods of direct action"; who paternalistically believes he can set the timetable for another man's freedom; who lives by a mythical concept of time and who constantly advises the Negro to wait for a "more convenient season." Shallow understanding from people of good will is more frustrating than absolute misunderstanding from people of ill will. Lukewarm acceptance is much more bewildering than outright rejection.

I had hoped that the white moderate would understand that law and order exist for the purpose of establishing justice and that when they fail in this purpose they become the dangerously structured dams that block the flow of social progress. I had hoped that the white moderate would understand that the present tension in the South is a necessary phase of the transition from an obnoxious negative peace, in which the Negro passively accepted his unjust plight, to a substantive and positive peace, in which all men will respect the dignity and worth of human personality. Actually, we who engage in nonviolent direct action are not the creators of tension. We merely bring to the surface the hidden tension that is already alive. We bring it out in the open, where it can be seen and dealt with. Like a boil that can never be cured so long as it is covered up must be opened with all its ugliness to the natural medicines of air and light, injustice must be exposed, with all the tension its exposure creates, to the light of human conscience and the air of national opinion before it can be cured.

In your statement you assert that our actions, even though peaceful, must be condemned because they precipitate violence. But is this a logical assertion? Isn't this like condemning a robbed man because his possession of money precipitated the evil act of robbery? Isn't this like condemning Socrates because his unswerving commitment to truth and his philosophical inquiries precipitated the act by the misguided populace in which they made him drink hemlock? Isn't this like condemning Jesus because his unique God-consciousness and never-ceasing devotion to God's will precipitated the evil act of crucifixion? We must come to see that, as the federal courts have consistently affirmed, it is wrong to urge an individual to cease his efforts to gain his basic constitutional rights because the quest may precipitate violence. Society must protect the robbed and punish the robber.

I had also hoped that the white moderate would reject the myth concerning time in relation to the struggle for freedom. I have just received a letter from a white brother in Texas. He writes: "All Christians know that the colored people will receive equal rights eventually, but it is possible that you are in too great a religious hurry. It has taken Christianity almost two thousand years to accomplish what it has. The teachings of Christ take time to come to earth." Such an attitude stems from a tragic misconception of time, from the strangely irrational notion that there is something in the very flow of time that will inevitably cure all ills. Actually, time itself is neutral; it can be used either destructively or constructively. More and more I feel that the people of ill will have used time much more effectively than have the people of good will. We will have to repent in this generation not merely for the hateful words and actions of the bad people but for the appalling silence of the good people. Human progress never rolls in on wheels of inevitability; it comes through the tireless efforts of men willing to be co-workers with God, and without this hard work, time itself becomes an ally of the forces of social stagnation. We must use time creatively, in the knowledge that the time is always ripe to do right. Now is the time to make real the promise of democracy and transform our pending national elegy into a creative psalm of brotherhood. Now is the time to lift our national policy from the quicksand of racial injustice to the solid rock of human dignity.

You speak of our activity in Birmingham as extreme. At first I was rather disappointed that fellow clergymen would see my nonviolent efforts as those of an extremist. I began thinking about the fact that I stand in the middle of two opposing forces in the Negro community. One is a force of complacency, made up in part of Negroes who, as a result of long years of oppression, are so drained of self-respect and a sense of "somebodiness" that they have adjusted to segregation; and in part of a few middle-class Negroes who, because of a degree of academic and economic security and because in some ways they profit by segregation, have become insensitive to the problems of the masses. The other force is one of bitterness and hatred, and it comes perilously close to advocating violence. It is expressed in the various black nationalist groups that are springing up across the nation, the largest and best-known being Elijah Muhammad's Muslim movement. Nourished by the Negro's frustration over the continued existence of racial discrimination, this movement is made up of people who have lost faith in America, who have absolutely repudiated Christianity, and who have concluded that the white man is an incorrigible "devil."

I have tried to stand between these two forces, saying that we need emulate neither the "do-nothingism" of the complacent nor the hatred and despair of the black nationalist. For there is the more excellent way of love and nonviolent protest. I am grateful to God that, through the influence of the Negro church, the way of nonviolence became an integral part of our struggle.

If this philosophy had not emerged, by now many streets of the South would, I am convinced, be flowing with blood. And I am further convinced that if our white brothers dismiss as "rabble-rousers" and "outside agitators" those of us who employ nonviolent direct action, and if they refuse to support our nonviolent efforts, millions of Negroes will, out of frustration and despair, seek solace and security in black-nationalist ideologies—a development that would inevitably lead to a frightening racial nightmare.

Oppressed people cannot remain oppressed forever. The yearning for freedom eventually manifests itself, and that is what has happened to the American Negro. Something within has reminded him of his birthright of freedom, and something without has reminded him that it can be gained. Consciously or unconsciously, he has been caught up by the Zeitgeist, and with his black brothers of Africa and his brown and yellow brothers of Asia, South America and the Caribbean, the United States Negro is moving with a sense of great urgency toward the promised land of racial justice. If one recognizes this vital urge that has engulfed the Negro community, one should readily understand why public demonstrations are taking place. The Negro has many pent-up resentments and latent frustrations, and he must release them. So let him march; let him make prayer pilgrimages to the city hall; let him go on freedom rides—and try to understand why he must do so. If his repressed emotions are not released in nonviolent ways, they will seek expression through violence; this is not a threat but a fact of history. So I have not said to my people: "Get rid of your discontent."

Rather, I have tried to say that this normal and healthy discontent can be channeled into the creative outlet of nonviolent direct action. And now this approach is being termed extremist.

But though I was initially disappointed at being categorized as an extremist, as I continued to think about the matter I gradually gained a measure of satisfaction from the label. Was not Jesus an extremist for love: "Love your enemies, bless them that curse you, do good to them that hate you, and pray for them which despitefully use you, and persecute you." Was not Amos an extremist for justice: "Let justice roll down like waters and righteousness like an ever-flowing stream." Was not Paul an extremist for the Christian gospel: "I bear in my body the marks of the Lord Jesus." Was not Martin Luther an extremist: "Here I stand; I cannot do otherwise, so help me God." And John Bunyan: "I will stay in jail to the end of my days before I make a butchery of my conscience." And Abraham Lincoln: "This nation cannot survive half slave and half free." And Thomas Jefferson: "We hold these truths to be self-evident, that all men are created equal. . . ." So the question is not whether we will be extremists, but what kind of extremists we will be. Will we be extremists for hate or for love? Will we be extremists for the preservation of injustice or for the extension of justice? In that dramatic scene on Calvary's hill three men were crucified. We must never forget that all three were crucified for the same crime— the crime of extremism. Two were extremists for immorality, and thus fell below their environment. The other, Jesus Christ, was an extremist for love, truth and goodness, and thereby rose above his environment. Perhaps the South, the nation and the world are in dire need of creative extremists.

I had hoped that the white moderate would see this need. Perhaps I was too optimistic; perhaps I expected too much. I suppose I should have realized that few members of the oppressor race can understand the deep groans and passionate yearnings of the oppressed race, and still fewer have the vision to see that injustice must be rooted out by strong, persistent and determined action. I am thankful, however, that some of our white brothers in the South have grasped the meaning of this social revolution and committed themselves to it. They are still all too few in quantity, but they are big in quality. Some—such as Ralph McGill, Lillian Smith, Harry Golden, James McBride Dabbs, Ann Braden and Sarah Patton Boyle—have written about our struggle in eloquent and prophetic terms. Others have marched with us down nameless streets of the South. They have languished in filthy, roach-infested jails, suffering the abuse and brutality of policemen who view them as "dirty nigger-lovers." Unlike so many of their moderate brothers and sisters, they have recognized the urgency of the moment and sensed the need for powerful "action" antidotes to combat the disease of segregation.

Let me take note of my other major disappointment. I have been so greatly disappointed with the white church and its leadership. Of course, there are some notable exceptions. I am not unmindful of the fact that each of you has taken some significant stands on this issue. I commend you, Reverend Stallings, for your Christian stand on this past Sunday, in welcoming Negroes to your worship service on a nonsegregated basis. I commend the Catholic leaders of this state for integrating Spring Hill College several years ago.

But despite these notable exceptions, I must honestly reiterate that I have been disappointed with the church. I do not say this as one of those negative critics who can always find something wrong with the church. I say this as a minister of the gospel, who loves the church; who was nurtured in its bosom; who has been sustained by its spiritual blessings and who will remain true to it as long as the cord of life shall lengthen.

When I was suddenly catapulted into the leadership of the bus protest in Montgomery, Alabama, a few years ago, I felt we would be supported by the white church. I felt that the white ministers, priests and rabbis of the South would be among our strongest allies. Instead, some have been outright opponents, refusing to understand the freedom movement and misrepresenting its leaders; all too many others have been more cautious than courageous and have remained silent behind the anesthetizing security of stained-glass windows.

In spite of my shattered dreams, I came to Birmingham with the hope that the white religious leadership of this community would see the justice of our cause and, with deep moral concern, would serve as the channel through which our just grievances could reach the power structure. I had hoped that each of you would understand. But again I have been disappointed.

I have heard numerous southern religious leaders admonish their worshipers to comply with a desegregation decision because it is the law, but I have longed to hear white ministers declare: "Follow this decree because integration is morally right and because the Negro is your brother." In the midst of blatant injustices inflicted upon the Negro, I have watched white churchmen stand on the sideline and mouth pious irrelevancies and sanctimonious trivialities. In the midst of a mighty struggle to rid our nation of racial and economic injustice, I have heard many ministers say: "Those are social issues, with which the gospel has no real concern." And I have watched many churches commit themselves to a completely otherworldly religion which makes a strange, un-Biblical distinction between body and soul, between the sacred and the secular.

I have traveled the length and breadth of Alabama, Mississippi and all the other southern states. On sweltering summer days and crisp autumn mornings I have looked at the South's beautiful churches with their lofty spires pointing heavenward. I have beheld the impressive outlines of her massive religious-education buildings. Over and over I have found myself asking: "What kind of people worship here? Who is their God? Where were their voices when the lips of Governor Barnett dripped with words of interposition and nullification? Where were they when Governor Wallace gave a clarion call for defiance and hatred? Where were their voices of support when bruised and weary Negro men and women decided to rise from the dark dungeons of complacency to the bright hills of creative protest?"

Yes, these questions are still in my mind. In deep disappointment I have wept over the laxity of the church. But be assured that my tears have been tears of love. There can be no deep disappointment where there is not deep love. Yes, I love the church. How could I do otherwise? I am in the rather unique position of being the son, the grandson and the great-grandson of preachers. Yes, I see the church as the body of Christ. But, oh! How we have blemished and scarred that body through social neglect and through fear of being nonconformists.

There was a time when the church was very powerful—in the time when the early Christians rejoiced at being deemed worthy to suffer for what they believed. In those days the church was not merely a thermometer that recorded the ideas and principles of popular opinion; it was a thermostat that transformed the mores of society. Whenever the early Christians entered a town, the people in power became disturbed and immediately sought to convict the Christians for being "disturbers of the peace" and "outside agitators." But the Christians pressed on, in the conviction that they were "a colony of heaven," called to obey God rather than man. Small in number, they were big in commitment. They were too God-intoxicated to be "astronomically intimidated." By their effort and example they brought an end to such ancient evils as infanticide and gladiatorial contests.

Things are different now. So often the contemporary church is a weak, ineffectual voice with an uncertain sound. So often it is an archdefender of the status quo. Far from being disturbed by the presence of the church, the power structure of the average community is consoled by the church's silent—and often even vocal—sanction of things as they are.

But the judgment of God is upon the church as never before. If today's church does not recapture the sacrificial spirit of the early church, it will lose its authenticity, forfeit the loyalty of millions, and be dismissed as an irrelevant social club with no meaning for the twentieth century. Every day I meet young people whose disappointment with the church has turned into outright disgust.

Perhaps I have once again been too optimistic. Is organized religion too inextricably bound to the status quo to save our nation and the world? Perhaps I must turn my faith to the inner spiritual church, the church within the church, as the true *ekklesia* and the hope of the world. But again I am thankful to God that some noble souls from the ranks of organized religion have broken loose from the paralyzing chains of conformity and joined us as active partners in the struggle for freedom. They have left their secure congregations and walked the streets of Albany, Georgia, with us. They have gone down the highways of the South on tortuous rides for freedom. Yes, they have gone to jail with us. Some have been dismissed from their churches, have lost the support of their bishops and fellow ministers. But they have acted in the faith that right defeated is stronger than evil triumphant. Their witness has been the spiritual salt that has preserved the true meaning of the gospel in these troubled times. They have carved a tunnel of hope through the dark mountain of disappointment.

I hope the church as a whole will meet the challenge of this decisive hour. But even if the church does not come to the aid of justice, I have no despair about the future. I have no fear about the outcome of our struggle in Birmingham, even if our motives are at present misunderstood. We will reach the goal of freedom in Birmingham and all over the nation, because the goal of America is freedom. Abused and scorned though we may be, our destiny is tied up with America's destiny. Before the pilgrims landed at Plymouth, we were here. Before the pen of Jefferson etched the majestic words of the Declaration of Independence across the pages of history, we were here. For more than two centuries our forebears labored in this country without wages; they made cotton king; they built the homes of their masters while suffering gross injustice and shameful humiliation—and yet out of a bottomless vitality they continued to thrive and develop. If the inexpressible cruelties of slavery could not stop us, the opposition we now face will surely fail. We will win our freedom because the sacred heritage of our nation and the eternal will of God are embodied in our echoing demands.

Before closing I feel impelled to mention one other point in your statement that has troubled me profoundly. You warmly commended the Birmingham police force for keeping "order" and "preventing violence." I doubt that you would have so warmly commended the police force if you had seen its dogs sinking their teeth into unarmed, nonviolent Negroes. I doubt that you would so quickly commend the policemen if you were to observe their ugly and inhumane treatment of Negroes here in the city jail; if you were to watch them push and curse old Negro women and young Negro girls; if you were to see them slap and kick old Negro men and young boys; if you were to observe them, as they did on two occasions, refuse to give us food because we wanted to sing our grace together. I cannot join you in your praise of the Birmingham police department.

It is true that the police have exercised a degree of discipline in handling the demonstrators. In this sense they have conducted themselves rather "nonviolently" in public. But for what purpose? To preserve the evil system of segregation. Over the past few years I have consistently preached that nonviolence demands that the means we use must be as pure as the ends we seek. I have tried to make clear that it is wrong to use immoral means to attain moral ends. But now I must affirm that it is just as wrong, or perhaps even more so, to use moral means to preserve immoral ends. Perhaps Mr. Connor and his policemen have been rather nonviolent in public, as was Chief Pritchett in Albany, Georgia, but they have used the moral means of nonviolence to maintain the immoral end of racial injustice. As T. S. Eliot has said: "The last temptation is the greatest treason: To do the right deed for the wrong reason."

I wish you had commended the Negro sit-inners and demonstrators of Birmingham for their sublime courage, their willingness to suffer and their amazing discipline in the midst of great provocation. One day the South will recognize its real heroes. They will be the James Merediths, with the noble sense of purpose that enables them to face jeering and hostile mobs, and with the agonizing loneliness that characterizes the life of the pioneer. They will be old, oppressed, battered Negro women, symbolized in a seventy-two-year-old woman in Montgomery, Alabama, who rose up with a sense of dignity and with her people decided not to ride segregated buses, and who responded with ungrammatical profundity to one who inquired about her weariness: "My feets is tired, but my soul is at rest." They will be the young high school and college students, the young ministers of the gospel and a host of their elders, courageously and nonviolently sitting in at lunch counters and willingly going to jail for conscience' sake. One day the South will know that when these disinherited children of God sat down at lunch counters, they were in reality standing up for what is best in the American dream and for the most sacred values in our Judaeo-Christian heritage, thereby bringing our nation back to those great wells of democracy which were dug deep by the founding fathers in their formulation of the Constitution and the Declaration of Independence.

Never before have I written so long a letter. I'm afraid it is much too long to take your precious time. I can assure you that it would have been much shorter if I had been writing from a comfortable desk, but what else can one do when he is alone in a narrow jail cell, other than write long letters, think long thoughts and pray long prayers?

If I have said anything in this letter that overstates the truth and indicates an unreasonable impatience, I beg you to forgive me. If I have said anything that understates the truth and indicates my having a patience that allows me to settle for anything less than brotherhood, I beg God to forgive me.

I hope this letter finds you strong in the faith. I also hope that circumstances will soon make it possible for me to meet each of you, not as an integrationist or a civil-rights leader but as a fellow clergyman and a Christian brother. Let us all hope that the dark clouds of racial prejudice will soon pass away and the deep fog of misunderstanding will be lifted from our fear-drenched communities, and in some not too distant tomorrow the radiant stars of love and brotherhood will shine over our great nation with all their scintillating beauty.

Yours for the cause of Peace and Brotherhood,

MARTIN LUTHER KING, JR.

For Discussion

1. According to King, when is a law unjust?
2. What is King's implicit definition of anarchy?
3. To what extent does King's letter reflect the spirit of the black people today? Which specific examples of discrimination are still valid?
4. How is King's letter similar to the Declaration of Independence? Consider both the assumptions about the nature of man and the development of the argument.
5. Explain the difference between an "I-it" and an "I-thou" relationship. Suggest other examples of "I-it" relationships in current society.
6. What is King's purpose in comparing the Civil Rights movement to early Christian agitation?
7. How does King universalize the Negro struggle?
8. What does King say about the moral relationship between means and ends?
9. In what important respects does King agree with Gandhi? With Thoreau?
10. What qualities that made Martin Luther King, Jr. a leader of his people are reflected in this letter?
11. Compare the style of the final paragraph to that of Cleaver's closing remarks in "A Letter from Jail" and Baldwin's in "My Dungeon Shook."
12 King's voice is reflective because he is personally involved in exploring his own thoughts. However, one might argue that he is also discursive. Why?

HUNTER S. THOMPSON

Conclusion to "Hell's Angels"

Born in Louisville, Kentucky, Hunter S. Thompson is a free-lance writer whose work has appeared in *The Reporter, The Nation,* and *Esquire.* The following selection, the concluding chapter of his book *Hell's Angels,* is the result of more than a year of close association with the outlaw motorcycle gangs of California.

> He who makes a beast of himself gets rid of the pain of being a man.
>
> —Dr. Johnson

> The neighborhood suddenly exploded with excited, morbid crowds. Hysterical women surged forward in a frenzy, screeching in almost sexual ecstasy, scratching and fighting the agents and police in their attempt to reach the body. One fat-breasted woman with stringy red hair broke through the cordon and dipped her handkechief in the blood, clutched it to her sweaty dress and waddled off down the street . . .
>
> —From an account of the death of John Dillinger

Toward Christmas the action slowed down and the Angels dropped out of the headlines. Tiny lost his job, Sonny got involved in a long jury trial on the attempted-murder charge,[1] and the El Adobe was demolished by the wrecker's ball. The Angels drifted from one bar to another, but they found it harder to establish a hangout than to maintain one. In San Francisco it was just as slow. Frenchy spent three months in General Hospital when a can of gasoline blew up on him, and Puff went to jail after a fracas with two cops who raided an Angel birthday party. Winter is always slow for the outlaws. Many have to go to work to stay eligible for next summer's

[1] Which ended with a hung jury and eventual reduction of the charge to "assault with a deadly weapon"—to which Barger pleaded guilty and served six months in jail.

unemployment insurance, it is too cold for big outdoor parties, and the constant rain makes riding an uncomfortable hazard.

It seemed like a good time to get some work done, so I dropped off the circuit. Terry came by now and then to keep me posted. One day he showed up with a broken arm, saying he'd wrecked his bike, his old lady had left him and the niggers had blown up his house. I'd heard about the house from Barger's wife, Elsie, who was handling the communications post at their home in Oakland. During one of the sporadic flare-ups between the Hell's Angels and the Oakland Negroes somebody had thrown a home-made bomb through the window of the house that Terry was renting in East Oakland. The fire destroyed the house and all of Marilyn's paintings. She was a pretty little girl about nineteen, with long blond hair and a respectable family in one of the valley towns. She'd been living with Terry for nearly six months, covering the walls with her artwork, but she had no stomach for bombs. The divorce was effected soon after they moved to another dwelling. "I came back one night and she was gone," said Terry. "All she left was a note: 'Dear Terry, Fuck it.'" And that was that.

Nothing else happened until January, when Mother Miles got snuffed. He was riding his bike through Berkeley when a truck came out of a side street and hit him head on, breaking both legs and fracturing his skull. He hung in a coma for six days, then died on a Sunday morning, less than twenty-four hours before his thirtieth birthday—leaving a wife, two children and his righteous girl friend, Ann.

Miles had been president of the Sacramento chapter. His influence was so great that in 1965 he moved the whole club down to Oakland, claiming the police had made life intolerable for them by constant harassment. The outlaws simply picked up and moved, not questioning Miles' wisdom. His real name was James, but the Angels called him Mother.

"I guess it was because he was kind of motherly," said Gut. "Miles was great, great people. He took care of everybody. He worried. You could always depend on him."

I knew Miles in a distant kind of way. He didn't trust writers, but there was nothing mean about him, and once he decided I wasn't going to get him locked up somehow, he was friendly. He had the build of a pot-bellied stevedore, with a round face and a wide, flaring beard. I never thought of him as a hoodlum. He had the usual Hell's Angel police record: drunk, disorderly, fighting, vagrancy, loitering, petty larceny and a handful of ominous "suspicion of" charges that had never gone to trial. But he wasn't plagued by the same demons that motivate some of the others. He wasn't happy with the world, but he didn't brood about it, and his appetite for revenge didn't extend beyond specific wrongs done to the Angels or to him personally. You could drink with Miles without wondering when he was going to swing on somebody or lift your money off the bar. He wasn't that way. Booze seemed to make him more genial. Like most of the Angels' leaders, he had a quick mind and a quality of self-control which the others relied on.

When I heard he'd been killed I called Sonny to ask about the funeral, but by the time I finally got hold of him the details were already on the radio and in the newspapers. Miles' mother was arranging for the funeral in Sacramento. The outlaw caravan would form at Barger's house at eleven on Thursday morning. The Angels have gone to plenty of funerals for their own people, but until this one they had never tried to run the procession for ninety miles along a major highway. There was also a chance that the Sacramento police would try to keep them out of town.

The word went out on Monday and Tuesday by telephone. This was not going to be any Jay Gatsby funeral; the Angels wanted a full-dress rally. Miles' status was not the point; the death of any Angel requires a show of strength by the others. It is a form of affirmation—not for the dead, but the living. There are no set penalties for not showing up, because none are necessary. In the cheap loneliness that is the overriding fact of every outlaw's life, a funeral is a bleak reminder that the tribe is smaller by one. The circle is one link shorter, the enemy jacks up the odds just a little bit more, and defenders of the faith need something to take off the chill. A funeral is a time for counting the loyal, for seeing how many are left. There is no question about skipping work, going without sleep or riding for hours in a cold wind to be there on time.

Early Thursday morning the bikes began arriving in Oakland. Most of the outlaws were already in the Bay Area, or at least within fifty or sixty miles, but a handful of Satan's Slaves rode all of Wednesday night, five hundred miles from Los Angeles, to join the main caravan. Others came from Fresno and San Jose and Santa Rosa. There were Hangmen, Misfits, Presidents, Nightriders, Crossmen and some with no colors at all. A hard-faced little man whom nobody spoke to wore an olive-drab bombardier's jacket with just the word "Loner" on the back, written in small, blue-inked letters that looked like a signature.

I was crossing the Bay Bridge when a dozen Gypsy Jokers came roaring past, ignoring the speed limit as they split up to go around me on both sides of the car. Seconds later they disappeared up ahead in the fog. The morning was cold and bridge traffic was slow except for motorcycles. Down in the Bay there were freighters lined up, waiting for open piers.

The procession rolled at exactly eleven—a hundred and fifty bikes and about twenty cars. A few miles north of Oakland, at the Carquinez Bridge, the outlaws picked up a police escort assigned to keep them under control. A Highway Patrol car led the caravan all the way to Sacramento. The lead Angels rode two abreast in the right lane, holding a steady sixty-five miles an hour. At the head, with Barger, was the scruffy Praetorian Guard:

Magoo, Tommy, Jimmy, Skip, Tiny, Zorro, Terry and Charger Charley the Child Molester. The spectacle disrupted traffic all along the way. It looked like something from another world. Here was the "scum of the earth," the "lowest form of animals," an army of unwashed gang rapists . . . being escorted toward the state capital by a Highway Patrol car with a flashing yellow light. The steady pace of the procession made it unnaturally solemn. Not even Senator Murphy could have mistaken it for a dangerous run. There were the same bearded faces; the same earrings, emblems, swastikas and grinning death's-heads flapping in the wind—but this time there were no party clothes, no hamming it up for the squares. They were still playing the role, but all the humor was missing. The only trouble en route came when the procession was halted after a filling-station owner complained that somebody had stolen fourteen quarts of oil at the last gas stop. Barger quickly took up a collection to pay the man off, muttering that whoever stole the oil was due for a chainwhipping later on. The Angels assured each other that it must have been a punk in one of the cars at the rear of the caravan, some shithead without any class.

In Sacramento there was no sign of harassment. Hundreds of curious spectators lined the route between the funeral home and the cemetery. Inside the chapel a handful of Jim Miles' childhood friends and relatives waited with his body, a hired minister and three nervous attendants. They knew what was coming—Mother Miles' "people," hundreds of thugs, wild brawlers and bizarre-looking girls in tight Levis, scarves and waist-length platinum-colored wigs. Miles' mother, a heavy middle-aged woman in a black suit, wept quietly in a front pew, facing the open casket.

At one-thirty the outlaw caravan arrived. The slow rumble of motor-cycle engines rattled glass in the mortuary windows. Police tried to keep traffic moving as TV cameras followed Barger and perhaps a hundred others toward the door of the chapel. Many outlaws waited outside during the service. They stood in quiet groups, leaning against the bikes and killing time with lazy conversation. There was hardly any talk about Miles. In one group a pint of whiskey made the rounds. Some of the outlaws talked to bystanders, trying to explain what was happening. "Yeah, the guy was one of our leaders," said an Angel to an elderly man in a baseball cap. "He was good people. Some punk ran a stop sign and snuffed him. We came to bury him with the colors."

Inside the pine-paneled chapel the minister was telling his weird congregation that "the wages of sin is death." He looked like a Norman Rockwell druggist and was obviously repelled by the whole scene. Not all the pews were full, but standing room in the rear was crowded all the way back to the door. The minister talked about "sin" and "justification," pausing now and then as if he expected a rebuttal from the crowd. "It's not my business to pass judgment on anybody," he continued. "Nor is it my business to eulogize anybody. But it *is* my business to speak out a warning that *it will happen to you!* I don't know what philosophy some of you have about death, but I know the Scriptures tell us that God takes no pleasure in the death of the wicked . . . Jesus didn't die for an animal, he died for a man . . . What I say about Jim won't change anything, but I can preach the gospel to you and I have a responsibility to warn you that you will all have to *answer to God!*"

The crowd was shifting and sweating. The chapel was so hot that it seemed like the Devil was waiting in one of the anterooms, ready to claim the wicked just as soon as the sermon was over.

"How many of you—" asked the minister, "how many of you asked yourselves on the way up here, 'Who is next?' "

At this point several Angels in the pews rose and walked out, cursing quietly at a way of life they had long ago left behind. The minister ignored these mutinous signs and launched into a story about a Philippian jailer. "Holy shit!" mumbled Tiny. He'd been standing quietly in the rear for about thirty minutes, pouring sweat and eying the minister as if he meant to hunt him down later in the day and extract all his teeth. Tiny's departure caused five or six others to leave. The minister sensed he was losing his audience, so he brought the Philippian story to a quick end.

There was no music as the crowd filed out. I passed by the casket and was shocked to see Mother Miles clean-shaven, lying peacefully on his back in a blue suit, white shirt and a wide maroon tie. His Hell's Angels jacket, covered with exotic emblems, was mounted on a stand at the foot of the casket. Behind it were thirteen wreaths, some bearing names of other outlaw clubs.

I barely recognized Miles. He looked younger than twenty-nine and very ordinary. But his face was calm, as though he were not at all surprised to find himself there in a box. He wouldn't have liked the clothes he was wearing, but since the Angels weren't paying for the funeral, the best they could do was make sure the colors went into the casket before it was sealed. Barger stayed behind with the pallbearers to make sure the thing was done right.

After the funeral more than two hundred motorcycles followed the hearse to the cemetery. Behind the Angels rode all the other clubs, including a half dozen East Bay Dragons—and, according to a radio commentator, "dozens of teen-age riders who looked so solemn that you'd think Robin Hood had just died."

The Hell's Angels knew better. Not all of them had read about Robin Hood, but they understood that the parallel was complimentary. Perhaps the younger outlaws believed it, but there is room in their margin for one or two friendly illusions. Those who are almost thirty, or more than that, have been living too long with their own scurvy image to think of themselves as heroes. They understand that heroes are always "good guys," and they have seen enough cowboy movies to know that good guys win in the end. The myth didn't seem to include Miles, who was "one of the best." But all he got in the end was two broken legs, a smashed head and a tongue-lashing from the preacher. Only his Hell's Angels identity kept him from going to the grave as anonymously as any ribbon clerk. As it was, his funeral got nationwide press coverage: *Life* had a picture of the procession entering the cemetery, TV newscasts gave the funeral a solemn priority, and the *Chronicle* headline said: HELL'S ANGELS BURY THEIR OWN—BLACK JACKETS AND AN ODD DIGNITY. Mother Miles would have been pleased.

Moments after the burial the caravan was escorted out of town by a phalanx of police cars, with sirens howling. The brief truce was ended. At the city limits the Angels screwed it on and roared back to Richmond, across the Bay from San Francisco, where they held an all-night wake that kept police on edge until long after dawn. On Sunday night there was a meeting in Oakland to confirm Miles' successor, Big Al. It was a quiet affair, but without the grimness of the funeral. The banshee's wail that had seemed so loud on Thursday was already fading away. After the meeting there was a beer party at the Sinners Club, and by the time the place closed they had already set the date for the next run. The Angels would gather in Bakersfield, on the first day of spring.

> ALL MY LIFE MY HEART HAS SOUGHT
> A THING I CANNOT NAME.
> —*Remembered line
> from a long-forgotten poem*

Months later, when I rarely saw the Angels, I still had the legacy of the big machine—four hundred pounds of chrome and deep red noise to take out on the Coast Highway and cut loose at three in the morning, when all the cops were lurking over on 101. My first crash had wrecked the bike completely and it took several months to have it rebuilt. After that I decided to ride it differently: I would stop pushing my luck on curves, always wear a helmet and try to keep within range of the nearest speed limit . . . my insurance had already been canceled and my driver's license was hanging by a thread.

So it was always at night, like a werewolf, that I would take the thing out for an honest run down the coast. I would start in Golden Gate Park, thinking only to run a few long curves to clear my head . . . but in a matter of minutes I'd be out at the beach with the sound of the engine in my ears, the surf booming up on the sea wall and a fine empty road stretching all the way down to Santa Cruz . . . not even a gas station in the whole seventy miles; the only public light along the way is an all-night diner down around Rockaway Beach.

There was no helmet on those nights, no speed limit, and no cooling it down on the curves. The momentary freedom of the park was like the one unlucky drink that shoves a wavering alcoholic off the wagon. I would come out of the park near the soccer field and pause for a moment at the stop sign, wondering if I knew anyone parked out there on the midnight humping strip.

Then into first gear, forgetting the cars and letting the beast wind out . . . thirty-five, forty-five . . . then into second and wailing through the light at Lincoln Way, not worried about green or red signals, but only some other werewolf loony who might be pulling out, too slowly, to start his own run. Not many of these . . . and with three lanes on a wide curve, a bike coming hard has plenty of room to get around almost anything . . . then into third, the boomer gear, pushing seventy-five and the beginning of a windscream in the ears, a pressure on the eyeballs like diving into water off a high board.

Bent forward, far back on the seat, and a rigid grip on the handlebars as the bike starts jumping and wavering in the wind. Taillights far up ahead coming closer, faster, and suddenly—zaaapppp—going past and leaning down for a curve near the zoo, where the road swings out to sea.

The dunes are flatter here, and on windy days sand blows across the highway, piling up in thick drifts as deadly as any oil-slick . . . instant loss of control,. a crashing, cartwheeling slide and maybe one of those two-inch notices in the paper the next day: "An unidentified motorcyclist was killed last night when he failed to negotiate a turn on Highway I."

Indeed . . . but no sand this time, so the lever goes up into fourth, and now there's no sound except wind. Screw it all the way over, reach through the handlebars to raise the headlight beam, the needle leans down on a hundred, and wind-burned eyeballs strain to see down the centerline, trying to provide a margin for the reflexes.

But with the throttle screwed on there is only the barest margin, and no room at all for mistakes. It has to be done right . . . and that's when the strange music starts, when you stretch your luck so far that fear becomes exhilaration and vibrates along your arms. You can barely see at a hundred; the tears blow back so fast that they vaporize before they get to your ears. The only sounds are wind and a dull roar floating back from the mufflers. You watch the white line and try to lean with it . . . howling through a turn to the right, then to the left and down the long hill to Pacifica . . . letting off now, watching for cops, but only until the next dark stretch and another few seconds on the edge . . . The Edge . . . There is no honest way to explain it because the only people who really know where it is are the ones who have gone over. The others—the living—are those who pushed their control as far as they felt they could handle it, and then pulled back, or slowed down, or did whatever they had to when it came time to choose between Now and Later.

But the edge is still Out there. Or maybe it's In. The association of motorcycles with LSD is no accident of publicity. They are both a means to an end, to the place of definitions.

For Discussion

1. Characterize the mode of life portrayed in the first two-thirds of this selection.
2. What qualities of Miles are typical of the Angels? Why are they admired?
3. How does the funeral dramatize the Angels as dissenters?
4. How does the image of the Angels which Thompson projects differ from that usually presented by the news media?
5. What makes the description of the ride to Sacramento vivid?
6. Discuss the relevance of the three epigraphs.
7. What is Thompson's feeling in the final episode? How does it relate to what has gone before?
8. What is "the edge"? What does it say about Hell's Angels? (Also see Boorstin on the sensation-oriented society.)
9. In what way does this selection express dissent? How does it differ from others in the book?

LAWRENCE FERLINGHETTI

Prison Diary

Lawrence Ferlinghetti, born in Paris in 1920, is best known as a poet. He is also a painter, translator, publisher, and founder of the City Lights Bookstore in San Francisco, the first all-paperback bookstore in the United States. He currently heads City Lights Publications, an avant garde press. The following piece, originally titled "Santa Rita Journal," was written after his arrest for taking part in an antiwar protest at the Oakland Induction Center in 1967.

Santa Rita Rehabilitation Center, January 4, 1968—what are we doing here in this dank tank? Probing the limits of legitimate political dissent in this unenlightened country? Nonviolent gesture of blocking the entrance to war at Oakland Army Induction Center hereby judged beyond that limit. Rehabilitate us, please. . . . First rough impressions of anybody's first time in jail: suddenly realizing what "incarcerated" really means. Paranoid fear of the unknown, fear of not knowing what's going to happen to your body, fear of getting thrown in The Hole. . . . Routine of being booked, fingerprinted, mugged, shunted from bullpen to bullpen itself a shock for any "first offender." . . . Naive vestigial illusions about the inherent goodness of man fly out the barred window. . . . From Oakland jail, shunted through a series of sealed boxes, the first on wheels—long gray bus, windows blinded, 50 inmates behind locked grate, the freeway where yesterday we rode free now visible only through holes in grate. . . . Prison sighted half hour later on a forlorn plain at Pleasanton. . . . Barbed wire fences and watchtowers. Poor man's concentration camp? . . . Shunted through another series of holding cells, several more hours of not knowing one's immediate fate, just as likely you'll be put in "Graystone" maximum security pen as in General Compound. . . . I take the easier way out: I don't refuse to shave or work. Reforming the prison system is another issue.

Rather have a pen than a beard (and so keep this journal). Pen mightier than beard. Opportunity to infiltrate general prison population with non-violent ideas? Another naive liberal illusion!

The prison is about two-thirds black, and the other third is Mexican, Pachuco and white North American. They've got their own problems and their own enemies, and they've no use for "nonviolence." The jungle is full of felons and, as for the war, most of them have the attitudes of their jailers and think what we're doing in Vietnam is great, violence being one way of life they fully understand. This sure deflates the myth promoted by Our President equating anti-war demonstrations with "crime in the streets" and with ghetto wars. If there were any blacks busted this time at the Oakland Induction Center, I didn't see them. (And if I were black, in Oakland, I'd stay away too). . . .

January 5—There's not a political prisoner in my barracks. The most "uncooperative" of the demonstrators are in Graystone, two in a cell or in The Hole on bread and skimmed milk. A larger group is in Compound 8 with no privileges and a meal-and-a-half a day. A little incident happened today when they were marching back from the mess hall. The last in the line suddenly went limp and sat down in the middle of the Compound street. He was a kid of about 20 with medium-long hair he'd refused to cut. One officer ran up to him and tried to make him get up. He would not. The officer made a signal and four other officers wearing black leather gloves came at the double up the center of the street from the gate. They had no guns or night sticks. Each took an arm or a leg of the boy and started dragging him. He was a big kid, and they couldn't get his tail off the ground. They got him out of sight in a hurry. When I got back to barracks, someone had an Oakland Tribune with a photo of four Marines carrying a dead Marine buddy away from a Vietnam battlefield in the same style. . . .

January 6—I told them I had printing experience, and they put me stencilling pants! "Santa Rita" in pure white on every pair. "Gives us something to aim at!" the deputy told me, laughing, sighting his fingers at the stencil marks. Very funny. Holy prison, named for a Spanish saint. . . . Goya should have seen a place like this. He did, he did. Goya faces in the morning chowline, a thousand of them sticking out of blue denims, out of Goya's "Disasters of War." These are the disasters of peace. Down rows and rows of long wooden tables, half of skid row mixed with Oakland ghettos and the backwash of various nearby penitentiaries, long-term cons now here hung up on short-term crimes—petty boosters, bad check artists, child molesters, freeway drag-racers, car thieves, armed robbers, mail frauds, sex-freaks, winos, hypes, pushers, you name it. And political prisoners. . . . Sit swine-like at the trough, gobbling the chow from metal trays. Great place to keep from getting too refined; dig these myriad beat faces. . . . Here comes "Orfeo"—very handsome young Negro dude with a fine great black beard. Walked out of a Genet prison novel. Just stood there smiling like a black angel without wings when they told him to shave or get thrown in The Hole. They came back later and took him away. Now he shows up again in the mess hall, looking as wild and gentle as ever. I believe he is truly mad and they know it. I don't believe he understood anything they told him. They let him keep his beard. He'll fly away over the rooftops one day, to a shack on a hillside above Rio and live with a beautiful mulatto and tend goats, blowing a wreathed horn. And the horn full of grass. . . .

Another face in the gallery across the table from me: enormous ragged gray head, with hogshead snout, on a 200-pound body in ragged jeans. Great hams of white hands. But the face, the face: white stubble from shaggy hair to throat, rum-pot eyes. Small pig-eyes, but not mean looking. Just dumb and staring. This is what has become of "The Man with the Hoe." Long, heavy jaw with great, protruding rows of white teeth. Grunted and snuffled as he slurped his pancakes. When he called for the coffee pitcher, his voice came out in a thin squeal. Man, what have you done to this man? Man, who made you like that? Man, has Mother ever seen you, seen what has become of you? Man, you still alive inside? (I hear your stentor breath.) Man, are you to be born again? Live again, love again? Man. Who is there to redeem you. Fidel Castro? The true revolutionary, Fidel said, is one whose first concern is the *redemption* of mankind. . . . Faces fallen out of wombs somewhere, long ago. Now rolled down streets and come to rest among writhing bodies in a painting by Bosch, Garden of Paradise. . . . Feed and shuffle out, doubles of models Goya used in a Toledo madhouse. "By Graystone's foetid walls." . . . One doesn't eat here to consume food; one eats to consume time. And time is life. . . .

January 7—Sunday in the Compound, and "religious services": let them explain away the existence of evil here. The older one gets, the more one learns to believe in the very real existence of evil. This place proves it. The making of criminals. The redemption of mankind? The rehabilitation of man? They put 19-year-old Judith Bloomberg and Joan Baez on bread and milk for three days. (On the men's side, Gary Lisman fasted for 12 days.) These kids are the greatest. They are busted for disturbing the "peace" and are hauled away. They plead *nolo contendere*. They do not wish to contend. They are telling their elders they can have it. They are telling the Establishment that they want nothing to do with its power structure and refuse even to dispute the legal terms of that evil. . . . As long as there are guns, they will shoot, telescopically. . . . At the weekly movie tonight, the inmates spy Joan Baez through a crack in the curtain hiding the balcony where the women prisoners sit. A hundred felons turn and raise their hands in the Peace Sign and shout, "We love you, Joan!"

January 8—The Enormous Room of my barracks: a black inmate is reading "Synanon" (the place is full of junkies). He doesn't realize what an elite place Synanon may be. Diedrich, the founder, must have read Hermann Hesse's *Magister Ludi* (the Bead Game) and seized upon the conception of an elite world-within-a-world depicted by Hesse in Germany—Castallia being the name of the German intellectual elite created to govern society, with its own special *esprit de corps,* its own hierarchy, its own pecking order—a self-contained world of its own—Synanon also having developed its own cadre of first leaders framed on the wall, approval and status in its society dependent on length of residence, etc., the drug user rejected by the outside straight world here able to reject that society himself in favor of Synanon's own hierarchy: the Bead Game on its own level. And the prison system with its own Bead Game. . . . Shigeyoshi Murao comes to see me during visiting hours and tells me it looks just like the prisoner of war camps they kept Nisei in during World War Two.

January 9—Obscenity: violation of the Penal Code: today in the Commissary line when I tried to exchange a word with Dr. Lee Rather (a political prisoner), Officer Dykes hollered at me: "Get your fucking ass out of here, you motherfucker!"

January 10—Back in the barracks, the sealed life goes on. We are on some blind ship, all portholes sealed. Siren sounds and loudspeaker barks. Up for the count. Then down again, felon shipmates stretched in their bunks, staring at the overhead. . . . You spend a lot of time staring at nothing in a place like this. Great place to develop the Tragic Sense of Life. "Lucy in the Sky with Diamonds" comes over the barracks radio, and I picture myself in a boat on a river, where newspaper taxis await on the shore, waiting to take me away. . . .

January 11—Awakened at exactly three a.m. by a guard with a flashlight and told to get up and stand by my bunk. "You're going to court today." From three to eight a.m. I wait in a bullpen with over 50 other inmates going to court. The cell is 20′ by 15′, and over half the inmates have to stand up all the time. I talk to one black felon who has been gotten up like this three days in a row, and if he wants to fight his case this is the way he can do it. . . . Life goes on at Santa Rita. Or death. . . . I got the Santa Rita blues. . . .

Afterthoughts and vituperations: Really realize how a hole like this literally makes criminals: 18-year-old first-offender thrown in for disturbing society's deep sleep now making his first hard connection with hard drugs (they are shooting it up in the john!) and enforced homosexuality (bend over, buddy!). . . .

Guards with hard-edge voices careful not to show any human feelings for inmates, on the watch for the slightest lack of obsequiousness on the part of prisoners, now and then goading them a bit with a choice obscenity . . . a slip of the tongue in return, and you're in The Hole with your tongue hanging out. . . .

Plus mail officers with German names withholding mail and books at will, first class letters opened and censored. . . . Working in the mailroom I note two books (sent directly to an inmate from City Lights Bookstore) withheld: Debray's *Revolution in the Revolution?* and *Black Power.* . . . Burn, baby, burn—but in here, baby, it's you who'll be burning. . . . Later, when I am loose, I send *Gandhi on Non-Violence* to an inmate felon, and it comes back stamped "Unacceptable."

Unhappy Dehabilitation Center, man-made excrescence befouling the once-beautiful landscape in the shadow of distant Mount Diablo: Devil's mount!

If only revolution can blot out such scenes, let there be revolution; but not a revolution of hate leading in the end to just another super-state. . . .

For Discussion

1. Much of the power of this writing derives from personal observations of prison life. What images does Ferlinghetti present of buildings, food, other prisoners, guards? Describe the cumulative effect of these details.
2. The irony depends in part on a familiarity with some of Ferlinghetti's literary and artistic allusions. Which can you identify? Why are they ironic?
3. What other examples of irony can you find?
4. What do you know about Synanon? The Nisei in World War II?
5. Comment on the paragraph dealing with "the disasters of peace." How might this idea compare to Darrow's thesis?
6. Ferlinghetti obliquely refers to himself as a "political prisoner." To what extent do you agree?
7. What unifying principle guided Ferlinghetti in his selection of details?
8. How does the fact that this is a journal influence Ferlinghetti's style and voice?

STEPHEN H. WILDSTROM

Mugged by Sheriffs: An Anecdote

Stephen H. Wildstrom, the 1968–69 managing editor of the Michigan Daily, is now doing research in the field of police-community relations. In writing of his personal experience with the police, he focuses on a subject which drew national attention during the 1968 Democratic convention in Chicago and which has been of increasing public concern.

When I was growing up in a pleasant, tree-shaded part of near-suburban Detroit, I was taught that policemen are our friends. Once a year, friendly Sergeant somebody or another from the Youth Bureau would come to a school assembly with his trained dog to teach us how to cross streets safely and show us how friendly cops were. Like most middle-class kids, I believed the line.

It was in high school that I began to doubt. I saw Bull Connor's cops do their stuff in Birmingham, but that was only on television and anyway the cops up North weren't like that. Then in the summer of 1967, I was a wire service reporter during the Detroit riot and I got a first-hand look at cops unleashed. I began to think maybe the talk I'd heard about police brutality was more than just rhetoric. My negative view of police was reinforced when I saw the Detroit police mount a cavalry charge into a group of unarmed, peaceful members of the Poor People's March last spring.

But it took the Washtenaw County (Michigan) sheriff's department to bring it all home.

In September 1968 a group of welfare mothers staged a series of demonstrations at the County Building to protest Aid to Dependent Children payments which were insufficient to buy their children school clothes. The demonstrations culminated in the arrest of more than 200 mothers and University of Michigan students. As managing editor of the *Michigan Daily,*

Reprinted by permission of *Dissent* and the author.

I went over to the County Building on the second day of the protest to complain to the sheriff about the continued harassment of our reporters by his deputies.

I walked up to the door and found it guarded by a group of helmeted deputies, the same cops who had given me a hard time the day before. When I attempted to open the door, I was told I couldn't go in. I explained who I was and what I wanted and asked why a person could not enter a public building during normal business hours. "You can't go in," they repeated. When I tried to argue the point further, I was jumped from behind by one of the deputies, pushed face down against the concrete pavement, and generally beaten.

When they felt I had been adequately pummeled, I was handcuffed and dragged over to the jail. After a couple of hours, I was set free on bond of $25, waiting arraignment that will probably never come, on a charge of assault and battery that would be funny if someone else were the defendant.

Though I've never been a victim of a mugging—crime in the streets variety—I imagine it is a terrifying experience. But to receive the equivalent of a mugging at the hands of a duly deputized law officer is probably the most terrifying experience in modern American society.

There is no situation in which a citizen can feel more helpless than when a man with a badge lands a solid blow to his stomach, and another pushes his face into a concrete curbstone. At least when attacked by a civilian mugger, you can make an effort to fight back. To do so against a cop is to invite a charge of resisting arrest or, in most states, of assaulting an officer, which is a felony.

The incident at the County Building cost me two nights of sleep and a couple of weeks of soreness. Slowly, the terror gave way to anger—anger which turned to rage as I discovered that I had virtually no legal recourse. I decided to throw the book at the cops who beat me, but that book turned out to be exceedingly thin.

I was lucky to know the name of the ringleader of the group of deputies and to have had a good enough look at the others to identify one or two on sight. It seemed the first thing to do was to file criminal assault charges against the deputies. Naively, I filed such a complaint with the city police; it disappeared into a bureaucratic morass. Relations between the city police and the sheriff's department are none too good in Ann Arbor, but a cop is a cop and they don't like stepping on one another's jurisdictions. A citizen can't bring a complaint against another unless a State's attorney issues a warrant. So much for that angle.

Next, I was going to file a civil suit for false arrest and damages. But I was informed that no one in recent memory had won a false arrest suit in this county, and that even if I won the case legal fees would far exceed anything I could hope to collect in damages.

Finally, there is a state statute which makes it a felony to commit a legal act in an illegal manner and an obscure 19th-century federal civil rights law which makes it a misdemeanor to conspire to deprive a citizen of civil rights under color of law without due process. But conspiracy was well-nigh impossible to establish in this case, and going through the Justice Department on the federal charge seemed of very limited utility.

So here I am, still raging and still without redress. About the best I can hope for at this point is to get the still pending criminal charge against me dropped and my arrest records destroyed, thus clearing my record.

A current theory has it that urban blacks have suffered so much for so long at the hands of city cops because they are ignorant of their rights. The truth is much simpler: the citizen doesn't have any viable rights in such cases. As a white middle-class student with some background in the law, I was no better able to obtain redress than a 16-year-old black kid roughed up by cops in the ghetto.

American society will never be peaceful so long as significant portions of that society are systematically terrorized by the police. There will be no peace because, as blacks have learned and students are learning, the cops are above the law, and the only satisfying way to respond to their violence is with violence of one's own. And no matter what kind of pronouncements come down from the police brass, the terror will continue as long as individual cops are immune from attempts by citizens to make them responsible for their acts. Despite the assertions of commissioners, chiefs and mayors, police departments have proved themselves to be at best unable, and at worst unwilling, to discipline their own.

The only hope is true civilian community control of the police. Not just a police review board but a community control board which would hire and fire officers and which would have full disciplinary powers. Considering the powerful vested interests of the cops and the widespread belief in the white community that the cops are always right, that day will be a long time coming.

For Discussion

1. Characterize the speaker. Why is his identity important?
2. Enumerate the legal courses of action open to Wildstrom after the mugging and evaluate his decisions concerning them.
3. What conditions does Wildstrom stipulate for a peaceful society? What evidence can you offer that some of these conditions are being met?

4. Comment on Wildstrom's recommendation for a "community control board."

5. What do you think has caused such widespread publicity of police brutality?

6. Wildstrom tells his story in order to argue inductively. How valid is his conclusion?

7. Discuss the effect of Wildstrom's use of narrative to argue his point.

THE IRONIC *NO*

*We are all in the same pot, we are all
guilty, or innocent, depending on whether
we take the frog's view or the Olympian
view.*

HENRY MILLER
Letter to Mr. J. Hirsch

The ironic writer plays with his subject and reader. By deliberately
distorting his material or placing his reader in an unexpected or
novel position to it, he manipulates his reader into recognizing a
new dimension of experience, into seeing in a way he never saw
before. When this art of manipulation is used to ridicule human
weakness, stupidity, or cruelty, it is called *satire*. When it is not
used for purposes of ridicule, the larger term *irony* is employed.
But whether it is comic or not, irony always involves a disparity
or tension between what appears to be true and what is true, between what is said and what is actually meant, between what is
pretended and what is real.

    Like the discursive writer, the ironic writer makes an appeal
to our minds. He wants the reader to see beneath the surface
appearance of men's behavior and to recognize, through laughter
or shock, the contradictions between what men say they are and
what they really are. He does this by using various ironic "arts":
invective (abusive language), sarcasm (caustic or bitter distor-
tion of one's meaning with an intent to injure or strike back),
hyperbole (exaggeration or overstatement), understatement (saying less than one means), and Socratic irony (pretended ignorance

or innocence while exposing someone else's pretense). All of these methods are used to throw the reader off balance, to confound or surprise him into seeing the subject under ridicule—which may be the reader himself.

Most of us do not like to be laughed at. For this reason, the satirist often "tricks" his reader by setting up a situation in which the reader is unknowingly led to adopt a point of view different from his customary one, thus making him laugh at what he would ordinarily find offensive or threatening. As Henry Miller says, the satirist tries to make the reader see himself as he is—from "the frog's view"—and not as he would like to see himself—from "the Olympian view." This often unflattering picture of humanity can be disagreeable, even when it is funny. But in a sense the satiric writer is perhaps the most flattering of all writers because he depends upon the reader's sense of humor in its broadest application—his ability to laugh even "when it hurts," even when what he is laughing at turns out to be his most cherished beliefs.

By its very nature, all satire is dissent, and in its objection to and exposure of human folly, it has great social value. Furthermore, it enables the writer to vent his anger in a communicable form and to channel his strong feeling in a way which might otherwise be less constructive. For these reasons, irony can be a healthful and humanizing experience; it is a positive way of attacking social ills. And when the reader shares in it, he benefits.

The essays which follow are excellent examples of varied ironic voices. Some of the writers will shock you; others will make you laugh; still others will do both. But each writer will be trying to make you see his protest in an original and often surprising way.

JONATHAN SWIFT

A Modest Proposal

for preventing the children of poor people
in Ireland from being a burden to their
parents or country, and for making them
beneficial to the public

Born in Ireland in 1667 of English parents, Jonathan Swift graduated from Trinity College and was ordained as an Anglican priest, taking a parish near Dublin. Swift preferred England, however, where in spite of his success as a political writer, he received only an appointment as Dean of Saint Patrick's Cathedral in Dublin, a position he held until his death in 1745. Although Swift wrote serious and satirical verse, he is best known for his prose satires. *Gulliver's Travels, The Battle of the Books, The Tale of a Tub,* as well as the following selection, published in 1729, illustrate the logic and brilliance of his satire.

It is a melancholy object to those who walk through this great town or travel in the country, when they see the streets, the roads, and cabin doors, crowded with beggars of the female-sex, followed by three, four, or six children, all in rags and importuning every passenger for an alms. These mothers, instead of being able to work for their honest livelihood, are forced to employ all their time in strolling to beg sustenance for their helpless infants, who, as they grow up, either turn thieves for want of work, or leave their dear native country to fight for the Pretender in Spain, or sell themselves to the Barbadoes.[1]

I think it is agreed by all parties that this prodigious number of children in the arms, or on the backs, or at the heels of their mothers, and

[1] As indentured servants in order to pay for their emigration to a colony. [Ed.]

frequently of their fathers, is in the present deplorable state of the kingdom a very great additional grievance; and therefore whoever could find out a fair, cheap, and easy method of making these children sound, useful members of the commonwealth would deserve so well of the public as to have his statue set up for a preserver of the nation.

But my intention is very far from being confined to provide only for the children of professed beggars; it is of a much greater extent, and shall take in the whole number of infants at a certain age who are born of parents in effect as little able to support them as those who demand our charity in the streets.

As to my own part, having turned my thoughts for many years upon this important subject, and maturely weighed the several schemes of other projectors, I have always found them grossly mistaken in their computation. It is true, a child just dropped from its dam may be supported by her milk for a solar year, with little other nourishment; at most not above the value of two shillings, which the mother may certainly get, or the value in scraps, by her lawful occupation of begging; and it is exactly at one year old that I propose to provide for them in such a manner as instead of being a charge upon their parents or the parish, or wanting food and raiment for the rest of their lives, they shall on the contrary contribute to the feeding, and partly to the clothing, of many thousands.

There is likewise another great advantage in my scheme, that it will prevent those voluntary abortions, and that horrid practice of women murdering their bastard children, alas, too frequent among us, sacrificing the poor innocent babes, I doubt, more to avoid the expense than the shame, which would move tears and pity in the most savage and inhuman breast.

The number of souls in this kingdom being usually reckoned one million and a half, of these I calculate there may be about two hundred thousand couples whose wives are breeders; from which number I subtract thirty thousand couples who are able to maintain their own children, although I apprehend there cannot be so many under the present distresses of the kingdom; but this being granted, there will remain an hundred and seventy thousand breeders. I again subtract fifty thousand for those women who miscarry, or whose children die by accident or disease within the year. There only remain an hundred and twenty thousand children of poor parents annually born. The question therefore is, how this number shall be reared and provided for, which, as I have already said, under the present situation of affairs, is utterly impossible by all the methods hitherto proposed. For we can neither employ them in handicraft or agriculture; we neither build houses (I mean in the country) nor cultivate land. They can very seldom pick up a livelihood by stealing till they arrive at six years old, except where they are of towardly parts; although I confess they learn the rudiments much earlier, during which time they can however be looked upon only as probationers, as I have been informed by a principal gentleman in the county of Cavan, who protested to me that he never knew above one or two instances under the age of six, even in a part of the kingdom so renowned for the quickest proficiency in that art.

I am assured by our merchants that a boy or a girl before twelve years old is no salable commodity; and even when they come to this age they will not yield above three pounds, or three pounds and half a crown at most on the Exchange; which cannot turn to account either to the parents or the kingdom, the charge of nutriment and rags having been at least four times that value.

I shall now therefore humbly propose my own thoughts, which I hope will not be liable to the least objection.

I have been assured by a very knowing American of my acquaintance in London, that a young healthy child well nursed is at a year old a most delicious, nourishing, and wholesome food, whether stewed, roasted, baked, or boiled; and I make no doubt that it will equally serve in a fricassee or a ragout.

I do therefore humbly offer it to public consideration that of the hundred and twenty thousand children, already computed, twenty thousand may be reserved for breed, whereof only one fourth part to be males, which is more than we allow to sheep, black cattle, or swine; and my reason is that these children are seldom the fruits of marriage, a circumstance not much regarded by our savages, therefore one male will be sufficient to serve four females. That the remaining hundred thousand may at a year old be offered in sale to the persons of quality and fortune through the kingdom, always advising the mother to let them suck plentifully in the last month, so as to render them plump and fat for a good table. A child will make two dishes at an entertainment for friends; and when the family dines alone, the fore or hind quarter will make a reasonable dish, and seasoned with a little pepper or salt will be very good boiled on the fourth day, especially in winter.

I have reckoned upon a medium that a child just born will weigh twelve pounds, and in a solar year if tolerably nursed increaseth to twenty-eight pounds.

I grant this food will be somewhat dear, and therefore very proper for landlords, who, as they have already devoured most of the parents, seem to have the best title to the children.

Infant's flesh will be in season throughout the year, but more plentiful in March, and a little before and after. For we are told by a grave author, an eminent French physician,[2] that fish being a prolific diet, there are more children born in Roman Catholic countries about nine months after Lent than at any other season; therefore, reckoning a year after Lent, the markets

[2] Rabelais.

will be more glutted than usual, because the number of popish infants is at least three to one in this kingdom; and therefore it will have one other collateral advantage, by lessening the number of Papists among us.

I have already computed the charge of nursing a beggar's child (in which list I reckon all cottagers, laborers, and four fifths of the farmers) to be about two shillings per annum, rags included; and I believe no gentleman would repine to give ten shillings for the carcass of a good fat child, which, as I have said, will make four dishes of excellent nutritive meat, when he hath only some particular friend or his own family to dine with him. Thus the squire will learn to be a good landlord, and grow popular among the tenants; the mother will have eight shillings net profit, and be fit for work till she produces another child.

Those who are more thrifty (as I must confess the times require) may flay the carcass; the skin of which artificially dressed will make admirable gloves for ladies and summer boots for fine gentlemen.

As to our city of Dublin, shambles may be appointed for this purpose in the most convenient parts of it, and butchers we may be assured will not be wanting; although I rather recommend buying the children alive, and dressing them hot from the knife as we do roasting pigs.

A very worthy person, a true lover of his country, and whose virtues I highly esteem, was lately pleased in discoursing on this matter to offer a refinement upon my scheme. He said that many gentlemen of this kingdom, having of late destroyed their deer, he conceived that the want of venison might be well supplied by the bodies of young lads and maidens, not exceeding fourteen years of age nor under twelve, so great a number of both sexes in every county being now ready to starve for want of work and service; and these to be disposed of by their parents, if alive, or otherwise by their nearest relations. But with due deference to so excellent a friend and so deserving a patriot, I cannot be altogether in his sentiments; for as to the males, my American acquaintance assured me from frequent experience that their flesh was generally tough and lean, like that of our schoolboys, by continual exercise, and their taste disagreeable; and to fatten them would not answer the charge. Then as to the females, it would, I think with humble submission, be a loss to the public, because they soon would become breeders themselves: and besides, it is not improbable that some scrupulous people might be apt to censure such a practice (although indeed very unjustly) as a little bordering upon cruelty; which, I confess, hath always been with me the strongest objection against any project, how well soever intended.

But in order to justify my friend, he confessed that this expedient was put into his head by the famous Psalmanazar, a native of the island Formosa, who came from thence to London above twenty years ago, and in conversation told my friend that in his country when any young person happened to be put to death, the executioner sold the carcass to persons of quality as a prime dainty; and that in his time the body of a plump girl of fifteen, who was crucified for an attempt to poison the emperor, was sold to his Imperial Majesty's prime minister of state, and other great mandarins of the court, in joints from the gibbet, at four hundred crowns. Neither indeed can I deny that if the same use were made of several plump young girls in this town, who without one single groat to their fortunes cannot stir abroad without a chair, and appear at the playhouse and assemblies in foreign fineries which they never will pay for, the kingdom would not be the worse.

Some persons of a desponding spirit are in great concern about that vast number of poor people who are aged, diseased, or maimed, and I have been desired to employ my thoughts what course may be taken to ease the nation of so grievous an encumbrance. But I am not in the least pain upon that matter, because it is very well known that they are every day dying and rotting by cold and famine, and filth and vermin, as fast as can be reasonably expected. And as to the younger laborers, they are now in almost as hopeful a condition. They cannot get work, and consequently pine away for want of nourishment to a degree that if at any time they are accidentally hired to common labor, they have not strength to perform it; and thus the country and themselves are happily delivered from the evils to come.

I have too long digressed, and therefore shall return to my subject. I think the advantages by the proposal which I have made are obvious and many, as well as of the highest importance.

For first, as I have already observed, it would greatly lessen the number of Papists, with whom we are yearly overrun, being the principal breeders of the nation as well as our most dangerous enemies; and who stay at home on purpose to deliver the kingdom to the Pretender, hoping to take their advantage by the absence of so many good Protestants, who have chosen rather to leave their country than to stay at home and pay tithes against their conscience to an Episcopal curate.

Secondly, the poorer tenants will have something valuable of their own, which by law may be made liable to distress, and help to pay their landlord's rent, their corn and cattle being already seized and money a thing unknown.

Thirdly, whereas the maintenance of an hundred thousand children, from two years old and upwards, cannot be computed at less than ten shillings a piece per annum, the nation's stock will be thereby increased fifty thousand pounds per annum, besides the profit of a new dish introduced to the tables of all gentlemen of fortune in the kingdom who have any refinement in taste. And the money will circulate among ourselves, the goods being entirely of our own growth and manufacture.

Fourthly, the constant breeders, besides the gain of eight shillings sterling per annum by the sale of their children, will be rid of the charge of maintaining them after the first year.

Fifthly, this food would likewise bring great custom to taverns, where the vinters will certainly be so prudent as to procure the best receipts for dressing it to perfection, and consequently have their houses frequented by all the fine gentlemen, who justly value themselves upon their knowledge in good eating; and a skillful cook, who understands how to oblige his guests, will contrive to make it as expensive as they please.

Sixthly, this would be a great inducement to marriage, which all wise nations have either encouraged by rewards or enforced by laws and penalties. It would increase the care and tenderness of mothers toward their children, when they were sure of a settlement for life to the poor babes, provided in some sort by the public, to their annual profit instead of expense. We should see an honest emulation among the married women, which of them could bring the fattest child to the market. Men would become as fond of their wives during the time of their pregnancy as they are now of their mares in foal, their cows in calf, or sows when they are ready to farrow; nor offer to beat or kick them (as is too frequent a practice) for fear of a miscarriage.

Many other advantages might be enumerated. For instance, the addition of some thousand carcasses in our exportation of barreled beef, the propagation of swine's flesh, and improvement in the art of making good bacon, so much wanted among us by the great destruction of pigs, too frequent at our tables, which are no way comparable in taste or magnificence to a well-grown, fat, yearling child, which roasted whole will make a considerable figure at a lord mayor's feast or any other public entertainment. But this and many others I omit, being studious of brevity.

Supposing that one thousand families in this city would be constant customers for infants' flesh, besides others who might have it at merry meetings, particularly weddings and christenings, I compute that Dublin would take off annually about twenty thousand carcasses, and the rest of the kingdom (where probably they will be sold somewhat cheaper) the remaining eighty thousand.

I can think of no one objection that will possibly be raised against this proposal, unless it should be urged that the number of people will be thereby much lessened in the kingdom. This I freely own, and it was indeed one principal design in offering it to the world. I desire the reader will observe, that I calculate my remedy for this one individual kingdom of Ireland and for no other that ever was, is, or I think ever can be upon earth. Therefore let no man talk to me of other expedients: of taxing our absentees at five shillings a pound: of using neither clothes nor household furniture except what is of our own growth and manufacture: of utterly rejecting the materials and instruments that promote foreign luxury: of curing the expensiveness of pride, vanity, idleness, and gaming in our women: of introducing a vein of parsimony, prudence, and temperance: of learning to love our country, in the want of which we differ even from Laplanders and the inhabitants of Topinamboo[3]: of quitting our animosities and factions, nor acting any longer like the Jews, who were murdering one another at the very moment their city was taken: of being a little cautious not to sell our country and conscience for nothing: of teaching landlords to have at least one degree of mercy toward their tenants: lastly, of putting a spirit of honesty, industry, and skill into our shopkeepers; who, if a resolution could now be taken to buy only our native goods, would immediately unite to cheat and exact upon us in the price, the measure, and the goodness, nor could ever yet be brought to make one fair proposal of just dealing, though often and earnestly invited to it.

Therefore I repeat, let no man talk to me of these and the like expedients, till he hath at least some glimpse of hope that there will ever be some hearty and sincere attempt to put them in practice.

But as to myself, having been wearied out for many years with offering vain, idle, visionary thoughts, and at length utterly despairing of success, I fortunately fell upon this proposal, which, as it is wholly new, so it hath something solid and real, of no expense and little trouble, full in our own power, and whereby we can incur no danger in disobliging England. For this kind of commodity will not bear exportation, the flesh being of too tender a consistence to admit a long continuance in salt, although perhaps I could name a country which would be glad to eat up our whole nation without it.

After all, I am not so violently bent upon my own opinion as to reject any offer proposed by wise men, which shall be found equally innocent, cheap, easy, and effectual. But before something of that kind shall be advanced in contradiction to my scheme, and offering a better, I desire the author or authors will be pleased maturely to consider two points. First, as things now stand, how they will be able to find food and raiment for an hundred thousand useless mouths and backs. And secondly, there being a round million of creatures in human figure throughout this kingdom, whose sole subsistence put into a common stock would leave them in debt two millions of pounds sterling, adding those who are beggars by profession to the bulk of farmers, cottagers, and laborers, with their wives and children who are beggars in effect; I desire those politicians who dislike my overture, and may perhaps be so bold to attempt an answer, that they will first ask the parents of these mortals whether they would not at this day think it a great happiness to have been sold for food at a year old in the manner I prescribe, and thereby have avoided such a perpetual scene of misfortunes as they

[3] A district in Brazil.

have since gone through by the oppression of landlords, the impossibility of paying rent without money or trade, the want of common sustenance, with neither house nor clothes to cover them from the inclemencies of the weather, and the most inevitable prospect of entailing the like or greater miseries upon their breed forever.

I profess, in the sincerity of my heart, that I have not the least personal interest in endeavoring to promote this necessary work, having no other motive than the public good of my country, by advancing our trade, providing for infants, relieving the poor, and giving some pleasure to the rich. I have no children by which I can propose to get a single penny; the youngest being nine years old, and my wife past childbearing.

For Discussion

1. The irony of the essay arises from our recognition that there is a difference between Swift himself and the Speaker who makes the proposal. The two different voices address two different audiences and actually make two different arguments. Describe the voices, the audiences, and the arguments.
2. How does the Speaker's language reveal his personality?
3. The Speaker's argument cannot be destroyed by pointing to any fallacies in reasoning or lack of supporting evidence. On what grounds, then, can one argue with his proposal?
4. What does this argument do that any good argument should do?
5. Of what purpose are the grisly arithmetic and other specific details?
6. What advantages other than economic does the Speaker propose?
7. Archibald MacLeish has said that the purpose of poetry is to make "facts felt." Discuss the essay in the light of this idea.
8. In this essay murder is disguised as humanitarianism. What evidences of similar arguments can you find in contemporary life?
9. What reasons might you have for placing this essay in *The Impassioned NO? The Discursive NO?*

MARK TWAIN

The War Prayer

"The War Prayer" is an example of Twain's later work in the vein of *The Mysterious Stranger, The Damned Human Race,* "The Man Who Corrupted Hadleyburg," and other darkly satiric works. (See the introduction to "Reflections on Religion" for biographical information on Twain.)

It was a time of great and exalting excitement. The country was up in arms, the war was on, in every breast burned the holy fire of patriotism; the drums were beating, the bands playing, the toy pistols popping, the bunched firecrackers hissing and spluttering; on every hand and far down the receding and fading spread of roofs and balconies a fluttering wilderness of flags flashed in the sun; daily the young volunteers marched down the wide avenue gay and fine in their new uniforms, the proud fathers and mothers and sisters and sweethearts cheering them with voices choked with happy emotion as they swung by; nightly the packed mass meetings listened, panting, to patriot oratory which stirred the deepest deeps of their hearts and which they interrupted at briefest intervals with cyclones of applause, the tears running down their cheeks the while; in the churches the pastors preached devotion to flag and country and invoked the God of Battles, beseeching His aid in our good cause in outpouring of fervid eloquence which moved every listener. It was indeed a glad and gracious time, and the half-dozen rash spirits that ventured to disapprove of the war and cast a doubt upon its righteousness straightway got such a stern and angry warning that for their personal safety's sake they quickly shrank out of sight and offended no more in that way.

Sunday morning came—next day the battalions would leave for the front; the church was filled; the volunteers were there, their young faces alight with martial dreams—visions of the stern advance, the gathering momentum, the rushing charge, the flashing sabers, the flight of the foe, the tumult, the enveloping smoke, the fierce pursuit, the surrender!—then home

From *Europe and Elsewhere* by Mark Twain. Copyright 1923, 1951 by The Mark Twain Company.

from the war, bronzed heroes, welcomed, adored, submerged in golden seas of glory! With the volunteers sat their dear ones, proud, happy, and envied by the neighbors and friends who had no sons and brothers to send forth to the field of honor, there to win for the flag or, failing, die the noblest of noble deaths. The service proceeded; a war chapter from the Old Testament was read; the first prayer was said; it was followed by an organ burst that shook the building, and with one impulse the house rose, with glowing eyes and beating hearts, and poured out that tremendous invocation—

> "God the all-terrible! Thou who ordainest,
> Thunder thy clarion and lightning thy sword!"

Then came the "long" prayer. None could remember the like of it for passionate pleading and moving and beautiful language. The burden of its supplication was that an ever-merciful and benignant Father of us all would watch over our noble young soldiers and aid, comfort, and encourage them in their patriotic work; bless them, shield them in the day of battle and the hour of peril, bear them in His mighty hand, make them strong and confident, invincible in the bloody onset; help them to crush the foe, grant to them and to their flag and country imperishable honor and glory—

An aged stranger entered and moved with slow and noiseless step up the main aisle, his eyes fixed upon the minister, his long body clothed in a robe that reached to his feet, his head bare, his white hair descending in a frothy cataract to his shoulders, his seamy face unnaturally pale, pale even to ghastliness. With all eyes following him and wondering, he made his silent way; without pausing, he ascended to the preacher's side and stood there, waiting. With shut lids the preacher, unconscious of his presence, continued his moving prayer, and at last finished it with the words, uttered in fervent appeal, "Bless our arms, grant us the victory, O Lord our God, Father and Protector of our land and flag!"

The stranger touched his arm, motioned him to step aside—which the startled minister did—and took his place. During some moments he surveyed the spellbound audience with solemn eyes in which burned an uncanny light; then in a deep voice he said:

"I come from the Throne—bearing a message from Almighty God!" The words smote the house with a shock; if the stranger perceived it he gave no attention. "He has heard the prayer of His servant your shepherd and will grant it if such shall be your desire after I, His messenger, shall have explained to you its import—that is to say, its full import. For it is like unto many of the prayers of men, in that it asks for more than he who utters it is aware of—except he pause and think.

"God's servant and yours has prayed his prayer. Has he paused and taken thought? Is it one prayer? No, it is two—one uttered, the other not. Both have reached the ear of Him Who heareth all supplications, the spoken and the unspoken. Ponder this—keep it in mind. If you would beseech a blessing upon yourself, beware! lest without intent you invoke a curse upon a neighbor at the same time. If you pray for the blessing of rain upon your crop which needs it, by that act you are possibly praying for a curse upon some neighbor's crop which may not need rain and can be injured by it.

"You have heard your servant's prayer—the uttered part of it. I am commissioned of God to put into words the other part of it—that part which the pastor, and also you in your hearts, fervently prayed silently. And ignorantly and unthinkingly? God grant that it was so! You heard these words: 'Grant us the victory, O Lord our God!' That is sufficient. The *whole* of the uttered prayer is compact into those pregnant words. Elaborations were not necessary. When you have prayed for victory you have prayed for many unmentioned results which follow victory—*must* follow it, cannot help but follow it. Upon the listening spirit of God the Father fell also the unspoken part of the prayer. He commandeth me to put it into words. Listen!

"O Lord our Father, our young patriots, idols of our hearts, go forth to battle—be Thou near them! With them, in spirit, we also go forth from the sweet peace of our beloved firesides to smite the foe. O Lord our God, help us to tear their soldiers to bloody shreds with our shells; help us to cover their smiling fields with the pale forms of their patriot dead; help us to drown the thunder of the guns with the shrieks of their wounded, writhing in pain; help us to lay waste their humble homes with a hurricane of fire; help us to wring the hearts of their unoffending widows with unavailing grief; help us to turn them out roofless with their little children to wander unfriended the wastes of their desolated land in rags and hunger and thirst, sports of the sun flames of summer and the icy winds of winter, broken in spirit, worn with travail, imploring Thee for the refuge of the grave and denied it—for our sakes who adore Thee, Lord, blast their hopes, blight their lives, protract their bitter pilgrimage, make heavy their steps, water their way with their tears, stain the white snow with the blood of their wounded feet! We ask it, in the spirit of love, of Him Who is the Source of Love, and Who is the ever-faithful refuge and friend of all that are sore beset and seek His aid with humble and contrite hearts. Amen.

(*After a pause*) "Ye have prayed it; if ye still desire it, speak! The messenger of the Most High waits."

It was believed afterward that the man was a lunatic, because there was no sense in what he said.

For Discussion

1. List the assertions about war which are stated or implied in the first two paragraphs. What mood is created?
2. Look at the language of both prayers. How does the phrasing of each

determine the audience's response? What generalizations about the nature of communication can be inferred from your analysis?

3. Twain said, "The difference between the right word and the almost right word is the difference between real lightning and a lightning bug." Find examples of Twain's use of the "right" word.

4. As closely as you can, describe Twain's ironic technique. What adjective best describes the tone of Twain's irony? How is it reflected in the last sentence?

D. H. LAWRENCE

Benjamin Franklin

The following essay about an American, Benjamin Franklin, is illustrative of Lawrence's interest in personality as a reflection of culture. (See the introduction to "Sex versus Loveliness" for biographical information on Lawrence.)

The Perfectibility of Man! Ah heaven, what a dreary theme! The perfectibility of the Ford car! The perfectibility of the Ford car! The perfectibility of which man! I am many men. Which of them are you going to perfect? I am not a mechanical contrivance.

Education! Which of the various me's do you propose to educate, and which do you propose to suppress?

Anyhow I defy you. I defy you, oh society, to educate me or to suppress me, according to your dummy standards.

The ideal man! And which is he, if you please? Benjamin Franklin or Abraham Lincoln? The ideal man! Roosevelt or Porfirio Diaz?

There are other men in me, besides this patient ass who sits here in a tweed jacket. What am I doing, playing the patient ass in a tweed jacket? Who am I talking to? Who are you, at the other end of this patience?

Who are you? How many selves have you? And which of these selves do you want to be?

Is Yale College going to educate the self that is in the dark of you, or Harvard College?

The ideal self! Oh, but I have a strange and fugitive self shut out and howling like a wolf or a coyote under the ideal windows. See his red eyes in the dark? This is the self who is coming into his own.

The perfectibility of man, dear God! When every man as long as he remains alive is in himself a multitude of conflicting men. Which of these do you choose to perfect, at the expense of every other?

Old Daddy Franklin will tell you. He'll rig him up for you, the pattern American. Oh, Franklin was the first downright American. He knew what he was about, the sharp little man. He set up the first dummy American.

At the beginning of his career, this cunning little Benjamin drew up for himself a creed that should "satisfy the professors of every religion, but shock none."

Now wasn't that a real American thing to do?

"That there is One God, who made all things."

(But Benjamin made Him.)

"That He governs the world by His Providence."

(Benjamin knowing all about Providence.)

"That He ought to be worshiped with adoration, prayer, and thanksgiving."

(Which cost nothing.)

"But—" But me no buts, Benjamin, saith the Lord.

"But that the most acceptable service of God is doing good to men."

(God having no choice in the matter.)

"That the soul is immortal."

(You'll see why, in the next clause.)

"And that God will certainly reward virtue and punish vice, either here or hereafter."

Now if Mr. Andrew Carnegie, or any other millionaire, had wished to invent a God to suit his ends, he could not have done better. Benjamin did it for him in the eighteenth century. God is the supreme servant of men who want to get on, to *produce*. Providence. The provider. The heavenly storekeeper. The everlasting Wanamaker.

And this is all the God the grandsons of the Pilgrim Fathers had left. Aloft on a pillar of dollars.

"That the soul is immortal."

The trite way Benjamin says it!

But man has a soul, though you can't locate it either in his purse or his pocketbook or his heart or his stomach or his head. The *wholeness* of a man is his soul. Not merely that nice comfortable bit which Benjamin marks out.

It's a queer thing, is a man's soul. It is the whole of him. Which means it is the unknown him, as well as the known. It seems to me just funny, professors and Benjamins fixing the functions of the soul. Why the soul of a man is a vast forest, and all Benjamin intended was a neat back garden. And we've all got to fit in to his kitchen garden scheme of things. Hail Columbia!

The soul of man is a dark forest. The Hercynian Wood that scared the Romans so, and out of which came the white-skinned hordes of the next civilization.

Who knows what will come out of the soul of man? The soul of man is a dark vast forest, with wild life in it. Think of Benjamin fencing it off!

Oh, but Benjamin fenced a little tract that he called the soul of man, and proceeded to get it into cultivation. Providence, forsooth! And they think that bit of barbed wire is going to keep us in pound forever? More fools them.

This is Benjamin's barbed wire fence. He made himself a list of virtues, which he trotted inside like a grey nag in a paddock.

1. *Temperance.* Eat not to fullness; drink not to elevation.
2. *Silence.* Speak not but what may benefit others or yourself; avoid trifling conversation.
3. *Order.* Let all your things have their places; let each part of your business have its time.
4. *Resolution.* Resolve to perform what you ought; perform without fail what you resolve.
5. *Frugality.* Make no expense but to do good to others or yourself—i.e., waste nothing.
6. *Industry.* Lose no time, be always employed in something useful; cut off all unnecessary action.
7. *Sincerity.* Use no hurtful deceit; think innocently and justly, and, if you speak, speak accordingly.
8. *Justice.* Wrong none by doing injuries, or omitting the benefits that are your duty.
9. *Moderation.* Avoid extremes, forbear resenting injuries as much as you think they deserve.
10. *Cleanliness.* Tolerate no uncleanliness in body, clothes, or habitation.
11. *Tranquillity.* Be not disturbed at trifles, or at accidents common or avoidable.
12. *Chastity.* Rarely use venery but for health and offspring, never to dullness, weakness, or the injury of your own or another's peace or reputation.
13. *Humility.* Imitate Jesus and Socrates.

A Quaker friend told Franklin that he, Benjamin, was generally considered proud, so Benjamin put in the Humility touch as an afterthought. The amusing part is the sort of humility it displays. "Imitate Jesus and Socrates," and mind you don't outshine either of these two. One can just imagine Socrates and Alcibiades roaring in their cups over Philadelphian Benjamin, and Jesus looking at him a little puzzled, and murmuring: "Aren't you wise in your own conceit, Ben?"

"Henceforth be masterless," retorts Ben. "Be ye each one his own master unto himself, and don't let even the Lord put his spoke in." Each man his own master" is but a puffing up of masterlessness.

Well, the first of Americans practiced this enticing list with assiduity, setting a national example. He had the virtues in columns, and gave himself good and bad marks according as he thought his behavior deserved. Pity these conduct charts are lost to us. He only remarks that Order was his stumbling block. He could not learn to be neat and tidy.

Isn't it nice to have nothing worse to confess?

He was a little model, was Benjamin. Doctor Franklin. Snuff-colored little man! Immortal soul and all!

The immortal soul part was a sort of cheap insurance policy.

Benjamin had no concern, really, with the immortal soul. He was too busy with social man.

1. He swept and lighted the streets of young Philadelphia.
2. He invented electrical appliances.
3. He was the center of a moralizing club in Philadelphia, and he wrote the moral humorisms of Poor Richard.
4. He was a member of all the important councils of Philadelphia, and then of the American colonies.
5. He won the cause of American Independence at the French Court, and was the economic father of the United States.

Now what more can you want of a man? And yet he is *infra dig*, even in Philadelphia.

I admire him. I admire his sturdy courage first of all, then his sagacity, then his glimpsing into the thunders of electricity, then his common-sense humor. All the qualities of a great man, and never more than a great citizen. Middle-sized, sturdy, snuff-colored Doctor Franklin, one of the soundest citizens that ever trod or "used venery."

I do not like him.

And, by the way, I always thought books of Venery were about hunting deer.

There is a certain earnest naïveté about him. Like a child. And like a little old man. He has again become as a little child, always as wise as his grandfather, or wiser.

Perhaps, as I say, the most complete citizen that ever "used venery."

Printer, philosopher, scientist, author and patriot, impeccable husband and citizen, why isn't he an archetype?

Pioneer, Oh Pioneers! Benjamin was one of the greatest pioneers of the United States. Yet we just can't do with him.

What's wrong with him then? Or what's wrong with us?

I can remember, when I was a little boy, my father used to buy a scrubby yearly almanack with the sun and moon and stars on the cover. And it used to prophesy bloodshed and famine. But also crammed in corners it had little anecdotes and humorisms, with a moral tag. And I used to have my little priggish laugh at the woman who counted her chickens before they were hatched, and so forth, and I was convinced that honesty was the best policy, also a little priggishly. The author of these bits was Poor Richard, and Poor Richard was Benjamin Franklin, writing in Philadelphia well over a hundred years before.

And probably I haven't got over those Poor Richard tags yet. I rankle still with them. They are thorns in young flesh.

Because although I still believe that honesty is the best policy, I dislike policy altogether; though it is just as well not to count your chickens before they are hatched, it's still more hateful to count them with gloating when they *are* hatched. It has taken me many years and countless smarts to get out of that barbed wire moral enclosure that Poor Richard rigged up. Here am I now in tatters and scratched to ribbons, sitting in the middle of Benjamin's America looking at the barbed wire, and the fat sheep crawling under the fence to get fat outside and the watchdogs yelling at the gate lest by chance anyone should get out by the proper exit. Oh America! Oh Benjamin! And I just utter a long loud curse against Benjamin and the American corral.

Moral America! Most moral Benjamin. Sound, satisfied Ben!

He had to go to the frontiers of his State to settle some disturbance among the Indians. On this occasion he writes:

> We found that they had made a great bonfire in the middle of the square; they were all drunk, men and women quarreling and fighting. Their dark-colored bodies, half naked, seen only by the gloomy light of the bonfire, running after and beating one another with fire-brands, accompanied by their horrid yellings, formed a scene the most resembling our ideas of hell that could well be imagined. There was no appeasing the tumult, and we retired to our lodging. At midnight a number of them came thundering at our door, demanding more rum, of which we took no notice.
>
> The next day, sensible they had misbehaved in giving us that disturbance, they sent three of their counselors to make their apology. The orator acknowledged the fault, but laid it upon the rum, and then endeavored to excuse the rum by saying: "The Great Spirit, who made all things, made everything for some use; and whatever he designed anything for, that use it should always be put to. Now, when he had made rum, he said: 'Let this be for the Indians to get drunk with.' And it must be so."
>
> And, indeed, if it be the design of Providence to extirpate these savages in order to make room for the cultivators of the earth, it seems not improbable that rum may be the appointed means. It has already annihilated all the tribes who formerly inhabited all the seacoast. . . .

This from the good doctor, with such suave complacency is a little disenchanting. Almost too good to be true.

But there you are! The barbed wire fence. "Extirpate these savages in order to make room for the cultivators of the earth." O, Benjamin Franklin! He even "used venery" as a cultivator of seed.

Cultivate the earth, ye gods! The Indians did that, as much as they needed. And they left off there. Who built Chicago? Who cultivated the earth until it spawned Pittsburgh, Pa.?

The moral issue! Just look at it! Cultivation included. If it's a mere choice of Kultur or cultivation, I give it up.

Which brings us right back to our question, what's wrong with Benjamin, that we can't stand him? Or else, what's wrong with us, that we find fault with such a paragon?

Man is a moral animal. All right. I am a moral animal. And I'm going to remain such. I'm not going to be turned into a virtuous little automaton as Benjamin would have me. "This is good, that is bad. Turn the little handle and let the good tap flow," saith Benjamin and all America with him. "But first all extirpate those savages who are always turning on the bad tap."

I am a moral animal. But I am not a moral machine. I don't work with a little set of handles or levers. The Temperance-silence-order-resolution-frugality-industry-sincerity-justice-moderation-cleanliness-tranquility-chastity-humility keyboard is not going to get me going. I'm really not just an automatic piano with a moral Benjamin getting tunes out of me.

Here's my creed, against Benjamin's. This is what I believe:

"That I am I."

"That my soul is a dark forest."

"That my known self will never be more than a little clearing in the forest."

"That gods, strange gods, come forth from the forest into the clearing of my known self, and then go back."

"That I must have the courage to let them come and go."

"That I will never let mankind put anything over me, but that I will try always to recognize and submit to the gods in me and the gods in other men and women."

There is my creed. He who runs may read. He who prefers to crawl, or to go by gasoline, can call it rot.

Then for a "list." It is rather fun to play at Benjamin.

1. *Temperance.* Eat and carouse with Bacchus, or munch dry bread with Jesus, but don't sit down without one of the gods.
2. *Silence.* Be still when you have nothing to say; when genuine passion moves you, say what you've got to say, and say it hot.
3. *Order.* Know that you are responsible to the gods inside you and to the men in whom the gods are manifest. Recognize your superiors and your inferiors, according to the gods. This is the root of all order.

4. *Resolution.* Resolve to abide by your own deepest promptings and to sacrifice the smaller thing to the greater. Kill when you must, and be killed the same: the *must* coming from the gods inside you, or from the men in whom you recognize the Holy Ghost.

5. *Frugality.* Demand nothing; accept what you see fit. Don't waste your pride or squander your emotion.

6. *Industry.* Lose no time with ideals; serve the Holy Ghost; never serve mankind.

7. *Sincerity.* To be sincere is to remember that I am I, and that the other man is not me.

8. *Justice.* The only justice is to follow the sincere intuition of the soul, angry or gentle. Anger is just, and pity is just, but judgment is never just.

9. *Moderation.* Beware of absolutes. There are many gods.

10. *Cleanliness.* Don't be too clean. It impoverishes the blood.

11. *Tranquillity.* The soul has many motions, many gods come and go. Try to find your deepest issue, in every confusion, and abide by that. Obey the man in whom you recognize the Holy Ghost; command when your honor comes to command.

12. *Chastity.* Never "use" venery at all. Follow your passional impulse, if it be answered in the other being; but never have any motive in mind, neither off-spring nor health nor even pleasure, nor even service. Only know that "venery" is of the great gods. An offering-up of yourself to the very great gods, the dark ones, and nothing else.

13. *Humility.* See all men and women according to the Holy Ghost that is within them. Never yield before the barren.

There's my list. I have been trying dimly to realize it for a long time, and only America and old Benjamin have at last goaded me into trying to formulate it.

And now I, at least, know why I can't stand Benjamin. He tries to take away my wholeness and my dark forest, my freedom. For how can any man be free, without an illimitable background? and Benjamin tries to shove me into a barbed-wire paddock and make me grow potatoes or Chicagoes.

And how can I be free, without gods that come and go? But Benjamin won't let anything exist except my useful fellow-men, and I'm sick of them; as for his Godhead, his Providence, He is Head of nothing except a vast heavenly store that keeps every imaginable line of goods, from victrolas to cat-o-nine tails.

And how can any man be free without a soul of his own, that he believes in and won't sell at any price? But Benjamin doesn't let me have a soul of my own. He says I am nothing but a servant of mankind—galley-slave I call it—and if I don't get my wages here below—that is, if Mr. Pierpont Morgan or Mr. Nosey Hebrew or the grand United States Government, the great US, US OR SOMEOFUS, manages to scoop in my bit along with their lump—why, never mind, I shall get my wages HEREAFTER.

Oh Benjamin! Oh Binjum! You do NOT suck me in any longer.

And why oh why should the snuff-colored little trap have wanted to take us all in? Why did he do it?

Out of sheer human cussedness, in the first place. We do all like to get things inside a barbed-wire corral. Especially our fellow-men. We love to round them up inside the barbed-wire enclosure of FREEDOM, and make 'em work. "Work, you free jewel, WORK!" shouts the liberator, cracking his whip. Benjamin, I will not work. I do not choose to be a free democrat. I am absolutely a servant of my own Holy Ghost.

Sheer cussedness! But there was as well the salt of a subtler purpose. Benjamin was just in his eyeholes—to use an English vulgarism meaning he was just delighted—when he was at Paris judiciously milking money out of the French monarchy for the overthrow of all monarchy. If you want to ride your horse to somewhere you must put a bit in his mouth. And Benjamin wanted to ride his horse so that it would upset the whole apple-cart of the old masters. He wanted the whole European apple-cart upset. So he had to put a strong bit in the mouth of his ass.

"Henceforth be masterless."

That is, he had to break-in the human ass completely, so that much more might be broken, in the long run. For the moment it was the British Government that had to have a hole knocked in it. The first real hole it ever had: the breach of the American rebellion.

Benjamin, in his sagacity, knew that the breaking of the old world was a long process. In the depths of his own under-consciousness he hated England, he hated Europe, he hated the whole corpus of the European being. He wanted to be American. But you can't change your nature and mode of consciousness like changing your shoes. It is a gradual shedding. Years must go by, and centuries must elapse before you have finished. Like a son escaping from the domination of his parents. The escape is not just one rupture. It is a long and half-secret process.

So with the American. He was a European when he first went over the Atlantic. He is in the main a recreant European still. From Benjamin Franklin to Woodrow Wilson may be a long stride, but it is a stride along the same road. There is no new road. The same old road, become dreary and futile. Theoretic and materialistic.

Why then did Benjamin set up this dummy of a perfect citizen as a pattern to America? Of course he did it in perfect good faith, as far as he knew. He thought it simply was the true ideal. But what we *think* we do is not very important. We never really know what we are doing. Either we are materialistic instruments, like Benjamin or we move in the gesture of creation, from our deepest self, usually unconscious. We are only the actors, we are never wholly the authors of our own deeds or works. IT is the author, the unknown inside us or outside us. The best we can do is to try to hold ourselves in unison with the deeps which are inside us. And the worst we can do is to try to have things our own way, when we run counter to IT, and in the long run get our knuckles rapped for our presumption.

So Benjamin contriving money out of the Court of France. He was contriving the first steps of the overthrow of all Europe, France included. You can never have a new thing without breaking an old. Europe happens to be the old thing. America, unless the people in America assert themselves too much in opposition to the inner gods, should be the new thing. The new thing is the death of the old. But you can't cut the throat of an epoch. You've got to steal the life from it through several centuries.

And Benjamin worked for this both directly and indirectly. Directly, at the Court of France, making a small but very dangerous hole in the side of England, through which hole Europe has by now almost bled to death. And indirectly in Philadelphia, setting up this unlovely, snuff-colored little ideal, or automaton, of a pattern American. The pattern American, this dry, moral utilitarian little democrat, has done more to ruin the old Europe than any Russian nihilist. He has done it by slow attrition, like a son who has stayed at home and obeyed his parents, all the while silently hating their authority, and silently, in his soul, destroying not only their authority but their whole existence. For the American spiritually stayed at home in Europe. The spiritual home of America was and still is Europe. This is the galling bondage, in spite of several billions of heaped-up gold. Your heaps of gold are only so many muck-heaps, America, and will remain so till you become a reality to yourselves.

All this Americanizing and mechanizing has been for the purpose of overthrowing the past. And now look at America, tangled in her own barbed wire, and mastered by her own machines. Absolutely got down by her own barbed wire of shalt-nots, and shut up fast in her own "productive" machines like millions of squirrels running in millions of cages. It is just a farce.

Now is your chance, Europe. Now let Hell loose and get your own back, and paddle your own canoe on a new sea, while clever America lies on her muck-heaps of gold, strangled in her own barbed-wire of shalt-not ideals and shalt-not moralisms. While she goes out to work like millions of squirrels in millions of cages. Production!

Let Hell loose, and get your own back, Europe!

For Discussion

1. How does Lawrence immediately set himself at odds with Franklin?
2. Contrast Lawrence's and Franklin's ideas of the soul. Discuss the metaphors used to illustrate each. How does Lawrence's metaphor fit his idea of "mystery" in "Sex Versus Loveliness"?

3. Discuss Lawrence's objection to honesty as the best policy.
4. What purpose does the illustration of the Indian uprising serve?
5. Discuss Lawrence's creed in terms of its value to the individual. To society.
6. What analysis does Lawrence make of Franklin's negotiations with France?
7. What do you think is at the heart of Lawrence's dislike of Franklin?
8. What does Lawrence find to admire in Franklin?
9. Determine Lawrence's focus in the final paragraphs. What insight does this give you into the real purpose of the satire?
10. Locate descriptive phrases in which the word choice reveals Lawrence's attitude toward Franklin.
11. Make an argument for including this piece in *The Impassioned No; The Reflective NO.*

H. L. MENCKEN

The Politician

H. L. Mencken was born in Baltimore in 1880. After gradua-
tion from high school at sixteen, he began newspaper work at the
Baltimore *Evening Herald,* becoming managing editor at the age
of twenty-five. In 1906, he joined the staff of the Baltimore *Sun,*
where he maintained staff relations until 1941, in the meantime
launching *The American Mercury* with George Jean Nathan, an
association that was to last nine years. An iconoclastic critic and a
celebrated stylist, Mencken exerted a powerful influence on the
press of the nation during the first half of this century. Perhaps
our greatest satirical journalist, he continually attacked the
"*boob*oisie," a term which he used to epitomize American middle-
class values. His linguistic study, *The American Language,* is
probably his best known work, but the force of his personality
can be strongly noted in his six volumes of *Prejudices,* in Volume
IV of which this essay appears.

Half the sorrows of the world, I suppose, are caused by making false
assumptions. If the truth were only easier to ascertain the remedy for them
would consist simply of ascertaining it and accepting it. This business, alas,
is usually impossible, but fortunately not always: now and then, by some
occult process, half rational and half instinctive, the truth gets itself found
out and an ancient false assumption goes overboard. I point, in the field of
the social relations, to one which afflicted the human race for millenniums:
that one, to wit, which credited the rev. clergy with a mysterious wisdom
and awful powers. Obviously, it has ceased to trouble all the superior varieties
of men. It may survive in those remote marches where human beings go to
bed with the cows, but certainly it has vanished from the cities. Asphalt and
the apostolic succession, indeed, seem to be irreconcilable enemies. I can
think of no clergyman in any great American city today whose public dignity

and influence are much above those of an ordinary Class I Babbitt. It is hard for even the most diligent and passionate of the ancient order to get upon the first pages of the newspapers; he must make a clown-show, discreditable to his fraying cloth, or he must blush unseen. When bishops began launching thunderbolts against heretics, the towns do not tremble; they laugh. When elders denounce sin, sin only grows more popular. Imagine a city man getting a notice from the ordinary of his diocese that he had been excommunicated. It would trouble him far less, I venture, than his morning *Katzenjammer*.

The reason for all this is not hard to find. All the superior varieties of men—and even the lowest varieties of city workmen are at least superior to peasants—have simply rid themselves of their old belief in devils. Hell no longer affrights and palsies them, and so the magic of those who profess to save them from it no longer impresses them. That profession, I believe, was bogus, and its acceptance was therefore a false assumption. Being so, it made men unhappy; getting rid of it has delivered them. They are no longer susceptible to ecclesiastical alarms and extortions; *ergo*, they sleep and eat better. Think of what life must have been under such princes of damnation as Cotton Mather and Jonathan Edwards, with even bartenders and metaphysicians believing in them! And then compare it to life under Bishop Manning and the Rev. Dr. John Roach Straton, with only a few half-wits believing in them! Or turn to the backwoods of the Republic, where the devil is still feared, and with him his professional exterminators. In the country towns the clergy are still almost as influential as they were in Mather's day, and there, as everyone knows, they remain public nuisances, and civilized life is almost impossible. In such Neolithic regions nothing can go on without their consent, on penalty of anathema and hell-fire; as a result, nothing goes on that is worth recording. It is this survival of sacerdotal authority, I begin to believe, and not hookworm, malaria or the event of April 9, 1865, that is chiefly responsible for the cultural paralysis of the late Confederate States. The South lacks big cities; it is run by its country towns—and in every country town there is some Baptist *mullah* who rules by scaring the peasantry. The false assumption that his pretensions are sound, that he can actually bind and loose, that contumacy to him is a variety of cursing God—this false assumption is what makes the yokels so uneasy, so nervous, and hence so unhappy. If they could throw it off they would burn fewer Aframericans and sing more songs. If they could be purged of it they would be purged of Ku Kluxry too.

The cities got rid of that false assumption half a century ago, and have been making cultural progress ever since. Somewhat later they got rid of its brother, to wit, respect for government and, in particular, respect for its visible agents, the police. That respect—traditional, and hence irrational—had been, for years, in increasingly unpleasant collison with a great body of obvious facts. The police, by assumption austere and almost sacrosanct, were gradually discovered to be, in reality, a pack of rogues and but little removed, save by superior impudence and enterprise, from the cut-throats and purse-snatchers they were set to catch. When, a few decades ago, the American people, at least in the big cities, began to accept them frankly for what they were—when the old false assumption of their integrity and public usefulness was quietly abandoned and a new and more accurate assumption of their roguery was adopted in its place—when this change was effected there was a measurable increase, I believe, in the public happiness. It no longer astonished anyone when policemen were taken in evildoing; indignation therefore abated, and with it its pains. If, before that time, the corps of Prohibition enforcement officers—*i.e.*, a corps of undisguised scoundrels with badges—had been launched upon the populace, there would have been a great roar of wrath, and much anguished gnashing of teeth. People would have felt themselves put upon, injured, insulted. But with the old false assumption about policemen removed from their minds, they met the new onslaught calmly and even smilingly. Today no one is indignant over the fact that the extortions of these new *Polizei* increase the cost of potable alcohol. The false assumption that the police are altruistic agents of a benevolent state has been replaced by the sound assumption that they are gentlemen engaged assiduously, like the rest of us, in finding meat and raiment for their families and in laying up funds to buy Liberty Bonds in the next war to end war. This is human progress, for it increases human happiness.

So much for the evidence. The deduction I propose to make from it is simply this: that a like increase would follow if the American people could only rid themselves of another and worse false assumption that still rides them—one that corrupts all their thinking about the great business of politics, and vastly augments their discontent and unhappiness—the assumption, that is, that politicians are divided into two classes, and that one of those classes is made up of good ones. I need not argue, I hope, that this assumption is almost universally held among us. Our whole politics, indeed, is based upon it, and has been based upon it since the earliest days. What is any political campaign save a concerted effort to turn out a set of politicians who are admittedly bad and put in a set who are thought to be better? The former assumption, I believe, is always sound; the latter is just as certainly false. For if experience teaches us anything at all it teaches us this: that a good politician, under democracy, is quite as unthinkable as an honest burglar. His very existence, indeed, is a standing subversion of the public good in every rational sense. He is not one who serves the common weal; he is simply one who preys upon the commonwealth. It is to the interest of all the rest of us to hold down his powers to an irreducible minimum, and to reduce his compensation to nothing; it is to his interest to augment his powers at all hazards, and to make his compensation all the traffic will bear. To argue that these aims are identical is to argue palpable nonsense. The politician, at his ideal best, never even remotely approximated in practice, is a necessary evil; at his worst he is an almost intolerable nuisance.

What I contend is simply that he would be measurably less a nuisance if we got rid of our old false assumption about him, and regarded him in the cold light of fact. At once, I believe, two-thirds of his obnoxiousness would vanish. He would remain a nuisance, but he would cease to be a swindler; the injury of having to pay freight on him would cease to be complicated by the insult of being rooked. It is the insult and not the injury that makes the deeper wounds, and causes the greater permanent damage to the national psyche. All of us have been trained, since infancy, in putting up with necessary evils, plainly recognized *as* evils. We know, for example, that the young of the human species commonly smell badly; that garbage men, bootblacks and messenger boys commonly smell worse. These facts are not agreeable, but they remain tolerable because they are universally assumed—because there is no sense of having been tricked and cozened in their perennial discovery. But try to imagine how distressing fatherhood would become if prospective fathers were all taught that the human infant radiates an aroma like the rose—if the truth came constantly as a surprise! Each fresh victim of the deception would feel that he had been basely swindled—that his own child was somehow bogus. Not infrequently, I suppose, he would be tempted to make away with it in some quiet manner, and have another—only to be shocked again. That procedure would be idiotic, admittedly, yet it is exactly the one we follow in politics. At each election we vote in a new set of politicians, insanely assuming that they are better than the set turned out. And at each election we are, as they say in the Motherland, done in.

Of late the fraud has become so gross that the plain people begin to show a great restlessness under it. Like animals in a cage, they trot from one corner to another, endlessly seeking a way out. If the Democrats win one year, it is a pretty sure sign that they will lose the next year. State after state becomes doubtful, pivotal, skittish; even the solid South begins to break. In the cities it is still worse. An evil circle is formed. First the poor taxpayers, robbed by the politicians of one great party and then by those of the other, turn to a group of free-lance rogues in the middle ground—nonpartisan candidates, Liberals, reformers or whatnot: the name is unimportant. Then, flayed and pillaged by these gentry as they never were by the old-time professionals, they go back in despair to the latter, and are flayed and pillaged again. Back to Bach! Back to Tammany! Tammany reigns in New York because the Mitchel outfit was found to be intolerable—in other words, because the reformers were found to be even worse than the professionals. Is the fact surprising? Why should it be? Reformers and professionals are alike politicians in search of jobs; both are trying to bilk the taxpayers. Neither ever has any other motive. If any genuinely honest and altruistic politician had come to the surface in America in my time I'd have heard of him, for I have always frequented newspaper offices, and in a newspaper office the news of such a marvel would cause a dreadful tumult. I can recall no such tumult. The unanimous opinion of all the journalists that I know, excluding a few Liberals who are obviously somewhat balmy— they all believed, for example, that the late war would end war—is that, since the days of the national Thors and Wotans, no politician who was not out for himself, and for himself alone, has ever drawn the breath of life in the United States.

The gradual disintegration of Liberalism among us, in fact, offers an excellent proof of the truth of my thesis. The Liberals have come to grief by fooling their customers, not merely once too often, but a hundred times too often. Over and over again they have trotted out some new hero, usually from the great open spaces, only to see him taken in the immemorial mal-practices within ten days. Their graveyard, indeed, is filled with cracked and upset headstones, many covered with ribald pencilings. Every time there is a scandal in the grand manner the Liberals lose almost as many general officers as either the Democrats or Republicans. Of late, racked beyond endurance by such catastrophes at home, they have gone abroad for their principal heroes; losing humor as well as hope, they now ask us to venerate such astounding paladins as the Hon. Béla Kun, a gentleman who, in any American state, would not only be in the calaboose, but actually in the death-house. But this absurdity is only an offshoot of a deeper one. Their primary error lies in making the false assumption that some politicians are better than others. This error they share with the whole American people.

I propose that it be renounced, and contend that its renunciation would greatly rationalize and improve our politics. I do not argue that there would be any improvement in our politicians; on the contrary, I believe that they would remain substantially as they are today, and perhaps grow even worse. But what I do argue is that recognizing them frankly for what they are would instantly and automatically dissipate the indignation caused by their present abominations, and that the disappearance of this indignation would promote the public contentment and happiness. Under my scheme there would be no more false assumptions and no more false hopes, and hence no more painful surprises, no more bitter resentment of fraud, no more despair. Politicians, in so far as they remained necessary, would be kept at work—but not with any insane notion that they were archangels. Their rascality would be assumed and discounted, as the rascality of the police is now assumed and discounted. Machinery would be gradually developed to limit it and counteract it. In the end, it might be utilized in some publicly profitable manner, as the insensitiveness to filth of garbage men is now utilized, as the reverence of the clergy for capitalism is now utilized. The result, perhaps, would be a world no better than the present one, but it would at least be a world more intelligent.

In all this I sincerely hope that no one will mistake me for one who shares the indignation I have spoken of—that is, for one who believes that politicians can be made good, and cherishes a fond scheme for making them so. I believe nothing of the sort. On the contrary, I am convinced that the art and mystery they practice is essentially and incurably anti-social—that they must remain irreconcilable enemies of the common weal until the end of time. But I maintain that this fact, in itself, is not a bar to their employment. There are, under Christian civilization, many necessary offices that demand the possession of anti-social talents. A professional soldier, regarded realistically, is much worse than a professional politician, for he is a professional murderer and kidnaper, whereas the politician is only a professional sharper and sneak-thief. A clergyman, too, begins to shrink and shrivel on analysis; the work he does in the world is basically almost indistinguishable from that of an astrologer, a witch-doctor or a fortune-teller. He pretends falsely that he can get sinners out of hell, and collects money from them on that promise, tacit or express. If he had to go before a jury with that pretension it would probably go hard with him. But we do not send him before a jury; we grant him his hocus-pocus on the ground that it is necessary to his office, and that his office is necessary to civilization, so-called. I pass over the journalist delicately; the time has not come to turn state's evidence. Suffice it to say that he, too, would probably wither under a stiff cross-examination. If he is no murderer, like the soldier, then he is at least a sharper and swindler, like the politician.

What I plead for, if I may borrow a term in disrepute, is simply *Realpolitik, i. e.,* realism in politics. I can imagine a political campaign purged of all the current false assumptions and false pretenses—a campaign in which, on election day, the voters went to the polls clearly informed that the choice before them was not between an angel and a devil, a good man and a bad man, an altruist and a go-getter, but between two frank go-getters, the one, perhaps, excelling at beautiful and nonsensical words and the other at silent and prehensile deeds—the one a chautauqua orator and the other a porch-climber. There would be, in that choice, something candid, free and exhilarating. Buncombe would be adjourned. The voter would make his selection in the full knowledge of all the facts, as he makes his selection between two heads of cabbage, or two evening papers, or two brands of chewing tobacco. Today he chooses his rulers as he buys bootleg whiskey, never knowing precisely what he is getting, only certain that it is not what it pretends to be. The Scotch may turn out to be wood alcohol or it may turn out to be gasoline; in either case it is not Scotch. How much better if it were plainly labeled, for wood alcohol and gasoline both have their uses—higher uses, indeed, than Scotch. The danger is that the swindled and poisoned consumer, despairing of ever avoiding them when he doesn't want them, may prohibit them even when he does want them, and actually enforce his own prohibition. The danger is that the hopeless voter, forever victimized by his false assumption about politicians, may in the end gather such ferocious indignation that he will abolish them teetotally and at one insane swoop, and so cause government by the people, for the people and with the people to perish from this earth.

For Discussion

1. What examples of false assumptions does Mencken discuss in the first three paragraphs?
2. Explain the false assumptions that Americans hold about politicians.
3. What assumptions does Mencken provide as alternates? To what extent do you agree that these are valid?
4. According to Mencken, how would a more "realistic" attitude affect politics and politicians?
5. What would happen if American society discarded its false assumptions regarding politicians, press, police, and clergy? What changes would have to be made?
6. Although Mencken was writing in the early 1920's, many present day political observers have noted a similar "gradual disintegration of Liberalism among us." Discuss Mencken's reasoning in regard to this trend and try to account for its existence today.
7. Identify the following allusions:
    a) Babbitt
    b) Katzenjammers
    c) Cotton Mather
    d) Buncombe
8. What point is Mencken making in his analogy of bootleg whiskey? How valid is his point?
9. Locate five sentences which illustrate ironic epigram, irreverent broadside, or hyperbole (for example, the sentence in paragraph three beginning "The police . . .").
10. How does Mencken create irony?

HENRY MILLER

The Staff of Life

The only formal education Henry Miller received, apart from two months at New York City College, was in public schools in Brooklyn, where he was born in 1891. The rest of his impressive and varied knowledge was acquired through reading and travel. In 1930 he went to Paris where his controversial career began with his first novel, *Tropic of Cancer* (1934), banned in the United States, along with many later books, until recent court decisions reversed the restrictions. Despite the long-existing ban, Miller continued to be widely read all over the world. First praised by the "beat" generation, whose prophet he unwillingly became, he now enjoys an enthusiastic following, even in the "academy," where he was ignored for so long. Famous for his realistic and surrealistic descriptions of his expatriate days in Paris, Miller wrote on subjects ranging from oriental philosophy to recipes—all with an equal hilarity, zest, and erudition. "The Staff of Life," now an American classic, develops the idea expressed in Ecclesiastes: "Eat thy bread with joy and drink thy wine with a merry heart."

Bread: prime symbol. Try and find a good loaf. You can travel fifty thousand miles in America without once tasting a piece of good bread. Americans don't care about good bread. They are dying of inanition but they go on eating bread without substance, bread without flavor, bread without vitamins, bread without life. Why? Because the very core of life is contaminated. If they knew what good bread was they would not have such wonderful machines on which they lavish all their time, energy and affection. A plate of false teeth means much more to an American than a loaf of good bread. Here is the sequence: poor bread, bad teeth, indigestion, constipation, halitosis, sexual starvation, disease and accidents, the operating table, artificial limbs, spectacles, baldness, kidney and bladder trouble, neurosis, psychosis, schizo-phrenia, war and famine. Start with the American loaf of bread so beauti-fully wrapped in cellophane and you end on the scrap heap at forty-five. The only place to find a good loaf of bread is in the ghettos. Wherever there is a foreign quarter there is apt to be good bread. Wherever there is a Jewish grocer or delicatessen you are almost certain to find an excellent loaf of bread. The dark Russian bread, light in weight, found only rarely on this huge continent, is the best bread of all. No vitamins have been injected into it by laboratory specialists in conformance with the latest food regulations. The Russian just naturally likes good bread, because he also likes caviar and vodka and other good things. Americans are whiskey, gin and beer drinkers who long ago lost their taste for food. And losing that they have also lost their taste for life. For enjoyment. For good conversation. For everything worth while, to put it briefly.

What do I find wrong with America? Everything. I begin at the be-ginning, with the staff of life: bread. If the bread is bad the whole life is bad. Bad? Rotten, I should say. Like that piece of bread only twenty-four hours old which is good for nothing except perhaps to fill up a hole. Good for target practice maybe. Or shuttlecock and duffle board. Even soaked in urine it is unpalatable; even perverts shun it. Yet millions are wasted ad-vertising it. Who are the men engaged in this wasteful pursuit? Drunkards and failures for the most part. Men who have prostituted their talents in order to help further the decay and dissolution of our once glorious Republic.

Here is one of the latest widely advertised products: Hollywood Bread. On the red, white and blue cellophane jacket in which it is wrapped, this last word in bread from the American bakeries, it reads as follows:

BAKED WITH

whole wheat flour, clear wheat flour, water, non-diastatic malt, yeast, salt, honey, caramel, whole rye flour, yeast food, stone ground oatmeal, soya flour, gluten flour, barley flour, sesame seed, and a small quantity of de-hydrated (water free) vegetables including celery, lettuce, pumpkin, cabbage, carrots, spinach, parsley, sea kelp, added for flavor only.

The only thing missing from this concoction is powdered diamonds. How does it taste? Much like any other American product. Of course, this is a reducing bread of which one should eat two slices a day three times a day and not ask how it tastes. Grow thin, as in Hollywood, and be thankful it doesn't taste worse. That's the idea. For several days now I have been trying to get a whiff of some of those ingredients—sea kelp especially—which were included "for flavor only." Why they were not added for health too I don't know. Naturally all these delicious-sounding items amount to about one ten-thousandth part of the loaf. And on the second day, stale, flat and unprofitable, this marvelous new bread is no more attractive to the palate or the stomach than any other loaf of American bread. On the second day it is good for replacing a missing tile on the roof. Or to make a scratchboard for the cat.

The second day! If the first is given to creation, to light, let us say, the second (in America) is given up to garbage. Every second day is garbage day in America. I know because I have had lots to do with garbage. I've hauled it, for pay, and I've eaten it upon necessity. I learned to distinguish between one kind of bread and another by salvaging dry crusts from the garbage can. I don't know which is worse—the day of creation, when everything turns to gas and bilge, with its concomitants dandruff, constipation, halitosis, false teeth, artificial limbs, psychic impotency, and so on, or the second day, given up to garbage, when all creation turns out to be nothing but a mirage and a disillusionment. It has been said, and I have no doubt it is true, that the garbage accumulated by one big American city would feed certain of the little countries of Europe handsomely. I know no quicker way to kill off the warring nations of Europe than to feed them our garbage. The pygmies might thrive on it, possibly even the Chinese coolie, who is supposed to thrive on anything, but I cannot see the Danes, the Swiss, the Swedes, the Greeks, the Albanians, or the Austrians thriving on it. No Sir. I would sooner feed them buzzards than the left-overs from the American table. Already, with our canned food products, our cold storage meat, our dehydrated vegetables, we have brought about a tremendous deterioration in these sturdy people of Europe. From these to the machine and thence to war is but a step. Then, famine, plague, pestilence, dung heaps. And monuments, of course. All sorts of monuments. Done by second or third rate artists.

The care and affection which once was bestowed on the human body now goes to the machines. The machines get the best food, the best attention. Machines are expensive; human lives are cheap. Never in the history of the world was life cheaper than it is to-day. (And no pyramids to show for it either.) How natural, then, that the staff of life should be utterly without value. I begin with bread and I shall end with bread. I say we make the foulest bread in all the world. We pass it off like fake diamonds. We advertise it and sterilize it and protect it from all the germs of life. We make a manure which we eat before we have had time to eliminate it. We not only have failed God, tricked Nature, debased Man, but we have cheated the birds of the air with our corrupt staff of life. Everytime I fling the stale bread over the cliff I beg forgiveness of the birds for offering them our American bread. Perhaps that is why they are not singing any more as they used to when I was a child. The birds are pining and drooping. It's not the war, for they have never participated in our carnages. It's the bread. The stale, flat, unprofitable bread of the second day. It shortens their wing-span, weakens their umbrella-ribs, reduces the scope of their swoop, blunts their beaks, deteriorates their vision, and finally—it kills their song! If you don't believe me, ask any ornithologist. It's a known fact. And how Americans love facts!

Another fact. . . . Food, when it is not enjoyed, kills. The best diet in the world is useless if the patient has no appetite, no gusto, no sensuality. On the whole, Americans eat without pleasure. They eat because the bell rings three times a day. (I omit mention of the clay eaters of the South and other poor whites who live on rats, snakes, and cow-dung.) They don't eat because they love food. To prove it you have only to shove a glass of whiskey before them. See which they reach for first! And now, with vitamins and all the other life-savers, food has become even less important. Why bother trying to squeeze a bit of life out of our worn-out products of the soil? Why pretend? Throw anything down the hatch to stop the gnawing and swallow a dozen vitamins. That way you'll make sure you've had your proper dose of the vital essentials. Should the vitamins fail, see a surgeon. From there to the sanitarium. And from there to the nut-house—or the dung heap. Be sure to get a Hollywood funeral. They're the loveliest, the duckiest, the most sanitary, the most inspiring. And no more expensive than ordinary ground burial. You can, if you like, have your dear lost one propped up in a natural reclining position, her cheeks rouged, a cigarette to her lips, and a phonograph record talking to you just as she once talked to you in life. The most wonderful fake imaginable. Jolly, what? O death, where is thy sting? What's more, she can be kept that way for an unspeakably long period; the cigarette is guaranteed not to rot away before the lips or the buttocks. You can come back and have a second, a third, a twenty-fifth look at the beloved. Still smoking a cigarette. Or you can have her reading a book, the *Iliad,* say, or the *Bhagavad Gita*—something uplifting like that.

I remember when I used to be served a slice of homemade bread with butter and sugar smeared over it. Glorious days! That bread really had a taste. *Schmecht gut, nichtwahr? Yah! Sehr gut. Wunderbar. Ausgezeichnet.* With a piece of bread like that I used to sit and read *Pinocchio* or *Alice Through the Looking Glass* or Hans Christian Andersen or *The Heart of a Boy.* Mothers had time in those days to make good bread with their own hands, and still do the thousand and one things which motherhood demands of a woman. To-day they haven't time to do anything, and hardly a bloody mother in the bloody land knows how to bake a loaf of bread. Mother gets up early now to work in an office or a factory. She's busy doing nothing all day, which is to say—earning a living. Earning a living has nothing to do with living. It's the belt line to the grave, without a transfer or a stopover. A one-way passage via the frying pan and the cookerless cooker. A child is an accident—bad rubber goods or else too much drink and recklessness. Any way, it's there and it has to be fed. You don't bake bread for accidents, do you? And why bother to produce milk from the breast when the cows are working over-time for the dairy companies of America?

Day by day the morons, epileptics and schizoids multiply. By accident, like everything else. Nothing is planned in America except improvements. And all improvements are for the machine. When a plenum is reached war is declared. Then the machine really gets going. War is a Roman Holiday for the machine. Man becomes even less than nothing then. The machine is well fed. The food products become plastics and plastics are what make the world go round. Better to have a good steering wheel than a good stomach. In the old days an army advanced on its stomach; now it advances in tanks or spitfires or super-fortresses. Civilians never advance. Civilians always rot and help make insurance companies richer.

But bread. . . . Let's not forget, it's bread we want—and children that are not accidents brought about by defective rubber or bathtub gin. How to get it? Bread, I mean. By putting a monkey wrench in the machine. By going backwards on all fours, like giraffes with broken necks. By praying for life now and not hereafter. By exercising freedom and not inventing four, five or six freedoms won by the slaughter and starvation of twenty or thirty millions. Begin today by baking your own bread. First of all you need a stove. A wood or coal stove. Not a gas range. Not an electric apparatus. Then let the flies in. Then roll your sleeves up and get your hands in the dough. Lick your fingers. Never mind if you lose your job. Eat your bread first, then maybe you won't want to work in an office or a factory. Life begins with bread. And a prayer. Not a begging prayer, but a prayer of thanks. Don't bless the block-busters. Bless God for his favors—air, water, sun, moon. God wants you to enjoy the bread of life. He never meant you to go out all day working at a job you loathe so that you can buy a loaf of store bread wrapped in cellophane. God gave us germs as well as air and water and sun. Germs attack only what is already rotting. Man is rotting in every fibre of his being: that is why he is a prey to germs. And that is why he is allergic to everything that is for his own good.

Before Communism was there was Communion and before that there was God and God said let there be light and there was light. And what a glorious light it was. It lasted for aeons, and then came the scientific age and darkness fell upon the land everywhere. Now everything can be proved backwards and out of existence and instead of soaring with our own wings or on the backs of our giant birds we make things of metal and plastics which spread havoc and destruction in their wake. We throw bones to the dogs and eat the dogs instead of the bones. Not one step has been taken towards improving the flow of milk from the mammary glands. Only mothers and wet nurses give milk, whereas with time and experimentation every one could give milk and the food problem would be solved for eternity. We wouldn't even need to sit down to eat: now and then a step-ladder might be necessary, but nothing more. Why hasn't any one thought of that? Is it so improbable? Ants have their own milk cows—how did that happen? Anyway, with human milk the universal food, with manna falling from heaven, and nectar and ambrosia for dessert, think what a lot of work would be eliminated. Think too of the gratitude the animals would show, once they got on to the new scheme of things. All we would need, men and animals, would be one huge grass plot. No more dairy companies, no more containers, no more bottles, plates, knives and forks, spoons, pots, pans, stoves. The solution of the food problem would throw a monkey wrench into the entire economic and social system; our mores would change, our religions would disappear, our money become valueless. One can hardly imagine what the cause for war would then be, though doubtless a good excuse will always be found.

Outside of the foreign quarters, then, take it for granted that there is no good bread to be had. Every foreign group has introduced into our life some good substantial bread, even the Scandinavians. (Excepting the English, I should add, but then we hardly think of them as foreign, though why we shouldn't I don't know, for when you think of it the English are even less like us than the Poles or Latvians.) In a Jewish restaurant you usually have a basket filled with all kinds of bread from which to choose. In a typical American restaurant, should you ask for rye, whole wheat or any other kind of bread but the insidious unwholesome, and unpalatable white, you get white bread. If you insist on rye bread you get whole wheat. If you insist on whole wheat you get graham bread. Once in a great while you come upon nut bread; this is always a sheer accident. Raisin bread is a sort of decoy to lure you into eating unpalatable, perfidious and debilitating white bread. When in doubt go to a Jewish restaurant or delicatessen; if necessary, stand up and eat a sandwich made of sour rye, sweet butter, pastrami and pickle. A Jewish sandwich contains more food value than an eighty-five cent meal in the ordinary American restaurant. With a glass of water to wash it down you can walk away feeling fit. Don't sit down and eat a Jewish meal, because the Jews are bad cooks despite their great concern about food, which amounts to a neurosis. It is curious, though, how the desire to survive has made the Jews keen about preserving the staff of life. It is even more curious that they are just as much riddled with disease as the other members of the community—more so, in fact, judging purely from personal observation. They not only have all the physical ailments which other white peoples are heir to but they have all the mental and nervous ailments. Often they have everything at once, and then they concentrate upon food with even greater acuity and despair. It is only when they become revolutionary that they begin to lose interest in food. The real American, on the other hand, though totally unrevolutionary at heart, seems born with an indifference to food. One can serve a white American food which would make an Igorote turn up his nose. Americans can eat garbage, provided you sprinkle it liberally with ketchup, mustard, chili sauce, tabasco sauce, cayenne pepper, or any other condiment which destroys the original flavor of the dish. On the other hand, olive oil which the French eschew when preparing salads because it has too strong a flavor, Americans hardly ever use in their salads. Nothing on God's earth is more uninviting, more anaemic, than the American salad. At its best it is like refined puke. The lettuce is a joke: even a canary would refuse to touch it. This concoction, mind you, is usually served before the meal, together with the coffee which is cold by the time you are ready to drink it. The moment you sit down at a table in the ordinary American restaurant, the moment you begin scanning the menu, the waitress asks you what you wish to drink. (If by chance you should say "cocoa" the whole kitchen would be thrown out of gear.) To this question I usually counter with another: "Do you have anything but white bread?" If the answer is not a flat No, it is: "We have whole wheat," or "We have graham bread." Whereupon I usually mumble under my breath: "You can stick that up your ass! When she says: "What did you say?" I reply, "Do you have rye bread by any chance?" Then, before she can say no, I launch into an elaborate explanation of the fact that I don't mean by rye bread the ordinary rye bread, which is no better than white, graham, or whole wheat, but a succulent, tasty, dark, sour rye such as the Russians and the Jews serve. At the mention of these two suspect nationalities a scowl spreads over her face. While she is saying in her most sarcastic voice that she is sorry but they do not have that kind of rye bread or any rye bread, for that matter, I begin asking about the fruit, what kinds of fruit, fresh fruit, they have on hand, knowing damned well that they haven't any. Nine times out of ten her answer will be: "We have apple pie, and peach pie." ("Stick it up your ass!") "I beg your pardon?" she says. "Yes, fruit . . . you know, the kind that grows on trees . . . apples, pears, bananas, plums, oranges . . . something with skin on it that you peel." Whereupon a light dawns and she hastens to interpolate: "Oh, but we have apple sauce!" ("Fuck your apple sauce!") "I beg pardon?" Here I look leisurely round the room, surveying the shelves, the counter, the pie plates. Finally, resting my gaze upon a bowl of artificial fruit, I exclaim with glee: "Like that over there, *only real!*"

Sometimes, upon scanning the menu and knowing that it will only give me a belly-ache, I ask immediately if they can serve me a large bowl of fresh fruit. Here, incidentally, let me call attention to the dishes of mixed fruit prepared early in the morning which stand rotting in disgusting sweet canned juices until lunch or dinner hour. In the Automat type of restaurant one sees the counter piled with these vile stews. These, like the salads mentioned a moment ago, and like the pies fabricated by the wholesale bakers (who are probably responsible for more deaths than all our wars put together), are peculiar to the American temperament. There is not the least food value in any of them. The salad is at its worst when served in one of those delightful little inns run by spinsters in villages of imaginary charm, such as one is supposed to find in Vermont, Maryland, or Connecticut. Here everything looks immaculate and is immaculate, and therefore without value, without flavor, without joy. One suddenly feels like a canary which has been castrated and can no longer warble or differentiate between seed and salad. Beginning with this obscene salad one just knows that the meal is going to end with a charming little dessert such as prune whip or vanilla ice cream. To ask for a grape or a herring in one of these places is like committing sacrilege. There are certain things you must never ask for in an American restaurant. Never. One is good sour rye such as the Russians and the Jews make. Another is a cup of strong coffee. (Exceptions: French and Italian restautrants, and Louisiana. In Louisiana you can get a cup of coffee that is like liquid dynamite. But it tastes good; it has chicory in it. And chicory is excellent, despite all opinion to the contrary.) A third is cheese. A fourth is grapes. A fifth is nuts. Never have I seen a bowl of assorted and uncracked nuts put on the table in an American restaurant. Now and then, rarely, very rarely, one sees nuts in an American home. Usually, however, they are there as decoration. The fruit likewise. Fruit and nuts belong on the sideboard for the children, when there are any, to nibble at. The mixed fruit, or fruit salad, as they have the impudence to call it in America, reaches the height of abomination in the arm-chair Automat type of restaurant. Have you ever noticed the derelicts who frequent these eating places, sitting in the show window munching their lunch or dinner? Is there any more lugubrious sight on earth? (The corollary to it is the cheap traveling salesman type of hotel where all day long the weary commercial traveler sits in an enormous leather armchair staring vacantly out on the street. This is the type who gets orders for useless commodities which the American slave toils his ass off to accumulate, which he sells to his own kind and pretends thereby that he is earning an honest living. This is the type that votes the Democratic or Republican ticket year in and year out, in lean years and fat years, in war and in peace, and is always complaining that business is bad. This is the most traveled man in the world, and yet he knows nothing, absolutely nothing, and brags about it. This is the type who when you mention China says immediately—"coolies." If there is any more ignominious coolie than the traveling salesman I have yet to know him. The fact that he reads the "Digest" or some other compilation of facts gives him the illusion that he is informed and a useful member of society.)

But it's the pie that takes the cake. The pie is at its worst in the Greek restaurant, often called "New York Café," and encountered in every village and hamlet throughout the length and breadth of the land. In fact, everything is at its worst in this type of eating place. But it's here that the pie becomes positively obsessive. Often there is nothing to offer the weary traveler but pie. There they stand, row upon row of pie plates, all filled with gangrene and arsenic. The crust looks like scurf and is scurf, usually of the finest rancid grease made by the Criscomaniacs of America. Here and there one can detect in a whole pie a piece of fruit, such as apple or peach; it is surrounded by a clot of phlegm swimming in a mess of undefinable paste. The pie of apple or peach is sourish, billious, gaseous, having no more resemblance to the apple or peach in its native state than corn whiskey has to corn on the cob. The Greek proprietor delights in serving white Americans this unholy dish; he despises them for eating it, but, canny business man that he is, he believes in giving them what they ask for. He himself has a totally different cuisine, a damned good one, too, I must say, if you ever make a friend of him and get invited to his home. On his table you will see olives, real olives, okra, olive oil, fruits of all kinds, nuts, rice, vine leaves, the tenderest lamb imaginable, wines of all kinds, including retsina, and cognac, Greek cognac, and other delicacies.

Let us digress here a moment. . . . How is it that Americans, composed of nothing but foreign nationalities, living amongst people accustomed to the most varied cuisines, people who have made an art of cooking from time immemorial, continue to be the worst cooks in the world, continue to open one foul restaurant after another? Explain it, if you can. To me it's an enigma. The more mixed becomes the blood in our veins, the more American we become. And by American I mean the more set, crass, conservative, prejudiced, stupid, narrow-minded, unexperimental and unrevolutionary. In every big city we have Chinese, Italian, French, Hungarian, Russian, German, Swedish restaurants. Do we learn anything from these skilled restaurateurs? No, not a thing. We go our way, serving pies, mixed fruit salads, hamburgers, baked beans, steak and onions, vicious veal cutlets, whether breaded or unbreaded, and so on. Has any one ever had a good stew in an American restaurant? The peasants of Europe have thrived on stews for centuries. Here a stew means a couple of spoonfuls of superannuated meat swimming in a tiny pool of grease and bilge with bloated potatoes as a garniture. One hasn't begun to eat when the meal is over. It's an imaginary stew at the best. And the most imaginary part of it is the vegetables without which no stew is complete: leeks, carrots, turnips, onions, celery, parsley, and so on. If you find a tiny piece of any other vegetable than the potato you are indeed a lucky individual.

All right, steak then! Steak is the great American dish. Steak and onions. Fine. Nothing better, I say. Where can you get it? I mean without paying $2.50 per person! The first and only time I got the real flavor of steak was when I passed through Denver. Up till then I never knew what a real steak tasted like. The meat companies are for convincing us that meat from the refrigerator, meat that has been on ice several years, is the best meat of all. The whole world is being shipped and fed this cold storage meat, thanks to Armour & Co. and their subsidiary hog-butchers. In France I used to eat *filet de boeuf* practically every other day. It cost, for one person, a good portion, mind you, from twelve to eighteen cents, at the rate of exchange prevailing in the late thirties. It was delicious meat, and I knew how to prepare it (Americans as a rule know only how to spoil a good piece of meat in cooking it.) When I came to America, in 1940, I went to the butcher one day and asked for my customary *filet de boeuf*. A piece for two people came to $1.10, so help me God. I couldn't believe my ears. And this was in a cheap butcher shop on Third Avenue, New York. Christ only knows what it would have cost in the Park Avenue neighborhood. I took it home and I fried it. I did everything just as I used to at the Villa Seurat. I had wine with it too, the best I could buy for $1.25 the bottle. I also had grapes and nuts, and a salad prepared with the best olive oil. I had several kinds of cheese, including roquefort and camembert. Despite all precautions the meal didn't taste the same. There was something lacking. As a matter of fact, all the essentials were lacking. A piece of lettuce grown in America is like a piece of lettuce grown in France only in looks and name. American fruit, the most sensational looking fruit in the world (barring the tropics), is practically tasteless compared to the sicklier looking European fruits. American cheeses look delicious, and God knows the Kraft Brothers have tickled them up inordinately, but they do not have the flavor of the cheeses they are made to imitate. A stale piece of Camembert in a dirty French restaurant is worth a whole box of beautiful looking fresh Camembert put out by the crafty cheese-makers of Wisconsin. The flat Dutch cheeses are of course still more flat and tasteless when you eat them in America, being as they are the product of the most pampered cows in all the world. Wines, even when they are good, and in the realm of ordinary table wines America makes some of the best, do not taste as good as in Europe, perhaps because the atmosphere, the violence, the tempo of American life destroys whatever blessing wine confers.

Wine with the meal, in America, produces the wrong result. What is required, when attempting to digest American food, is strong spirits—whiskey, gin, cocktails. The correct procedure is to get soused beforehand; this enables one to eat without noticing how vile the food is. It gets one flushed and excited, and the food is forgotten. It makes one argumentative, which aids in bringing on indigestion, dyspepsia, flatulence, constipation, hemorrhoids, and finally the operating table. Whichever road you take, in America, you always wind up at the surgeon's door. If you buy an automobile it's the surgeon you have to reckon with eventually. If you take a good-paying job, it's the surgeon who will bleed you to death. If you economize and eat in armchair restaurants, or the Greek restaurants (where American food is served—not the real Greek restaurant), you meet the surgeon sooner or later, generally sooner. If you take to the soil and live the outdoor life, you first must have all your teeth pulled out and plates inserted. Farmers have about the worst teeth of all, even worse than factory workers. They have all the physical ailments, too, and are often as not undernourished. Farmers die of inanition in the midst of plenty. There isn't anything you can do, in America, by way of earning a living whereby you can escape dire taxation, disease, accident, misery and humiliation. At the end of every road stands the surgeon, who is for Americans what Nemesis was for the Greeks. The whole culture of America springs from two lunatics: the Marquis de Sade and Sacher Masoch. Justice, always retributive, is apotheosized by the surgeon. His henchmen are the dentists. If you have an ache or pain never mention it to the dentist, or he will immediately extract all your teeth. Nowadays even cowboys are proud of their false teeth. Scarcely any hard-working American, however splendid his physique, is without plates or bridges after forty. Hardly any normal American has a full head of hair after forty. Hardly any American over twenty-one, whether he works hard or takes it easy, is without eye-glasses. Almost every American suffers from hemorrhoids. Practically every American over forty has a bad heart. Cancer, syphilis, arthritis, tuberculosis, schizophrenia are so prevalent that we accept them as part of the bargain—i.e., the American way of life. Nearly every family boasts of one moron among its members, one lunatic, one drunkard, one pervert. All the food advertisements boast of the vitamin contents of their products. All the medicaments advertised boast of their cure for every thing under the sun. It is obvious that our foods lack the proper vitamins, just as it is obvious that in employing these health foods so rich in vitamins we nevertheless are afflicted with all the diseases known to man. We die young, mortgaged to the hilt, insolvent, despite all the insurance policies issued by all the insurance companies whose tentacles reach into every avenue of com-mercial and industrial life. It is also evident that, despite the fact this is the land of opportunity where freedom reigns, where every one has the right to worship and the right to vote for the wrong candidate, that the zest for life is so low that less than one child per family is now produced, except among certain Indian tribes, certain religious communities, certain strata of poor whites, and among the Negroes as a whole. Even the Jews, known for their big families as well as their good bread, are beginning to have less children—in America. And when the Jew loses his desire to perpetuate his own kind there must indeed be something seriously wrong with the national life. In the poorest countries of Europe the Jews still remained fertile; here, with everything in his grasp, except recognition by the Gentiles, he withers away. Only among the American Indians, and there only in certain tribes, is the population on the increase. It is said that this is due in part to the practice of polygamy. And here we touch another tender subject, one almost as potent as bread. I mean the fear among native white Americans of in-dulging in any other form of marriage but that sponsored by the Christian churches. Why not polygamy? Why not polyandry? Why not any kind of marriage, including love marriages? With polygamy the Mormons were fast on the way to building an empire. Nobody can say that the Mormons are, or ever were, an undesirable element in the great American community. They were and still are one of the few communities in this country where poverty is relatively unknown. They produce less criminals than other parts of the country—and less morons, and less idiots, and less trouble of any nature. And God knows they were never, never more immoral than the other members of the community. On the contrary, they were not only more law-abiding, more peaceful, more prosperous, more social-minded and far-visioned than the other communities of America, but they were absolutely more moral in the strictest sense of the word, that is, in the sense that they actually practiced what they preached.

But to get back to bread. . . . Today the mailman brought three kinds of bread: Italian bread, a milk loaf, and pumpernickel. (No sour rye, of course, no corn bread.) The bread comes from Monterey, the nearest town, which is fifty miles away. In Monterey there is no Jewish grocer or delica-tessen, worse luck. In Monterey there are Mexicans, Portuguese and Filipinos, but who gives a damn what these poor devils eat? The Mexicans have their tortillas, the Portuguese their garlic, and the Filipinos . . . well, among other things they have all our bad habits. Nobody in Monterey has a good slice of bread to eat. Nor in Carmel either, unless it's Robinson Jeffers, and that would be a sacramental bread. Just outside of Carmel lives Edward Weston, the photographer. And that leads me to speak of another kind of bread: photographic bread. Have you ever noticed that even the photographic bread tastes poorly? Have you ever seen a piece of bread photographed by our advertising maniacs which you would like to bite into? I haven't. Edward Weston could undoubtedly make you the most wonderful photographic bread conceivable—*but could you eat it?* The bread you hang on your wall is not the bread you want to eat at table. Even a piece of bread by Man Ray would prove unpalatable, particularly if he just happened to be reading his favorite author, the Marquis de Sade. Sacher Masoch might have made a good bread, if he had lived long enough. It has a Kosher sound, *Sacher Masoch*. But in the long run I have a feeling it would make one morbid and introspective, this Sacher Masoch bread.

I have now found that the only way to eat our most unwholesome, un-palatable and unappetizing American bread, the staff of our unsavory and monotonous life, is to adopt the following procedure. This is a recipe, so please follow instructions to the letter.

To begin with, accept any loaf that is offered you without question, even if it is not wrapped in cellophane, even if it contains no kelp. Throw it in the back of the car with the oil can and the grease rags; if possible, bury it under a sack of coal, *bituminous coal*. As you climb up the road to your home, drop it in the mud a few times and dig your heels into it. If you have a dog with you, let him pee on it now and then. When you get to the house, and after you have prepared the other dishes, take a huge carving knife and rip the loaf from stem to stern. Then take one whole onion, peeled or unpeeled, one carrot, one stalk of celery, one huge piece of garlic, one sliced apple, a herring, a handful of anchovies, a sprig of parsley, and an old toothbrush and shove them into the disemboweled guts of the bread. Over these pour first a thimbleful of kerosene, a dash of Lavoris and just a wee bit of Clorox; then sprinkle guts liberally with the following—molasses, honey, orange marmalade, vanilla, soy bean sauce, tobasco sauce, ketchup and arnica. Over this add a layer of chopped nuts, assorted nuts, of course, a few bay leaves (whole), some marjoram, and a stick of licorice cut into fine pieces. Put the loaf in the oven for ten minutes and serve. It it is still lacking in taste whip up a chili con carne piping hot and mix bread well with it until it becomes a thick gruel. If this fails, piss on it and throw it to the dog. But under no circumstances feed it to the birds. The birds of North America are already on the decline, as I pointed out earlier. Their beaks have become dull, their wingspan shortened; they are pining and drooping, moulting in season and out. Above all, they no longer sing as they used to; they make sour notes, they bleat instead of tweeting, and sometimes, when the fogs set in, they have been heard to cackle and wheeze.

For Discussion

1. What specific qualities in American bread are characteristic of American society? Look at the adjectives chosen to describe the bread.
2. Analyze Miller's palate. What specific American foods does he hate? What evidence can you cite that American taste is moving farther from —or nearer to—his liking?
3. What does Hollywood bread symbolize? Hollywood funeral? Photographic bread?
4. Look at the digressions on foreign ghettos, Greek restaurants, and ordinary American restaurants. What does each contribute?
5. What purpose do the numerous references to machines serve?
6. In what ways is this essay dated? In what ways not?
7. Find examples of hyperbole and invective. Look at the sections charting the sequence of bread leading to famine.
8. Sarcasm is a kind of irony. Find examples which illustrate Miller's mastery of this art. (Also see Mencken.)
9. Look up the word *paean*. How does this essay qualify as a paean?
10. What relationship does Miller establish with the reader? How does he do it?
11. Miller's attitude toward his subject becomes more apparent when portions of the essay are read aloud. Listen to the last paragraph. What is its tone, and how is it consistent with that of the whole essay?

LENNY BRUCE

Pills and Shit: The Drug Scene

In his short life—1926 to 1966—Long Island born nightclub entertainer Lenny Bruce became a legend. He is considered by many to be the most passionate and active advocate of free speech in our time, for which he was constantly harrassed by police wherever he entertained audiences with personal monologues expressing defiance of various taboos—objectionable language, sex, dope, and politics. His tragic life, full of unhappiness and turmoil, ended in a hotel bathroom where he was found dead from an overdose of drugs (his friend Jerry Tallmer said "an overdose of police"). Critic Ralph J. Gleason has called him "one of the most brilliant social satirists [with] a moral conscience second to none." An account of Bruce's life and difficulties with the courts and police can be found in his autobiography, *How to Talk Dirty and Influence People*. The selection which follows is a verbatim transcript of one of his nightclub routines.

Oh! I got busted since I've seen you. I'm going to lay that on you first. I got two arrests. One: illegal use and possession of dangerous drugs—which is a lie. They're *not*, they're *friendly*.

Lemme get serious with that for a moment. That's how weird I am: I could never discuss or support anything I'm involved with.

I don't smoke pot at all. I don't dig the high. The reason I don't smoke shit is that it's a hallucinatory high, and I've got enough shit going around in my head; and second, it's a *schlafedicker*[1] high, and I like being *with* you all the time. So therefore I can talk about pot, and champion it.

Marijuana is rejected all over the world. Damned. In England heroin is all right for out-patients, but marijuana? They'll put your ass in jail.

Reprinted by permission of Douglas International and the Lenny Bruce Estate.

[1] Sleepy, low, drowzy, sluggish. Yiddish words and expressions are often impossible to translate, but the footnotes provided will give the reader a working approximation of their meanings as Bruce uses them in context. [Ed.]

I wonder why that is? The only thing I can think of is DeQuincy—the fact that opium is smoked and marijuana is smoked, and there must be some correlation there. Because it's not a deterrent. In all the codes you'll always see, "Blah-blah-blah with all the narcotics *except* marijuana." So the legislature *doesn't* consider it a narcotic. Who does?

Well, first: I think that there's no *justification* for smoking shit. Alcohol? Alcohol has a medicinal justification. You can drink rock-and-rye for a cold, pernod for getting it up when you can't get it up, blackberry brandy for cramps, and gin for coming around if she didn't come around.

But marijuana? The only reason could be: *To Serve The Devil—Pleasure!* Pleasure, which is a dirty word in a Christian culture. Pleasure is Satan's word.

> CONDEMNING VOICE: What are you doing! You're *enjoying* yourself? Sitting on the couch smoking shit and *enjoying* yourself? When your mother has *bursitis!* And all those people in China are suffering, too.
> GUILTY VOICE: I'm enjoying it a *little* bit, but it's bad shit, anyway. And I got a headache and I'm eating again from it.

If we were to give Man A three glasses of whiskey a day, and Man B were to smoke the necessary amount of marijuana to produce a euphoria like that the alcohol brings, and we do this now for ten years straight, stop them cold one day—Pow!

The guy who juiced will suffer some absence syndromes—he'll need a taste, physically need a taste. The guy that smoked the pot will suffer no discomfort. He is not addicted. Healthwise, the guy who juiced is a little screwed up; and the pot smoker may have a little bronchitis. Maybe.

Since marijuana is not a deterrent, no more than cigarettes, it seems inhumane that they *schlep*[2] people and put them in jail with it.

> "Well, maybe marijuana's not *bad* for you, but it's a stepping stone. It leads to heavier drugs—heroin, etc."

Well, that syllogism has to work out this way, though: The heroin addict, the bust-out junkie that started out smoking pot, says to his cell-mate:

> "I'm a bust-out junkie. Started out smoking pot, look at me now. By the way, cell-mate, what happened to you? There's blood on your hands. How'd you get to murder those kids in that crap game? Where did it all start?"
> "Started with bingo in the Catholic Church."
> "I see."

[2] Drag or move.

Now lemme tell you something about pot. Pot will be legal in ten years. Why? Because in this audience probably every other one of you knows a law student who smokes pot, who will become a senator, who will legalize it to protect himself.

But then no one will smoke it any more. You'll see.

Do me a favor. I don't want to take a bust. The code reads that *I* talk, *you* smoke, *I* get busted. So don't smoke—drop a few pills, but don't smoke.

Did you see the *Post* reviews? It said that

"His regulars consist of mainlining musicians, call girls and their business managers."

Isn't that a little bit libelous?

I know that Californians are very concerned with the modern. Seven years ago there was a narcotics problem in New York, fifteen years ago in Los Angeles. Now in L.A. it's been like this:

They have a rehabilitation center, and they got this group to attack these narcotic drug addicts. Now, this group is attacking, and getting good at attacking. They mobilize. They get good at it, and better and better and better. First they learn the orthodox way to attack. Then, by hanging out with these deterrents, these felons, they learn *un*orthodox ways. They become bitchy-good attackers—unorthodox, orthodox—and they're wailing their ass off.

Suddenly:

CALIFORNIA LOSING ITS WAR

AGAINST DRUG ADDICTS

There are eighteen hundred empty beds at the rehabilitation center.

"*Schmuck,*[3] you're winning!"
"No, we're *losing*. We gotta fill up the beds!"
"You didn't make one win? In fifteen years?"
"No. We're losing, we're losing!"

Well, I assume there's only one junkie left.

Narcotics? Now they've finished with heroin—I think in 1951 there were probably about fifty narcotic officers and seven thousand dope fiends in this state. Today, probably, there are about fifteen thousand narcotics officers

[3] A jerk, a stupid or dull person.

and four dope fiends. Fifteen thousand Nalline testing stations, loop-o meters, and they got four dopey junkies left, old-time 1945 hippies.

O.K. One guy works for the county, undercover; the other guy works for the federal heat. O.K. So, finally, finally they went on strike:

> JUNKIE: Look, we don*wanna* use dope any more. We're *tired!*
> AGENT: Come on, now, we're just after the guys who sell it.
> JUNKIE: *Schnook,*[4] don'tya remembuh me? Ya arrested me last week.
> I'm the undercover guy for the federals.

It's like Sambo, running around the tree. *He* works for the federals, *he* works for the county.

> AGENT: Look, we're after the guys who sold it to you. O.K.?
> JUNKIE: But *nobody* sold it to me. I bought it from *him,* I told you
> that. . . .
> AGENT: Well, will ya just point out one of the guys?
> JUNKIE: Don't you *know* him? There's four of us! I told ya that.
> AGENT: Just tell us the names of the guys. Cooperate now. Tell us
> everybody.
> JUNKIE: [*gives up*]: O.K. He was a Puerto Rican. Drove a green
> Buick. Hangs out in Forster's.
> AGENT: We'll wait for him.
> JUNKIE: O.K.
> Three days with the investigation:
> AGENT: Is that him?
> JUNKIE: No, I think it's, hm, ah, I think he was Hawaiian, anyway.
> AGENT: O.K. Don't forget. If you hear from him—
> JUNKIE: O.K. I'll call ya the first thing.
> AGENT: O.K.

So now they've finished up that nonsense, and the guy says:

> "You mean to tell me that you guys are gonna screw up our rehabilitation
> program? If *you're* not using any dope, you certainly *know* some people that
> need help."
> JUNKIE: We don't know anybody. We don't know *anybody. Please.*
> *I can't use any more dope.* I don't *like* it any more.
> AGENT: Well, you really are selfish. You don't care about anybody
> but yourself. Do you know we have a center to rehabilitate people with
> fifteen hundred empty beds?
> JUNKIE: I know, I'm shitty that way. I'll try.

---

[4] A well-meaning jerk.

I loved that when he got arrested. He was a dope fiend—Bela Lugosi. It was the worst advertisement for rehabilitation: he was a dope fiend for seven years; he cleaned up; and dropped dead.

There're no more narcotic drug addicts, so we're moving now to dangerous drugs. Dangerous drugs—no opiates, nothing to send you to that lethal mania, but the mood elevators, the amphetamines.

The big connections of the dangerous drugs are Squibb and Park-Lilly, Olin Mathison and Merc and Wyeth. Do they know that? Does the legislature know that? I wonder why they're not apprised of that situation. Dangerous drugs—that's the legal phrase—relates to all these medications that are mood elevators, not made for sores or boils. They are made not in Guatemala, but in factories and for a purpose.

Then I said, "These senators, they come from the South. Southerners don't take pills. Nor do Southern doctors prescribe pills." I'll bet you that when all those people were dying of spinal meningitis at Moffet Field—and heretofore sulpha drugs had worked—you wondered what happened. Guys are dying there:

"They're spitting out the pills!"
"They're *what*? Whatsa matter with you guys?
You're *dying* and you're spitting out the sulpha drugs!"
"Look. I'm a Lockheed worker, and I read all about it in the *Herald Express,* about those dangerous drugs. I'm not filling my body fulla those poisons! I got spinal meningitis, I'll get rid of it the natural way—take an enema. I'll sweat and I'll run around. Not gonna take none of that horse-shit."

O. K. Now, dangerous drugs. Now, the insanity in that area is that the reason that heroin is *verboten* is that it's no good for people. It destroys the ego, and the only reason we get anything done in this country is that you want to be proud of it and build up to the neighbors. And if the opiate *schleps* all that away, then the guy goes up to the guy who builds a new building and he'll say,

DETACHED HIPPY VOICE: Hey, that's cool.

And that's it. So it's no good. And that's why it's out.

You know what I'd like to investigate? Zig-zag cigarette paper. Yeah. Bring the company up:

DEEP AGGRESSIVE VOICE: Now we have this report, Mr. Zig-zag . . .

Certainly it must have seemed unusual to you, that Zig-zag papers have been in business for sixteen years, and Bugler tobacco has been out of business for five years! . . .

This committee comes to the conclusion . . . that the people are using your Zig-zag cigarette papers, to . . . roll marijuana tobacco in it."

"Oh, shit."

"That's right. Lots of it—rolling it and smoking it."

Dig. The beautiful part about it is that so many neighborhood grocery stores have been kept in business for years—the *schmucks* don't know that, right?

> YOUNG VOICE [*trying to sound nonchalant*]: O.K. I'll have Delsey toilet tissues, and, ah, another six cans of soup, and a broom, and, ah . . . some cigarette papers.
>
> OLD JEWISH VOICE: I dunno, ve stay in business so long, it's terrific. All the markets—but ve screw em, we chahge top prices, and the people come in here anyway. They *like* me.

O.K. where does this go on? At a place called Alfie's. Alfy's. Open 24 Hours. Cigarettes, cigars, old Jewish man behind the counter:

> YOUNG WISE GUY: Pa?
>
> ANCIENT JEW: Yuh?
>
> WISE GUY: Pa, do you sell many cigarette papers here?
>
> OLD JEW: Uh.
>
> WISE GUY: What do you assume that people are doing with the cigarette papers they're buying?
>
> OLD JEW: De're rollink cigarettes.
>
> WISE GUY: They're rolling cigarettes? In these flamboyant times you assume people are *rolling* cigarettes?
>
> OLD JEW: Uhhh, so vut are you doink mit cigarette papuhs?
>
> WISE GUY: You don't know?
>
> OLD JEW: No.
>
> WISE GUY: They're rolling *pot!*
>
> OLD JEW: Vus?
>
> WISE GUY: Pot.
>
> OLD JEW: *Vus machts du* pop?[5]
>
> WISE GUY: Marijuana, *schmuck!*
>
> OLD JEW: Marijuana? Hey! Uh, agh, *vus?* Hey—

Always talking to some *schmuck* in the back who's not there.

> —you heard dot? Marijuana. All dese years I never knew dot. Marijuana.

---

[5] "Are you making *pop?*"

Sig-sag papuhs, marijuana, roll the marijuana, *meschugenah*,[6] marijuana.

Next night an eighty-year-old pensioner walks to the stand:

> OLD PENSIONER: "Hullo? Hullo? Solly, in the bek? Hullo? Dingaling-alingalinga?"
> OLD JEW: Hullo.
> PENSIONER: Listen, gimme a peckege Bugler's and some Sig-sag papuhs.
> OLD JEW: *Vus?* Sig-sag papuhs? Justa momunt . . . . [*Aside*] Hullo, policeman? Is gecamein a junkie![7]

All right. The kid, six years old, played by George McCready:

> "Well, let's see now. I'm all alone in my room, and it's Saturday, and Mother's off in Sausalita freaking off with Juanita, so I'll make an airplane. Yes. What'll I do . . . I'll make, ah, an Me-110, that's a good structure. I'll get the balsa wood . . . cut it out there . . . there we go . . . rub it up . . . Now, I'll get a little airplane glue, rub it on the rug, and, uh, uh, . . . hmmmmmm, I'm getting loaded! . . . Is this possible? Loaded on airplane glue? Maybe it's stuffy in here. I'll call my dog over.
> "Felika! Felika, come here, darling, and smell this rag. Smell it! You freaky little doggy . . . smell the rag Felika . . . Felika! Felika! IT WORKED! I'M THE LOUIS PASTEUR OF JUNKIEDOM! I'm out of my skull for a dime!
> "Well, there's much work to be done now . . . horse's hooves to melt down, noses to get ready . . ."

CUT TO, the toy store. The owner, Albert Wasserman. The kid walks in:

> *tinglelingleling!*
> KID [*affected innocent voice*]: Hello Mr. Shindler. It's a lovely store you've got here . . . Ah, why don't you let me have a nickel's worth of pencils, and a big boy tablet, hm? A Big-Little Book? Some nail polish remover, and, ah, [*voice changes to a driven madness*] *two thousand tubes of airplane glue!*
> OWNER [*old Jew*]: Dot's very unusual! Ve haff nefer sold so much airplane glue before. I'm an old man—don't bring no heat on the place! And save me a taste, you know? I vouldn't burn you for no bread, you know?

---

[6] A daft, screwy, or nutty person.

[7] Roughly interpreted, this sentence would read: "I have a junkie here!" or "A junkie has come in!"

Cut to Paul Cotes, Confidential File:

"This is Paul Cotes, Confidential File, and next to me, ladies and gentlemen of the viewing audience on television, is a young boy who's been sniffing airplane glue. Could be your kid, anybody's kid, whose life has been destroyed by the glue. I hope you can sleep tonight, Mr. LePage. Pretty rotten, a young kid like this. What's your name, sonny?"

"I'm Sharkey, from Palo Alto."

"Well, it's obvious that Sharkey feels a lot of hostility for the adult world. Sharkey, how did it all start, kid? How did you start on this road to ruin? With airplane glue."

"Well, I foist started chippying round wit small stuff—like smellin' sneakuhs, doity lawndry, Mallowmar boxes . . ."

"A little Krafft-Ebbing in there . . . That's very interesting, Sharkey. You've been sniffing it for six months?"

"At's right."

"Are you hooked?"

"No. I'm stuck."

This *schmuck* here was hooked on morphine suppositories. Like that? Honest to God. If heroin is a monkey on the back, what's a morphine suppository?

When I was in England all these faggots were strung out on sleeping pill suppositories. *Emmis.*[8] So I says to this cat, I says, "Do they really make you sleep, man?"

He says, "Are you kidding? Before you get your *finger* outta your *athth* you're *athleep,* Mary."

That's a beautiful ad:

BEFORE YOU GET YOUR FINGER OUT OF YOUR ASS—
YOU'RE ASLEEP!
NEBYALTAL

"What is *that?* What did he need *that* for?"

"He's *weird,* that's all. He's on it, that's all. He's on it."

"How can you tell?"

"You can tell when they're on it. He's standing on it right now. He *has* to have it. They gotta have it. They kill their mothers for it in the mornings. They get the strength of a madman."

How does he take it?

[*Deep bass voice, with pride*] "I take it in the suppository form."

Haha! I got high just before the show:

[*Urgently*] "Get it up there, Phil!"

"O.K."

"Hurry up! Hurry up! Somebody's coming!"

Now the reason why I take it in the suppository form is that I have

[8] An exclamation used for emphasis, like *Really!* or *No kidding!*

found that even with the most literate doctors, it's not the *substance*, it's the *method of administration,* because if this man would take a ton of opiates through a suppository, the imagery is: "If he takes rubicane in the arm, it's monstrous; but the guy takes it in the ass—what can it be? The *tuchus* . . ."[9]

This is a benzedrex inhaler. I know the inventor, who invented amphetamine sulphate, which was originally used for just shrinking the mucus membrane, you know, the air passage, but some fellows found out that you could crush these benzedrine inhalers and—you've done it—and put them in coca-colas, and it would become a cerebral depressant. So, somehow they took out the benzedrine and put in benzedrex.

The old thing—one guy ruined it for the rest.

Now, if you notice, it has a date when it's exhausted. Your nose? No. The inhaler. Smith, Klein and French.

Now it's sort of weird, you know. I put this, and you know, sniff it up there. But it's about a year old, and it's probably exhausted; so I don't know if I just did that, or sticking things in my nose, you know? Or maybe I'm just hooked on smelling my pocket!

Actually, it is lewd? That goes back to taste. You know that it's just not good taste to blow your nose in public or put one of these in your nose in public. And I've never done it in front of anybody. But I just feel like I wanna do it tonight.

For the first time, being recorded on tape, a man sticking a Smith Klein French inhaler in his nose!

"Ladies and gentlemen, we're here at Fax No. Two. A hush is going over the crowd. He's reaching in his pocket. His neck is tightening. Some ladies sitting ringside, traumatically, are sweating. He's taking it out, giggling nervously. Will he stick it up there? Nervous laughs emit from the crowd. He's a degenerate. Two D.A.R. women are throwing up. There go the people from the Mystery Bus Tour."

'We want our $5.75 back!'

"There he goes, folks, he's sniffing!

'Hi, Howard, hi! Zowie! We're really high now, Howard. We certainly are. We've solved the world's problems.' "

And you're only twelve months old, you little bugger!

Exploitation Films present: I WAS A TEEN-AGE REEFER-SMOKING PREGNANT YORTSITE CANDLE. With Sal Mineo and Natalie Wood. See Sal Mineo as the trigger-happy Arty, the kid who knew but one thing— how to *love*, how to *kill!* And see Fatlay Good as Theresa, the girl who knew the other thing, tenderness, and love. And see Lyle Talbot as Gramps, who

[9] The behind, the buttocks.

liked to watch. A picture with a message, and an original Hollywood theme—narcotics.

The film opens as we find Nunzio locked in the bathroom with the stuff, the *baccala*, the marijuana. Cut to the exterior—Youngstown kitchen, there's the wife, you know, the factory-worker wife, the whole bit. He comes home,

> WIFE [*delighted*]: Put me down, you big nut! Oh, tee hee . . .

That scene, you know? Looking at her,

> HUSBAND [*tenderly*]: Where's our son, where's Ralph?
> WIFE [*concerned*]:He's in the bathroom again. And I dunno whatsa-matter with him. He's nervous and listless, and he's not bothering with any of his friends, and he's falling off in his studies . . .
> HUSBAND: In the bathroom again, eh? Tsk Tsk. Hmmm. . . . [*knocks on the door*] Ralph? What are you doing in there?
> RALPH [*sucking in a big drag, then trying to hold it in as he answers*]: Usta minud, I beyout in a minud.
> WIFE: He's got asthma.
> HUSBAND: Will you stop with that, you nitwit! He's on the stuff!

O.K. Suddenly we hear a knock at the door, a whistle; and he takes the marijuana, throws it in the toilet, rushes to the door—there's no one there! He's thrown it away! It's *gone*, it's *too late!* Beads of perspiration are break-ing out on his forehead.

> RALPH: It's gone! There's only one thing left to do—*smoke the toilet!*

For Discussion

1. Throughout history satirists have ridiculed men's follies and hypocrisies. What universal human foibles does Bruce satirize?
2. What do you think of Bruce's stated reason for not smoking pot? Is it inconsistent with his defense of marijuana? What might be his opinion of LSD? (Also see Fort.)
3. What common arguments against marijuana does Bruce satirize?
4. How does Bruce relate drugs to pleasure? To ego?
5. What is Bruce's concept of lewd behavior? What is yours?
6. Examine the logic in
   a) the case of the crap game murderer
   b) the rehabilitation center fantasy
   c) the use of drugs in treating illness.

7. What things does Bruce satirize in the fantasies involving
    a) the old Jew, the wise guy, and the old pensioner?
    b) the agent and the junkie?
8. What does Bruce's language tell you about his background? His attitude toward social convention? How might hearing this piece in its original setting—a nightclub—affect your reaction to it?
9. Bruce was continually harassed for his use of objectionable subject matter and language, eventually to the point where no nightclub would hire him. What arguments can you give in Bruce's defense?
10. Compare the attitudes of Lennie Bruce, Henry Miller, and D. H. Lawrence toward pleasure.

DICK GREGORY

America Is My Momma

Dick Gregory, born in 1932, one of the first black satirists, has entertained in night clubs, on television and radio; has lectured to college audiences; and has campaigned for the Presidency of the United States as a peace candidate. Gregory's social satire is available on recordings as well as in his books, which include *From the Back of the Bus, Nigger, What's Happening?, Write Me In!,* and *The Shadow That Scares Me,* from which the following selection is taken.

> And the tongue is a fire. . . . With it we bless the Lord and Father, and with it we curse men, who are made in the likeness of God. From the same mouth come blessing and cursing. My brethren, this ought not to be so.
>
> James 3:6, 9–10

The Apostle James describes well what I have experienced in the church all my life. The tongue, the words we say or sing and do not mean, and the verses of scripture we interpret to fit our own prejudices, stains the whole body and sets on fire the cycle of nature. The same words are used to praise God and to curse men; to justify evil and to condemn it.

A popular song in the church is "The Battle Hymn of the Republic." Really listen to the words of that song and you will realize that very few people have the right to sing it. The day a person does decide to sing it should be the last day of his life. That is what the words of the song imply: "As He died to make men holy, let us die to make men free." If the Enforcer swept through the church today and said, "Put up or shut up," I only know about five folks who could sing that song and mean it. And three of them are already dead.

"As He died to make men holy, let us die to make men free." We do just the reverse. We will try to *kill* to make men free. But the song doesn't say that. It says, "Let us *die* to make men free." This refusal to live by our words makes a laughingstock out of the church, Good Friday, and Easter. Another song which amuses me is "Onward, Christian Soldiers." Church folks seem to think a Christian soldier is a Marine who prays. When you sing, "Onward, Christian Soldiers," you are not *really* talking about a man who will follow the cause of right to his death.

The church today has become a sick comedy. I tell my own kids to go to church only as a form of entertainment. The church is in such sad condition today that I cannot justify their attendance for any other reason. If my momma had told me that the church was a form of entertainment, I could have understood those old sisters sitting in the front pew of my church looking so evil. We never had a picture of the Devil in my house; only pictures of Jesus. But if we had a picture of the Devil, I'm sure it would have looked like one of those front pew sisters.

take a prostitute to church

The church is supposed to be so pure, much more pure than the nightclub. Yet I can take a prostitute to the nightclub with me and nobody will automatically assume I have been sleeping with her. It isn't strange to see a prostitute in a nightclub and she is welcome. My wife can walk into the nightclub with a pimp and nobody will assume she has been sleeping with him. But I defy you women to pick up an old wino out of the gutter on your way to church some Sunday and bring him along with you to hear the message of God. When you arrive, just listen to the sisters whisper.

And you men, I defy you to invite the town prostitute some Sunday morning, "Sister, would you like to come with me to church and hear my minister?" If she accepts the invitation, the minute you walk in the front door people will start whispering that you must have been with her all night. This is the church. It doesn't happen in a nightclub, a pool hall or a tavern. It makes me think they put the crosses on the wrong buildings.

why Judas?

When I was a kid, I used to ask my momma why the church accused a Jew of killing Christ. In Sunday school they taught me that all Judas did was *kiss* Christ. I asked "Momma, if you kiss me on the cheek and Daddy takes a gun and pulls the trigger on me, who are they going to get for murder?" Momma answered, "Daddy, of course." That bothered me, because

I could not understand why the Good Book kept accusing the kisser. Why not get that Roman soldier's name; the one with the nails and the hammer. He is the real killer. Just as it is today, nobody ever wants to accuse the man with the gun.

Of course, Momma knew her Bible and she had an explanation. She said, "They didn't know what Jesus looked like and if Judas hadn't kissed him, he couldn't have been arrested. That is why Judas gets blamed for killing Christ." The story I learned in Sunday school did not say that Christ was invisible. He walked out in the open every day. Thousands of people saw him and heard him teach. Two thousand years later we have his picture on the wall and claim to know what he looked like. We don't have pictures of Judas.

So I said to Momma, "Do you mean to tell me that the king and the queen, who own the Army, the Navy, the CIA, and the secret police, were so stupid that they didn't know what the boss looked like but they could recognize his helper?" If you can believe that, you can believe anything. The power structure had enough sense to know that if Jesus had lived he would have hurt them. But they didn't know what he looked like. Even as a child that explanation didn't make sense to me.

When you start twisting the words of the Bible around, the church and the whole world are in trouble. The Christian soldiers are pictured on the front page of the newspaper with their heads bowed worshiping with the chaplain immediately after a good kill. The Christian soldier prays to his God. His buddy on the other side of the firing line called the "enemy," prays to his God. And they are both praying at the same time! Man really puts God on the spot on the front line of the battlefield.

If I was silly enough to go to war, I would give God better treatment than that. I wouldn't take a Bible to battle with me and I wouldn't pray. My last prayer would be just before I shipped out. I would tell God, "Okay, Brother. I am going to do for myself for about four or five years. You'll hear from me when I get back."

When I was a kid, religion made con-men out of everyone in our house. I flatly refused to pray the Lord's Prayer. It just did not make sense to pray to God, "Give us this day our daily bread," when sometimes there was six months' food supply in the pantry. I used to listen to my momma pray. She would start out with the Lord's Prayer. Since everything is really covered in that prayer, she should have stopped while she was ahead. But she would start improvising. She would pray, "Bless the sick and shut-in," which she knew she wasn't going to visit, and then she would start her thirty-minute beg. "Lord, you know the rent is due, the bills have to be paid; and if you will just do *this* for me, let me tell you what I'll do for *you.*"

Hearing a prayer like that used to make me wonder who God is. Momma would always try to work out deals with Him. But at the end of every prayer, Momma would always give God a cop-out: "Lord, let not my will but thine be done." Next week the rent still would be due and Momma would say, "I guess the Lord knew what He was doing." On those church radio services I heard prayers which were even safer. I heard a woman pray, "Lord, thank you for all the good you have done to me and the evil too." That *really* made me wonder who God is. It is a vicious God whom you have to thank for wrong.

I finally came to the conclusion that I couldn't go to school and to church too. At school I would be taught to prove everything to the *n*th degree. When I asked questions in church, looking for proof, the minister would say, "What's wrong with you, boy?" So I decided if I had to go to church, I would make some money at it. Back in the 1940's when I was a kid, my church used to take up a special collection every Sunday for African missionary work. The church didn't even have a back wall in it yet and there was much more work to do on the building, so I knew the money was not going to Africa. I used to sneak back and wipe out that collection every Sunday. It was the only way I could justify spending my time in church when they wouldn't explain things to me.

Joseph and Mary at the Hilton

I never could understand the story of Christmas. People used to weep and wail every year over the fact that "there was no room for Mary in the inn." Every Christmas the innkeeper took a beating in my church for the way he treated poor Mary and Joseph. But Mary was pregnant. Suppose Mary and Joseph came back today and walked into the lobby of the Conrad Hilton and said to the desk clerk, "This is Mary and I am Joseph. We're not married, but let me tell you about this dream we had." You know they would be thrown out immediately. The dream might be legitimate, but you don't tell the desk clerk about it and then get mad because he doesn't believe you. You can't go into a hotel today with a pregnant woman to have a baby. Nor can you check into the hospital just to have a place to sleep. It is just the reverse. You go to the hospital to have the baby and go to the hotel to read the Bible—there is one in every room. The government has taken the Bibles out of the schools, but it left them in the hotel rooms. So maybe the government knows which place is more hip.

My momma could never understand how white folks could twist the words of the Bible around to justify racial segregation. Yet she could read the Ten Commandments, which clearly say, "Thou shalt not kill," and still justify eating meat. Momma couldn't read the newspaper very well, but she sure could interpret the Word of God. "God meant you shouldn't kill people," she used to say. But I insisted, "Momma, he didn't say that. He said, 'Thou shalt not kill.' If you leave that statement alone, a whole lot of things would be safe from killing. But if you are going to twist the words about killing to mean what you want them to mean, then let white folks do the same thing with justifying racial segregation."

"You can't live without eating meat," Momma would persist. "You'd starve." I couldn't buy that either. You get milk from a cow without killing it. You do not have to kill an animal to get what you need from it. You get wool from the sheep without killing it. Two of the strongest animals in the jungle are vegetarians—the elephant and the gorilla. The first two years are the most important years of a man's life, and during that period he is not involved with eating meat. If you suddenly become very ill, there is a good chance you will be taken off a meat diet. So it is a myth that killing is necessary for survival. The day I decide that I must have a piece of steak to nourish my body, I will also give the cow the same right to nourish herself on human beings.

There is so little basic difference between animals and humans. The process of reproduction is the same for chickens, cattle, and humans. If suddenly the air stopped circulating on the earth, or the sun collided with the earth, animals and humans would die alike. A nuclear holocaust will wipe out all life. Life in the created order is basically the same and should be respected as such. It seems to me the Bible says it is wrong to kill—period.

If we can justify *any* kind of killing in the name of religion, the door is opened for all kinds of other justifications. The fact of killing animals is not as frightening as our human tendency to justify it—to kill and not even be aware that we are taking life. It is sobering to realize that when you misuse one of the least of Nature's creatures, like the chicken, you are sowing the seed for misusing the highest of Nature's creatures, man.

if you had to kill your own hog

Animals and humans suffer and die alike. If you had to kill your own hog before you ate it, most likely you would not be able to do it. To hear the hog scream, to see the blood spill, to see the baby being taken away from its momma, and to see the look of death in the animal's eye would turn your stomach. So you get the man at the packing house to do the killing for you. In like manner, if the wealthy aristocrats who are perpetrating conditions in the ghetto actually heard the screams of ghetto suffering, or saw the slow death of hungry little kids, or witnessed the strangulation of manhood and dignity, they could not continue the killing. But the wealthy are protected from such horror. They have people to do the killing for them. The wealthy profit from the daily murders of ghetto life but they do not see them. Those who immerse themselves in the daily life of the ghetto see the suffering—the social workers, the police, the local merchants, and the bill collectors. But the people on top never really see.

By the time you see a piece of meat in the butcher shop window, all of the blood and suffering have been washed away. When you order a steak in the restaurant, the misery has been forgotten and you see the finished product. You see a steak with butter and parsley on it. It looks appetizing and appealing and you are pleased enough to eat it. You never even consider the suffering which produced your meal or the other animals killed that day in the slaughterhouse. In the same way, all the wealthy aristocrats ever see of the black community is the finished product, the window dressing, the steak on the platter—Ralph Bunche and Thurgood Marshall. The United Nations or the Supreme Court bench is the restaurant and the ghetto street corner is the slaughterhouse.

Life under ghetto conditions cuts short life expectancy. The Negro's life expectancy is shorter than the white man's. The oppressor benefits from continued oppression financially; he makes more money so that he can eat a little better. I see no difference between a man killing a chicken and a man killing a human being, by overwork and forcing ghetto conditions upon him, both so that he can eat a little better. If you can justify killing to eat meat, you can justify the conditions of the ghetto. I cannot justify either one.

Every time the white folks made my momma mad, she would grab the Bible and find something bitter in it. She would come home from the rich white folks' house, after they had just called her "nigger," or patted her on the rump or caught her stealing some steaks, open her Bible and read aloud, "It is easier for a camel to pass through the eye of a needle than for a rich man to get into Heaven." When you get involved with distorting the words of the Bible, you don't have to be bitter. The same tongue can be used to bless and curse men.

the Lord knew there would be needles

When Momma used to curse the rich white folks with the judgment against rich men, I used to try to point out the contradictions. "Momma," I would say, "they didn't have needles when the Bible was written." And she would say, "The Lord knew they would one day." Now I thought it was terribly unfair to write something that couldn't possibly be understood for a few thousand years. So I used to prod Momma for more answers. "What about those people at the time of Christ? How were they supposed to understand the Bible?" That just wasn't Momma's immediate problem. "They ain't here now," she would say. Then I would try to explain that the eye of a needle was an arch in the old Arabian cities and when a camel came through, the bigger the load the more the camel would have to stoop to get through. The rich man had more trouble getting through the eye because his load was bigger than the poor man's. But Momma wouldn't listen. She wanted *all* rich men cursed, because of what one rich man had just done to her.

Momma always had the Bible under her arm. If she was flat broke and found a nickel on the street, she would fall on her knees and say, "Thank God!" But on payday, if she found a dollar, she wouldn't even think to thank Him, because finding money didn't mean anything when there was already money in her purse. Even though the Bible clearly says, "Thou shalt not steal," Momma could always justify stealing from the white folks' pantry. She knew her kids were hungry and she used to try to justify her stealing to us. "If I didn't steal, you would starve to death. The white folks aren't paying me enough anyway." It is so easy for people to justify what they want to believe. Sophisticated Negroes today who are embarrassed by the rioting and looting in the ghetto can still justify their grandma raiding the white folks' pantry for survival. The ghetto brother is fighting for survival also. If you can justify one kind of stealing, you can justify any manifestation of theft that suits your particular fancy. But right is right and wrong is wrong.

If the same Negroes who are embarrassed by the rioting and looting in the ghetto picked up the newspaper one morning and read that the First National Bank of Kansas City was held up by five well-dressed, collegiate-looking Negroes pulling off the biggest bank robbery in history, they would not be embarrassed. They would wink at each other that morning at work and talk about how clever those cats were in Kansas City. But a Brooks Brothers suit does not change the complexion of looting. You cannot justify stealing because the thieves were brilliant and looked respectable, any more than you can justify stealing as necessary for survival. "Thou shalt not steal" means that stealing is wrong. The Bible goes further in talking about how man should treat his fellow man. It clearly condemns the conditions of life which cause a man to steal for survival. But stealing itself is still wrong. When the same tongue can bless one man's stealing and curse another man's stealing, all hell breaks loose, to paraphrase the Epistle of James!

illegitimate parents

My momma and my church always taught me that illegitimacy is something wrong. My society tells me that it is something "colored." Society is forever reminding me of the rate of illegitimacy in Negro neighborhoods. Statistically this is true. Negro women in America represent 20 percent of the illegitimacy rate and white women represent 2 percent. But if Negroes could ever get their hands on that white man's abortion credit card, those statistics would change.

But if illegitimacy is wrong and colored, then Christ was colored and a sinner. Because the story in the Good Book clearly shows that He was illegitimate. Either church folks should admit that Christ Himself shared in the wrong or they should stop slandering the ghetto mother. The only way for the current church attitude to be consistent with the Bible is to interpret the Christmas story this way: Illegitimacy is wrong, unless the illegitimate child ends up being the religious boss—the Son of God. You cannot bless one illegitimate birth and curse another one. The Apostle James said, "From the same mouth come blessing and cursing. My brethren, this ought not to be so." He was speaking to both church and society.

In America, we have a habit of cursing the underdog and branding the defenseless. The term "illegitimate child" is a contradiction. All children are the product of the same sexual act. The legitimate result of that sexual act is the birth of a child. The child born out of wedlock is the natural product of an illegitimate sexual act. Yet the statistics speak of "illegitimate children" and not "illegitimate mothers and fathers." We curse the underdog and brand the defenseless.

America's obsession with the Negro crime rate is another example of cursing the underdog and branding the defenseless. Billions of dollars made from dope, gambling, and prostitution are stolen from the greatness of America and all by white men. There are no Negroes in the Cosa Nostra. Just as there are very few Negro cops. At the time of the Watts riot, for example, there were fifty-one hundred cops in Los Angeles. Only 205 were Negro. And there were only four Negro cops in the 77th Precinct which is responsible for law enforcement in the Watts section of Los Angeles. In the history of the Los Angeles Police Department, a Negro had never been graduated above the rank of lieutenant.

When you speak of a Negro crime rate, you are really talking about a "Negro-arrested-by-the-police-and-convicted" rate! Go into any traffic court and you will see twice as many Negroes as whites. When I consider the population proportion, I refuse to believe that Negroes do twenty-eight times more speeding than white folks. America must ask herself the question: what would the white crime rate look like if the overwhelming majority of cops were Black Muslims?

"relief" or "foreign aid"?

America curses the underdog on relief. "Relief" has become a dirty word in this country. An atmosphere has been created where people are ashamed to be on relief. If relief embarrasses or shames America, let it be called foreign aid. America is never embarrassed to send money all over Europe, for health projects and the like, and it is nothing but relief. A white man once asked me about the shame of the increasing number of colored folks on the relief rolls. I asked him, "Do you know any Africans on relief?" He answered, "No." So I said, "Then why didn't you leave us over there?"

I personally feel that all Negroes in this country should be on relief, regardless of their income. Relief is like my coming into your barn and stealing a horse. I put him in my stable. When the stolen horse gets hungry, I have to feed him. I would have to be a fool to come by your house and demand oats. Nor should the horse be expected to feed himself or be embarrassed that he is hungry. When a man decides to steal, he must accept the consequences of his theft. Relief is America paying her just dues for theft. It is the theft which is shameful, not the dues. I am tired of America balancing her wrongs by cursing my natural rights.

The irony is that the "curse" is really the "blessing." Having been on relief for twenty years, I have a personal resentment against it and wish that relief would be eliminated. Five minutes after my momma received her relief check, it was in the hands of that Right Wing bigot. He owned the business where Momma spent her money. Some seventeen million dollars a month is spent on relief in the state of Illinois. Though white folks curse relief, in all honesty the State of Illinois has to bless it. If relief were terminated, in ten months' time it would cost the State of Illinois $170 million. Knock that kind of revenue out of a state's economy and it is doomed.

when the state kills

We speak of separation of church and state. I personally believe that the state has completely taken over the church. Even if you accept my momma's interpretation of "Thou shalt not kill" as covering only *human* life, the church is a long way from converting the state. The state is still allowed to kill the man who has killed. We still allow capital punishment in America. But two wrongs do not make a right. Have you ever stopped to consider who leads the condemned man to the killer? The minister or the priest! The state has completely taken over the church and uses it as a moment of final comfort for those whom the state would kill. I have often wondered what the clergyman says to the condemned man at the last moment before the execution. "Is there anything more I can do for you, son?" I would tell him, "Yes, Father. Stand here next to the electric chair and hold my hand." My Baptist preacher was always putting his foot in his mouth. I can just hear him saying to the condemned man as they are strapping him into the electric chair, "Well, son, this is as far as I go. I really don't know what to say, but more power to you."

Capital punishment is a disgrace. For the church to allow it to continue is an even greater disgrace. It is wrong for the church to tell me I should not kill and still be unwilling to make the same demand of the state. The greatest contradiction of all is for the clergyman to be present at the hour of the state's vengeance. If that same clergyman would go all the way and jump into the electric chair just once, it would end capital punishment immediately. Such an act would be a "sit-in" to end killing.

One of the most sacred acts of a Christian society is the act of marriage. Yet it is possible to bypass the church completely and get married by city hall. If you do go to the church to get married, you had better get things straight with city hall first.

A friend of mine was getting married and I was to be the best man. When we got to city hall, the old Justice of the Peace was sitting in his office surrounded by all those soldiers with their pregnant girls. And he was tired of it all. When my friend, his bride, and I walked into the office, the Justice never even looked up. He just mumbled his formalities and ended up with, "I now pronounce you man and wife." Then he looked up for the first time and told *me* to kiss the bride. That is how sacred marriage is in society today.

I cannot help but question how anything as sacred as marriage can depend upon the payment of a ten-dollar fee. If you went to city hall, got married, kissed your bride, and then told the Justice, "I'm not paying you," he probably would say, "Then it doesn't count." And you would not be married. Marriage has become that automatic and commercial and yet people wonder about the breakdown of the family.

President Johnson, backed by the statistics and findings of the Moynihan Report, has said that a breakdown of the family is responsible for the plight of the Negro in America. He is absolutely correct. America is my momma. And my momma was America to me. Since the United States Constitution is the farthest thing from the Negro in America, it is the last thing to be blamed for his plight. State, city, and county governments are closer, but they are still distant. My momma, as head of the family, was the only authority my America allowed me to touch. When my momma stole food from white folks, and justified it as necessary for survival, I did not blame the system. I did not blame a country where the black man is denied his constitutional rights; where Momma was stripped of her womanhood and Daddy of his manhood. I blamed Momma for stealing.

We got on the bus or streetcar and Momma always put my age back. The only thing a poor ghetto kid has is his God-given birthday. I was robbed of that. As Momma was robbed of her womanhood and Daddy of his manhood, I was robbed of my childhood. As a child, I didn't blame the system; I blamed Momma.

America was momma's momma

Now that I am a man, I have "given up childish ways." I realize that America is my momma and America was Momma's momma. And I am going to place the blame for injustice and wrong on the right momma. Even today, when I leave my country to appear on television and make other public appearances in foreign countries, I find it difficult to speak of the injustices I experience in this country. Because America is my momma. Even if Momma is a whore, she is still Momma. Many times I am asked if I would go to war if drafted. I always answer, "Yes, under one condition; that I be allowed to go to the front line without a gun. Momma is worth dying for, but there is nothing worth killing for. And if I ever change my opinion about killing, I will go to Mississippi and kill that sheriff who spit in my wife's face."

America is my momma. One Fourth of July, I want to go to the New York harbor and talk to Momma—the Statue of Liberty. I want to snatch that torch out of her hand and take her with me to the ghetto and sit her down on the street corner. I want to show her the "tired, the poor, the huddled masses yearning to breathe free." I want to show Momma what she has been doing to her children. And Momma should weep. For the grief of the ghetto is the grief of the entire American family.

For Discussion

1. What purpose does the Biblical quotation at the beginning serve?
2. Why does Gregory object to the "Christian soldier"? Would Mark Twain agree? (See "War Prayer" and "Reflections on Religion.")
3. What specific accusations does Gregory level against the church? Is he irreligious?
4. Discuss Gregory's demonstration of the "forked tongue" in regard to
    a) prostitution
    b) theft
    c) illegitimacy
    d) relief
    e) capital punishment
5. What is Gregory's purpose in using recollections of his childhood, particularly of his religious training?
6. Gregory's objections to killing are developed in several ways. Discuss these objections and comment on the strength of his arguments.

7. How valid are the analogies of the ghetto owner to the meat eater and the welfare recipient to the stolen horse?
8. Identify and discuss each of the "momma's" Gregory develops.
9. Gregory's use of contradictions and pairings of opposites reveal his ironic voice, which for the most part is humorous. How does his tone change in the final section?
10. Discuss Gregory's use of colloquialism in his paraphrasing of Biblical stories.

ARTHUR HOPPE

The Perfect Solution
to Absolutely Everything

Arthur Hoppe of the San Francisco *Chronicle* writes a daily
column which is syndicated throughout the United States. In
addition, he is the author of two collections of political satire,
The I Love Everybody* Crusade and *The Perfect Solution to
Absolutely Everything*, from which the following excerpts are
taken.

our sacred commitments

The Middle East Crisis has stimulated some public interest in our Sacred
Commitments. Many informed citizens were mildly surprised to learn that
several of our Presidents, including the incumbent, had made Sacred Commitments to defend not only the territorial integrity of Israel, but also that
of Egypt, Jordan, Syria, Lebanon and other nations. Like Vietnam, Laos,
Thailand . . . .

So, in order to clarify any lingering confusion in the public mind, I
dropped over to the National Archives of Sacred Commitments in the
basement of the Washington Monument for a chat with its curator, Dr.
Homer T. Pettibone, D.V.M. I found Dr. Pettibone happily surrounded by
stacks upon stacks of Sacred Commitments of all shapes, sizes and degrees
of yellowed age. I said I was surprised to find that the Archives contained
more than one kind of Sacred Commitment.

"Oh, they come in hundreds of different varieties," said Dr. Pettibone
polishing his pince-nez. "But we file them under three general headings:
Very Sacred Commitments, Plain Old Sacred Commitments, and Casual
Sacred Commitments."

Could he explain the difference?

From *The Perfect Solution to Absolutely Everything* by Arthur Hoppe. Copyright ©
1968 by Arthur Hoppe. Reprinted by permission of Doubleday & Company, Inc.

"Surely," he said, reverently drawing forth an impressive one labeled "NATO Agreement."

"Now here is a Very Sacred Commitment. As you can see, our President pledges us to go to war in behalf of a whole passel of countries in Western Europe. Naturally, under our Constitution, this treaty had to be ratified by the Senate after long and solemn debate over the wisdom of making such a grave promise."

"Naturally," I said. And what did a Plain Old Commitment look like?

"Well, here's one," he said, pulling out a letter addressed, "To the Premier of Vietnam Whom It May Concern."

"As you can see, a Plain Old Commitment is a letter or public statement made by a President to go to war for somebody if asked."

But if both kinds pledged the Nation to go to war, what was the difference?

"I thought I explained that," said Dr. Pettibone irritably. "The first kind is ratified by the Senate."

"Now here," he continued, flicking on a tape recorder, "is a Casual Sacred Commitment."

A familiar voice said, "And if there's anything we can ever do for you, you just ask."

"Now, let's see," said Dr. Pettibone, frowning, "did he say that to the Ambassador for Upper Volta at a garden party or the Foreign Minister of Outer Mongolia over root beer? We really should know so that we don't go to war with the wrong country."

"My," I said, "we certainly had a lot of Sacred Commitments."

"Oh, we have Sacred Commitments," said Dr. Pettibone with a true curator's pride, "with countries you never heard of."

And would we honor them all?

"Like any great nation with its honor at stake, we stand ready when the time comes to keep sacred each and every one of our Sacred Commitments," said Dr. Pettibone with dignity, "that we can't get out of."

some missiles are inscrutable

The news that we are probably going to build an Anti-Chinese Ballistic Missile system (A-CBM) has caused some questions to arise in the public mind, such as: "What the hell's an Anti-Chinese Ballistic Missile?"

This is a good question. The answer, of course, is that an Anti-Chinese Ballistic Missile is not an Anti-Russian Ballistic Missile. And we hope that everyone, particularly the Russians, will understand this clearly drawn distinction. This is crucial because the Secretary of Defense doesn't want to build an expensive Anti-Russian Ballistic Missile system. The Russians, he says, would simply build more Russian Ballistic Missiles, then we'd have to build more antis, which would make them build more. . . . And who knows where it would all end? We do, don't we?

So this firm stand makes sense. Unfortunately, we have a lot of generals and such who are just crazy to have an Anti-Ballistic Missile system of some sort for their very own—never having had one before. So the Secretary kind of sighs and says, well, then, let's build a cheap, shoddy, little system fit only to shoot down cheap, shoddy Chinese missiles. After all, the Chinese are already building missiles as fast as they can anyway.

But the Russians! Right away they get suspicious and say, "How do we know your Anti-Chinese Ballistic Missiles won't shoot down our missiles, too?"

Obviously, we must convince the Russians their missiles will be safe in making an attack on us. The only conceivable solution is to encourage Russian spies to slip stealthily into our Anti-Chinese Ballistic Missile factories and steal the plans for the extraordinary sensory equipment these missiles will employ to distinguish a wily, inscrutable Chinese missile from a husky, stolid Russian one. This should reassure the Russians that their missiles have nothing to fear from us. Indeed, it could well lead to the dawn of a new day of mutual trust:

"There're three hundred thermonuclear missiles passing overhead, sir," says the Corporal on the Distant Early Warning Line, his finger poised nervously over the Anti-Chinese Ballistic Missile button. "Are you sure they're Chinese? They all look alike to me."

"Hold your fire, son," says the Captain, peering through his binoculars. "They're only Russian friendlies heading for New York."

Some problems remain to be solved, however. What if the devious Chinese start building Russian missiles to penetrate our defense system. And if we build Anti-Russian Ballistic Missiles to counter this threat, what if the Russians should counter-counter with a buildup of Afghanistanian missiles? It's a well-known top secret that we don't have a single Anti-Afghanistanian Ballistic Missile even on the drawing board. Then, if we counter-counter-counter by speeding production of Anti-Afghanis . . . .

But let's not get mired down in petty details. After all, in any logical discussion of the inexorable steps inherent in the strategy of nuclear deterrence, we instinctively know where we're all going to wind up. Don't we?

thou shalt not

(SCENE: The summit of Mt. Sinai.

TIME: The present. Moses, holding two stone tablets in his hand, enters nervously.)

MOSES: Sorry to bother you again, Sir. But I'm afraid we need another revision in the original copy.

THE LORD (WITH A SIGH): Another? What now?

MOSES: Well, Sir, it's where You say here, "Thou shall not kill."

THE LORD: That seems perfectly clear and concise.

MOSES: But it's causing an awful haggle among Your theologians, Sir. The Catholics feel it applies to spermatozoa and ova; the Conservatives, only after the union of the two; the Moderates would reserve it for twenty-week-old embryos and up; and the Liberals feel it takes effect precisely at the moment of birth.

THE LORD (puzzled): But why would anyone want to kill an unborn child?

MOSES: Primarily, Sir, on the chance it might emerge deformed.

THE LORD: In that case, why don't they wait to see whether it does before they kill it?

MOSES: Oh, all theologians oppose killing children after they're born. Except, of course, at a distance of more than 500 yards.

THE LORD: Why 500 yards?

MOSES: In wartime, Sir, it is a terrible thing to kill a child with a rifle bullet and an atrocity to do so with a bayonet. But all recognized theologians agree that it is permissible, if regrettable, to blow them up with high explosives or incinerate them with jellied gasoline, as long as it is dropped from an airplane or fired from an artillery piece—particularly, the Christians feel, if you do so to save them from Godless Communism.

THE LORD: I suppose it does do that.

MOSES: Of course, once a male child reaches the age of eighteen he may be killed in virtually any fashion on the battlefield except with poison gas. The use of poison gas in war, all theologians agree, is the greatest atrocity.

THE LORD: Then where do they use it?

MOSES: Only in state-operated gas chambers. It is used there, with the approval of theologians, because it is the most humane way to kill people.

THE LORD: But if it's the most humane. . . . Never mind. Is that all?

MOSES: I almost overlooked germ warfare. It is also unconscionable to save people from Godless Communism by inflicting them with any fatal sickness—except radiation sickness, which causes a lingering and painful death.

THE LORD (shaking his head): Moses, I don't know what to do.

MOSES (briskly): Well, first off, Sir, I'd suggest setting aside a five-mile stretch of the Pasadena Freeway.

THE LORD: Whatever for?

MOSES: You certainly aren't going to get the necessary revisions on one of these stone tablets, Sir. Now, I've got a rough draft here of an effective compromise that should mollify all factions. It begins: "Thou shall not kill any person between the ages of minus four months (see Appendix) and eighteen years (asterisk) at a distance of less than 500 yards (see Footnote 7a, Chapter Three), with any of the following . . . ."

THE LORD (*in measured tones*): Never mind, Moses. I have a better idea. Gabriel? Gabriel, come here. And bring your trumpet.

For Discussion

1. What is being satirized in each of these pieces?
2. What method does Hoppe use to develop his satire in "Some Missiles are Inscrutable"? What point does the development make?
3. Hoppe uses an ironic *no* in "Thou Shalt Not." Evaluate the force of his *no*.
4. Characterize Dr. Pettibone in "Our Sacred Commitments." How does he contribute to the irony?
5. Where does Hoppe combine the expected and unexpected to achieve irony and humor?
6. How does Hoppe's technique in using situation and character create humor?
7. What makes Hoppe's language particularly effective? Consider his vocabulary in terms of his subject matter.

JERRY FARBER

The Student as Nigger

Presently on the English faculty at San Diego State College,
Jerry Farber has become a familiar name among college students,
principally for the following controversial essay, which was widely
read in underground editions before it was included in a book
of the same title, written by Farber, containing this and other
works. Like Kunen and other younger writers, Farber is a spokesman for a new generation of dissenters from traditional educational philosophy.

Students are niggers. When you get that straight, our schools begin to
make sense. It's more important, though, to understand why they're niggers.
If we follow that question seriously enough, it will lead us past the zone of
academic bullshit, where dedicated teachers pass their knowledge on to a new
generation, and into the nitty-gritty of human needs and hang-ups. And
from there we can go on to consider whether it might ever be possible for
students to come up from slavery.

First let's see what's happening now. Let's look at the role students
play in what we like to call education.

At Cal State L.A. where I teach, the students have separate and unequal
dining facilities. If I take them into the faculty dining room, my colleagues
get uncomfortable, as though there were a bad smell. If I eat in the student
cafeteria, I become known as the educational equivalent of a niggerlover. In
at least one building there are even restrooms which students may not use.
At Cal State, also, there is an unwritten law barring student-faculty love-
making. Fortunately, this anti-miscengenation law, like its Southern counterpart, is not 100 percent effective.

Students at Cal State are politically disenfranchised. They are in an
academic Lowndes County. Most of them can vote in national elections—their
average age is about 26—but they have no voice in the decisions which affect

The story "The Student as Nigger" is reprinted with permission of Contact Books, 6340
Coldwater Canyon Boulevard, North Hollywood, California. The book *The Student as
Nigger* is copyrighted (Copyright © 1969) by Jerry Farber and published by Contact
Books, 6340 Coldwater Canyon Boulevard, North Hollywood, California ($2.95).

their academic lives. The students, are, it is true, allowed to have a toy government of their own. It is a government run for the most part by Uncle Toms and concerned principally with trivia. The faculty and administrators decide what courses will be offered; the students get to choose their own Homecoming Queen. Occasionally, when student leaders get uppity and rebellious, they're either ignored, put off with trivial concessions, or maneuvered expertly out of position.

A student at Cal State is expected to know his place. He calls a faculty member "Sir" or "Doctor" or "Professor"—and he smiles and shuffles some as he stands outside the professor's office waiting for permission to enter. The faculty tell him what courses to take (in my department, English, even electives have to be approved by a faculty member); they tell him what to read, what to write, and, frequently, where to set the margins on his typewriter. They tell him what's true and what isn't. Some teachers insist that they encourage dissent but they're almost always jiving and every student knows it. Tell the man what he wants to hear or he'll fail your ass out of the course.

When a teacher says "jump" students jump. I know of one professor who refused to take up class time for exams and required students to show up for tests at 6:30 in the morning. And they did, by God! Another, at exam time, provides answer cards to be filled out—each one enclosed in a paper bag with a hole cut in the top to see through. Students stick their writing hands in the bags while taking the test. The teacher isn't a provo; I wish he were. He does it to prevent cheating. Another colleague once caught a student reading during one of his lectures and threw her book against the wall. Still another lectures his students into a stupor and then screams at them in a rage when they fall asleep.

Just last week, during the first meeting of a class, one girl got up to leave after about ten minutes had gone by. The teacher rushed over, grabbed her by the arm, saying "This class is NOT dismissed!" and led her back to her seat. On the same day another teacher began by informing his class that he does not like beards, mustaches, long hair on boys, or capri pants on girls, and will not tolerate any of that in his class. The class, incidentally, consisted mostly of high school teachers.

Even more discouraging than this Auschwitz approach to education is the fact that the students take it. They haven't gone through twelve years of public school for nothing. They've learned one thing and perhaps only one thing during those twelve years. They've forgotten their algebra. They're hopelessly vague about chemistry and physics. They've grown to fear and resent literature. They write like they've been lobotomized. But, Jesus, can they follow orders! Freshmen come up to me with an essay and ask if I want it folded and whether their name should be in the upper right hand corner. And I want to cry and kiss them and caress their poor tortured heads.

Students don't ask that orders make sense. They give up expecting things to make sense long before they leave elementary school. Things are true because the teacher says they're true. At a very early age we all learn to accept "two truths" as did certain medieval churchmen. Outside of class, things are true to your tongue, your fingers, your stomach, your heart. Inside class, things are true by reason of authority. And that's just fine because you don't care anyway. Miss Wiedemeyer tells you a noun is a person, place or thing. So let it be. You don't give a rat's ass; she doesn't give a rat's ass.

The important thing is to please her. Back in kindergarten, you found out that teachers only love children who stand in nice straight lines. And that's where it's been at ever since. Nothing changes except to get worse. School becomes more and more obviously a prison. Last year I spoke to a student assembly at Manual Arts High School and then couldn't get out of the goddamn school. I mean there was NO WAY OUT. Locked doors. High fences. One of the inmates was trying to make it over a fence when he saw me coming and froze in panic. For a moment, I expected sirens, a rattle of bullets, and him clawing the fence.

Then there's the infamous "code of dress." In some high schools, if your skirt looks too short, you have to kneel before the principal, in a brief allegory of fellatio. If the hem doesn't reach the floor, you go home to change while he, presumably, jacks off. Boys in high school can't be too sloppy and they can't even be too sharp. You'd think the school board would be delighted to see all the spades trooping to school in pointy shoes, suits, ties and stingy brims. Uh-uh. They're too visible.

What school amounts to, then, for white and black kids alike, is a 12-year course in how to be slaves. What else could explain what I see in a freshman class? They've got that slave mentality: obliging and ingratiating on the surface but hostile and resistant underneath.

As do black slaves, students vary in their awareness of what's going on. Some recognize their own put-on for what it is and even let their rebellion break through to the surface now and then. Others—including most of the "good students"—have been more deeply brainwashed. They swallow the bullshit with greedy mouths. They honest-to-God believe in grades, in busy work, in General Education requirements. They're pathetically eager to be pushed around. They're like those old grey-headed house niggers you can still find in the South who don't see what all the fuss is about because Mr. Charlie "treats us real good."

College entrance requirements tend to favor the Toms and screen out the rebels. Not entirely, of course. Some students at Cal State, L.A. are expert con artists who know perfectly well what's happening. They want the degree or the 2-S and spend their years on the old plantation alternately laughing and cursing as they play the game. If their egos are strong enough they cheat a lot. And, of course, even the Toms are angry down deep somewhere. But it comes out in passive rather than active aggression. They're unexplainably thick-witted and subject to frequent spells of laziness. They misread simple questions. They spend their nights mechanically outlining history chapters while meticulously failing to comprehend a word of what's in front of them.

The saddest cases among both black slaves and student slaves are the ones who have so thoroughly introjected their masters' values that their anger is all turned inward. At Cal State these are the kids for whom every low grade is torture, who stammer and shake when they speak to a professor, who go through an emotional crisis every time they're called upon during class. You can recognize them easily at finals time. Their faces are festooned with fresh pimples; their bowels boil audibly across the room. If there really is a Last Judgment, then the parents and teachers who created these wrecks are going to burn in hell.

So students are niggers. It's time to find out why, and to do this, we have to take a long look at Mr. Charlie.

The teachers I know best are college professors. Outside the classroom and taken as a group, their most striking characteristic is timidity. They're short on balls.

Just look at their working conditions. At a time when even migrant workers have begun to fight and win, college professors are still afraid to make more than a token effort to improve their pitiful economic status. In California State colleges the faculties are screwed regularly and vigorously by the Governor and Legislature and yet they still won't offer any solid resistance. They lie flat on their stomachs, with their pants down, mumbling catch phrases like "professional dignity" and "meaningful dialogue."

Professors were no different when I was an undergraduate at UCLA during the McCarthy era; it was like a cattle stampede as they rushed to cop out. And in more recent years, I found that my being arrested in sit-ins brought from my colleagues not so much approval or condemnation as open-mouthed astonishment. "You could lose your job!"

Now, of course, there's the Vietnamese war. It gets some opposition from a few teachers. Some support it. But a vast number of professors who know perfectly well what's happening, are copping out again. And in the high schools, you can forget it. Stillness reigns.

I'm not sure why teachers are so chickenshit. It could be that academic training itself forces a split between thought and action. It might also be that the tenured security of a teaching job attracts timid persons who are unsure of themselves and need weapons and the other external trappings of authority.

At any rate teachers ARE short of balls. And, as Judy Eisenstein has eloquently pointed out, the classroom offers an artificial and protected environment in which they can exercise their will to power. Your neighbors may drive a better car; gas station attendants may intimidate you; your wife may dominate you; the State Legislature may shit on you; but in the classroom, by God, students do what you say—or else. The grade is a hell of a weapon. It may not rest on your hip, potent and rigid like a cop's gun, but in the long run it's more powerful. At your personal whim—any time you choose—you can keep 35 students up for nights and have the pleasure of seeing them walk into the classroom pasty-faced and red eyed carrying a sheaf of type-written pages, with title page, MLA footnotes and margins set at 15 and 91.

The general timidity which causes teachers to make niggers of their students usually includes a more specific fear—fear of the students them-selves. After all, students are different, just like black people. You stand exposed in front of them, knowing that their interests, their values and their language are different from yours. To make matters worse, you may suspect that you yourself are not the most engaging of persons. What then can pro-tect you from their ridicule and scorn? Respect for Authority. That's what. It's the policeman's gun again. The white bwana's pith helmet. So you flaunt that authority. You wither whisperers with a murderous glance. You crush objectors with erudition and heavy irony. And, worst of all, you make your own attainments seem not accessible but awesomely remote. You conceal massive ignorance—and parade a slender learning.

The teacher's fear is mixed with an understandable need to be admired and to feel superior, a need which also makes him cling to his "White supremacy." Ideally, a teacher should minimize the distance between himself and his students. He should encourage them not to need him . . . eventually or even immediately. But this is rarely the case. Teachers make themselves high priests of arcane mysteries. They become masters of mumbo-jumbo. Even a more or less conscientious teacher may be torn between the need to give and the need to hold back, the desire to free his students and the desire to hold them in bondage to him. I can find no other explanation that accounts for the way my own subject, literature, is generally taught. Literature, which ought to be a source of joy, solace and enlightenment, often becomes in the classroom nothing more than a source of anxiety—at best an arena for expertise, a ledger book for the ego. Literature teachers, often afraid to join a real union, nonetheless may practice the worst kind of trade-unionism in the classroom; they do to literature what Beckmesser does to song in Wagner's "Meistersinger." The avowed purpose of English departments is to teach literature; too often their real function is to kill it.

Finally, there's the darkest reason of all for the master-slave approach to education. The less trained and the less socialized a person, the more he constitutes a sexual threat, and the more he will be subjugated by institutions such as penitentiaries and schools. Many of us are aware by now of the sexual neurosis which makes white man so fearful of integrated schools and neighborhoods and which makes the castration of Negroes a deeply en-trenched Southern folkway. We should recognize a similar pattern in education. There is a kind of castration that goes on in schools. It begins, before school years, with parents' first encroachment on their children's free unashamed sexuality and continues right up to the day when they hand you your doctoral diploma with a bleeding, shriveled pair of testicles stapled to the parchment. It's not that sexuality has no place in the classroom. You'll find it there but only in certain perverted and vitiated forms.

How does sex show up in school? First of all, there's the sado-masochistic relationship between teachers and students. That's plenty sexual, although the price of enjoying it is to be unaware of what's happening. In walks the teacher in his Ivy League equivalent of a motorcycle jacket. In walks the teacher—a kind of intellectual rough trade—and flogs his students with grades, tests, sarcasm and snotty superiority until their very brains are bleeding. In Swinburne's England, the whipped school boy frequently grew up to be flagellant. With us the perversion is intellectual but it's no less perverse.

Sex also shows up in the classroom as academic subject matter—sanitized and abstracted, thoroughly divorced from feeling. You get "sex education" now in both high school and college classes: everyone determined not to be embarrassed, to be very up to date, very contempo. These are the classes for which sex, as Feiffer puts it, "can be a beautiful thing if properly administered." And then, of course, there's still another depressing manifestation of sex in the classroom: the "off-color" teacher, who keeps his class awake with sniggering sexual allusions, obscene titters and academic innuendo. The sexuality he purveys, it must be admitted, is at least better than none at all.

What's missing, from kindergarten to graduate school, is honest recognition of what's actually happening—turned-on awareness of hairy goodies underneath the petti-pants, the chinos and the flannels. It's not that sex needs to be pushed in school; sex is push enough. But we should let it be, where it is and like it is. I don't insist that ladies in junior high lovingly caress their students' cocks (someday, maybe); however, it is reasonable to ask that the ladies don't, by example and stricture, teach their students to pretend that those cocks aren't there. As things stand now, students are psychically castrated and spayed—and for the very same reason that black men are castrated in Georgia: because they're a threat.

So you can add sexual repression to the list of causes, along with vanity, fear and will to power, that turn the teacher into Mr. Charlie. You might also want to keep in mind that he was a nigger once himself and has never really gotten over it. And there are more causes, some of which are better described in sociological than psychological terms. Work them out. It's not hard. But in the meantime what we've got on our hands is a whole lot of niggers. And what makes this particularly grim is that the student has less chance than the black man of getting out of his bag. Because the student doesn't even know he's in it. That, more or less, is what's happening in higher education, And the results are staggering.

For one thing damn little education takes place in the schools. How could it? You can't educate slaves; you can only train them. Or, to use an even uglier and more timely word, you can only program them.

I like to folk dance. Like other novices, I've gone to the Intersection or to the Museum and laid out good money in order to learn how to dance. No grades, no prerequisites, no separate dining rooms; they just turn you on to dancing. That's education. Now look at what happens in college. A friend of mine, Milt, recently finished a folk dance class. For his final exam, he had to learn things like this: "The Irish are known for their wit and imagination, qualities reflected in their dances, which include the jig, the reel and the hornpipe." And then the teacher graded him A,B,C,D, or F, while he danced in front of her. That's not education. That's not even training. That's an abomination on the face of the earth. It's especially ironic because Milt took that dance class trying to get out of the academic rut. He took crafts for the same reason. Great, right? Get your hands in some clay? Make something? Then the teacher announced that a 20-page term paper would be required—with footnotes.

At my school we even grade people on how they read poetry. That's like grading people on how they fuck. But we do it. In fact, God help me, I do it. I'm the Adolph Eichmann of English 323. Simon Legree on the poetry plantation. "Tote that iamb! Lift that spondee!" Even to discuss a good poem in that environment is potentially dangerous because the very classroom is contaminated. As hard as I may try to turn students on to poetry, I know that the desks, the tests, the IBM cards, their own attitudes toward school and my own residue of UCLA method are turning them off.

Another result of student slavery is equally serious. Students don't get emancipated when they graduate. As a matter of fact, we don't let them graduate until they've demonstrated their willingness—over 16 years—to remain slaves. And for important jobs, like teaching, we make them go through more years, just to make sure. What I'm getting at is that we're all more or less niggers and slaves, teachers and students alike. This is a fact you want to start with in trying to understand wider social phenomena, say, politics, in our country and in other countries.

Educational oppression is trickier to fight than racial oppression. If you're a black rebel, they can't exile you; they either have to intimidate you or kill you. But in high school or college, they can just bounce you out of the fold. And they do. Rebel students and renegade faculty members get smothered or shot down with devastating accuracy. In high school, it's usually the student who gets it; in college, it's more often the teacher. Others get tired of fighting and voluntarily leave the system. This may be a mistake, though. Dropping out of college for a rebel, is a little like going North, for a Negro. You can't really get away from it so you might as well stay and raise hell.

How do you raise hell? That's a whole other article. But just for a start, why not stay with the analogy? What have black people done? They have, first of all, faced the fact of their slavery. They've stopped kidding themselves about an eventual reward in the Great Watermelon Patch in the sky. They've organized; they've decided to get freedom now, and they've started taking it.

Students, like black people, have immense unused power. They could, theoretically, insist on participating in their own education. They could make academic freedom bilateral. They could teach their teachers to thrive on love and admiration, rather than fear and respect, and to lay down their weapons. Students could discover community. And they could learn to dance by dancing on the IBM cards. They could make coloring books out of the catalogs and they could put the grading system in a museum. They could raze one set of walls and let life come blowing into the classroom. They could raze another set of walls and let education flow out and flood the streets. They could turn the classroom into where it's at—a "field of action" as Peter Marin describes it. And, believe it or not, they could study eagerly and learn prodigiously for the best of all possible reasons—their own reasons.

They could. Theoretically. They have the power. But only in a very few places, like Berkeley, have they even begun to think about using it. For students as for black people, the hardest battle isn't with Mr. Charlie. It's what Mr. Charlie has done to your mind.

For Discussion

1. Why does Farber use the word *nigger?*
2. This essay follows a clear pattern of organization. Analyze the main divisions.
3. The student-nigger analogy is the basis of Farber's argument. In what specific ways does he develop this analogy? Discuss each point of comparison.
4. What specific criticisms does Farber make of faculty. Of administration? Of students?
5. How valid is Farber's observation about the slave mentality—"obliging and ingratiating on the surface but hostile and resistant underneath"— as it applies to students?
6. How does your own experience contradict or support Farber's characterization of the teacher as timid? As tyrannical?
7. Discuss the teaching of literature as Farber describes it. How might his criticism be applied to other subjects?

8. What is Farber saying about the place of sex in the school? What do you think should be its proper place?
9. In what ways is the black man better off than the student-nigger?
10. Does Farber's criticism of education extend to what is being taught as well as how it is being taught? Explain.
11. Discuss Farber's use of invective, obscenity, and hyperbole. How does each affect the force of his argument? The logic of his argument?
12. What does Farber's language say about his attitude toward his subject and his audience?
13. Analogies are never conclusive as arguments and are valid only insofar as they point to essential likenesses. Perhaps by constructing other analogies you can gain insight into the validity of Farber's comparison. Consider, for example, "The Child As Nigger," "The Patient As Nigger," "The Laborer As Nigger," "The Wife As Nigger."

DATE DUE

GAYLORD			PRINTED IN U.S.A.